HIGH SEAS
HIGH STAKES

HIGH SEAS
HIGH STAKES

ALEX BENNETT

Published by Alex Bennett in 2010

ISBN 978-0-9567808-0-5

Printed by Fujifilm using a Colour 1000 digital press.
Finished by Duplo UK using the Ultra 200 UV Coater and the DPB-500 PUR Perfect Binder.

Dedicated to my loving parents David and Virginia, without whom I would never have achieved my dreams. You have been there to share the adventures and pick up the pieces during dark days. I love you beyond words. This book is dedicated to you both.

Everything in my life has led me to this point. Some say, 'be careful what you wish for', but I say 'bring it on'; life is for living and out here I feel alive. I'm master and commander of my own environment. Yes, it's scary at times, but solo ocean racing is an extreme sport. I live for this stuff. I was born to sail. It's in my blood and this is my story.

EARLY DAYS

Ever since I was a young child I wanted to be a professional yachtsman. I read the books of round-the-world adventurers like Sir Robin Knox Johnston and Sir Chay Blyth and from a young age I knew I wanted that way of life. I would sit in the maths lessons at school with a copy of Yachting World tucked inside the text book, pretending to listen to the teacher when really I was dreaming of adventure on the high seas. Sometimes the teacher caught me out, other times she had no idea.

When I did get caught, I would get the same lecture: "Sailing will never do anything for you Alex, but you must learn maths to give yourself a good foundation in life". She was right of course, or at least half-right. Maths was important but I always knew I wanted to tread a different path to the norm and I'm glad I did.

I was not really a brainy kid at school. I knew I would never be an academic but that didn't bother me. I took notice of what did interest me and blanked out the rest. Even at the time when we were all asked what we wanted to become when we grew up I knew I would be OK. My dad gave me the best education I could ever want. He made sure I was no mug. Streetwise at a young age, I knew how many beans made five. It worked for me.

One day it would be me who would sail across oceans, I told myself.

In those early days it was the mystery and spirit of the ocean that captivated and inspired me. The appeal of yacht racing – let alone solo ocean racing – had not yet embedded itself into my mind.

My father first took me on board a boat at the tender age of two. At that point we had a 27-foot fly bridge power boat on the River

A very young me, already playing with boats.

1981 steering Dad's boat.

Thames, moored at Penton Hook near Windsor. Despite being so young I do have memories of those early days. They were great times. As a family we would regularly enjoy cruising along the River Thames. Apparently I was captivated by the essence of speed – Dad would regularly open up the throttles of the twin-engine boat and give it some stick just to see the smile on my face. The rebel in me is definitely something I inherited from my father.

It was another three years before I first felt the wind on my face on a sailboat. That was a 26-foot Westerly Centaur called *Zephyr*, a beautiful little yacht, solid, sound and safe. My first experiences of sailing were in the Solent, the stretch of water separating the Isle of Wight from the mainland on the south coast of England. My dad and I would take short weekend adventures from Portsmouth to Cowes on the Isle of Wight. It was a journey of only about seven miles or so, but at that age it didn't matter, we were on the high seas together. My poor mum, though, is ever the long-suffering wife when it comes to all things nautical. She came along as much as she could, but the sea just doesn't agree with her and to this day she suffers terribly from seasickness.

I guess at the time my parents had no idea of the impact sailing and their introduction to boats would have on my life. The only significant sportsman in our family was my grandfather, who was an amateur boxer. He became Business House Champion in the 1920s then went on to challenge for the Golden Gloves boxing championship, which he unfortunately lost on points. He was a real 'tough guy' and later became a successful businessman.

At the age of nine we moved house from London to Whitby on the north east coast, my mother's birthplace and the town where Captain Cook's famous vessel HMS Endeavour was built in 1767. This was the

Making my first raft aged eight.

perfect setting for a young boy to acquire a love for the sea and it was here that I started to develop what has since become an all-consuming passion for ocean racing. My parents joined the Whitby Yacht Club in 1989 and I promptly enrolled into the Cadet series of dinghy races within the confines of Whitby harbour. This was my first introduction to the sport of sailboat racing.

My parents could see sailing was becoming more than just a casual interest. Realising the benefit of having a dinghy of my own, my father went to the London International Boat Show and purchased what he thought would be a great little first boat for me to learn in.

At the time I was aware that Dad was away for a few days on business but suspected, thanks to a tip-off from Mum, that if I was good he might return with a dinghy for me. There had been talk about it previously and I was excited by the prospect.

Dad arrived the next day with a huge van, the bow of a little boat sticking out of the back. Wow, here it was, my first boat. I had watched Arthur Ransome's Swallows and Amazons on television and had been dreaming of some adventures of my own. This little boat represented a ticket to my very own Narnia and I planned to make the most of it.

My memories of sailing *The Toad* are of mixed emotions. The boat itself was an ideal craft in which to learn to sail, but she was fat and slow and not in the least bit suited to racing. My first summer was intense. I was a fast learner and quickly wanted to explore beyond the boundaries of this little boat. Dad and I had planned our latest trip, a summer excursion from the mouth of the River Esk in Whitby harbour all the way to Ruswarp Bridge where the river ceased to be navigable.

We packed everything we thought we might need: lifejackets, warm clothes, some of Mum's fairy cakes – thereafter known as 'boat cakes' – as well as a couple of torches, just in case. We cast off just after lunch on a fresh summer day, bound for unknown upstream adventures.

The plan was to sail to Ruswarp and back before nightfall. Progress was slow with all that extra weight on board but we eventually ghosted up to Ruswarp Bridge on the last of the tide just before darkness came upon us.

At first, Dad was all for leaving the boat at Ruswarp until the next day but I managed to convince him that a night-time trip back down the river was just what was required to make us real explorers. I cast off

The Toad, my first command 1988, aged twelve.

the bow line before he could reconsider, quickly waved a goodbye kiss to Mum, who had come to meet us with fresh supplies of boat cakes and tea, and we were off back down the river.

The river lacked the reassuring glow of the moon to guide us. It was pitch black but I didn't mind. I wasn't scared, I was with my dad and knew that just like our other adventures, we would make it. Despite not being able to see much past the front of the boat, those few hours passed much more quickly than the daylight part of the trip and it wasn't long before we were approaching the slipway. Now we were guided by the blinding lights of Mum's Land Rover. She had spotted our torches in the dark. Good old Mum, ever the guiding light in my life.

It was only a few miles, but that trip was the foundation of my passion for a life at sea. I was hooked. I made another trip up the river in *The Toad* before the end of the summer, this time solo. However, I was quickly outgrowing that little boat. The competitive side of the sport was starting to dominate my thoughts. I sailed *The Toad* in just two races. The first time was in the Whitby Yacht Club Winter Frostbite series where I came last and promptly sailed to shore, declaring, "I will never sail this boat again". It's become a family joke now, but at the time I felt frustrated. I knew I could do better but I needed the right tools.

Enjoying a good day's sailing on my laser off Whitby Harbour.

The boat I really wanted was a Topper, a sleek yet robust little dinghy constructed from injection moulded polypropylene. It's a recognised design on the youth sailing circuit. A Topper provides the ideal progression into racing and is virtually indestructible, a useful consideration when young children are involved. I had to wait a few months for the new boat to arrive. My parents knew I had outgrown *The Toad* but were also mindful of the fact that I should appreciate the value of money. I knew this already but was certainly willing to do what was necessary to get the new boat.

The last straw came when I managed to finish a windless Frostbite race in first place only to be disqualified by the race committee because I was sculling the rudder, waggling it from side to side to make the boat move through the water. On a windless day it's actually quite effective for making a small boat move forward, but unfortunately for me, quite illegal in the world of racing.

I couldn't believe it. I thought I had won my first race only to find that what I was doing was illegal. I thought all Hell was about to break loose between my dad and the race committee members. It must have taken half an hour for the committee to explain the rules and calm everyone down. In my father's eyes, his lad had won fair and square and that was that. These people were trying to cheat us out of a win. This, however, was not the case and a good lesson was learned. The Topper arrived a couple of weeks after that.

What a difference! This boat was the challenge I needed. It wasn't long before I was winning races in the Frostbite series and challenging the club's long-timers who were seen as the pros. I progressed through various types of dinghy after that. I gained invaluable experience in Lasers, Enterprises and Larks before moving onto the bigger boats, competing in local events in the North-East .

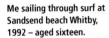

Me sailing through surf at Sandsend beach Whitby, 1992 – aged sixteen.

My first chance to race on board a yacht at sea came one evening while I was in the yacht club. A club member was scouting for crew for the following day's coastal race from Whitby to Boulby Bouy and back. I jumped at the chance and introduced myself. Before I knew it, I had made friends with the skipper of the *Red Trappeze*.

Dave Hutchinson was a bear of a man, seven feet tall, or at least he seemed to be. A Geordie with a big moustache and blood-red face, he had a reputation for being a hard man who didn't pull any punches. He played to win, told it how it was and went to sea in all weathers. Fearless and unpredictable, Red Ned, as he had been affectionately nicknamed, was the sort of guy who didn't take any crap and could drink the pants off the best of them.

I remember that first race well. Dave asked me if I wanted to steer for a while so he could light his pipe. He always smokes a pipe, it was as important to him as the sailing. I took the helm while we were sail-ing into the wind and waves along the coast towards Tees Bay. The wind was up and we were starting to get overpowered sailing on the port tack.

The lads were sitting out on the high side of the boat as is the custom when racing. The extra weight of the crew sitting on the high side helps to improve the speed of the boat, albeit only marginally. The lee rail was starting to become awash. We needed to reduce sail, and fast. Red Ned gave the call to head into the wind and went forward to attend to the sail.

In my haste to impress, I steered into the wind rather too quickly. The boat tacked through the wind, laying flat in the water on the other side, dunking the guys on the rail into the sea in the process. I scrambled to the other side of the cockpit, having let go of the tiller in favour of holding on for dear life. What had I done? By the time the boat came upright Red Ned was screaming blue murder. He grabbed the tiller from me, swearing. I knew I had messed up. Not a word was said to me for the entire trip back to Whitby. I couldn't believe how stupid I had been. It was an elementary mistake and I should have known better.

I assumed I had blown it, but to my surprise on reaching the dock in Whitby Red Ned seemed pleased with the day's events: "Thanks for coming, son. Fancy it again next week?" His gesture took me by surprise. I thought he would be glad to see the back of me, but as I would later come to realise, that was just his way.

I spent two great action-packed seasons racing on *Red Trappeze* and can honestly say there was never a dull moment. We competed in the North East Cruiser Racers Association or NECRA series of events, one of the most memorable of which was the annual North Sea race from Scarborough to Holland.

We had crossed the start line off Scarborough amongst a competitive fleet of like-minded sailors bound for the Dutch coast. Twenty-four hours into the race, we were sailing past the numerous gas rigs that litter the North Sea when I realised that the other crew members on board had only been recruited the night before in Red Ned's local pub in Middlesbrough.

The only form of liquid sustenance on board was a skilfully considered selection of beer and premium lager. The only two people aboard who were bona-fide sailors were me and Red Ned. By now I had come to just accept this way of life on board *Red Trappeze* and duly dismissed it, putting it down to experience.

Approaching the Dutch mainland late the following evening, I noticed a rather perplexed look on Red Ned's face. We were in the final stages of the race and we all knew we were quickly approaching the finish line. The end of the race was marked by a buoy set just off the entrance to Ijmuiden harbour. This marks the start of the North Sea canal which eventually winds its way to Amsterdam.

"Alex, get up on the bow and keep an eye out. Let me know what you see, lad." Red Ned's tone indicated there was some uncertainty about our position. We were close to the shore, we knew that much. I was crouched down at the very front of the boat, holding onto the pulpit rail, looking intently into the darkness, unsure of what I was actually looking out for.

Suddenly I heard what sounded like breaking waves on a shoreline, the first indication of looming trouble. It was faint and I couldn't be sure. Then out of the darkness came a sight I will never forget – the shoreline. Panic quickly followed: "Shit, it's the beach!" I shouted back to the guys in the cockpit. As if on cue, like someone flicking on a light switch, the low-lying Dutch coastline popped into view.

Red Trappeze was under full sail at six knots with our spinnaker set by a following wind, pushing us directly towards an unknown beach. "Alex, get ready to catch the spinnaker. Hurry, lad!" The words from Red Ned sent me into action. I grabbed one of the control lines for the sail on the bow, the lads let the halyard go and the sail started to fall into the sea. I was grabbing chunks of sailcloth in my hands in an effort to break the world record for the quickest unaided recovery of a spinnaker. The noise of the waves on the shoreline was now very loud and intimidating.

Most of the sail ended up in the water, but I had retrieved enough sailcloth for Red Ned to steer us out of danger. Regrouping in the cockpit, our adrenaline was pumping. Red Ned handed me the helm and started to light his pipe. "I'm going below to work out where we are," he said. It turned out we had pitched up several miles down the coast from the finish line. We eventually found Ijmuiden and the finish line in the early daylight hours and unexpectedly, we ended up winning the race. Sailing with Red Ned was always going to be an experience I was unlikely to forget. But I loved every minute of it.

Red Trappeze leaving Scarborough harbour at the start of the North Sea race.

MY FIRST BIG BREAK

y first opportunity to take part in a big event came towards the
end of 1991. I was fifteen years old and very keen to broaden
my horizons. My parents and I were attending an end-of-season
prize-giving party at Hartlepool Yacht Club. I heard through the grape-
vine that a well-known local yachtsman called Harold Usherwood was
tentatively looking for a new crew for a serious assault on the following
year's Round Britain and Ireland Race, organised by the Royal Ocean
Racing Club. This was the opportunity I had been looking for and it had
dominated my thoughts for the previous two weeks.

I knew Harold would be at the prize-giving dinner and that this
would be the perfect opportunity to declare my ambition to be his
right-hand man. Harold was looking for serious commitment and dedication but, as with most opportunities, there was more to it than that.
Another slight problem was that my source had told me Harold would
not take on board anyone under seventeen.

As I was only fifteen at the time, this problem played on my mind.
I just had to get on board that boat. I chewed it over longer than I
should have done and before I knew it I was standing in the yacht
club with my parents and at least a couple of hundred other people.
Tonight was the night; I knew I had to approach Harold now but was
still having trouble thinking about dealing with the age issue.

I could see Harold on the far side of the room. He was standing
about thirty feet away engrossed in a conversation with a group of
people. My dad noticed I had been gazing across the room towards
Harold. "If you want it that much Alex, just go and ask him," Dad said.
My parents knew full well just how much this opportunity meant to me.

Up until now I had neglected to tell them about the age issue but now I needed a second opinion. I shared my concerns with Dad there and then in the crowded noisy room. He considered for a moment, then leaning over toward my ear, eyes fixed in Harold's direction, before saying, "Tell him you're seventeen, Alex". Dad has a great ability to simplify even the seemingly most complicated situation.

Telling a lie was not high on my agenda. However, I knew if I admitted to not being seventeen when I approached Harold I would not have a chance. There was no way I was going to let someone else take my place just because of the small matter of age. I remembered my grandfather had been rather economical with the truth about his age in order to sign up for the Navy during the Second World War. He had his own goals and ambitions. There was no way he was going to be compromised by age, so what was good enough for grandfathers was good enough for me. I walked across the room and seized the moment.

Harold Usherwood was a gentleman, close to retirement age with a big heart and admirable character, with good old-school values – the type of chap who placed merit on a firm handshake and good eye contact. He had years of sailing experience under his belt, most recently having won a big race from the UK to Cadiz in southern Spain. He had raced across the infamous Bay of Biscay and he was well-known and respected.

Our first encounter was fairly brief. It was a busy night at the yacht club, lots of laughter and singing being the main aim of the evening. After a formal introduction I said my piece, outlining my willingness to commit there and then.

Harold, listening intently, explained that he was looking for a firm commitment for the whole season, not just for the one race. That was the perfect scenario as far as I was concerned. The subject of age came up briefly but I managed to skirt around it with dubious skill. To this day, I am not sure whether he knew I had been economical with the truth, but the subject was not broached again. I think he must have known.

The conversation concluded with a loose invitation to attend a crew meeting scheduled for the following weekend at Hartlepool Marina. I duly accepted without any thought of how I would actually get from Whitby to Hartlepool but hey, in the worst scenario I would walk or ride my bike there. Harold was aware that I lived in Whitby, some 25 miles away by sea and even further by road. He must have thought that if I was keen enough to turn up I must be at least half serious.

Time passes very slowly when you're a teenager waiting for something to happen. I had school first thing Monday morning and knew that the following week would probably drag on and on. I was on the brink of the adventure of a lifetime. Nothing was cast in stone yet but I could see I was in a good position to secure my place on board Harold's boat and with it, a shot at the big time.

Fyling Hall School is set in an idyllic location, sandwiched between wooded forests just off the main road out of Robin Hood's Bay towards the North Yorkshire moors, about six miles from Whitby. It is in a stunning spot, looking out over the bay towards the North Sea on one side and the beauty of the moors on the other. An old bus would collect the day pupils from Whitby town centre every morning and head off to school, collecting more of us along the way.

A quality private school for day pupils and long-term boarders, this was the place where my mother received her schooling in the late 1950s. She was a day pupil, living with her parents in Whitby where they ran a successful fruit and vegetable store. The school had not changed much since then.

It was a rugby school through and through. For the games teachers, Mr Blackwell and Mr Lewis, it was all about the rugby and as a team we were pretty successful. A few of us even had an opportunity to attend trials for the North Yorkshire youth team. Mr Blackwell was given the nod by a group of scouts that if we attended trials and played the quality of rugby we had been delivering throughout the season there would be a very good chance to progress to the next level. This was like a red rag to a bull for the games teachers but it wasn't for me. I had a sailing opportunity to pursue.

I was tempted, though. I really enjoyed rugby. It suited my character but I loved sailing more and it was difficult to see a path where I could enjoy competing in both sports at a high level. Maybe that was my crossroads, that time in your life when you are presented with the choice of two avenues to pursue, knowing that realistically you can choose only one.

Deciding to bin the rugby trials in favour of sailing brought a lot of heat down on me. Even the headmaster got involved. At the time I was devastated that the school didn't share my enthusiasm for my sailing but looking back, rugby was for them the obvious activity to build character and discipline. As a school, Fyling Hall was skilled at that and participation in competitive sailing was just not part of the official way of thinking. To this day I'm glad I made the choice I did, although I ended up playing a lot of rugby for the school and thoroughly enjoying the experience, especially when we won. I didn't realise at the time – does anyone? – but my days at Fyling Hall gave me some of the best experiences of my youth.

One thing I have learned to appreciate with the passage of time is that Fyling Hall didn't just teach me the National Curriculum; it helped me develop some of the essential life skills required to make my own way in this world. We had so much freedom in those days and I am thankful I was in the lucky position to be able to experience schooling at its finest.

The Sunday meeting at Hartlepool came around more quickly than I expected. I had convinced my parents to drive me to the meeting. They were keen to see me succeed and were on my side from the beginning and so didn't require much persuasion. As we parked at the marina I couldn't wait to get out of the car and give it my best shot.

April Storm was a Westerly Storm 33, a production design built to cater for both the cruising and racing fraternity. She was not an extreme design of boat by any means but, at thirty-three feet in length she was a capable craft, and had a white hull with a thick dark blue stripe running around the top section. Harold had owned the sleek and immaculate boat from brand new, having specified a taller mast and deeper keel to improve her competitive ability. I would later find out that *April Storm* also had a bespoke set of new racing sails to complete her inventory, a revelation for me at the time.

I could see *April Storm* as I walked down the gangplank leading to the pontoon. She was being hauled out of the water for the winter and Harold needed several keen hands to help with the lifting-out procedure. The day passed very quickly and with darkness approaching it was not long before the time had come to say goodbye to some new-found friends and head back to the car park to find Mum and Dad. I was buzzing with excitement. Harold had noticed I got on well with everyone and seemed to fit in.

The day certainly had been successful. I had earned a place on board for some early season races. Harold was happy to let me take part in the first two to see how things worked out. He naturally didn't want to commit until he had seen how competent I was. It was at that moment I knew I had a real chance of being part of the team.

Once we started sailing early the following year it wasn't long before I was given the official seal of approval and formally offered a place in the crew for the whole season, including the Round Britain. We had just completed a 190 mile offshore race from Blyth in Northumberland, around the Bass Rock in the mouth of the Firth of Forth and back to Blyth. The Bass Rock race is a summer classic, held annually in the North East and an event not to be missed in that part of the world.

The news of my acceptance as a team member was a big relief but was also tinged with a bit of sadness. I had earned my place on board *April Storm* but the days of sailing with Red Ned had come to a natural end.

The Round Britain and Ireland race is a gruelling two thousand miles from start to finish. It is split into four legs with stopovers in Cork in southern Ireland, Lerwick in the Shetlands and for the 1992 event there was a penultimate pit stop in Hartlepool before sailing south down through the Dover Straights and along the English Channel to Cowes on the Isle Of Wight. It was to be an international event like nothing I had experienced before.

The start was electric. I was used to the close-quarters manoeuvres so typical just before a race, but this was the Solent, arguably the home of yachting in the UK and we were now mixing it up with the big boys. We were amongst a fleet with no less than twenty-eight of some of the most experienced offshore sailors in Europe. There was the likes of Mike Slade, the millionaire businessman and passionate offshore yachtsman on his eighty-foot maxi yacht *Ocean Leopard*. He was always a serious contender, someone with real chance of overall success in this race, although his team would have to fight off some serious competition for an outright win.

There was also a young Matt Humphreys heading up a youth team and campaigning for a future Whitbread Round the World Race. He would later go on to compete in the Whitbread as the skipper of the sixty-foot yacht *Dolphin and Youth*, firmly establishing himself on the pro yachting scene in the process.

We were one of the smaller sized yachts competing in Class Two. Despite being dwarfed by the biggest boats in the fleet, everyone on board *April Storm* was determined to make a good start. This meant keeping well out of the way of the big boys. That's easier said than done, though, when every boat is vying for the best position in the final moments before the gun fires. In this case the guns were no less than the cannons of the Royal Yacht Squadron situated at the western entrance to Cowes. Membership there is by invitation only and some would say it's the most prestigious yacht club in the world.

As we started counting down the final five minutes before the start, everything suddenly became more real. I could hear crew members on board some of our competitors' boats shouting commands to each other relating to the close proximity of approaching vessels: "head up a bit, steer to port, down ten." 'Down ten' means steer away from the wind by ten degrees to avoid a big crash. Usually one crew member stands at the front of the boat looking behind the foresail, barking orders to the team in the cockpit so the helmsman can steer a clean course towards the start line. On a well-sailed boat with good team players, this process can be a precise and invaluable tactic, resulting in a good clean start. With poor communication however, everything can quickly go to pieces.

Harold had experience on his side. He knew this was a two thousand-mile race which would not be won on this start line, but could quite possibly be lost there. A collision with another competitor now would mean the end of a year-long campaign and it would be several more years before we'd have another chance to compete in this race. The stakes were high, so we took a moderately conservative approach.

The smoke from the shore-side cannons signified the game was afoot a couple of seconds before we heard the boom. Not a poor start by any means – we were middle of the pack. Safe and sound, we knew our objectives. I briefly wondered why we were not getting stuck into the thick of the fight from the beginning but didn't say anything. I was busy enough trimming sails and trying to absorb the whole experience. I think Harold had made his decision about our tactics for the start before he even stepped on board the previous day.

Sailing west down the Solent towards the Needles channel we were on good form, keeping pace with the bulk of the fleet. The next stop would be Cork, three hundred and forty miles away. At this stage we didn't know for sure who was hot and who was not, but we had an idea. The big boats seemed to shoot off down the Solent like greyhounds out of the trap, and would soon be over the horizon.

It doesn't take long before life on board settles into a routine and we had soon put our watch system into practice with half the crew on port watch and the other on starboard. Our first dramatic experience came close to midnight while sailing across the Celtic Sea. We had been pushing hard all day, revelling in the windy conditions. We had a following sea and wind, surfing down the waves at speeds reaching well into the double digits under spinnaker and full mainsail. I had been off-watch for about twenty minutes or so. Lying in my bunk in the aft cabin area, feet pointing toward the back of the boat, I could feel the strain *April Storm* was under as she surfed down the waves.

The wind had been steadily building all evening. There had been talk of dropping the spinnaker just before darkness but the desire to push on prevailed. We were over-pressed, flying a full canvas of sail when most cruising yachtsman would be well reefed down. My watch had seen several big surfs, propelling *April Storm* down the face of waves into the troughs at nearly sixteen knots. That's very fast for a boat that was never really designed to sail at more than nine knots or so. Drifting off to sleep I knew it would not be too long before we would have to reduce sail.

Suddenly and violently I awoke to a loud crash. *April Storm* had been knocked down heavily onto her starboard side. I was no longer lying on the bunk, I was now wedged into the cockpit side walls. As I opened my eyes and looked forward it was clear we were lying flat on our side. The masthead must have been close to the water. It was very dark in the cabin but the faint glow of red light coming from the chart table area provided just enough ambient light to watch the galley cooker break its mounts and fly across the cabin.

I struggled to get out of my bunk as the call came through: "Everyone on deck, all hands, get the spinnaker down." Harold's voice cut clearly through the dark cabin. He had been catnapping at the chart table and had narrowly missed being squashed by the cooker as it made its bid for freedom. My fight to get to the companionway steps seemed to take a lifetime, the noise of the spinnaker violently ragging in the wind could be felt throughout the boat. The crew on deck were obviously in trouble. We all were.

There was no time to get my waterproofs on. I couldn't find my lifejacket in the darkness. I remember feeling exhilarated by the experience and was keen to impress. I was the first of the off-watch crew to get to the companionway entrance. I shot up the steps and poked my head out of the hatch. It was pitch black and raining. I felt the full force of the wind on my face. It was really kicking. *April Storm* was lying right over on her side, the crew in the cockpit holding on as best they could.

I knew it was my job to get up on the bow and retrieve the spinnaker but, in those winds, it would take more than just one man. I sensed one of the guys climbing up the companionway steps behind me and, having frozen for a split second to absorb the enormity of the situation, I climbed up onto the high side and started to work my way towards the bow. People were shouting orders all over the place. It was difficult to know who was in charge but I understood the general idea – get shot of the spinnaker, and quickly.

Reaching the heavily-inclined bow and wedging my feet onto the pulpit rail I prepared myself for the sail drop. By now the spinnaker had been flogging for probably three or four minutes. The sheer strength of wind was preventing the guys in the cockpit from being able to steer away from the wind and get *April Storm* back on her feet. We were slowly sliding sideways through the water. The spinnaker was systematically wrapping itself around the forestay wire, creating a tight knot. I shouted into the darkness at the top of my voice in the vague direction of the cockpit, "it's wine-glassed around the forestay".

I'm not sure anyone heard the call. The guys in the cockpit had already let the halyard go so the spinnaker could be retrieved. I was now joined by two of the lads, who had realised I would be out of my depth on my own up there on the bow. Reaching out for the sail, I lost my footing on the steep angled deck. In an instant I slipped through the pulpit rail, my legs hanging off the side of the boat. I was up to my waist in water, struggling to maintain my grip on the stainless steel rail. There was no time for regrets. Luckily for me one of the guys reached out and grabbed my arm, preventing me from becoming fully detached from the boat. A close call indeed.

Time was running out, the spinnaker was progressively winding itself around the forestay and we would soon discover that there was no way we would be able to retrieve the sail intact. It took a couple of hours to get the boat sorted and sailing again. We lost the spinnaker, eventually retrieving what was left of the torn sail. By the time we had cut the last of it from the forestay, it looked like it had been put through a paper shredder. What a nightmare. With the wind now gusting over forty knots we spent the rest of the night under a deeply reefed mainsail and small working jib. The knock-down and subsequent loss of the spinnaker had cost us a lot of time. Our competitors would undoubtedly have made significant gains during our ordeal, but we took comfort in the knowledge that this was a long race with plenty of opportunity to catch up.

On reaching Cork our spirits were lifted when we heard news of other competitors having struggled too in the testing conditions. The Celtic Sea had proved to be a short, sharp introduction to the race. It had been a harsh trip for all of us, with reports of damage of one kind or another being the main topic of conversation in the Royal Cork Yacht Club bar.

The Round Britain Race was living up to its reputation of being a tough event, and the stories of damage set a trend that would last the whole way around the British Isles. Some would feel the hand of Lady Luck, some would not. In ocean racing, you can have the best boat with the best equipment and still have the sweet smell of success taken away from you in an instant.

This is exactly what happened to the team of the fifty-foot yacht *Dumptruck*. They were racing in Class 1 with high hopes of being at the top of the leader board going into the third leg of the race. Their main rival was the much larger heavyweight brute *Ocean Leopard*. At eighty feet long, *Ocean Leopard* was on paper the faster vessel. That gave a time allowance to the smaller but fast and lightweight fifty-footer. The pair had been head-to-head all the way around the British Isles and were now locked into a fierce duel for overall line honours. They were regularly in sight of each other as they tacked their way down the North Sea coastline, crossing each other's paths.

Approaching Coquet Island near Amble off the Northumbrian coast, the skipper of *Dumptruck* made a tactical decision that would mean the end of their race and effectively hand the overall line honours to Mike Slade on *Ocean Leopard*. *Dumptruck* was doing well and based on the handicap ratings, very likely had the measure of the larger vessel. The forth leg stopover of Hartlepool was fast approaching and it was becoming unlikely that *Ocean Leopard* could pull ahead far enough to take the win on handicap.

The team on board *Dumptruck* could not only smell victory, they wanted a taste of overall glory and line honours, as first boat to finish the leg. Visibility was less than perfect off the Amble coast but the opportunity to gain a margin over *Ocean Leopard* was too much too ignore. The team elected to sail close to the shoreline for tactical advantage. They must have known it was a risky manoeuvre but often reward does not come without risk. Whether they sailed inshore to get out of the adverse effects of the tidal currents or to capitalise on a better direction of wind so close to the shore, I never found out. By contrast, *Ocean Leopard* stayed farther out to sea in deeper water.

Dumptruck's gamble did not pay off. It wasn't long before the crew found themselves aground on the rocks, within sight of the harbour. They eventually had to abandon the stricken yacht in the interests of safety. The event proved to be big news, not just on the race circuit but it also made the regional television headlines. The race was over for those guys and the fight for overall line honours would soon become a distant memory.

Meanwhile, further back in the fleet, we had no idea of the commotion going on ahead of us. We had not long departed Lerwick, locked in our own private duel with another identical boat, a sailing school entry owned and operated by a company called Five Star Sailing. Their boat, *Jade*, was crewed by sailors paying for the privilege to compete. Nonetheless they were a good team and proved to be a formidable adversary.

The stopover in Lerwick had offered a welcome respite and a much longed-for trip to the pub. We arrived exhausted from several days at sea, racing the eight hundred and forty miles in varying sea and wind conditions. The crew, including me, were all tired and keen to get a quick pint before a long-awaited sleep.

Walking into the pub, the smoke-filled room was full of hardcore Scottish fishermen. Weathered, unshaven and still wearing our sailing kit, we must have looked like a bunch of drowned rats. The lady bartender, wiping the bar with a damp cloth, asked what we all wanted to drink. 'Beer all round' was the quick response.

There had been much talk of a well-earned beer earlier in the day as we made the final approach into port. But I couldn't think of drinking anything worse, my days sailing with Red Ned had been enough to put me off beer for life and despite looking older than I actually was, I was still only just sixteen. "Not for me," I answered, asking instead, "do you have any milk? I would love a pint of milk."

The look on the bartender's face said it all. Everyone in the pub seemed to stop what they were doing and turn around. "Milk? Are you sure? I don't think we have any..." She was obviously perplexed by my unusual request and stared at me intently. "Yes, I really fancy a pint of milk," I said.

It was about now I was starting to realise what I had just said. For a moment you could have cut the air with a knife. The silence was quickly broken by the bartender replying in a strong Scottish accent, "Well, if it's milk you want, milk you shall have". With that she disappeared from behind the bar, ran across the road to the corner shop and came back with a bottle of the finest local white stuff, poured it into a pint glass and handed it to me. "Cheers," one of the locals shouted, laughing with an approving nod. I got away with that one.

Back in the race, we had cleared the southern tip of the Shetland Islands and were pushing south through the numerous gas and oil rigs that litter that part of the North Sea. We were really in the swing of things and it was to be a very good leg of the race for us. Motivated by the thought of bringing *April Storm* into our home port of Hartlepool in the lead, we had no trouble finding our form. We were on home territory now, sailing in familiar waters.

If there was one leg of this epic race that we definitely wanted to do well in it was the Lerwick-to-Hartlepool section. We knew there would be a healthy crowd of well-wishers awaiting our arrival whatever the result, but how much sweeter it would be if we rocked up as the winner of our division.

Approaching the outermost edge of the beautiful Farne Islands off the Northumbrian coast, the home of one of the largest colonies of grey seals in Europe and the scene of Grace Darling's famous sea rescue all those years ago, we were starting to feel the effects of fatigue. An aggressive low pressure weather system had the majority of the fleet trapped in an iron grip. Once again we were battling into rough conditions with an unwelcome side serving of torrential rain under the cover of darkness. Despite the conditions *April Storm* was holding up well and we all knew it was now only a matter of hours before we would be able to share our stories with our families and friends.

I knew my parents would be waiting for me, and were probably in Hartlepool already. Dad would be pacing the dock, determined not to miss the arrival of his son. This dock-pacing ritual would become a familiar process for Dad in the coming years.

Crossing the penultimate leg finish line in Hartlepool we knew we had done well, but at that moment were unaware that a trophy had our name on it. We had sailed a blinder. As we motored into the lock at the entrance of the then-new harbour development we could see the crowds of well-wishers. Several larger race boats had joined us for the lock through into the new harbour, having waited for the tide to rise in the old marina at Kafiga Wharf.

Throwing our lines up to the dockmen I looked up to the top of the lock walls and noticed my parents. Mum was waving while Dad gave a loud cheer. He was holding a bottle of champagne and was busy shaking the bottle while expertly pushing the cork out of the top. With a loud pop the cork shot out, flying across the dock and as if controlled by a missile guidance system, it bounced off the side of our mast and landed on the deck. This was a complete fluke, as I knew Dad's aim was not the most accurate in the world, but it didn't matter. It all added to the excitement of the moment.

We had been received by a big crowd, many more people than we expected. Even when you take the rest of the crew's friends and family into account there was still loads of people there I didn't know at all. Moving into the inner harbour I noticed *Ocean Leopard* and remember thinking what I would have given to have a sail on her. She was a real Goliath of a boat. Our personal entourage of friends and family followed us around to our berth and were waiting to take our mooring lines as we tied up. We had created quite a buzz, and it was not long before news came that we had won our class for this particular leg and were told that the local media were interested in our story.

This was my first opportunity to talk to the media, something that is nowadays a regular part of life. They were interested in the bad weather we'd experienced off the Farne Islands and how we felt coming into our home port in first place. We all felt like a million dollars. We had finally found our form. We still had the last leg of the race ahead of us but we were armed with a new-found energy to succeed. Boy, would we need it.

The last leg would be the toughest of all, partly because of the length of time we had already been at sea and partly due to some truly diabolical conditions in the English Channel.

The Dover Straits are the eastern entrance to the Channel, one of the busiest shipping lanes in the world. From here we had a mere 115 miles to sail to the finish. Our battle with *Jade*, the sailing school boat, continued. We were in sight of each other as we approached Dover, engaged in our own private match race. The weather, as forecast, had been slowly deteriorating and we were now once again sailing into the wind and waves. At this point the conditions were challenging but not severe. We were well acclimatised to this kind of sailing by now, it had become the norm.

It was here that I was to learn an interesting lesson. John Horn, the skipper of *Jade*, had noticed that the conditions inside the breakwater of Dover harbour were quite clement, in stark contrast to the weather we were bashing into just a few hundred yards south of the breakwater entrance. Suddenly, they changed course and headed through the eastern entrance for the confines of the harbour. Suspecting they had some kind of problem on board, we continued on our way, keeping a careful eye out for any fast-moving commercial shipping.

It wasn't until we noticed *Jade* reappear ahead of us by a considerable margin that we realised they had sailed into the confines of the harbour to gain shelter from the rough seas and then sailed toward the western entrance, popping out the other side with an advantage. Cheeky buggers, we all thought. We were not sure if the stunt was even legal. Either way, we had to admire their spirit.

The final leg of the race was proving to be relentless. The English Channel is actually quite a shallow stretch of water and coupled with gale-force winds can produce a very nasty, steep sea. This was exactly our problem. With the wind speed now well into gale force eight, the motion onboard *April Storm* was becoming quite violent as we bounced off each and every wave. Standing by the galley with one hand braced against the edge of the sink and the other holding onto the companionway steps, I was getting ready to start my shift on deck.

Harold had been sitting at the chart table considering our options. It was clear he was considering pulling into a safe port to shelter from the worst of the weather. In his mind we were clearly sailing close to the limit. At that moment without thinking I blurted out, "We can't stop now, we're almost home". Harold was tired and visibly quite stressed,

as we all were. His reply was immediate and quite abrupt. I realised I had upset him. It was the only time I ever saw Harold lose his cool.

Me and the crew onboard ***April Storm.***

We slammed down hard off the top of a particularly steep wave. The whole cabin vibrated with the shock. On deck, the water cascading over the boat. One of the lads had been catnapping in the saloon bunk on the low side of the cabin. Curled up in his sleeping bag, he was bombarded with several cans of tinned food.

One of the saloon lockers had burst open with the force of impact as we crashed into the waves. I remember feeling an uncontrollable urge to laugh as the food achieved a direct hit on the guy in the bunk. I felt guilty afterwards, but for a split second it was funny. Harold also found the situation mildly amusing, unlike our fellow crewmember who looked thoroughly fed-up. In those conditions all you can do is just hang on and do your best to get through the day.

For us the final twenty-four hours seemed to take forever but, eventually we found ourselves sailing up the Solent, sheltered by the Isle of Wight. We had made it. *April Storm* had taken a real pasting in the final hours but our faithful steed had held together to the end. We managed a podium finish for the final leg and a respectable fourteenth overall out of the original twenty-eight that started. We had completed this tough challenge, done well and I had experienced my first big ocean race.

3
THE WARRIOR QUEEN

resh from my experience of racing around the British Isles I was hungry for more, but initially faced an important decision of a different kind. My time at Fyling Hall was rapidly coming to an end. Having completed my GCSE exams I was facing the now very real prospect of having to go out into the world and make my way, or go to college and further my education. I was all for leaving school and jumping on board the next boat I could find, but in reality, I knew it would not be that simple. It rarely is.

My parents really wanted me to go to college and although I wasn't initially very keen on the idea, I was eventually persuaded that it made sense. Despite my pretty average exam results I was offered a place at Scarborough Sixth Form College. I still had several months to go before I would be able to start learning to drive a car and by going to college I could continue sailing at Whitby and keep my folks happy at the same time. Life was easy and it gave me plenty of opportunity to plot my next adventure.

The first time I met John Beattie was on the marina pontoon in the upper harbour at Whitby. John was at that time a fairly inexperienced sailor and a recent convert from the armchair group of yachtsmen. He had recently purchased the *Warrior Queen*, a 35-foot long-keeled cruising yacht. Conservative in every aspect of her design, the *Warrior Queen* was constructed from fibreglass and came with a design pedigree of proven passage-making qualities.

The *Warrior Queen* was not a new yacht. In fact, she was quite the opposite. She had a deep central cockpit with wheel steering as opposed to a tiller and a separate aft cabin. Not obviously showing her age at first glance, she was certainly in need of a refit before any serious sailing could be considered, but *Warrior Queen* certainly had the potential to make a quality cruising yacht. John had some pretty serious plans. He invited me on board for a chat and as we sat in the cockpit with a cup of tea it wasn't long before his dreams began to ignite fires in my heart.

John was a college lecturer, originally from Belfast and now living in Whitby, frustrated with life and keen to see his aspirations of some twenty-five years finally flourish. It was a case of now or never for him. He had decided to make that leap of faith that proves to be the dividing line for most armchair sailors and had purchased a yacht with the genuine intention of sailing around the world.

Before he could set off there was much preparation to be done to both boat and skipper. John's plan was defiantly bold; he was short on both money and time but I could see he was determined to live out his dreams. Listening intently, I remember thinking about how I could fit in. Then, out of the blue, John mentioned he was looking for crew to help with the preparation of the boat as well as a transatlantic trip to the Caribbean. This was my chance.

An ocean passage to the Caribbean! "Wow, now you're talking," I thought. Although John wasn't proposing any kind of racing along the way, the idea of a transatlantic crossing was thrilling. It would be a huge undertaking and at just sixteen I felt it would be my ultimate challenge. I remember thinking this was a once-in-a-lifetime opportunity. A couple of months spent sailing across the Atlantic would give me more experience than I could gain sailing along the North-East coast in years. I decided to seize the moment. Sailing on board the *Warrior Queen* would indeed prove to be an experience, although not necessarily the one I expected. This particular trip would not go according to plan.

Convincing myself that a transatlantic ocean passage was a good idea was far easier than selling the prospect to my parents or my college tutors. I had only just started at the college and would need permission for time off. The Round Britain was one thing, an event where outside assistance, if needed, would never be far away, but going transatlantic was a whole different ball game: we would be completely on our own, cut off from the outside world and we would have to be totally self-sufficient for the whole passage. I felt this was a natural progression for me and headed home to talk it through with Mum and Dad.

Finding the money to purchase the *Warrior Queen* and prepare the boat for a round-the-world voyage had been a big financial commitment for John. He had been spending his hard-earned cash on the project for a long time before I met him and, unknown to the outside world, was starting to feel the pinch. It's a costly business – the paperback Admiralty charts necessary for navigating around the globe cost over a thousand pounds alone.

Dad had agreed to talk to John, and after an informal get-together at Whitby Yacht Club it was agreed that I and another friend of the family would join up, help prepare the boat and make the transatlantic passage. However, we would not be part of the crew sailing the boat from Whitby to Portugal. It was suggested that too much time away from my studies was not wise, whatever the opportunity. Reluctantly I agreed, pleased that I would get to do the transatlantic part of the trip. I later found out that my dad was concerned about the apparent lack of preparation and wanted to see the boat and crew undertake a serious passage before I joined. My dad has always had a way of smelling trouble before it arrives. He knew that any underlying problems would likely come to the fore on the crossing of the Bay of Biscay.

I was juggling college with the project. I had managed to square it with the headmaster who, despite bringing to my attention the fact I had only just joined, agreed it would be a good character-building exercise.

Bob Siggsworth, known to his friends as Siggy, was a member of Whitby Yacht Club and a well-known local yachtsman. I had first met him during the winter Frostbite sessions a few years earlier. We had hit it off from the start, sharing a passion for sailing. He was a lot older than me, with a wife and two kids plus a healthy level of sailing experience to draw upon. Siggy was always feeling the wrath of his wife Pauline for squandering the family savings on boats. They own Siggy's fish and chip bar on the quay just above the swing bridge at Whitby. It is still there today.

Siggy had so many boats pass thorough his hands you could almost say he was a yacht broker. He wasn't of course, he just hadn't been able to shake off those boyhood dreams that I was starting to turn into reality for myself. I liked Bob, he was a real laugh. He oozed an 'everything is possible' attitude. His stories of past adventures always brought a smile to my face. We had seen a few mini adventures of our own, but this project would be the first time both of us would face the enormity of an Atlantic ocean crossing.

The trip across the Bay of Biscay was not a particularly pleasurable experience for John Beattie. They saw some terrible weather and suffered a series of problems with the boat, including a heavy knockdown in rough seas that had really shaken John and damaged the self-steering system in the process. We were due to rendezvous in the Portuguese port of Lisbon. Having flown into Faro airport on Portugal's southern coast, Siggy and I were sitting on a noisy old train bound for Lisbon when he mentioned that the *Warrior Queen* was not actually there.

John was actually holed up in Porto, north of Lisbon. Situated at the mouth of the Rio Douro or River of Gold, this is the Portuguese region famous for producing port wine. Looking at the map we had picked up from the airport I could see Porto was miles up the coast. The steering problems must have been more of an issue than we had been led to believe. Siggy had decided not to tell me before we left Whitby in case my folks decided not to let me go, as he knew how much it meant to me and didn't want to screw things up.

Warrior Queen was tied up to a harbour wall in the old part of the town. The little boat was dwarfed by the surrounding buildings. Pleased to see us, John quickly invited us on board where we were greeted by Perry, the fourth crew member and new shipmate.

It quickly became apparent that the Biscay crossing had been a scary experience indeed and there was much to do before our departure the following day. The troubles with the self-steering gear were continuing and while John and Perry attended to that, Siggy and I set about repairing the mainsail which had been damaged a few days earlier. That night, while huddled around the cosy saloon table enjoying our first meal on board, John brought up the subject of their Biscay crossing.

The self-steering gear was not an isolated problem. There were also ongoing issues causing the main steering system to become stiff and heavy, making the *Warrior Queen* difficult but not impossible to steer manually. The ship's main electrical batteries were also a cause for concern, often not remaining charged for long enough to produce enough current to start the engine.

Our departure from Porto coincided with very little wind and a large, uncomfortable sea state left behind from some bad weather the region had seen a few days earlier. There was thick fog and we struggled to see the other side of the port as we motored out to sea. We should have waited until the conditions improved but John was keen to leave, muttering about the cost of mooring fees.

The plan was to sail to the Canary Islands and pull in for some re-stocking of supplies before setting out across the Atlantic. Everything sounded plausible enough to me. I had read several books in the lead up to our adventure. They all recommended sailing south beyond the Canary Islands 'until the butter melts and then turn right', heading west for the Caribbean some three thousand miles below the horizon.

This is the generally accepted method for a successful crossing of the Atlantic. Sailing south beyond the Canary Islands is mostly necessary in order to pick up the north-easterly trade winds flowing off the Sahara desert. Mariners have used these winds for centuries to help propel themselves across the wide expanse of the Atlantic towards the Americas.

Twenty-four hours into the trip we encountered the first of a string of problems. Our self-steering system which had already been repaired once now failed again. The system was an old but proven Hydrovane mechanical device that bolted to the stern of the boat. Unlike modern autopilot systems, this piece of equipment had no requirement for electricity and was a well-known and widely-used solution for steering small cruising yachts at sea for long periods. The knock-down in the Bay of Biscay had damaged the Hydrovane's rudder and it was not long before it snapped off completely, leaving John with no option but to manually steer *Warrior Queen* until he could reach a safe port.

Luckily for us, the thick fog the day before had lifted to reveal stunning bright sunshine and crystal blue seas. We were out of sight of land and completely on our own. It was obvious we would have to find a solution to the steering problem and that would most likely be found in the confines of a safe harbour rather than out here on the high seas.

Looking over the back of the boat we could see that the replacement rudder John and Perry had retro-fitted in Porto was damaged. Perry suggested going over the side into the ocean to check it out. I wasn't too sure about the idea but the weather was calm, so we all went along with it.

As Perry swam down to the base of the Hydrovane's rudder it

became clear that the laminated blade of plywood used as a replacement rudder was waterlogged and falling apart. Resources had been scarce in Porto and with limited funds John had made do with what he could find. Unfortunately, the chunk of plywood he had used didn't seem to be of a marine grade quality and lasted just a few hours before it failed.

We had plenty of hands on board to manually steer *Warrior Queen* to a safe port but had until now been relying on the Hydrovane as our primary steering system, as the main steering wheel in the cockpit was becoming fairly rigid and mostly unusable. We spent several hours effectively drifting on the ocean before we could rig up a successful repair.

It was decided that we would head for the Portuguese archipelago of Madeira. Closer than the Canary Islands, we could almost certainly buy a new and more suitable rudder for the Atlantic crossing there. Madeira was almost directly on our intended path so the detour would not cost us much time, or so we thought.

Warrior Queen on her way to Madeira. Siggy is steering with John in the foreground.

Approaching the islands, we were impressed by the beauty of Porto Santo, the most northern island of the archipelago, situated some twenty-seven miles north-east of Madeira itself. The good weather was holding and with a beautiful warm following wind we ghosted into the bay and soon found ourselves anchored off Porto Santo's beach, relaxing in our newly-found paradise.

Our stop off at Porto Santo was only meant to be a few hours, a chance for a bite to eat at anchor and a brief dip in the sea. With the sun on its way below the horizon, the time came to up anchor and get under way. The engine on board *Warrior Queen* was fairly old and despite having received an overhaul before leaving Whitby months earlier, had proved temperamental at times. Up until now the rusty old diesel had always spluttered into life after a bit of persuasion, but this time it seemed luck wasn't on our side. The batteries were drained flat and it became clear that we were going nowhere.

Once again it seemed destiny was trying to tell us something. It was apparent by now that the boat had significant problems. The night at anchor off the harbour was an unexpected respite that I was quite pleased to enjoy under the circumstances. The next day we went ashore by dinghy in search of a garage to recharge our flat batteries.

It turned out that John knew a thing or two about engines and with a few hours of spanners and grease behind us, a couple of squirts of Easy Start into the air intakes and a fully-charged set of batteries we heard the old girl kicking into life. We were on our way once again, bound for the harbour of Funchal on the main island.

Funchal is the capital of Madeira, a volcanic Island and natural safe haven, nestled into the base of huge mountains stretching into the sky. For mariners Funchal has provided excellent shelter from the Atlantic ocean for hundreds of years. It has become the equivalent of a motorway service station for yachtsmen and would be our best shot for a suitable long-term repair for the self-steering equipment.

Approaching Funchal, as if to add insult to injury the main steering system, already difficult to use, virtually seized up and became non-responsive. The mechanical link from the steering wheel in the cockpit to the rudder had become jammed. John struggled with the steering wheel and could hardly guide *Warrior Queen* as we motored into the harbour mouth. Just another problem for us to add to the list, I thought.

This voyage was turning into a nightmare and I was feeling a little uneasy about the whole thing. Siggy and I were hell-bent on completing an Atlantic crossing but here we were with a boat falling apart beneath our feet. It was becoming increasingly difficult for us to brush off the series of problems we were experiencing. Voicing my concerns to Siggy, I found that he too was struggling with the situation. We decided, after much debate, to stick with it until we reached the Canary Islands and then make a final decision. The Canaries would be the point of no return, so this made sense.

The Canary Islands are about three hundred miles south of Madeira and a good two-and-a-half days' sail with a fair wind. After some frantic exploration around Funchal we managed to find a local boatyard to machine up a suitable new rudder blade in exchange for what seemed like an extortionate amount of John's dwindling cash. To make matters worse, the measurements taken before we had the piece of mahogany made up were incorrect, and the result was a new rudder big enough to steer a battleship.

Despite directing our energies into repairing the boat, we found some time to paint the Whitby Yacht Club flag emblem onto the seawall in Funchal harbour. This has become a custom for passing yachts and is encouraged by the locals. Murals of sailboats and their crews illustrate colourful stories of past voyages. I believe ours is still there.

Money was obviously a real concern for John. It was clear that my and Siggy's financial contributions at the start of the trip were rapidly being eaten up with all the problems on board, while John's own reserves were dangerously low. Leaving Madeira, I could see the relief on John's face. At sea, there were no mooring fees to pay, no restaurant bills and no extortionate labour charges from locals to settle. We were free on the ocean, that much was clear.

I didn't know it at the time, but the second night at sea out of Madeira would be our last full night sailing on board the good ship *Warrior Queen*. We were cruising along under a moderate following wind as the sun started to set. It was lovely sailing and we were making good progress.

Throughout the trip John had insisted on using an old Tilley paraffin lamp to illuminate the cabin and reduce the amount of electricity taken from the batteries. It certainly was a lovely piece of kit and useful perhaps when at anchor, but I had been opposed from the outset to the idea of using it at sea, seeing it as a fire risk.

The lamp was illuminating the cabin, creating a warm inviting glow. Perry was sitting in the cockpit by the entrance to the cabin, enjoying the easy sailing and warm evening wind. John was in the aft cabin asleep and Siggy was up forward also enjoying some downtime. As we forged our way, southbound into the darkness, we suddenly noticed the light coming from the saloon. The intensity of the glow had changed. The motion of the boat had caused the lamp to crash into the vertical hand rail above the saloon table and burst into flames.

Within seconds that warm inviting glow threatened to turn into an inferno. "Bloody hell!" I shouted as I let go of the steering wheel, pushing past Perry who was staring into the cabin with equal astonishment, his eyes fixed on the flames as they engulfed the lamp.

I knew we had a matter of seconds before the most useful item of equipment on board would be our rubber life raft. There was no time to find a fire extinguisher. Leaping into the cabin I grabbed the nearest knife and with a cloth from the galley smothered the lamp. Cutting it away from the cabin head I ran up on deck, past Perry who had by now come into the cabin to help.

Entering the cockpit with this now subdued inferno in my hands I was all for throwing it over the side. John had been woken by the shouting and commotion. He popped his head out of the rear cabin hatchway with perfect timing, just as I was about to throw his beloved paraffin lamp into the sea for a one-way trip to the bottom. This event did nothing for crew morale and despite preventing a major fire on board I had managed to upset John by breaking the glass of the lamp and nearly throwing the whole lot over the side.

As we reached the tiny port of Los Gigantes on the west coast of Tenerife I was really struggling to see the trip going any further for me. The episode with the paraffin lamp was weighing heavily on my mind. It seemed that everything on board was showing signs of age and failing around us. I wanted the Atlantic so much, but not like this. My heart was saying one thing and my head was saying another. Once again I found myself motoring into a foreign port with a heavy heart.

We had just reached the safe confines of the harbour walls when John announced that we had lost all forward drive from the engine. What now, I thought. "Try reverse," said Siggy. Nothing happened. We had no forward or reverse gears. Drifting up to a pontoon, we took the decision to moor up there and then. Further inspection revealed that the propeller shaft had severed its connection to the engine.

The only thing stopping the shaft sliding out of the boat, leaving a

Warrior Queen being hauled out in the Canary Islands, note the huge rudder for the self-steering gear.

gaping hole and sending us to the bottom of the sea, was the fact that the shaft and propeller had become wedged into the forward section of the rudder stock. The following morning we arranged for the boat to be lifted out of the water with a view to fixing the problem. It became obvious *Warrior Queen* was not going anywhere for some time.

This was the final straw for me. I couldn't go back to sea. I knew the right choice would be to leave the boat here and fly home. The lure of the Atlantic was so strong but I felt overwhelmed by the problems and total lack of preparation. Siggy was thinking the same thing, but we both felt a real sense of commitment to John and could not just leave him high and dry without any help.

Several days later and with *Warrior Queen* now effectively impounded in the boatyard due to a lack of money to pay the boatyard bills, Siggy and I informed John of our reluctant decision to fly home. Our adventure had drawn to a premature conclusion and with it went our dreams of crossing the Atlantic.

John took the news rather well, all things considered, but you couldn't fail to notice reality had well and truly kicked in for him. He was dealing with many more pressing demons and I had the feeling we were the least of his problems. We felt terrible for leaving, but there was no way forward for us either. We couldn't put to sea even if we wanted to, and with time and money conspiring against us it was time to call it a day. This was a heartbreaking moment for me. Letting go of the Atlantic dream was so difficult. It was my first experience of having to make a tough decision under pressure, and despite knowing I had made the right choice, I flew back to England disappointed and deflated.

John eventually got the *Warrior Queen* sailing again and would later go on to refine his round-the-world sailing ambition to a circuit of the north Atlantic. Sailing home from Venezuela, he would stumble upon a small open rowing boat several hundred miles from St Lucia in the Caribbean. The boat contained a young but half-dead fisherman. He and his friend had been blown out to sea several days earlier while fishing. His friend had perished the day before from exposure and lack of fresh water. By pure chance, John had stumbled across their boat in the nick of time. He saved the fisherman's life, taking him back to St Lucia before going on to successfully complete his passage.

4

BANDIT

ollege for me was becoming an increasingly mundane activity. The thought of another two years at school was really starting to feel like a bad idea. I knew what I wanted from life and had a fair idea of how to achieve my goals. It was January 1993 and in April I would turn seventeen. The college was beginning to realise that my commitment lay elsewhere and it was only a matter of time before the headmaster's patience ran out. I had been reprimanded several times for not turning up for classes, going sailing with Siggy instead.

My mum and dad were aware of this and realised I was going through the motions for their sake more than mine. I was keen to get out into the world and had already declared my intention to become a professional yachtsman.

My dad knew that many people were drawn by the allure of the professional yachting scene but few actually succeeded in making the transition from budding amateur to fully-paid professional. He was keen to make sure I embraced life's opportunities, but mindful that I shouldn't throw the best years of my life away with nothing to show for it financially.

We agreed that I would stay on at college until I passed my driving test. I would then join Dad in the family car sales business in London, learning the ropes there while I pursued a career in sailing. This suited me just fine. I loved all things car and had grown up with Dad buying and selling them. The motor trade was the only other subject that I found interesting at the time. From my parents' point of view, I would have a back-up career option should the sailing not work out. Everyone was happy. All I had to do was get through the next few months.

A chance meeting at Whitby Yacht Club that winter with another member and sailing friend of my dad would present my first opportunity to take command of my own yacht. Roger Ellison was a keen sailor who until recently had always struggled to attract enough crew to race his small open keelboat. Dad often went sailing with Roger in the summer and I had sailed with them occasionally when they needed an extra person.

Roger had recently sold his boat and had been given the nod by a friend about a small yacht that was going for a song, somewhere in the depths of Ipswich. The owner had lost interest in sailing some time ago and having laid the boat up on his driveway, was keen to sell. Roger, a nice guy with a quiet nature, wanted to discuss the prospect of a partnership. Leaning across the table he asked, "How about going halves on the boat? He just wants to get shot of it and the price reflects that." Roger was no mug – he knew that by going in with me, he would never be short of enthusiastic crew.

The boat in question was a 23-footer, a lightweight flyer. It was designed by well-known and prolific naval architect Stephen Jones. I would later have a phone conversation with Stephen about the boat, in which he struggled to remember even designing such a craft. She had been designed in the late 1970s and despite being nearly fifteen years old, had not seen much action. She was in remarkable condition for her age; with a bit of spit and polish, she could be restored to her former glory.

I was in no position to make such an adult financial commitment but I did have the asset of my Laser sailing dinghy, which I knew one of my friends was keen to buy. I could see a way forward, but needed to have a sit-down with my parents to gauge their response. The new boat was so cheap that if I could sell my Laser and get a little support from Mum and Dad we would be in business.

I needn't have worried. I soon had my parents' contribution in the bag and, armed with the proceeds from the sale of my Laser, I had just enough cash to take care of my end and make the deal. Roger was pleased and made the necessary arrangements. Two weeks later, *Bandit*, as she would most affectionately become known, arrived on the back of a truck, having made the long, slow journey from Ipswich.

It was a big moment in our household. The imminent arrival of the boat that signified my new-found freedom had been the topic of conversation for days. We even went up on to the North Yorkshire moors in Mum's Land Rover, awaiting the grand arrival with a healthy supply of boat cakes and hot tea in thermos flasks. It was the middle of winter and a thick layer of beautiful virgin white snow covered the landscape.

I was impatient and keen to get straight to work on the refit. Roger and I wanted the boat to be ready for the upcoming season of races at Whitby Yacht Club, and I had already spoken to a few of my friends about the prospect of crewing aboard the good ship *Bandit*.

As we sat in the car within sight of RAF Fylingdales, the early warning centre for ballistic missile attack against the UK, I could hardly bear the suspense. The name of *Bandit* had been picked from a hatful of possible boat names by Roger's youngest daughter Amelia. I had originally wanted to call the boat Obsession, on account of my obsessive love of sailing, but *Bandit* had a better ring to it.

The sight of *Bandit*, also covered in snow, coming over the moors was a truly marvellous moment. She needed work, but somehow that made the occasion all the more pure. I remember the overwhelming feeling of excitement as we followed *Bandit* off the moors and into Coates marine boatyard in Whitby. You could have given me the keys to a brand new Ferrari that day and I would not have felt the same buzz, not even close.

Bandit making her way over the North Yorkshire moors.

We had three months before our first scheduled race and I was keen to make sure we would be in good shape by then. Most of the work required to get *Bandit* up and running was just cosmetic. Roger and I decided to change the thick beige hull stripe for a set of sparkling red racing stripes. We repainted the worn non-slip paint on the deck, changing the colour from a dirty white to an attractive light blue and with a few other minor tweaks our boat started to adopt her new persona. Within just a few weeks we had transformed *Bandit* from an old, tired and nameless boat into a sleek racing machine. We were ready for a season of competitive yacht racing.

With my new-found freedom came new responsibilities. By now I had a fair amount of sailing experience under my belt for my age, but this was the first time I would be in command of a boat and other people. I had taken my RYA Day Skipper course at Whitby Yacht Club the year before, when I was just sixteen. The course provided the basic but essential knowledge I would require in order to navigate *Bandit* safely along the North-East coast. Roger was only interested in sailing locally at Whitby and although I had more ambitious plans, the boat was ready to sail, so we settled on a loose agenda for the upcoming season.

We got off to a good start, and our results improved each time we went racing. *Bandit* was a real flying machine and I was in my element. Enjoying our success, I remember feeling I had the world in the palm of my hand. I was keen to have an all-youth team on board for the costal races but, before he would let me sail over the horizon, Dad decided to sit in on a couple of events to see how I managed things.

Our first costal event was a regatta hosted by the North East Cruiser Racing Association, a weekend of racing from Whitby to Hartlepool and returning the following day. This was my first trip away from Whitby with *Bandit*. With a couple of mates and Dad's wisdom we were soon racing across the Bay bound for Hartlepool. It was a pretty windy affair, with most of the small boats electing not to hoist their biggest sails.

We had the whole lot up. The spinnaker pulled us along at breathtaking speed towards Kettleness Point at the northern end of the Bay. I was already thinking of glory. Dad voiced his concerns about hoisting this amount of sail in the aggressive conditions but, keen to make a solid impression on the fleet, I wanted to go for it. Everyone on board apart from my father had a dinghy sailing background, and we were not in the least bit fazed by the strong conditions. I now realise that Dad was viewing the situation from a position of experience and maturity. He didn't want us to hoist the big spinnaker and knew it would not be long before something dramatic happened if we did.

We were ahead of the main bulk of the fleet, having started before the largest boats in the race and were certainly holding our own against everyone in our division. The motion on board was starting to become really skittish and it was clear that *Bandit* was being pushed to her limit with this amount of sail set. We were surfing down the waves with the wind behind us, but the bigger boats were gradually bearing down on us with their extra power and speed. They were close enough for us to hear the grinding of winches as their bows sliced through the rough sea like knives through butter.

I was steering, sitting at the back of the cockpit not saying a word, my mind fixed on keeping the boat on her feet and not wiping-out. I could feel the pressure on the tiller. It was exhilarating. Closing in on Runswick Bay some five miles north of Whitby we were really on the edge. Most of the biggest yachts were all around us when a couple of competitors further inshore wiped out under a big gust of wind. That same wind was rapidly coming out to sea towards us and it was clear that we were about to be engulfed. There was nothing we could do but hold on and hope for the best. Dad threw me a glance, looking worried. I did my best to reassure him, saying that this was normal for yacht racing. Dad was a cruising man and until recently had not experienced much racing other than with Roger. His reaction indicated that he didn't believe a word.

With savage force, the gust of wind smacked us. I shouted, "Here we go!" Full of expectation and confident we were about to be treated to the ride of our lives, I expected us to capitalise on this gust of wind and increase our lead in spectacular fashion. We were already standing out from the pack as one of the few smaller yachts flying a big spinnaker. Suddenly there was a loud tearing sound, similar to paper being torn, only much louder, followed by an unexpected calm. The boat instantly slowed, like a spaceship dropping out of hyperdrive. Not the outcome I had expected!

Our colourful yellow-and-white spinnaker had exploded under the force of the wind. The sail, its guts wrenched apart was flying like a flag, the jagged remains blowing in the wind. I was plucked from my private bubble of disbelief by Dad saying, "Thank the Lord for that, there is a God in Heaven after all."

Dad is not a religious man but the realisation that the crazy sleigh ride had come to a natural end was enough to make him shout aloud. Our race didn't end there however – we did make it to the finish, completing the race and learning another valuable lesson in the process.

Me and Dad enjoying a cup of tea on board after the spinnaker blew out.

It was only a matter of time before I would be given official permission from Mum and Dad to take *Bandit* to sea on my own. When the time came, my young crew and I were ready to go out and show the world what we were made of.

One of my regular team members was a young lad called Peter Franks. We nicknamed him Biff on account of his striking resemblance to the character Biff Tannen from the film Back to the Future. Biff was a loyal friend and keen sailor. Slightly younger than me, he was always part of the team on *Bandit* and played a pivotal role on board whenever we went racing.

There was also my next-door neighbour, Justin Scott, who was always up for anything exciting. He and his brother were mates of mine. We would often hang out together and Justin would come sailing regularly. There is only one way to describe Justin – a pure adrenaline junkie. This guy made Action Man look tame and was always up for anything crazy.

Justin is the epitome of 'extreme', but in a good way. A talented sculptor, he can make the most beautiful and elegant sculptures from ice or bronze and alongside his 'man and van' business he makes an honest living. We would go mountain biking together and one time, just for the hell of it, we decided to ride across Whitby golf course because the bunkers made great jumps. We must have had the whole club chasing us as we violated their green. I paid a fair price that day by cracking the frame of my mountain bike when I landed rather heavily after miscalculating the height of a bunker as we escaped from a group of irate golfers. We got away, but only just.

Justin was also a very competent canoeist and achieved a reputation for being a little bit mad after pushing his canoe and himself off the top of Whitby pier at low tide, just for the rush. The drop must have been over twenty feet. He's a great bloke who lives for the moment by squeezing the sponge of life to the full and is the sort that thinks nothing of jumping out of a plane with a parachute. We have similar characters and remain friends to this day.

By the middle of the summer I had outstayed my welcome at Scarborough College and decided to leave before I was told to. I passed my driving test a week after my seventeenth birthday and was now working in London with Dad in the family business. By day I would be washing and cleaning cars and by night I worked three shifts a week for Timberland in one of their warehouses near Heathrow airport. I needed the extra money to pay for new sails and was keen to have them before the big event of the season. Every Friday night Dad and I jumped in the car and headed back up to Whitby for the weekend to see Mum and go sailing. They were happy days.

One of my greatest memories of sailing *Bandit* was during the 190-mile Bass Rock race in 1993. The event started and finished in Blyth on the Northumbrian coast. It was the big offshore event of the season; we had been building up to it all year and were desperate for a good result.

The forecast prior to the start had promised rough weather and, fearing the worst, several local skippers from Whitby urged me to not put to sea, saying I had nothing to prove. Although this was true, and I didn't feel under any pressure to sail, we felt confident, and having just hired a new life raft specifically for the event, I wanted to be part of the action.

The course meant a long, hard slog sailing into the wind to the Bass Rock in the mouth of the Firth of Forth and would be pretty tough going on the fleet. Being one of the smallest boats in the race, it wasn't long before we found ourselves as one of the back markers. *Bandit* was a lightweight boat that didn't excel when sailing into the wind and waves, especially when the weather was rough. By the time we were in sight of the Bass Rock we were left in no doubt that we were last in the race.

We could only watch as the biggest boats and leaders sailed past

us on their way back from rounding the rock. They were enjoying the rough conditions, although they were sailing with heavily-reefed sails. We, on the other hand, were getting a real pasting. We were making slow progress and the waves had been getting progressively steeper as we closed in on the Rock. The lads were all feeling a bit seasick and somewhat demoralised by the sight of the leaders heading back. Biff wanted to go below to make a well-earned Pot Noodle, our only source of hot food during the race. He had been inside the small, cramped cabin less than thirty seconds before he started shouting: "The bow is flexing, the bow is flexing!"

I couldn't quite understand what he meant at the time but the tone of his voice suggested there was some urgency. Handing over the tiller to one of the lads, I climbed into the cabin and could scarcely believe my eyes. The whole forward section of *Bandit*'s hull was flexing dramatically each time we bounced off a wave. *Bandit* was a home-finished boat and up until now we had never given any thought to the lack of lateral support in the bow area. We'd certainly never seen the hull flexing like that. It was potentially a very serious situation and – with the benefit of hindsight – we should have turned around there and then to relieve the pressure on the boat. The weather was not gale force by any means, but the wind was blowing a good Beaufort Force 6 to 7. That's as good as a gale on a little boat like *Bandit*.

Nevertheless, the Bass Rock was only five miles away, which translated into just over an hour's sailing. Once we had gone around the Rock, the pressure on the hull would be a lot less and we could continue racing, but if we turned around now it would all be over. There was only one thing for it: I told Biff it was his duty to sit down in the bow, arms outstretched, applying pressure to each side of the hull to support the large sections as we continued on. Biff would have followed me off a cliff if I'd said it would keep us in the race. I was lucky to have such a good mate. We would later compete in the famous Fastnet race together.

By the time we rounded the Rock we must have been sailing for closer to two hours since the discovery of the hull problem. Down in the cabin things were pretty ugly for poor Biff. He had been sick several times because of the violent pitching motion of the boat. The cabin was a mess, vomit and equipment everywhere. Despite that, he had held his station until the danger had passed.

Competing in the Whitby Yacht Club Summer Series.

We had rounded the Rock within sight of most of our division and knew the next class with the 30-foot yachts were not that far away. This was our chance – it was downwind to the finish and this was the point of sail that *Bandit* liked. Cutting the corner of the Rock rather closer than I would have liked under normal circumstances, I asked for the spinnaker to be hoisted. Once again, we were well above the normal limit for such a sail and a mistake now would put us over on our backsides. But knowing that the lads wanted a result in this race more than any other, we went for it.

Justin hoisted the sail. He was my man in those conditions. Although at the time he was not a very experienced sailor, I knew he had balls of steel and was up for the job. The sail filled and with what seemed like instant acceleration, *Bandit* shot off down the waves like a missile. We soon overhauled the front-runners in our fleet who were adopting a cautious but seamanlike approach to the conditions, and it wasn't long before we were challenging the bigger 30-foot yachts. We were the only team flying a spinnaker.

We huddled together at the back of the cockpit in an effort to keep as much of the crew's weight as far from the front of the boat as possible. This helped prevent the bow being buried in the waves as we surfed into the troughs. *Bandit* was flying, but we were definitely pushing her to the limit. Talking about the incident afterwards, I learned that the lads were all waiting for something to go wrong and none of us was particularly surprised when it did.

We were approaching the towering cliffs of St Abbs Head on the Berwickshire coast when the big wipe-out – the kind that creates reputations – happened. Picked up by a particularly steep wave, the force sent *Bandit* careering down the face and into the trough at the bottom. The bow disappeared, raising the back of the boat high into the air. As the rudder lifted out of the water I knew we were in trouble. I had no way of controlling the situation. There was water covering the foredeck, right up to the foot of the mast.

We had almost sailed *Bandit* under the waves and with the stern sticking up in the air we twisted around and fell over onto our port side, lying flat in the water. Everyone was holding on for dear life. I remember thinking I was glad the cabin hatches were shut tight, otherwise we would be in real danger of filling up with water. That episode was our cue to get the spinnaker down and we recovered as best we could.

On our way to winning Whitby Regatta.

Sailing *Bandit* at Roker Regatta, Sunderland.

This incident would spark an interesting conversation at the yacht club bar several weeks later. My Dad was ordering a round of drinks when a fellow sailor who was propping up the bar, having had one too many, pointed towards me, saying, "You see that lad over there? He's a nutter." He went on to explain how we'd shot past him during the Bass Rock Race, only to have the biggest wipe-out he had ever seen.

My Dad told the guy that I was his son. The man nearly fell over with apologies. Dad found it amusing that I had gained a reputation for being crazy in such a short time. We had indeed made our mark.

They were great times sailing on *Bandit*. We had many exciting adventures and many close calls. It was without doubt seat-of-your-pants sailing. I only had a basic grasp of navigation but we would enjoy real success over the following two seasons. We cleaned out most of the Whitby Yacht Club silverware before my eighteenth birthday, taking the Whitby Regatta and Summer Series titles amongst others in the process. We were on a roll and life was great .

Our continued success with *Bandit* meant that I attracted the attention of numerous yacht owners and they asked me to sail with them. One such offer came from local yachtsman Don Cowen. He was the proud owner of a very sleek 34-foot racing yacht called *Applecore*. The yacht itself was a thoroughbred and required experienced hands to realise her full potential.

This was a constant problem for Don. The boat needed eight to ten people on board and finding a regular team for local racing had proved surprisingly difficult. Don was ambitious, at least at a club level, and for the 1994 season he decided to have a stab at the North Sea Race from Blyth to Mandal in Norway. As one of several that had been invited on board, I was appointed as crew boss. My role was similar to the position I was now used to on *Bandit*, the only difference being that on this boat the buck stopped with Don and not with me.

The North Sea Race that year was blessed with fairly light following winds from the west that gave us a downwind trip under our colourful spinnaker all the way to Norway. This suited our lightweight flying saucer very well. As the Norwegian coast line appeared, not only were we still just in sight of the leaders, but we knew we could win the race on handicap.

The last few miles had proved very slow for the much larger leading boats. They had managed to claw their way to within sight of the finish line off Mandal before losing the wind completely. The race had turned into a yacht car park. We, though, had managed to hold onto a zephyr of wind. It was just enough to coax *Applecore* along, although at little more than a snail's pace. However, it's all relative, especially when your opposition's not moving at all. Within a couple of hours we closed in on the fleet and circled the drifting yachts. We maintained our momentum and managed to win overall, even without handicap.

It was a proud moment for all of us, but even more special for Don who had struggled for so long to get *Applecore* onto the podium. He was on a high for a long time after that.

As the second season of sailing with *Bandit* drew to a close, it was becoming ever more apparent I needed to broaden my horizons.

The south coast was where it was at and I knew my time sailing out of Whitby was coming to an end. I had to make the hard decision to permanently relocate closer to the south coast. I had a great life in Whitby, with lots of friends and family all around me; I could quite easily have taken the easier option to stay put. To make matters worse, I had a steady girlfriend and knew that a decision to leave Whitby permanently would mean curtains for our relationship.

Ginny and I met when I had just turned seventeen. She was a bit older than me but we were attracted to each other from the first moment we met. Ginny worked in the family business with her brother. Together they managed a charming little harbour-front café on the pier at Whitby. It had stunning views across the bay into the North Sea. I would spend a lot of my time there while we were together. On the long, hot summer days when the café was packed full I would lend a hand and help out clearing the tables. The café was a great little business and Ginny managed the place with elegant efficiency.

They were happy days and leaving Whitby would be a hard but necessary decision if I was going to break into the professional yachting arena. We told each other that being apart for extended periods wouldn't matter but I think we both knew that at that time in our lives, it eventually would. Ginny knew how much I loved sailing and even said that one day she thought my path would take me far away from Whitby and from her. On my eighteenth birthday she presented me with a bottle of champagne. She knew I wasn't much of a drinker but whilst sitting on the beach outside the café she asked me to promise not to open it until a very special moment in my life.

There have been many special moments since that day but none that seemed worthy enough to pop the cork from that bottle. I still have it, unopened.

I remember the day we said goodbye to each other. It was a Sunday and I was due back in London the following morning for work. Ginny was standing outside the front door of her house. It was early evening and just getting dark. I could see her in the rear-view mirror of my car as I drove out of the drive and down the street. Waving goodbye to each other I could tell she was upset. We both were. Despite not formally agreeing it was over, I think we both knew it was. It was an emotional moment, but a life elsewhere was beckoning and it was time to start following my dreams, even though it meant leaving Whitby and Ginny.

5

GAINING EXPERIENCE

Fresh from winning the North Sea Race, I was approached by an ex-Royal Marine-turned-yacht delivery skipper called Bob. He was looking for a couple of enthusiastic people to help with the delivery of a 34-foot yacht from Vilamoura in Portugal to the Beaulieu River on the south coast of England. I rounded-up Justin as a last-minute shipmate and we were on our way to the Algarve for my first official sailing job.

Bob was not your average yacht delivery skipper. Short in stature and round in the belly, his arms were as big as my legs. He had a unique outlook on life and his own style of sailing and boat management. Bob liked his booze and seemed to view the yacht delivery business as a way to go out on the razz while being paid for the privilege. Since leaving the Royal Marines he had made his living this way and would always turn up with a fistful of money, having been given some up-front cash for 'expenses'. Unbeknownst to the boat owners, they were paying for him to have a good time along the way. Bob never seemed to have any problem mixing business with pleasure.

Bob was the kind of guy that always had a story to tell, but perhaps his most outrageous tale – or at least the one that is most vivid in my mind – was where he had to flee the island of Majorca after a night on the booze that ended in devastation. He had been on one of his legendary benders, drinking all day and night. On leaving the bar, he made a fateful decision to drive home in his pink Rolls-Royce.

He had been doing rather well for himself in Majorca. I never asked what kind of work had been so rewarding but realised it would not have been just yacht deliveries. The car probably belonged to the owner of some super yacht he had managed to blag his way onto, although he would always talk about it as if it were his own.

The outcome was not pretty. The resulting accident left him in a ditch with the Roller smashed almost beyond recognition. Looking back at a trail of destruction, the view was apparently enough to sober up any man. He left the doomed Rolls-Royce in the ditch, its pink paint leaving a signature well and truly imprinted on the other smashed vehicles he'd used as cushions along the road. The next day he did a runner.

I never knew whether that story was true or not, but having had first-hand experience of the man, I was inclined to believe him. It was just the sort of crazy stunt he would pull. Easy come easy go, that was Bob.

We arrived in Vilamoura to find the harbour font lined with several small cafés and bars. It was a nice place although at that time a little quiet as there were few people around. After completing a quick preliminary look over the boat and dumping our gear on board, it was time for a bite to eat. The sun was shining and with beer on tap, Bob was in Heaven. Walking at random into a harbour-side bar I had no idea we would end up being there until the early hours of the following morning. If I had, I would have picked a place with more comfortable seating.

Justin had said he was thirsty and Bob wasted no time in assuming he meant thirsty for alcohol. Within minutes of entering the bar, Bob had laid down a challenge that Justin could not resist. A simple drinking game, with personal pride as the prize. Bob was on the local beer and Justin was matching his every gulp with sips of sangria. I elected to sample the local ice cream, something I would come to regret after my seventh chocolate sundae. Bob insisted on me keeping up with the challenge, whatever I was drinking or eating. Bob wasn't one to argue with so I kept my end of the bargain – for a while.

At the time I thought that a few ice cream sundaes would be the lesser of two evils; getting drunk a matter of hours before we embarked on a commercial delivery was not the best way to start off. As it turned out, I think I would have had a better chance with the beer. I had managed to make myself feel quite ill, matching them pint for ice cream. Eventually, with my belly full, I couldn't take any more and switched to jugs of water in an effort to settle my stomach.

The bartender must have been rubbing his hands. By the end of the evening we had spent a small fortune in that bar. The beer and sangria were flowing from 12 noon until 1am. I didn't have a clue what we were celebrating. Late in the evening, when Justin had already been sick into the harbour, the pair were both showing signs of fatigue. Justin had been out of it for some time, spilling more sangria than was passing through his lips. I was starting to realise this man Bob was a bit of a maverick.

With the pair on their last legs, Justin poured himself his final glass of Sangria. In a toast to the upcoming voyage rather than drinking he promptly threw the whole lot over his shoulder without looking to see if anyone was sitting behind us. At that stage I don't think it would have mattered to him anyway. Unfortunately for us, there was someone there, a really big someone who was now covered from head to toe in Justin's sangria.

It didn't go down too well. Bob was rocking from side to side on his stool and banging his fist on the table. He found it hilarious and under a shower of his laughter I found myself having to reason with a very angry and dripping wet local who didn't speak a word of English. Having explained as best I could that my friend was drunk and how sincerely sorry we were, we managed to round ourselves up and vacate the bar before things really got out of control.

On the whole Bob was a good bloke, but there was no doubt he had a somewhat cavalier attitude towards life and unfortunately this approach leaked into his professional judgement at times. We had not long put to sea from Vilamoura when I discovered there were no navigation charts on board. Bob's reaction to my discovery was sharp: "We don't need charts, it's all in my head, and anyway, we have a GPS". What good was a GPS without charts I thought? Justin and I thought he was joking. We soon realised he was deadly serious.

We sailed that yacht nearly a thousand miles back to the UK, along the Portuguese coast and across the Bay of Biscay without any charts whatsoever and to our surprise, completed the passage unscathed. Without doubt this was more by luck than judgement. In the future I would make it my business to check the little details before putting to sea, especially when I was not in command.

Luck eventually runs out for most people and Bob's would ultimately run out in spectacular style. He crashed a beautiful 53-foot twin screw wooden motor launch into the submarine barriers outside Portsmouth harbour, nearly sinking a piece of history in the process. The boat was a near-pristine example of 1950s wooden splendour and Bob managed to very nearly write the whole thing off. That was the last time I went to sea with Bob.

Late in the November 1994 I was presented with another chance to go transatlantic. I had applied for a job with a company called Polaris Yacht Deliveries. The company was a thoroughly professional operation run by a guy called John Chandler. John, then in his 50s, was an ex-London cabbie turned delivery captain. He was a lovely guy and a hugely experienced mariner. Together with his wife, who arranged the shore-side logistics of the business, they had delivered all types of sailing yachts around the globe to places as far afield as Fiji and Tonga.

Our trip was a 4,000-mile delivery of a brand-new 40-foot catamaran from Les Sables d'Olonne on France's Biscay coast across the Atlantic to Tortola in the British Virgin Islands. John's approach to yacht deliveries was at the other end of the spectrum to my experiences with

Celebrating Christmas Day mid-Atlantic.

Bob: we took two days just to cover all the saloon cushions and laminated wooden furniture with protective plastic.

John had established a reputation for attention to detail. He wanted to minimise the risk of any damage to the boat, no matter how small. I had to admire this approach, thorough and methodical. By the time we left Les Sables d'Olonne we even had foam covering the rigging to protect the mainsail when it rubbed against the wires. This was a long trip and chafing on ropes and sails could become a real problem. John knew his stuff.

The voyage would deliver my first real experience of an ocean storm and my first Christmas away from my parents. I was living a dream and loving every minute of it. Twenty-two days after leaving Les Sables, I caught my first glimpse of Tortola as we motored up to the dock at Road Town. The voyage had gone as smoothly as clockwork and I now had my first transatlantic crossing under my belt. It felt awesome.

THE FASTNET YOUTH CHALLENGE

1995 would be a good year and the future was waiting to be written. Coming back from the transatlantic voyage, I had my sights set on the Fastnet Race. I had hatched a clear plan in my mind during those long, solitary nights on watch in the Atlantic. I wanted to head up a youth team entry into the famous event. At the time, the 605-mile race felt like the pinnacle of sailing endeavour. I had been toying with the idea for a few months and with the plan worked out, I started what would prove to be a long and tiring journey to secure a boat.

My business idea was sound, or at least I thought so. The plan was simple: we would charter a suitable yacht and pay for it by recruiting a team of youngsters all keen to pay a fee for such a rare opportunity. The main problem was that I was still only eighteen, and people just didn't like the idea of chartering an expensive yacht to a teenager. I tried tirelessly to secure a boat but without success. Close to throwing in the towel, I had arranged a last-minute meeting in Plymouth with one of my potential crewmates.

I had met Ellie Littlejohn the year before after making a last-minute decision to hitch a ride on a race boat at Torbay Regatta. I arrived at the harbour with nowhere to stay and not knowing anyone, but Ellie was kind enough to offer me a place to sleep for the night on board the boat she was sailing.

Ellie was a couple of years younger than me but turned out to be equally keen to be part of the Fastnet adventure. She came from a family of sailors who lived in Haybrook Bay, an idyllic and secluded hamlet overlooking the sea near Plymouth. Their house was the family home her father had built with his own hands before Ellie was born.

Ellie's father was a master carpenter and his creations from wood were truly works of art. He was one of the nicest men you could ever be fortunate enough to meet. Together as a family they always made me feel completely at home. The house would become team headquarters over the following year and Ellie would prove to be the glue that kept us together as a team.

I had come to Plymouth at Ellie's request in a last-ditch attempt to find someone willing to loan us a boat. She knew people in the area and was keen for us to do the rounds to see what support we could drum up. The situation in Plymouth was all too familiar, however. We just seemed to be too young for anyone to take us seriously. We were ready to jack the project in when we stumbled across the Plymouth Sailing School. Ellie suggested we have one last go and thinking 'what the hell', I agreed.

We had no preconceptions but I didn't think our chances were too good. The principal of the school was a softly-spoken man called Richard Brown. He was a yacht master examiner with vast experience of everything nautical. Together, he and another staff member listened to us babble on for the best part of half an hour. I could tell after the first few minutes that they were interested, at least enough to hear us out.

Ellie and I hit it off with Richard from the outset. There were issues to overcome but with the basic outline on the table Richard could see past the age issue. The deal was simple: we would buy some new sails for their yacht and would allow the revenue from two crew places to go directly to the sailing school. The cost of new sails would be our concern but the school would be able to keep them after the race. We also offered our free labour to help with the overhaul that their boat obviously required.

Amazingly, within an hour we had a deal and the basics agreed. One point Richard was keen to address was my lack of official yachting qualifications. He could see I didn't lack experience, but knew they would need to train me to at least a Royal Yachting Association (RYA) Coastal Skipper standard with commercial endorsement. This would keep them on the correct side of the law when we put to sea and also help me pursue my career after the Fastnet. Richard's willingness to help was almost overwhelming.

Walking out of the room, Ellie and I were ecstatic, we had done it. We had pulled a rabbit out of the hat when we had been about to give up. The Plymouth Sailing School had literally been the last point of call before admitting failure. There was much to do, but from that moment we knew we were on our way to the famous Fastnet Rock.

St Luke's Crusader was a Sigma 36, a solid but fairly tired old girl. She reflected the years of commercial service she had given to the sailing school, but we could see the potential and set about once again on a pre-season overhaul. Recruiting a team was also in the forefront of our minds. I had a couple of candidates from Whitby who bought into the project. Biff was an early teammate, eager to sign up, and along with Matt Robinson, another friend from the North-East, things were starting to fall into place.

Left to right: Matt Robinson, me, Peter Franks *aka* Biff, 1995.

Ellie brought in one of her friends, Darren Wills, a local guy who was a year older than me. Darren was a good sailor but did have a tendency to let off a little too much steam every now and again. We would eventually develop a mutual understanding and he would become my reliable second-in-command when at sea.

With three more crew slots up for grabs we sent out our first press release to the world, informing the media of our forthcoming endeavours. To our amazement, the local television network latched onto the project and after the first of our interviews for the BBC I received a call from the mother of a lad who wanted to join our campaign.

At just fifteen, Dave Barden was very young but as keen to be involved as the rest of us. Looking across the sailing school table with his mother almost pleading with me to give him a chance, I couldn't help thinking of the time when I had wanted the place on Harold Usherwood's boat for the Round Britain Race.

Accepting Dave and offering him a place on board was one of the best decisions I made during the project. It would not be long before the quiet, unassuming lad would develop into one of the most competent sailors on board.

Within a short space of time my vision of a youth team entry into the Fastnet had evolved from a pipe dream into reality. We had secured the boat and with the addition of Jeremy Rowells and Sam Clarke, the final crew places were now decided. Jeremy was a student at Southampton University doing a degree in yacht manufacture and design; Sam was keen to gain an apprenticeship as a sailmaker and saw the project as a good stepping-stone.

Together we formed an eight-strong team and called ourselves the Fastnet Youth Challenge. At the London Boat Show in January, when the project was still just an idea, I had been introduced to one of the managers of a company called Pro Rainer. They made foul-weather gear and had expressed an interest in sponsoring the project if it got off the ground. I made contact again, as we all needed foul-weather clothing and I was keen for us to look like a team with matching kit.

Phil Davies had warmed to the project from our first introduction. He could see the benefit of having a team sporting his company clothing whilst also having Pro Rainer splashed down the side of the boat. Soon we had our first sponsor and a set of brand new sailing clothes for the entire team.

The project was not full-time for all of us and we certainly didn't have the run of the boat every day. We had to share *St Luke's Crusader* with her charter commitments during the build-up to the Fastnet race. It was not the best arrangement, but we were lucky to be in the game at all. My RYA training was progressing well under the guidance of the sailing school. I had completed the classroom theory and was now facing my practical exam onboard *Crusader* in Plymouth Sound.

The examiner was a tough cookie who knew his stuff and any gaps in my knowledge would certainly be exposed. I was adamant that I wanted to come away with my RYA Yacht Master qualification and had been studying full-on for months. I felt like I was back at school.

There were several people on board the boat taking their sailing qualifications that day but I was the only one trying for the Yacht Master certificate. As soon as we had cleared the confines of the marina the examiner switched off the diesel engine, saying that it had developed a fault and was broken. Looking at him as if he was crazy I said, "No it's not, it's fine!" Smiling, he informed me that the examination had begun. I felt like a right idiot but I suppose it broke the ice. I called for the sails to be unfurled.

That exam seemed to last forever and to top it off, the weather in Plymouth was terrible, blowing a near-gale, and the examiner seemed to grill the hell out of me all day. The blind navigation exercise went well, which I was pleased about. It's an exercise in which the skipper remains at the chart table and has to efficiently navigate the vessel from below decks in the cabin, issuing commands to the crew on deck while plotting the progress on the chart by means of estimated position fixing. No navigational aids like GPS are permitted. A correctly calibrated speedometer and compass, together with an understanding of tidal flow and wind effects are essential if you are to keep an accurate course.

Then there was the 'man overboard' drill followed by some intricate navigation up the River Tamar. The day was exhausting but very exciting. Despite it being an exam, I loved the experience. It felt like trying to take on a master chess player and anticipate his every move.

The following day I was awarded my RYA Coastal Skipper qualification with a commercial endorsement. The examiner was keen to point out that while I was competent with solid leadership qualities, I should have been confident enough to command the boat along the River Lyhner under the cover of darkness. The Lyhner is a small tributary of the River Tamar. The examiner had asked me to take the boat upriver until I felt it was unsafe, or until he did.

Turning left into the river I could see nothing but darkness in front of us and, mindful of the fact the Yacht Master exam also tests your ability to make decisions whilst under pressure, I thought the examiner was looking to see if I would run the crew into danger. I called for

Crusader to be brought about and informed the examiner that I felt it too dangerous to proceed any further. He said nothing at the time and I thought I had made the right call.

It turned out he was expecting me to navigate along the river using the depth contours as a safe guide. Depth contour lines are marked on all nautical charts and in conjunction with an accurate depth gauge this is a very useful means of safe pilotage. He felt that I should have known this and that was the reason he only awarded my Coastal Skipper qualification instead of the Yacht Master.

It was a fair point and after a thorough debrief I felt pleased with the overall result, albeit a little disappointed that I had fallen short of my personal target. Nevertheless, I was commended for knowing my limitations and also for the amount of tea I had kept pouring down the throats of the crew during the day. It wasn't a joke – the ability to look after your crew is something an examiner looks for as part of the Yacht Master qualification. I re-took the Yacht Master's exam five years later and passed with flying colours.

As a team we were enjoying the fruits of our labour and with a deal done for a new suit of racing sails, paid for by everyone's £2,000 buy-in money, we were on course. The summer was flying by and with two successful races to France under our belts, our training was complete. We were ready to face the challenge we had all been holding our breath for.

The Fastnet race starts from Cowes during the last weekend of Cowes Week and is one of the most successful and long-established sporting events in the UK. We arrived in time to catch the last few days of action and join in with the festivities. We also had a photo shoot commitment with our new sponsor Pro Rainer, who wanted some photos of us sailing in the Solent wearing the kit they had supplied.

It was the middle of August and baking hot. The kit we had been given, whilst perfectly suited to the rigours of an offshore race like the Fastnet, was less than suitable for a windless, hot day in the Solent. We were all overheating inside our clothes, sweat running down our faces. It was rather funny sailing along togged-up in our offshore kit while everyone else was in t-shirts and shorts. Still, Pro Rainer got their pictures and we kept our end of the bargain. That evening we went into town to celebrate our arrival for the big race. Being Cowes Week there were numerous drinks promotions available in each and every bar. A game card in a bar offered the chance of winning a shot of Jameson Whiskey if you could guess what various code flags signified. Between the eight of us we guessed enough correct answers to win a whole bottle of the stuff.

The night went downhill from there. I passed out in the bar. I woke up the following morning on the boat with no memory of how I had got back there. Everyone found it highly amusing. Realising the experience was just not for me, I gave up alcohol there and then and to this day don't touch the stuff.

During the build-up to the race we had overheard several teams discussing our entry. They were taking bets as to whether we would actually find the Rock, let alone complete the course. Even then, with a boat and an entry into the race, some found us a rather amusing prospect.

The race itself was everything we had hoped for and was a varied challenge from the outset. We didn't see any of the diabolical weather that caused tragedy in 1979. In that infamous year, a big storm devastated the fleet. Fortunately, our race was somewhat different. We experienced some intense racing and were starting to enjoy the thrill of

Scrubbing the hull before the Fastnet Race. That's commitment.

Above **A matching team, showing off our ProRainer clothing at Cowes Week.**

Right **In the groove at Cowes Week 1995.**

the chase when we had a rather close call.

We were sailing west, blazing a trail along the Cornish coastline towards Land's End, in close company with several other yachts when a competitor directly in front of us sailed over the top of a group of rocks called the Runnelstones and crashed to a halt. We changed our course immediately and headed out to sea, all holding our breath. We did hit, but it was a soft glancing blow with no damage done other than to our egos.

Rounding the famous Fastnet Rock off the south-west tip of Ireland was a moment we should have taken more time to savour. But we were in the thick of it, competing amongst a tightly-contested fleet. There was no time to relax and we were actually doing rather well. The crew had really been pulling together as a team and I felt we had a real chance of a result.

Halfway back across the Celtic Sea our stamina began to dwindle. The team had given their all from the start and since rounding the Fastnet everyone had been on the deck working the boat, trimming sails and doing what was necessary to keep *St Luke's Crusader* sailing fast. Sleep had been a secondary consideration. We had changed headsails frequently during the night as the wind speed went up and down and were now starting to feel the effects of forty-eight hours with little sleep. Tiredness was setting in and every manoeuvre was taking that much longer to execute.

A couple of the lads were fighting off the effects of seasickness, but despite this and the obvious fatigue, we did have a good, upbeat feeling on board. However, I could see we would all be close to exhaustion by the time we sailed past the breakwater in Plymouth.

The final hours of the race were intense. We had drawn close to the land sailing past the Lizard Lighthouse, Britain's most southerly point, and were being shadowed by a couple of competitors. Under the cover of darkness we had a close call with a cargo ship steaming out of Falmouth Bay. We didn't notice the lights of the ship until the last moment and had to take evasive action rather later than we should have done. We had to change course very quickly to avoid a potential collision. The crew was great and despite being in a tricky situation reacted with real calm and professionalism.

The finish line at Plymouth was approaching and soon our glorious race would be over. Several of our parents were waiting on the dock, keen to witness our arrival. The final two miles were nail-biting. Since dawn we had been duelling with another competitor. They were really close, within shouting distance and as the sun came up their identity was revealed. They were on another Sigma 36 design just like ours. Looking at their sail numbers we knew they had been the lead boat in our class since rounding the Fastnet. Our hard work had paid off and here we were, locked in a drag race to the finish with the leader in our class.

It was the perfect finish to a tough race and exactly what our team needed to get the adrenaline pumping in the final stages. We had to change course and tack several times for the finish line and this provided an opportunity for us to gain the advantage. Within sight of the finish we stuck to our competitor like glue, doing our best to squeeze every ounce of performance out of our tired old warhorse.

When they changed course and tacked so did we, mirroring their every move. It was our chance to gain an advantage by executing the manoeuvre better than they did. It was extremely tight racing, separated at times by literally just a few feet. With only yards to go before we crossed the finish line and with no more scope to outmanoeuvre them, we squeezed *St Luke's Crusader's* bow ahead by a matter of half a boat-length. It was a solid victory and one the crew could rightly be proud of.

Our opposition had been outwitted by a group of young upstarts with an average age of just seventeen. I couldn't help but smile. We were the first Sigma 36 home but due to the handicapping system, would be placed second in class, with an overall placing of fifty-ninth out of a fleet of nearly two hundred and fifty boats. We were over the moon and quite the centre of attention when we tied up alongside the harbour wall at Queen Anne's Battery marina.

The sense of achievement was evident on all our faces. We had the result we had all been striving for and, to make the experience just that little bit sweeter, I was greeted on the dock by Harold Usherwood. He had also competed in the race and having finished only minutes before us he knew that we had beaten him on the handicap ratings. "Well done, young Alex, you have beaten us fair and square," he said, offering his hand in approval.

Our victory was even more special for Ellie's family. Her father had been suffering from cancer and unknown to us at the time, his condition was terminal. Although the physical effects of his illness were taking hold, he was adamant that he would be present for our arrival and had mustered every ounce of energy just to be there on the dock. His resilience was sufficient to hide the awful truth from young Ellie and the rest of us.

I am thankful that he was able to fight the illness long enough to witness his young daughter sail triumphantly into Plymouth Sound, having successfully completed the adventure of a lifetime. He was so proud of Ellie. Sadly, he passed away a few weeks later.

Our result in the Fastnet Race provided the perfect foundation for the crew to move forward with their personal aspirations. Seven of us would end up working professionally within the sailing community in one way or another, and the race provided a unique stepping stone of which we can all be proud. For one of the crew, the Fastnet was just the start. The project proved to be the making of Dave Barden. He had become a first-class yachtsman and our next adventure was just around the corner.

A successful result, the team pose for the camera in Plymouth after the Fastnet Race.

7

MAVERICK

ith the Fastnet having reached a very satisfactory conclusion, I returned to London and the car yard for the remainder of the year. I had managed to secure a part-time job with a company called Topper International, demonstrating their range of performance dinghies to prospective clients.

Working for Topper was quite a rewarding experience. The pay wasn't brilliant but there was always the opportunity to scoop some extra business from clients after they completed their purchase and realised the boat they had just bought was actually more of a challenge than first thought. This would usually dawn on them after their first sail in the new boat. They would often spend most of the morning capsized, swimming rather than sailing. Then back they would come, asking if I offered tuition.

My boss, Richard Parslow, was usually the first point of contact and he would pass them on to me. We had a slick operation running: whenever we had a client who was less than competent, it was my job to take them sailing and make them feel like a champion. Zooming up and down the reservoir I would do my best to make it look easy. It was then up to Richard to close the deal the minute we came ashore. On other occasions, we took out sailors who really knew their stuff, and that became a free lesson for me. That's the beauty of sailing – every day you can learn something new.

Richard is a technical genius as far as sailing is concerned. He is one of the lucky few that competed with legendary yachtsman Laurie Smith, a multiple champion of champions. I used the opportunity to soak up as much knowledge as I could.

I would later get the chance to compete with Richard in the Boss Euro Cup Regatta on Lake Garda in Italy. At the time, the Boss Skiff was the flagship boat in the Topper range. Constructed from carbon fibre, she was ultra-lightweight and sported a huge carbon fibre bowsprit with a large spinnaker. The Boss was a rocket ship alright, and despite being perhaps a slightly easier boat to master in comparison to her competition, there's no doubt that she was a beast.

The Euro Cup was my first racing experience in the Boss, and we enjoyed an unbelievable regatta. The sailing was just as spectacular as the scenery. Revelling in the strong, near 30-knot winds on Lake Garda we achieved second overall, losing only to the European champions who rather conveniently also worked for Topper International.

The experience was fantastic, but I knew offshore sailing was where my heart was. The pull of the ocean was sometimes overwhelming. I had been invited to Emsworth on the south coast for a post-race wash-up dinner with Phil Davies, our Fastnet sponsor, who was keen to hear all about the race first hand. During my stay I was introduced to Merfyn Owen. Merf, as he likes to be addressed by his friends, is a gentle giant and a talented naval architect. He co-owns the company Owen Clarke Design LLP and would later be responsible for some of the best Open 60 yacht designs afloat.

Merf seemed very interested in my future plans and was keen to offer some advice. Unlike France, there is no clear path for success in England if you have aspirations of becoming a pro solo yachtsman. The French have sailing centres dedicated to training skippers for solo offshore racing, and with events like the Mini Transat and the Figaro circuit there is plenty of scope for an up-and-coming sailor to hone his or her skills. After a discussion that lasted late into the night, Merf mentioned *Maverick*.

Maverick was a revolutionary 30-footer his company had designed and built as a showcase for the business. She was the epitome of extreme design and thinking, a very fast, ultra-wide saucer-shaped flying machine. She carried a huge amount of sail area and was fitted with water ballast tanks on each side of her hull. Filling the tanks with seawater had the same effect as having about seven heavy guys sitting on the side of the boat, increasing her speed dramatically. At thirty feet long, she was like nothing I had experienced before. With the wind on her side, this boat was electric and unstoppable. In essence, *Maverick* offered a glimpse into the future of sailboat design.

I nearly fell off my chair when Merf suggested I take charge of her for the coming season. That kind of opportunity just doesn't come along, especially for a teenager. It was suggested that we consider competing in the Scottish Peaks Race as part of our programme. The Peaks race is a combined sailing and fell-running event on the Scottish west coast. A true adventure race, it is not for the faint-hearted, but offers a real challenge for competitors.

Maverick was berthed at Ocean Village in Southampton. It was agreed that Merf would formally hand over the boat early in the New Year, which gave me enough time to get organised. I needed to round up some new crew and decide on a programme for the coming season. I wanted to be in Southampton, close to the boat so I could focus full-time on the project.

Several friends and a few new faces agreed to join the project and I took the decision to rent a flat in Bassett, a 10-minute drive from Ocean Village. Money was tight but, with the crew seemingly commit-ted to sharing the financial demands of the project as well as the expe-rience, we moved into our new crew pad. We all took evening jobs at a local supermarket, stacking the shelves late into the night and training on the boat by day. This provided enough cash to keep the landlord from the door and put food on the table.

The *Maverick* project would be a real learning experience for me. With the introduction of the new faces, I didn't seem to have the same bond with the crew as I'd had during the Fastnet. Several team members were older than me and had their own ideas of how the project should be managed. Living and working together would also have unforeseen repercussions.

We took part in the Hamble Winter Sailing Series on the Solent. Pro Rainer was still supporting us with crew clothing and I had secured a new sponsor to replace all of our tired ropes on board. English Braids Yacht Ropes is a specialist cordage company based in Malvern, Worces-tershire, established by Peter Earp in the early 1970s. Its high-tech factory makes all kinds of synthetic ropes and braided cords for both yachting and manufacturing industries. Their cordage for the yachting market was a small but rapidly-growing branch of the business. I had taken up an opportunity to talk to them to offer a simple exchange deal. We needed quality ropes and they needed exposure within the yachting market. Keen to support us, David Ierston, one of the sales managers, came down to Southampton to help out with replacing the ropes on *Maverick*. It was the start of a close relationship with the company, and they remain one of my longest-standing sponsors.

The plan for the season was to compete in a race on home turf from Plymouth to Falmouth during the early summer, before heading to Scotland for the Peaks Race. However, cracks were already appearing in team morale even before we left for Plymouth. It was clear that three months of sailing and living in each others' pockets was starting to take its toll. There was friction in the ranks and my authority was under attack from two of the older crew. I decided we needed a team meeting to defuse the situation.

Arranging for everyone to meet at the boat, my strategy was to use *Maverick* to demonstrate how lucky we were to have been given this chance. I decided to get everything out into the open and give everyone a chance to address the bad feelings. Despite my best intentions, the meeting was a disaster. Half the crew agreed with my way of thinking but the remaining guys were threatening to walk out if the project wasn't run their way. It certainly wasn't my finest hour.

The wonderful opportunity we had been given by Merf just months earlier was beginning to turn into a nightmare. Sitting on the quay looking down at the boat, I knew this was not my vision for the future. Until then, I had thought sourcing a boat would always be the biggest hurdle, but it was now clear that keeping people united as a team was a much greater challenge.

We needed to get *Maverick* down to the West Country for the Plymouth to Falmouth race but after making the phone calls to the team, it was apparent we would be sailing light. Two of the lads had thrown in the towel and quit.

Putting to sea with a heavy heart is never recommended, but I was determined to retrieve some kind of a result from the situation. The delivery to Plymouth was undertaken with a skeleton crew and sailing into Plymouth Sound, I remember feeling more upbeat after an uneventful delivery that was free from bickering.

The conditions for the start of the Plymouth to Falmouth race were perfect. We were blessed with strong north-easterly winds, the perfect setting for *Maverick* to excel. There was still a bit of a tense atmosphere, but our spirits were briefly lifted by recognising the chance of pulling off a result.

Maverick had turned out to be an all-or-nothing boat. If the conditions were right we would win by miles; if they weren't, we would be at the bottom of the results table. Her extreme design was not favoured by the handicapping rules and she had not been built for this kind of sailing. She had been designed to compete against similar craft, without the handicap rules, where first across the line wins.

Flying out of Plymouth Sound, we were on fire. *Maverick* was revelling in the conditions. It was not long before we were well ahead of the fleet, surfing down the race track at 18 knots. We were all smiles and cheers. For a few hours during that race we could see past the disagreements and worked really well as a team.

It was a horizon job. We arrived into Falmouth so far ahead of the fleet that we could hardly see them. We had taken the win on the water and overall on handicap. It was a great result. The following day, however, proved to be a role reversal. With headwinds it was a tough slog back to Plymouth and we were well and truly stuffed by the competition.

It was obvious the compatibility issues with the crew were not going to disappear. Returning to the flat I knew I had lost control of the situation. I was now facing what my father called a damage limitation scenario and knew the flat had to go. We certainly couldn't keep up with the bills and rent now that two of the crew had walked out. It was a difficult time and to make matters worse, my car had just been stolen from outside the flat. I had hit rock bottom and felt things could not get any worse.

However, there was still a chance we could make the Scottish Peaks Race, so I tried to focus on that. Wrapping up the flat was an easier task than I had expected. The landlord quite understood the situation and despite the fact we'd signed a contract for a year's rental, he agreed to let us walk away. It was a big weight off my mind and having arranged a meeting with Merf to discuss the Peaks Race, I decided to keep plugging away.

Merf knew things weren't going according to plan. He was also aware of my ambitions to compete in the big solo offshore races like the Singlehanded Transatlantic Race and Transat Jacques Vabre. Walking down the pontoon, he looked pleased to see me and *Maverick*. We were going for a quick sail along Southampton Water to have a chat and check out a new spinnaker for the boat. He said that a friend had given us the spinnaker and would be along shortly. Merf's mate turned out to be none other than Mike Golding. An ex-fireman turned professional yachtsman, Mike had made his name in the tough BT Global Challenge. He was already a household name within the yachting community after completing an east-to-west solo circumnavigation of the world and setting a new record. Mike would later become the IMOCA World Champion with his Open 60 yacht *Ecover*. It was the first time we had met in person.

Meeting Mike was a welcome opportunity. He had experienced exactly the kind of extreme sailing that I so much wanted to embrace. Talking to him in person helped revive my passion and determination. As we returned to the marina I was adamant I would achieve my ambitions.

With what remained of *Maverick*'s crew, we set off from Plymouth. The trip through the Irish Sea was tough going, with strong headwinds hampering our progress. *Maverick* was a lively boat at the best of times, and these rough conditions made the motion on board quite violent as we punched our way northwards into a strong seaway.

The boat was holding up fine, although the same couldn't be said

A good training session on board *Maverick*.

for one of the lads who was struggling with seasickness. Confined to his bunk, he could only muster enough strength to express his keenness to get back to dry land. Seasickness is always a horrible experience. It can leave people completely debilitated and can prove dangerous at sea; I am lucky that I rarely feel the effects of it. There was no doubt that the weather was horrible and faced with the prospect of a prolonged period bashing into a cauldron of confused sea, we decided to turn about and run for shelter.

Several hours later we found ourselves tied up within the safe confines of Holyhead harbour on Anglesey. Time had run out for the Peaks Race, as there was no way we could make the start in time. Taking the weather into account and, with everyone keen to get home, we arranged to leave *Maverick* in Holyhead for a few days.

The season was effectively over and with little in the way of results to show for it, I was pretty disappointed. Merf's generosity was unfailing but I knew it was time to draw a line under the whole incident and hand *Maverick* back. Back at the car yard in London I reluctantly made the phone call to Merf. There was an implicit moral obligation to bring *Maverick* home from Holyhead but we agreed that after that, Merf would take her. The project was effectively over and I was gutted.

For the return trip from Holyhead I called on my friend Janie who had been dying to get on board all year. Together with Matt from the Fastnet Youth Challenge crew we brought *Maverick* back to home waters. With a few days to go before the handover, there was just enough time to squeeze in a double-handed race around the Isle of Wight with Matt as my teammate. It was a last-minute affair but with a good mate on board we enjoyed a great action-packed few hours' sailing. We finished the race in first place, taking line honours, and after handicapping achieved a respectable fourth overall. It was a bittersweet ending to the season. I had walked a tricky path that year and having made mistakes, I was determined to learn by them as best I could. Next time would be better.

I was licking my wounds in London and spent the winter with Dad working at the car yard before my phone started to ring with offers of more yacht delivery work. The money was good and with time on my hands, I started to fly around, taking up every opportunity. Sometimes the boat owners would come along for the experience, providing the core of my crew. Other times, I was operating on my own and would

Where are we?
Navigating on board
Maverick with the Isle of
Wight in the background.

round up Biff or Matt to help.

It was easy work and really enjoyable. I was sailing other people's yachts and getting paid for it. It was a sweet gig but I was aware of the danger of becoming complacent. I had aspirations of making it as a different kind of professional sailor and knew the delivery work, while certainly a solid business prospect, was not the right road for me. It was something I could always pick up if I needed to, but professional ocean racing was where I wanted to be.

I needed another campaign and knew I had to get organised.

8

THE TWO-HANDED ROUND BRITAIN AND IRELAND RACE

I n between the yacht deliveries I had established myself on the dinghy racing circuit, competing on a skiff-like dinghy, the RS600. The RS was a great boat and a real challenge to master, providing the ideal opportunity to sharpen my sailing skills. I had been looking at upcoming offshore events, considering which race would be suitable and decided on the Two-Handed Round Britain Race. I knew the course, having already sailed around the British Isles with Harold Usherwood on *April Storm*. It provided the perfect chance to make a real impression in the sailing world and it would be a challenge just to get to the starting line.

The race is organised by the Royal Western Yacht Club in Plymouth and is one of the must-do events for yachtsman interested in shorthanded ocean racing. Over the years, big names such as Sir Robin Knox-Johnston and Sir Chay Blyth have competed in this epic test of endurance. 'It will now be my turn,' I told myself.

The event has a reputation for being a bit hardcore but this was exactly what I was looking for. Two thousand miles of racing around the British Isles with four stopover ports in Ireland, the Hebrides, the Shetland Isles and Lowestoft. It would be a race of endurance, testing my skills to the limit and providing an ideal platform for my debut into the world of shorthanded ocean racing.

Like most of my other projects, making my entry into this race a reality would not be easy. Firstly, I needed another boat and, keen not to make the same crew mistakes as previously, I wanted to pair with someone who shared my vision. Choosing the right boat for an event like the Round Britain is not straightforward, either. I was very much constrained by finances, so the size of the boat would be dictated by the budget. I would be looking at the smallest class in the race, Class 5, for 30- to 35-foot yachts.

The hardest part of any sailing campaign at this level is the process of raising the money. The race is the stage on which to excel, but just getting to the start line is a slog and sometimes by far the biggest challenge. There was little chance I would be able to raise the money to purchase a suitable yacht in time for the race. *Maverick* by now had other commitments and there was a real possibility I would be racing against her. I needed an equal to rival her performance if I was going to have a chance of success. In this race there are no handicapping rules – the first boat across the finish line wins. A fast, lightweight boat would be vital.

I knew of one boat that had a chance of putting up a good fight against *Maverick* and the other competition for the Class 5 title, *Modi Khola*. She was already a proven winner. At thirty feet long she had won her class in the race twice before. *Modi Khola* was a sensational little boat. Lightweight and very strong, she had been constructed for the 1989 race and had flattened the competition in her class.

She was the largest boat in her division in 1989. But for the 1998 Round Britain race, the rules for the class divisions had been modified, making larger yachts up to thirty-five feet eligible to race in the same class. Even with this lightweight flyer we would be up against it to secure overall class victory. Nevertheless, *Modi Khola* represented our best hope. The only trouble was she wasn't for sale.

Modi Khola had been moored on the Hamble River when we were sailing *Maverick* the year before, so I drove down to the marina to see if she was still there. Walking up to her I could see she was a special boat. I knew her by reputation but had not been this close before. Her beautiful white hull had a thick red stripe just above the waterline. She sported low, sleek lines and a razor-sharp plumb bow with a long deep cockpit. I was in love. This boat certainly had the capability to challenge the fleet. She was small, but given the right conditions she could shine.

I wanted to contact the owner to see if she would be available for sale. The marina managers were reluctant to give me his phone number so I suggested they pass mine to him with a message to call me. I didn't expect to hear anything further, but the next day I did receive a call.

The owner understandably had a lot of affection for the boat and plans of his own. However, he revealed that his wife was pregnant so with a baby on the way, he might consider selling. The reality was that he needed to sell; he was a nice guy and realised with a racer like *Modi Khola* that he was a mere custodian rather than an owner. At least that's how I saw it.

We spoke about money and I was honest about my situation, explaining I needed to know a price but wasn't yet in a position to commit. I must have sounded like a complete dreamer. Luckily for me, he took me seriously and with a figure in my head I started to think about raising the money. I had saved a little cash from the delivery work and had some savings in trust from a relative. I could cash the whole lot in but would still be short of the figure required to purchase *Modi Khola*.

My parents had previously spoken about the possibility of providing an interest-free loan for a small boat should the right opportunity present itself. I really didn't want to borrow money from the family but it was my best option. I considered looking for a bank loan but who in their right mind would lend money to a twenty-two year-old with no assets? If I wanted to be on that start line I would have to take up all options available to me. I was lucky that my parents were willing to help.

At the same time, the search for a commercial sponsor was continuing. Month after month I was writing letters to companies and meeting people in the hope of attracting a financial backer. I must have written hundreds of letters, all to no avail. Companies just didn't see the value in sponsoring a young lad in a yacht race where the boats sail across the horizon five minutes after the start and have no means to communicate with the outside world. I was sure the human interest story combined with the 'man against the elements' factor was enough to spark a glimmer of interest. After all, Britain conquered the world by sea. We live on an island surrounded by the sea. Surely my message would strike a chord with someone.

We had no problem attracting product sponsors willing to supply the equipment required for the race. Their support would be invaluable and greatly appreciated. But hard cash was a different matter. I was aware that there are many people out there with similar dreams, all saying the same thing. If I could just get a boat, I felt my genuine commitment would be more obvious. So I cashed in my savings and trust money and took Mum and Dad up on their loan offer. I left behind the world of dreams and crossed into the land of total commitment. There was no going back.

With the funds now available, I contacted *Modi Khola*'s owner to start the negotiations. Any money I could save at this stage would stay in my family's pockets so I was keen to get a good deal. Negotiations didn't take long. My lack of communication for several months had strengthened my position and with the imminent arrival of the owner's new baby, we agreed on a price there and then.

The following week I arranged for *Modi Khola* to be lifted out of the water for an inspection. Satisfied with the outcome, I shot off to Bristol with twenty grand in the boot of my car to finalise the purchase. To say I was pleased as I drove back from the owner's house along the M4 would be a huge understatement. Not only had I just secured a boat for the race, I'd got a great deal in the process. *Modi Khola* was mine and there was a good chance I could make a profit selling her after the race, which I could return to Dad as a bonus. I was euphoric. I felt like a winner.

My attention was now firmly fixed on the Round Britain. There was less than a year go to the start and I needed to find a suitable team-mate. I had two favourites and several back-ups. My first choice was Dave, who had showed so much commitment during the Fastnet race. He had problems at home though, and I initially thought they might divide his focus.

Dave lived with his mother in Torquay. His mum ran a kind of reha-bilitation centre for drug addicts wanting to change their lives and quit the smack. They all lived together in the wing of an ancient villa that was falling down around their ears. At times they barely had enough money to keep the lights on. The place had once been a hotel with a grand swimming pool in the grounds but had fallen into disrepair. By the time I laid eyes on the place the pool had long since been filled with rubbish rather than water.

They received a small amount of grant money from the govern-ment but it was never enough. The bank was always chasing them and the neighbours would regularly complain about one thing or another. Dave's father had left home when Dave was just a child, leaving his mum well and truly in the lurch. But she worked hard and made a real difference to the lucky few that found her roof over their heads. She rarely received any thanks and never got any recognition. It wasn't easy for them. Dave's mum had been physically attacked on more than one occasion by a junkie that had fallen back into the murky world of drugs. Despite this, she and Dave had an unbreakable bond and always managed to smile.

My second option and initial teammate was a guy I met through sailing the RS dinghy. The two of us regularly trained together and were good friends. He was interested in my ocean experiences and keen for an adventure of his own. Despite having little offshore experience, he was willing to commit there and then. I admired that.

He lived not far from me in London and was certainly willing to put in the hours preparing the boat. He seemed the ideal candidate, even pushing me to up our physical training programme. But once the sailing started his interest fizzled out because he suffered terribly from seasickness. The romance of ocean racing had not lived up to his expectations. He quickly threw in the towel, returning to the dinghy circuit. Ocean racing is like Marmite – you either love it or hate it.

The change in teammates didn't cause any problems. Dave jumped at the chance. We were a team again and if we could complete the course, we would set the record for the youngest pairing to ever finish the gruelling race. With the purchase of an expensive and shiny new laptop for use with our electronic navigation charts we were ready to start our training programme. I had agreed a deal with a company called EuroNav who would supply us with free electronic charting software for the race in return for their logo appearing on board.

Electronic charts were becoming more mainstream in the yachting world and I felt their addition would give us an edge on the race track. Interestingly, while the software was excellent, it would only have cost about £500 to buy. The laptop I had to purchase to use it cost me a cool £1800. I would have been better off buying the charts and finding a company to supply me a free laptop!

I had initially berthed *Modi Khola* in Brighton Marina. I'd agreed a deal for free moorings and use of facilities in exchange for some advertising space on board. The marina had recently been subject to a management buyout and the new boss was a nice, approachable chap who was keen to help.

With Dave on board I would have to relocate to the West Country for the final build-up to the race. This made life easier for Dave and left

us free to concentrate on training. The vibrant nightlife in Torquay also meant there was plenty of opportunity to party when we felt the need. We worked well together and shared the same level of commitment. It was great to be sailing with someone who really wanted a result.

Looking fantastic, *Modi Khola* comes out of the hangar after refit.

We were also keen to follow up on the media interest we had generated from the Fastnet and so started churning out press releases. We knew we needed to achieve as much exposure as possible before the big guns arrived in town and created their own fanfare.

There had been talk of Tony Bullimore entering the race. Tony was a past winner of the Round Britain and had recently shot to fame by surviving against the odds in his capsized boat in the Southern Ocean. He was rescued by the Australian Navy and the drama had made international news. I knew that as soon as the big names and fancy yachts turned up in Plymouth we would be overlooked and lose our advantage with the media. We needed to make the most of it while we could. In the end, Tony didn't compete in the race but the mere idea that he might was enough to steal column-inches in the papers.

Before we knew it, we had quite a media following. Television, radio and newspapers all wanted our story and we made sure we exploited

Dave and I standing on
the deck of *Modi Khola*.

every opportunity. With Dave living in Torquay and my connections with Plymouth from the Fastnet race, the West Country media adopted us as the local team. I found that amusing because, thanks to some creative PR, the same story was unfolding in Brighton and back home in the North-East. The Whitby Gazette was full of stories of their 'local boy' taking on new adventures on the south coast.

The week before the race start we moved the boat into the Race

Left **Returning to Queen Annes Battery marina after filming with the BBC, before the race.**

Village in Plymouth. I had tied up a last-minute deal with a company called BCB International who agreed to provide our freeze-dried food during the race. With everything ready and organised, all that was left to do was suss out the opposition and chase the media.

Mum had given me a little teddy bear for good luck and we named him Modi Bear. Even he managed to get into the spotlight, appearing in a newspaper article as our lucky mascot. He would later travel the world with me and twice be saved from certain doom in the Atlantic.

One interview I did for a local Plymouth newspaper read 'Round

Me and Mums Teddy bear on board *Modi Khola*.

Britain favourites, meet the professionals'. It struck me that this was the first time I had been referred to as a professional yachtsman. That article made my day. I was starting to be seen as something other than an amateur. My hard work was starting to pay off.

Unknown to me at the time, the media coverage we were enjoying had been noticed by Mark Orr, the business partner of Pete Goss. Pete had recently shot to fame after rescuing fellow Vendee Globe competitor Raphael Dinelli from certain death during a ferocious storm in the Southern Ocean. Raphael's yacht had been fatally damaged and would inevitably sink. Pete was one of the nearest competitors and risked his own life by sailing the one hundred and sixty miles back into hurricane conditions to save the young Frenchman. Pete received the Legion d'honneur for his bravery. He was by now a huge celebrity and was building a revolutionary 120-foot catamaran in Devon for a global event called 'The Race'.

I didn't know at the time that our result in the Round Britain would prove crucial to my career. Mark Orr was a competitor and I would be racing against him. It was an opportunity to make a good impression, although in the event Mark would not make it past the first leg stopover, due to problems with his boat. Also taking part was Andy Hindley, an ex-BT Global Challenge skipper, competing on one of the biggest yachts in the fleet with Nigel Musto, co-owner of Musto Clothing. These three people would feature heavily in my future.

Our immediate competition came from a different group. Dave and I had been quietly looking at the fleet and had deduced that a podium position in our class was a real possibility. We were up against some more experienced sailors but we did have a real shot.

The race start within Plymouth Sound was a busy affair with over forty yachts of all shapes and sizes jostling for position. The weather wasn't great and it would be a tough first leg sailing into the wind and waves towards Land's End. We managed a clean start but with all the traffic around us it was going to be difficult clearing the western end of Plymouth Breakwater without being buried amongst the fleet, not a good option.

Closing in on the giant man-made breakwater it became obvious we had to change course and tack to clear it. Looking over my shoulder, there was a wall of sails behind us, closing in like vultures circling their prey. We had to tack, but choosing the right moment would be critical from both a tactical and a safety point of view. Andy Hindley and Nigel Musto were rapidly carving their way through the myriad of smaller competitors and spectator vessels. They would soon be upon us, dwarfing us with their huge sails. There was a small chance we would have just enough time to tack and nip across their bows. If we were on their weather side when they sailed past we would have the advantage over our rivals.

The manoeuvre was highly risky. By crossing their bows and getting under their feet they would have nowhere to go if my calculations were wrong. If we collided, it would be my fault. They would cut us in half, sending us to the bottom of Plymouth Sound. I gave the call to tack, adding, "There's no time to mess this up, Dave."

It was a close call. The bow of the huge 60-footer was bearing down on us as we started to gain momentum on the new tack. For a moment it looked like we would not make it. With less than half a boat length to spare, we squeezed our trusty little steed through, getting away with a rather cheeky manoeuvre in the process. I caught a glimpse of Andy's face as we sailed by. I wasn't sure if he was annoyed or impressed. A press photographer caught the moment on film. It was a dramatic photo and was printed in Yachting World. From the photographer's viewpoint, it looked like we were toast.

The Round Britain proved to be as tough as I had expected. We had a hard slog into the wind. Approaching Bishop's Rock Lighthouse, four miles west of the Scilly Isles, the visibility had dramatically dropped to less than a mile. With rain pelting the decks we were waiting for the lighthouse to reveal itself. We were close, with perhaps a mile to go. We knew that as soon as we rounded it our course would take us roughly north-west, giving us a better angle to the wind and allowing *Modi Khola* to pick up her skirt and start flying.

This would be a good point of sail for us and our first chance to stretch our legs against our opposition. Finally, out of the mist and rain, the great lighthouse appeared, a 49-metre tower that has stood defiant against the full force of the Atlantic Ocean since 1858. Rounding Bishop's Rock is always a moment to remember but, in the rough conditions on that day, it was all the more impressive.

Thundering down the waves, we hoisted our spinnaker without hesitation. This is where we would make up the miles on the leaders and pull away from our immediate competition. These were just the conditions in which our little rocket ship excelled. With the wind flowing across our portside rear quarter we were really hauling the mail. Running before a strong breeze on any fast, lightweight sailboat is a magical experience and that day we were treated to some truly spectacular surfing. We careered across the Celtic Sea toward the first stopover port of Crosshaven in southern Ireland.

Approaching the Irish coast, we knew we were doing well. After enjoying several hours of very fast sailing we caught a glimpse of a yacht ahead sailing well reefed-down. Assuming it must be another competitor, Dave got the binoculars out to try and identify the boat. As we drew closer it became apparent that it was a yacht called Telegroup, a similar water ballast design to *Modi Khola*, but five feet longer. They were our direct competition and should have been way ahead in these conditions.

Exciting sailing across the Celtic Sea during the first leg of the Round Britain Race 1998.

We managed to close in on them before their helmsman turned around and got the shock of his life. They had been taking it easy with heavily-reefed sails. The battle was on and we had the bit between our teeth. We were so close we could see them spring into action. Within seconds, both crew members were on deck and started to hoist full sail. We were now match racing to the finish. Telegroup was the larger, more powerful boat and pulled ahead by just seven minutes. Rolling across the first leg finish line in Crosshaven we took second place in class 5.

Our battle with Telegroup would continue all around the British Isles. They would eventually pull ahead leaving us locked into a fight for second place against another 35-footer called Q2. Q2 is owned by an intrepid and vastly experienced yachtswoman called Mary Falk. Her yacht was designed to win the Single Handed Transatlantic Race and is a real force to be reckoned with when sailing into the wind under heavy conditions. The first two legs of the Round Britain had given us a fair amount of fast, downwind sailing. We had a lead of several hours over Mary and her young crewmate Ashley and initially felt comfortable about the third leg from Barra to Lerwick.

The race rules for the Round Britain required competitors to carry a separate inflatable dinghy for the whole race. This is fairly unusual in the world of yacht racing. The reason for it is that Barra has no harbour facilities and competitors must be entirely self-sufficient while at anchor in the bay.

In an effort to save on the weight of carrying a heavy dinghy I had taken advantage of the rules. They did not stipulate exactly what type of dinghy should be carried. We took a lightweight child's beach boat, the sort of thing you would take on a day trip to the seaside. I paid ten quid for it on the harbour-side in Torquay. It seemed like a good idea at the time. However, when we were in Barra, it proved useless and nearly drowned us, causing much amusement amongst the rest of the fleet. I would not make that mistake again.

A last-minute check of our mast in Barra had revealed several broken wire strands in the rigging. This posed a serious problem for us. Barra is effectively in the middle of nowhere, with no facilities to repair boats. Our mast would be in real danger of falling over the side if we put to sea with broken rigging.

With just a couple of hours before our scheduled restart we were faced with a difficult decision. We had serious gear failure and would either have to pull out of the race or lash up the rigging as best we could and take a chance. It was a hard decision, but with a fairly light wind forecast for the following few days we decided to go for it.

I went ashore to phone my dad while Dave started to lash up the rigging with some rope. Pulling out of the race was not an option as far as I was concerned, at least not until the mast was in the drink anyway. Dad suggested we measure the broken wires and he would travel up to the Shetland Islands and meet us in Lerwick with a new set. It was so good of Dad to drop everything and come up to our aid, especially as it would not be a straightforward journey: he had to travel from London to Brighton Marina, get the wires made up and then drive back to London to catch a plane to Aberdeen before jumping into a smaller twin-engine propeller-powered plane to the Shetland Islands. To top it all, he had to be waiting on the dock in Lerwick by the time we arrived there, in order to allow enough time to change the wires over.

There was no guarantee we would arrive with a mast intact, either. Putting to sea with a dodgy set of rigging was certainly not part of the Yacht Master school of sailing. However, we were racing and to me, a place on the podium was worth the risk.

We were lucky. For most of the trip we saw just light winds which allowed us to nurse *Modi Khola* around the course to Lerwick. Dad made it and was waiting on the dock as we arrived. Good old Dad, always there when I need him. We were shattered, despite the light weather. The trip had been quite stressful and Q2 had capitalised on our misfortune, managing to halve our lead.

The final two legs were not going to be easy. The larger boats were starting to reel us in and with the prospect of sailing against the wind all the way to Lowestoft we knew it would be a fight to the finish. *Modi Khola* was a wet boat. Even in moderate conditions waves would regularly sweep over the deck, and the North Sea proved to be relentless.

Having seen our significant lead evaporate before our eyes, we sailed into Lowestoft level with Q2. The hunters had become the hunted. We would struggle to defend our second place on the final leg.

Once again, headwinds greeted the fleet at Dover. We were fighting a losing battle, knowing that Q2 would eventually stretch her legs. Her extra five feet of hull length made all the difference in the gale-force conditions. It was soon her turn to disappear over the horizon, leaving us with a titanic struggle to keep up.

Our mainsail was also becoming a cause for concern. It was showing signs of fatigue and I was worried it might not last the remaining two hundred miles to the finish. The harsh conditions were causing the Mylar material to delaminate and the sail was literally falling apart. Despite being at the front of our class for most of the race, we were now struggling to hold onto a podium position.

The race had become a battle to stay on the fine line between keeping the boat in one piece and maintaining a competitive edge. We did our best to minimise the damage to the mainsail although we really had very little influence. Approaching Portland Bill, off the Dorset coast, we were faced with a tactical decision. There was a chance to perhaps claw back a few miles on Q2. The tidal current was against us. We either had to stay well out to sea in deep water, away from the tidal race of Portland Bill, or take the risky option and hope to capitalise on a west-flowing tidal current inside the Race. This course would require us to sail within metres of the shoreline and rocks. It was a risky manoeuvre and made all the more tricky as it was now dark.

The Portland Race is a stretch of water just to the south of Portland Bill. It's a notoriously dangerous place and mariners usually keep at least five miles to seaward. Steep breaking seas often develop in the Race and are very dangerous, but there is a very small channel on the inside of the Race that can offer more clement seas and a west-flowing tidal current at certain times. If we could get into that current it would push us around Portland Bill toward the finish line, gaining some miles on our opposition in the process. We decided to go for it.

We made our approach, tentatively heading into the land under the lighthouse. Conditions were starting to moderate, with the wind now down to around Force 6. I was well aware that a cruising yachtsman giving consideration to safe seamanship would never undertake this approach. Dave and I had agreed a clear plan of action in case the situation took a turn for the worse. With a mile to go until the rocks would be upon us, I was down below, continuously plotting our course on the charts.

Without warning and just when we needed the instruments the most, the GPS went offline. The system could not acquire a satellite fix to display our position. I had to dig deep for those skills I had learnt during my Coastal Skipper exam. Every second that passed took us closer to the rocky shoreline. Dave, the eyes on deck, was steering and calling the depth readings from the instruments in the cockpit. Teamwork had never been more important than now.

We made the inside channel and it was time to tack and make our move. It took a few seconds for my eyes to adjust to the dark as I climbed into the cockpit. We could make out the shoreline just metres away. It was an exhilarating moment. Despite the problems with the GPS, the operation went without a hitch and with Portland behind us we breathed a sigh of relief. The manoeuvre should have gained us some valuable time over the competition. But would it be enough?

Twenty-one days and eleven hours after the start, we arrived back in Plymouth. The final stages were tough on both the boat and us, but in spite of the awful weather *Modi Khola* held together and the mainsail lasted just long enough for me to throw it into a skip at the end of the race.

Nursing *Modi Khola* across the finish line, we took third place in our class. Our risky manoeuvre off Portland Bill had indeed made gains on the competition but both Telegroup and the girls on board Q2 had proved uncatchable in the rough weather. It could so easily have gone the other way, though. Regardless, Dave and I were over the moon. We had set the record for the youngest team to ever complete the arduous course.

THE 1999 MINI TRANSAT

I was invited back to the Royal Western Yacht Club that winter to give a talk about my experiences in the Round Britain. I suggested to Dave that we do it together but he was less than enthusiastic. Speeches just weren't his thing. It was my first ever talk, and I was a little nervous, but knew it was an opportunity not to be missed. Luckily, I had been given a couple of months' notice and I took the time to rehearse. Every night I would study my notes and even did a dry run with Mum and Dad to gauge their reaction and interest.

I was determined to give a good account of myself. The talk would last about forty-five minutes, with a further five minutes set aside for any questions the audience might have. At the time, talking to a room of nearly sixty people seemed a daunting prospect. I had seen other people give speeches and knew it would not be easy.

I decided to support the talk with some video footage we had taken during the race. That way I could let the action speak for itself, at least for a few minutes. It would also give the audience a real insight into life at sea.

As the day drew closer, I started to feel a little easier in myself. I had practiced the talk for so long I knew the words off by heart. I arrived at the clubhouse a couple of hours early. It was important that everything should go according to plan and I wanted to check that the video equipment was all set up and working. It would not be long before the place started to fill up with people. As the seconds ticked by, I started to feel a little nervous. What if I forgot my lines? A lot of people were coming to hear me speak and they would be expecting a good show.

Everything was in place and in the blink of an eye, it was time to begin. I was sitting in the corner of the room next to the television. We had a full house. All the seats had been claimed and there was standing room only at the back. I was surprised by the turnout and wondered nervously if the act of throwing rotten fruit at bad performers was still common practice.

The Commodore, Ann Hoskin, called for quiet and made the introductions, the crowd started to clap, and I was on. I could feel my heart pounding, but despite those initial nerves I settled into my routine and enjoyed the opportunity to tell our story. The hour passed quite swiftly and I managed to hold the crowd's attention. The video footage went down particularly well. I didn't exactly stick to the script, but gave a good account and thoroughly enjoyed the experience too. Then my first talk was behind me. It would be the first of many.

Today, public speaking is an integral part of professional sailing. The ability to communicate effectively is essential in order to give real value to commercial partners. Explaining the challenges of extreme ocean racing to an audience is a side of the business I now thoroughly enjoy. Very few people get the chance to experience life on the edge through sporting endeavour. I feel it's important to share such thrilling experiences with anyone interested enough to listen.

After that first speech people asked what my next adventure would be. It was an interesting question. The natural progression from the Round Britain would be an international event overseas. The obvious choice was the Mini Transat race, a 4,000-mile solo transatlantic sprint to the Caribbean. The boats are very small, at just 6.5 metres in length, which is not much bigger than an average family estate car. Despite their tiny appearance, in the right hands, Minis can be very capable machines and are more than up to the job of a transatlantic passage.

Nowadays, the Mini Transat race is an international event that attracts some of the best up-and-coming competitors from around the world. Usually dominated by the French, it was originally conceived as an affordable alternative to the existing big-budget transatlantic races of the day. The Mini Transat provides a unique challenge, via a mammoth event that is certainly not for the inexperienced or fainthearted.

Bob Salmon's original race in 1977 represented a huge leap into the unknown for the twenty-four solo sailors that left Penzance for the Caribbean island of Antigua. The inaugural event was more about the adventure than the racing. Twenty years on, the biennial race has evolved from its humble beginnings to become what is undoubtedly one of the toughest solo ocean challenges in existence.

These days, it's a challenge to even qualify to enter the Mini Transat. Competitors must meet stringent requirements relating to the safety of their boats and demonstrate their competence as solo skippers by competing in several dedicated class races during the season. An aspiring skipper must also complete a 1,000-mile solo non-stop qualification passage. Even after all that, the wannabe competitor still is not assured a place in this epic race.

The event is always oversubscribed. The maximum number of entries is usually set at around seventy, on a first-come, first-served basis. Then there are a few places given out at the discretion of the race committee. As a result, it offers one of the most competitive fleets of any ocean-going race. It's been the proving ground for many of the top French yachting heroes and I felt it provided the perfect opportunity for me to pit my skills against the best of the latest generation of yachtsmen and women. In terms of the scale of challenge, the event is second only to the Vendée Globe solo around-the-world race.

Modi Khola was now up for sale. She had served her purpose and I knew my adventures with her had come to an end. I needed a new set of tools, and with the proceeds from her sale I could buy a suitable Mini. Travelling down to the port of La Trinité-sur-Mer on the French north-west Atlantic coast, I looked over several available boats before making my final decision.

I was in familiar territory and there were plenty of boats available, but making the right choice would be very important. I wanted the best boat available but Minis, despite their small size, are not cheap. A top-of-the-range model would fetch more than twice the value of *Modi Khola* and once again, I had to make a decision based on budget.

I initially settled on a Mini that was for sale in La Trinité. The owner was keen to sell and the boat had already successfully completed an Atlantic crossing. She was a proven boat and would be a fair choice. Having finalised the sale on *Modi Khola*, I agreed terms with the owner of the Mini and was just about to send through the money when we were informed he had sold the boat to someone else. I was bitterly disappointed. I had missed a good opportunity through no fault of my own.

Looking at my options, one idea would be to build a boat from scratch. I have always wanted to build my own boat, but at the time I didn't have the necessary skills to undertake the work myself and knew that a build project would more than double my workload. I had been in close negotiations with a well-known naval architect and had taken a trip to Southampton to view a couple of their Minis already in build.

They were both state-of-the-art designs, constructed from carbon fibre, and they certainly looked the part. I could just about afford one of these new boats but time, or lack of it, was always on my mind. The deal on the table would allow for a skilled yard to build the boat, but the time pressure kept eating away at me.

Given enough time, I would have jumped at the chance, but the Mini Transat was just one sailing season away and I would need every hour to prepare myself with as much on-the-water training as possible. Success in this race is all about the preparation. Commencing a new build for the upcoming race, learning how to sail her and then qualifying would have been a tall order for someone with twice my experience.

I knew the second-hand route was the better option and by chance, while looking around the factory at the new boats, I noticed another Mini at the back of the yard. It was owned by Mark Turner, who is now Dame Ellen MacArthur's business partner. Both of them had competed in the Mini Transat the year before and although Mark hadn't used this boat in that race, I knew it was a good design. I had seen the boat a few months earlier in a boatyard in Cowes on the Isle of Wight. Then, she was painted blue and had had a gaping hole in her side. The boat had been struck by another vessel while moored in the Medina River. I remembered thinking how cool the boat looked, even with a hole in her.

Speaking to Mark, it was clear he had spent a small fortune on her refit. She had been re-painted white and with the damage repaired, would require a minimum amount of preparation to be competitive. Mark was keen to help, and although someone else was interested in the boat they had messed him around and not come up with the money. This was the boat for me; it offered the perfect platform for my aspirations. She would be the oldest boat in the fleet by the time I reached the start line of the Transat but she had been designed by legendary naval architects Group Finot. Mark and Ellen were also in the market for a car. Ellen had only recently passed her driving test and needed to get mobile. So with a suitable second-hand Vauxhall Astra courtesy of my family's car business thrown in, we shook hands right away.

The work-up for the Mini Transat would not be easy. I was still eagerly chasing potential sponsors and I really needed to secure some kind of financial backer sooner rather than later. I had spent virtually all the budget on securing the boat and with a massive learning curve ahead of me, I would need to focus full-time on the project if I was to be competitive.

One company who showed interest was our rope and cordage supplier English Braids. I sent them a sponsorship proposal a couple of weeks after finalising the deal with the boat. They invited me to their headquarters in Malvern to present the project to the head of the company, Peter Earp.

I had established a good working relationship with the sales manager David Ierston, who was my initial point of contact. David had mentioned that the company might be interested in sponsoring a sailing campaign, as they wanted to increase their profile within the industry. Having read my proposal, Peter wanted to meet and hear what I had to say.

Peter is a lovely guy with a warm and friendly character. Having built the company from scratch, he's the sort of man who likes to hear it straight, without any polish or spin. I arrived for the meeting armed with my proposal and newly-acquired knowledge of the rope industry. David led the way up the stairs from the reception hall to the conference room where Peter and several management staff were awaiting my arrival.

Even though he was engrossed in a conversation, Peter noticed me walk through the door and jumped up to say hello. Before I could introduce myself he said, "Ah, you must be Alex Bennett. Do you mind if I call you Gordon Bennett instead?" It took a couple of seconds for the joke to sink in. The only thing I could think of was, "Sure, as long as you don't mind being called Wyatt Earp". Shaking hands, we both laughed. My reply had been a rather boyish response, but the ice was broken and Peter introduced me to the rest of the management team.

Peter and I hit it off straight away. He was full of admiration for my ambitious plans to sail solo across the Atlantic. The management team looked at me in almost disbelief as I outlined the project, explaining that the boat was just 6.5 metres long. Looking me straight in the eyes, Peter asked if I thought I would achieve my goal. A reply of 'absolutely' was all that was needed to put his mind at rest. I was quite clear about my goals and aspirations for the project. Peter then wanted to know what was in it for them and asked why they should sponsor me. This was my chance to sell it. I took a deep breath and pitched my proposal.

Sponsoring my project would cost them less than a high quality conventional advertising campaign, which would only go so far in terms of reaching the target audience. My project had the ability to reach that audience in a way that would make exciting reading. I would be an ambassador for the company, endorsing their products. The project would provide a tailor-made and prolonged advertising campaign as well as offering the company the perfect opportunity to trial newly-developed cordage before offering it to the retail market. This point was something the head of product development, Peter Neale, was quick to pick up on. It was perfect, and above all a real bargain. Peter Earp always likes to get a good deal and this was a good deal for everyone.

They didn't agree to it straight away, but within the week I received a call from David saying they wanted to go for it. I was thrilled. I had just signed up my first major sponsorship deal for real money. Not just that, I would be working closely with the company to develop new products. My comments from the race track would provide an essential insight into the performance and durability of their ropes. It was a fantastic moment, and the start of a great relationship. That was the day I became a bona-fide professional yachtsman. I could now focus full-time on the project.

There was much to do. We had to re-logo the boat with the English Braids livery, organise the press releases and arrange an official project launch. It was an exciting time. The staff at English Braids really threw their weight behind the project. We were a team working towards a common goal. Peter was especially keen. He knew the project would help unite the workforce on the factory floor. During the race, the factory staff would be kept informed of my progress with daily position reports posted in the works canteen. The idea was to bring the staff together as a team and involve them in the excitement of the race.

I would make regular visits to the factory to meet the staff and bring everyone up to date with progress. It was a truly magical time – Peter and the team had shown real commitment in backing the project and I was determined to go well above and beyond expectations to deliver results both on the race track and with our media coverage.

The boat would be known as *English Braids* performance yacht ropes. The company name would be splashed along each side of the hull and after a professional photo shoot, the company would instigate a complete overhaul of its promotional material and product packaging. Virtually everything relating to the company would bear the image of our faithful little boat. Even the stands that displayed the ropes at trade shows would carry a photo of me on the boat. All that was needed now was a new suit of sails and we would be in business.

During the Round Britain race I'd made friends with a young competitor called Shaun Patterson. Shaun was a professional sailor and sailmaker who had carved a career out of managing racing yachts for wealthy owners. Shaun was based in America and offered to help me build a new set of sails for the Mini. This was an incredible act of kindness. It was a long way for me to travel, but the opportunity to build my own sails could not be passed up.

Shaun was friendly with a company based in Long Island called Banks Sails. They would provide the necessary design work and allow us to build the sails in their factory. They even arranged for the sail material to be supplied for free from another company called Dimension Polyant. I would in turn give them both some prominent advertising space on board and tell the sailing world that Banks Sails USA was my sailmaker of choice. It was a great deal, made all the sweeter by the fact I would have a hand in making the sails that would propel *English Braids* across the enormous expanse of the Atlantic ocean.

In New York we had just a week to build three sails. It was a tall order but I was blessed with a great team and Shaun really pulled out all the stops. We worked together around the clock. It was fascinating to see how yacht sails are assembled panel by panel. A design is created on a computer which is then sent to a plotter. The machine's laser precision-cuts the various intricate sections of fabric into a jigsaw of material ready for assembly. I was so lucky, not many people get the chance to skipper a yacht in a major transatlantic race and have the opportunity to build their own sails. I was living the dream.

My flight back to the UK was late on a Friday afternoon. It was going to be tight. We had to complete the final assembly of the 80-square-metre spinnaker and apply some sponsor logos to the main-sail. Despite the rush, we pretty much had everything under control by lunchtime. I left the sail loft with just enough time for a mad dash to the airport to catch my flight. It had been a whirlwind visit to the States but I was coming home with a brand new set of sails.

Back in England, the plans for the project launch were taking shape. I had suggested we hold the campaign launch ceremony at Brighton Marina. The marina was still supporting me with free moorings and I was keen to give them something back. It was agreed that the marina was a good location for *English Braids* to hold a press launch. They had companies in the area that stocked their rope and would invite them along to be part of the action. Also, as Brighton is on the south coast it was reasonable to expect a good turn out from the yachting media.

As the boat took on her new livery we planned the final touches to the naming ceremony. The plan was to have the boat on display out of the water, next to the crane in the boatyard. Brandishing her shiny new logos, everyone would congregate around the boat to witness the traditional breaking of champagne over the bows. With the marina team lowering her slowly into the water, everyone would then migrate into the yacht club for lunch and speeches. Afterwards, while the VIPs were enjoying the buffet, the press could take the opportunity to have a ride in the company helicopter and take photographs of me putting *English Braids* through her paces off the Brighton coast. It was a busy agenda, but we were all keen to make the most of such a rare oppor-tunity.

The naming ceremony was a day to remember. We were blessed with reasonable weather and more importantly, dry conditions. The guys from English Braids arrived early in the company van, keen to add as much weight to the day as they could. Soon Peter would arrive via helicopter with the remaining staff.

We were due to kick things off by mid-morning and as the time grew ever closer it became apparent that a lot of people had made significant journeys to come and be part of the day. I watched as the crowd built up around the boat. There were a lot of people from the media. Local newspapers, the yachting press and local radio journal-ists complemented a healthy turn-out from friends, family and well-wishers.

As soon as Peter cracked open the champagne and poured it over the bow of *English Braids* I had all kinds of people asking me questions and taking pictures. We made the front page of the Brighton Evening Argus that day and achieved some good column inches in the yachting press. Poor Peter must have given over a dozen helicopter rides though I think he secretly enjoyed it. Peter has a similar passion for flying as I do for sailing. The day was a complete success. Everyone's hard work had paid off and we had pulled off our first big press launch.

Peter Earp and I stand in front of *English Braids* during the naming ceremony.

The plan for the season would revolve around a lot of sailing. I needed to get over to France and start training with the fleet. There would be three qualifying races for me to take part in before I could relax as a fully-qualified competitor. The thought of not qualifying just couldn't be entertained.

Before the first of the official qualifying races commenced, we took the opportunity to compete in a couple of local cross-Channel events. We won the first and the second, which was a sprint across the English Channel to St Vaast in France. For the return journey back to England the plan was for me to sail solo as part of my training. Leaving St Vaast, I accepted a tow from another English competitor. He and his team were setting off back to the UK on their 30-foot yacht and offered to tow me out of the harbour into open water. Unlike most yachts, Minis don't have any kind of onboard engine and the harbour at St Vaast is secured by lock gates. It would be difficult to get out of the harbour without any kind of help.

Once through the lock gates, vessels must follow the buoyage system along the narrow channel in order to clear the surrounding rocks. We had just left the lock with *English Braids* under tow and another yacht behind me which was also being towed. For no apparent reason the skipper of the yacht providing the tow started to stray off course in a rather erratic fashion. I had spoken to him earlier in the marina and he had seemed a little too happy and joyful, but I had not thought much of it at the time. I started to shout at them. They were straying out of the channel and into danger, taking us with them. We were surrounded by rocks. If we left the channel, it would be a matter of seconds before we ran aground.

The skipper's course became more erratic. There was definitely something wrong. Shouting and laughing, he didn't seem to care what he was doing. By now we had left the channel and were heading for the hard stuff. I was sure we would hit at any moment. I was shouting at the guy to turn the boat around, but it was obvious he was not listening. The sailors on the boat behind me were all shouting the same alerts to the skipper. It was time to cut the tow line before it was too late, but in that instant the lead boat violently hit the bottom.

The force was enough to send the crew flying across the deck. 'Shit, I'm next,' I thought. There was nothing I could do. We were attached to a tow line and there was no time to cut it. We piled into the back of the stricken yacht, sending me flying across the deck. Then came the crash and we were hard aground. All I could do was watch in horror as the yacht behind me zig-zagged around the tow line in a desperate effort to avoid the same fate as the rest of us. I was terrified she would ram us. There was nothing anyone could do but brace for impact. The noise was horrible as the other yacht went aground just metres from the back of my boat. At least they didn't hit me.

I picked myself up and looked over the bow of *English Braids*. We were in trouble. The force of the impact had created a huge hole in the front of the boat. Luckily, we had a watertight bulkhead in place so I knew we would not start to sink. Looking up at the boat that had just caused the chaos I shouted to the skipper, "What the hell do you think you're playing at? Look what you've done!"

I wanted to climb aboard and punch the guy, I was so furious. But that kind of emotion would have to wait, at least for a while. We had more pressing issues to deal with. We were all hard aground on the rocks and to make matters worse, the tide was going out. It would not be long before the situation would become very serious. The skipper of the yacht that caused all the damage was obviously in some kind of shock. Despite being physically fine, he wasn't responding to anyone. He was sitting on the floor of the cockpit staring into space. It turned out that he was drunk and had been drinking all morning before departure. His crew was a team of very inexperienced people that had now completely lost the plot. One of the girls on board was in hysterics. She was obviously very frightened and traumatised. The rest of the crew were frantically asking "What shall we do? What shall we do?"

I climbed down into the cabin to check we were not taking on any water and directed the crew of the other boats to do the same. We were all OK for the moment. We had taken significant damage and I had to get *English Braids* back to the harbour as quickly as I could. Outside assistance would prove to be critical here. The other yachts were just as stranded as me and we were starting to bounce on the rocks, every crash of the waves followed by a horrifying vibrating sound as the noise dissipated through the hull structure. My fragile little boat could not endure much of this pounding before she would be reduced to a complete wreck. There was no way we would get off on our own. There was little wind, and with no engine there was only one option. I would have to send out a distress call.

With the VHF radio in my hands I took a moment to remember the drill. Everything had happened so fast. Five minutes ago I was looking forward to a night of sailing across the English Channel. Now I was aground on the rocks with a massive hole in the bow.

Sending a distress call over VHF radio is part of basic RYA training. It's relatively simple, with a specific procedure to follow. But when you have to do it for real, it becomes a whole different ballgame. I took a moment to think it through, then cleared my throat and took a deep breath. I pressed the transmit switch on the VHF radio and sent my first Mayday distress call.

The local French lifeboat was on scene within twenty minutes of my call for help. However, with the tide quickly ebbing, we were heeled quite far over, stuck hard and fast. The lifeboat wasted no time, quickly towing both of us into deeper water. I was conscious that we had missed the last lock for the day and I knew that we would end up on our side in the outer harbour once the tide had gone out. At the time, that was the least of my worries.

Once in deeper water, the boat that had caused the incident was left to motor up the channel towards the safe confines of the harbour. The people on board had managed to sort themselves out and were much calmer than before, although the skipper was still in a kind of trance.

The lifeboat crew, seeing me as the biggest casualty, wasted no time in towing me back to the harbour, while the third boat reattached their towline to the yacht that caused the incident. There was just enough water in the outer harbour for us to scrape in before we ran aground alongside the harbour wall. The others were not so fortunate. They ran aground in the channel and would be stuck there for several hours, unable to get ashore.

I had been catapulted into a nightmare world of trouble. How would I explain this to my sponsors and how would I get the boat back to the UK? With *English Braids* lying on her side in the mud, she looked stranded, like a beached whale accepting her fate. I secured everything as best I could and went ashore to find a phone and call Dad. I was soaked and covered in mud. The situation was not good, but it could have been much worse. The damage was limited to the bow area. We would need to arrange for the boat to be lifted out of the water and then take her back to the UK by road.

I had to call English Braids and break the bad news. It was a call I really didn't want to make but Peter was very supportive. He immediately offered the use of the company van to help with towing the boat back home and with an offer of help from a friend we formulated a plan. The next day I arranged for the boat to be lifted out of the water and I returned to the UK to collect the van and hire a suitable trailer.

Three days later, I returned with my friend John Wright to sort out the mess. John is ex-Special Forces and the ideal character to have around when trouble rears its ugly head. He would play a big part in my future adventures and is one of those few true friends that would drop everything at a moment's notice to help his mates. He is a rare breed and with his 'can-do' attitude, I knew we could handle the situation.

We loaded *English Braids* onto the trailer and set off back to England. There was no doubt we were in a fix. With just a few weeks to go before the qualifying series started in France, we were faced with an uphill struggle. The accident was not my fault and would be covered by the perpetrator's insurance but I had to find a yard to take on the repair job and get the work done in record time.

Out of disaster came a glimmer of hope. The very yard where I had initially found *English Braids* was willing to take on the job. I called the owner, who had been a fellow competitor in the Round Britain race and he understood my predicament. We dropped the boat off at the factory on the way home. The repair job would take three weeks to complete, making time very tight, but not impossible for us to get to the first race.

It was the longest three weeks of my life. Our calamity had caught the attention of some local press and despite being initially concerned about the media writing a negative story, we managed to gain some good PR from the situation. The headline 'Transatlantic yacht crashes' certainly sounded dramatic.

During the lay-up I also took the time to apply for a job with a syndicate who were building a revolutionary catamaran to compete in The Race, a no-holds-barred global drag race. Heading the project was Pete Goss, the famous adventurer and yachtsman. Mark Orr, whom I had first met during the Round Britain race, was Pete's business partner. Mark was curious as to why they had not received an application from me for one of the crew positions. It was suggested during a telephone conversation that I should apply quickly, before crew selection concluded.

Eventually the call came with conformation the repair job had been completed. The yard had worked a small miracle and *English Braids* was ready for sea. There was just enough time to get over to France to make the start of the first qualifying race.

The first race in the calendar was the Solitaire de Concarneau, a testing 300-mile solo dash around the Biscay coast. The race starts and finishes in Concarneau on the south Brittany coast with the course taking competitors through the Glenan Islands just south of the starting area then onto Île de Ré, a small island off the coast of La Rochelle, before returning to Concarneau. It would be my first solo race and our first chance to have a pop at the competition.

The pace from the start was fast and furious, with boats all around me. That first night was just insane. We were sailing under spinnaker for the first few hours and blasting along under the cover of darkness, the racing was awesome. I could see the silhouettes of the boats in the dark. They were everywhere, all pushing hard, trying to gain the advantage.

Every now and then someone would make a mistake and wipe-out, signalled by their little masthead navigation lights pitching up at a crazy angle. One boat wiped-out under spinnaker right next to me. I could tell the poor bugger had plenty on his plate, I could hear the sails flogging in the darkness. My boat-handling skills were holding up well but I was finding the navigation a challenge. We were definitely pushing the safety envelope as we sailed close to the rocky shoreline.

The generally accepted method of navigation on a Mini is to kneel in the cockpit with the Admiralty chart folded over on the floor so you can plot position fixes as the action unfolds. At night, a head torch becomes your best friend when tackling chart work. The race rules ban any form of chart-plotting device and GPS had only recently been allowed by the race committee. In earlier races, the competitors would sail across the Atlantic with just a sextant, which is not an easy piece of equipment to use on the pitching deck of a tiny boat.

We were now very close to the Îles des Glenan, a rocky archipelago just south of Concarneau. The islands were a mark of the course and we had to sail through narrow channels before reaching open water again. It was a crazy introduction into the world of Mini sailing. I could see the faint outline of rocks everywhere as they slid past the hull, just metres away. I hoped my navigation was up to scratch, as at these speeds there was very little margin for error. But I was in my element. Mini racing was right up my street.

Once clear of the Îles des Glenan, we had a pretty trouble-free trip down towards La Rochelle and around Île de Ré. The bulk of the fleet had found its pace and we were hanging in there with the leading pack. The first night had been pretty hectic, sailing past all those hazards, but with the wind moderating and changing direction to the south we were now enjoying some light wind sailing. The tricky passage around the Île de Ré passed without incident and we were now heading northward back towards the finish line at Concarneau.

I could see three competitors around me. One was further out to sea, roughly level with us, one was way inshore up on the coastline of the island and the third was almost on the horizon in front of us, with just his sails visible. He was several miles away but certainly catchable.

With the wind being so light during the early hours I had moved most of our equipment and redundant sails into the bow area of the cabin. This positioning of movable ballast is a good way of lifting the back of the boat just clear of the water, which increases speed by reducing the friction of the hull on the sea. An essential and effective task on such small lightweight boats, the correct placement of heavy equipment on board can help to improve performance in differing wind and sea conditions.

The trouble was the wind was now steadily building. I knew we would soon have to start shifting all that equipment toward the rear of the boat before our advantage turned into a hindrance. If the wind increased too much, that dead weight in the bow would start to drive the nose down under the waves and make steering very difficult. I thought I had plenty of time and set my sights on catching the competitor ahead. We were gaining ground and the boat on the horizon was gradually becoming bigger as we closed the gap.

In my haste to catch the prey ahead of me I was unwittingly running into trouble. I had left it too late to shift the weight in the cabin. The bow of the boat was starting to bury into the waves ahead, the load on the tiller was becoming heavier by the minute and I knew that the ideal moment to go below and move things around had passed.

I had overlooked the fact that the automatic pilot would struggle to keep the boat on a straight course in those conditions with all that weight up front. It's amazing how the little details are always dramatically amplified at sea. With the wind filling in from behind, our powerful spinnaker was starting to pull us across the ocean at near double-digit speeds.

I had to get below but the pilot would not steer the boat while I did so. This predicament was my own fault. Struggling with the autopilot in the cockpit, tiller between my legs, I planned everything in my mind. The minute I could get the pilot to take a straight line I would dash below decks, throw everything to the back of the boat and jump back on deck to regain control. The only other option was to slow down and drop the spinnaker, but that didn't appeal. I would soon learn the error of my ways.

The moment arrived. The wind seemed to steady long enough for me to engage the pilot and all seemed good. Letting go of the tiller,

I leapt into the hatchway ready to disappear below decks, but there was barely time to blink before the bow dived into the wave ahead. The first indication of trouble came from the autopilot alarm emitting a loud beeping noise, indicating that the system was off-course and struggling to keep control. Time seemed to freeze as I made a desperate lunge for the tiller. I was momentarily stuck in the confines of the hatchway and my attempts to grab hold of the tiller were in vain. Then, in an instant, *English Braids* rounded up under the force of the wind and laid over on her side. It was a big wipe-out. All I could do was hang on and climb back into the cockpit to deal with the mess.

I had to get the sail down, it was flogging itself to bits. With all that weight up forward we were in a right old pickle. First things first, I thought. Spinnaker down, regain some control, keep calm. Reaching forward to release the halyard that attached the spinnaker to the mast-head, I flicked open the clutch and started to retrieve the sail. It was not easy with the boat lying on her side and I had to be careful not to end up in the drink along with the sail. All I could think about was the competition who would surely be reeling me in now.

It took nearly twenty minutes to sort out. I managed to retrieve the spinnaker but not before the sail had filled with water and pulled the halyard completely out of the mast. This meant I would not be able to re-hoist the sail for the remainder of the race. We would have to carry on without our biggest sail. This incident would prove to be a costly mistake. With the sail stowed safely below decks and the equipment down below now stacked right at the back of the boat, we were on our way again. I was exhausted and covered in sweat. The wipe-out and subsequent recovery had really taken it out of me. Without the big spinnaker flying, I could only sit on the cockpit floor, gasping for air and watch as the boats that were once so close pull ahead under full sail.

I was furious with myself but would later put it down to experience. This had been a short, sharp introduction into the world of Mini racing. I thought this was tough, but it was nothing compared to the drama that lay ahead.

It was early days for me and the Transat was the real prize. Everything else was just the warm-up. At this level of competition it was apparent the slightest mistake could make the difference between top five and bottom twenty-five in the rankings. Late that afternoon as we limped across the Concarneau finish line, I was completely knackered but pleased to hear we had finished twelfth out of a fleet of over thirty. The closing stages of the race had produced some ultra-close racing with us coming out on top after an intense battle with several other boats. I knew that with some quality training we could be well on the pace by the start of the Transat.

Two days later, I sailed back to the UK on my own as part of my single-handed training. The trip from Concarneau to Brighton proved to be an exciting passage. The weather along the English Channel was pretty fresh. The shipping forecasts issued on BBC Radio 4 were warning of strong winds in our area. Apparently the tempestuous weather had wreaked havoc with several dinghy regattas in Weymouth Bay at the same time as I was surfing up the Channel. The wind was behind us and little *English Braids* was delivering an exciting ride.

As I closed in on Brighton Marina, I knew my father would be waiting on the pier-end in anticipation. I had called my parents before I left France to give them an estimated time of arrival and I knew I was slightly overdue. While Dad waited patiently at the end of the marina harbour wall, dodging the waves as they crashed over the piers, he was approached by two local policemen. They had seen him standing at the end of the pier looking out to sea and realised he had been there for a while. The weather was appalling and Dad was the only person out there. Apparently they thought he was a jumper, contemplating throwing himself into the ocean. It was only when they approached to ask if he was alright that they realised everything was OK. Dad told them what was going on and explained he was waiting for me to arrive. Much relieved, they all had a good chuckle about it. Soon after that I sailed into view and the police officers left, but not before commenting that perhaps I was the crazy one, out there on the rough seas. No doubt my father agreed.

A week later, out of the blue, I received a letter from Goss Challenges. I had been successful in passing through the initial stages of the crew selection process for The Race and now faced a formal interview with Pete Goss and his second-in-command Andy Hindley at the Goss Challenge headquarters in Totnes, Devon. The crew selection process would not be decided by just one interview, though. Pete had been inundated with applications from all around the world and was methodically working through a list of some six hundred applicants for the two crew places on offer. Some applications came from hugely experienced individuals, while others, inspired by Pete's company strapline 'Dare to Dream', were doing just that.

Having enjoyed a good first meeting in the boardroom, I was invited on board Aqua Quorum, the boat that Pete had sailed around the world in the Vendée Globe. Pete and Andy wanted to go for a sail and have a chat. The day provided the perfect opportunity to gauge whether I would fit in. We were also joined by another professional yachtsman and prospective candidate. That interview also went well, but driving back to London, I felt none the wiser as to whether I had done enough to secure a place on board.

While I was at the factory for my first interview, Pete had showed me around the giant catamaran. It was a truly awe-inspiring vessel and unlike anything anyone had seen before. She was a goliath, one of the first of a new generation of G class or Giant Catamarans. At one hundred and twenty feet long and seventy feet wide, she was the world's largest carbon fibre composite structure. Her twin rotating wing masts would tower nearly one hundred and fifteen feet above the deck, higher than the equivalent of ten double-decker buses stacked on top of each other. Sitting motionless in the hangar, the assembly of various component parts that would eventually form the complete structure was well under way.

This unique craft was truly state-of-the-art. She resembled a spaceship more than a sailboat and represented a unique insight into what the future of sailboat design and technology might bring. She was a generation ahead of her time, and I was so desperate to be part of that project that I would have done almost anything to sign up.

Several weeks would pass before I was invited back to Totnes for a final meeting with Pete. In the boardroom at the factory that was to become so familiar to me, I was formally offered a place on board as full-time race crew. I was so excited that I nearly knocked over the tea tray on the table next to me. Pete shared my enthusiasm, but impressed upon me the need to keep the news a secret until he and the management team could finalise the details and decide on a suitable date for the team to be announced. I was on board but couldn't tell a soul other than my parents.

With my focus back on the Mini project I competed in several other qualification events during the build-up to the Mini Transat. Our results showed steady and consistent improvement. We achieved a seventh

Powering along under full sail.

Training off Plymouth.

place ranking out of nearly eighty competitors in the 700-mile Mini Fastnet race and succeeded in qualifying for the Transat with plenty of time to spare.

By the time we eventually found ourselves tied up in the race village in Concarneau, a week before the start, we were more than ready to take on the mighty Atlantic. I had sailed the boat over from England a week before the deadline for competitors to be present in the race village. I wanted to arrive early to avoid any last-minute problems and needed return to Devon during that week to join Pete and the team back at Goss Challenges. The date for introducing the crew to the world's media had been set and required all of us to be present. Pete would be announcing the two final crew members and Philips Electronics as our new title sponsor for the bid to win The Race. It was major news and essential that everyone pull their weight to ensure that the day went smoothly.

It was a busy period but I was loving every minute. This was the big time, and I had a place booked for the adventure of a lifetime. I had just bagged the coolest job on the planet. It felt like I was standing on the moon looking down at the Earth, just waiting for the most awesome rollercoaster ride to kick in. Sometimes life is so sweet. I thought I was to be one of the world's luckiest men, those who would take this already iconic breath-taking beast around the world.

The press conference at Goss Challenge headquarters was a huge affair, with hundreds of people present. I had never seen so many media and satellite trucks in one location. All the major news networks were there. Standing on the stage alongside Pete and the lads it was difficult to take in the enormity of the day. I looked at the crowd. Hundreds of people were staring right back at us. I suddenly realised that a result in the Mini Transat was now even more crucial. I was carrying the pride and faith of my new-found employers, as well as that of my sponsors at English Braids.

Back in the race village, our little *English Braids* might well have been the oldest boat in the fleet but she didn't look it. I had lived, slept and breathed the project all year and with the unstinting support of Peter Earp's company the boat looked and performed like a well-oiled piece of precision machinery. I had systematically improved my skills as a skipper over the season and as a team we had developed the quality and reliability of the ropes on board. There was now nothing left to do but the pre-race scrutineering and talking to the media. I took some time to reflect. I was proud of our achievements so far and excited that we were just days away from the start of an oceanic marathon.

Looking around the race village, I could see the level of competition. It was a massive fleet. I counted about eighty boats in the marina. One thing was for sure – everyone who had gotten this far was good. The fleet represented the best of the best. Competitors had travelled from as far afield as Australia and New Zealand. As well as a lone Finnish entry, one guy had even made it all the way from Japan. Unsurprisingly, most of the fleet was made up of French sailors, all keen to make their mark. The level of individual preparation varied from professionally-prepared boats that were totally sorted to ones that were in complete chaos, with the majority of competitors fitting into the 'reasonably well-prepared' category.

Right to left: me standing next to competitor Nick Maloney, Nick's girlfriend and Chris Sayer another competitor.

The pre-race festivities were in full swing. The French take their ocean racing very seriously, with the public treating the skippers more like football stars than just yachtsmen. In France, the Mini Transat is a huge 'must-see' event, drawing visitors from across the country. It's big news there, in total contrast to the public perception of ocean racing in Britain, despite the fact that we live on an island surrounded by the sea.

It always amazes me that the British and their media don't share the same passion for ocean racing as the French. In the race village, people kept asking for my autograph and to stand next to me for their picture to be taken. It was a remarkable experience, and the one thing

I had not prepared for. We were even adopted by a local primary school whose pupils hand-painted a motif of a dolphin jumping through a hoop onto our mainsail. The idea was that they would follow my progress across the Atlantic and learn about the ocean and the spirit of adventure.

In the final days before the start everyone became consumed by news that we were in for a blow. The French meteorological centre, Meteo France, and the UK Met Office were both forecasting south-westerly gale-force winds with the possibility of severe gales for the Bay of Biscay within twelve hours of the race commencing. That was not an encouraging forecast, but I remained confident. We had seen gales during our training and *English Braids* was well-sorted.

As the final countdown to the start began, reality started to set in for all the competitors. Some skippers were voicing safety concerns and asked the race organisers to postpone the start until the worst of the weather has passed by. The mood on the dock had certainly taken a dive. People were starting to realise that from the very start we would be setting out into the teeth of a full-on Atlantic gale.

Despite these concerns, the decision was taken to start as sched-uled. Meteo France was forecasting no more than thirty-five knots of wind, gale force eight. As competitors in a race like the Mini Transat, skippers should be more than capable of dealing with such weather. In any case, the race rules state that 'it is the sole and inescapable respon-sibility of the skipper to decide whether to start or continue in a race'. The organisers would only postpone the event if it were dangerous to get out of the harbour.

The night before the race, we received a last minute spot-check. The race committee wanted to check the size of our water ballast tanks. Class rules allow a volume of two hundred litres of seawater to be pumped into each side of the boat to increase stability and speed. We had been measured previously and despite sailing all season with the same setup, we were now found to be over the limit. I struggled to understand how this could be and was more than a little annoyed at the finding. However, at this late stage it was pointless trying to argue. We just had to reduce the size of our ballast tanks. Easier said than done, but after some quick thinking with Peter Earp, who had just arrived to take part in the final evening's festivities, we hatched a plan.

We would simply put polystyrene blocks into the ballast tanks to reduce the amount of water that could occupy the space. I will never forget the sight of Peter on his hands and knees beside the boat, hacksaw in hand, cutting through blocks of polystyrene whilst wearing an expensive business suit and shoes. This was typical of Peter, rolling up his sleeves and diving straight in to help make everything happen. I knew then why he had been so successful in business. I was blessed to be surrounded by people who believed in our project.

With the last-minute frustrations behind us, we were ready for action. Setting off from the dock is always an emotional moment. Friends and family waving goodbye, their faces showing the inevitable signs of worry. I had already seen it so many times, but this day was potentially more worrisome than previous occasions. Everyone knew the weather would be rough for the first few hours. My dad told me to keep my safety harness attached to the boat at all times, one last

Mum and me enjoying a hug before the Mini Transat start.

119

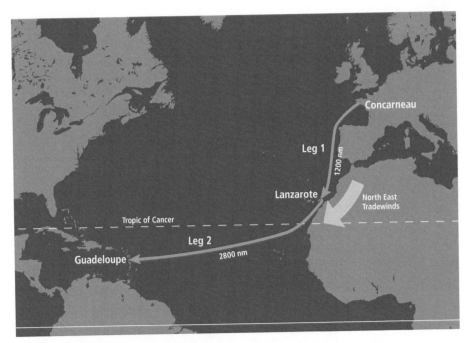

Race route of the 1999 Mini Transat.

reminder to his son before he disappeared over the horizon.

The starting area was a frantic place to be. Eighty of the world's most competitive sailors were all fired-up and competing for the best starting position. Once underway, the fleet had to pick its way through the minefield of spectator boats, sail into the bay towards the beach and then pass through the narrow channel, surrounded by rocks. A marker buoy anchored just off the beach was a mandatory turning mark of the course and would provide a perfect view for the twenty thousand spectators lining the shore as the fleet passed by. Only then could we make our way out to sea.

Going into the final five minutes before the start I had a close call with another boat, passing within feet of each other. I could hear the French skipper swearing as we avoided a collision more by luck than judgement. Others were not so lucky and there were numerous collisions on the start line.

The boom from the cannon on the committee boat signified that the 1999 Mini Transat was underway. This was everything we had worked towards over the last twelve months and we got away clean

– just. Sailing towards the harbour the fleet was glued together. It was chaos. People were hoisting their colourful spinnakers to gain an advantage. Some hoisted them upside-down in their frantic attempts to make everything happen faster than humanly possible.

We managed to get ours hoisted relatively smoothly. The channel was very narrow and with so many boats, there was a real possibility of a pile-up at the turning mark off the beach. I decided to drop the spin-naker early in favour of a controlled rounding at the mark, conscious that the eyes of the world were upon us.

Looking over my shoulder, I could see an armada of sails thunder-ing down on top of us, an impressive sight. We were in the top twelve. Those first thirty minutes of the Mini Transat are firmly imprinted in my mind as some of the most exhilarating moments of my life. I was surrounded by competition and felt so alive.

Within just a few hours of the start, as the fleet punched its way into the infamous Bay of Biscay, the cloud base started to lower dramat-ically. The barometer was taking an ominous dive and my expectations of the worst were being confirmed. It soon became apparent that we were heading into a ferocious storm. By nightfall, the wind was already near gale force eight and increasing. The motion on board was rough going but not extreme. This was what we had prepared for, and I felt confident as we plunged into the pitch black with heavily-reefed sails.

I knew the weather was going to deteriorate further. Conditions were manageable but something gave me the feeling that now was time to get into my survival suit and be prepared for action. Survival suits are commonly used on these types of boats. Being so small, Minis are somewhat susceptible to the elements. Water washes over the decks right back to the cockpit on a regular basis, even in moderate conditions. On a cold late-September night like this, alone in the Bay of Biscay, I knew I needed to keep as warm and dry as possible.

It was a real circus act trying to get into my one-piece suit. The waterproof zips were located on the rear of the suit, with one zip running across the top of my back. Easy enough to zip up for two people helping each other, but try it on your own in a small boat in complete darkness in the confines of a cramped cabin, while being tossed around on the ocean. It was near-impossible, but I eventually emerged from the cabin, zipped up and ready for the night ahead.

It was a long first night at sea. By morning, fifteen competitors had

Testing my shiny new
survival suit. It didnt leak!

returned to the confines of Concarneau harbour, beaten back by the
tough conditions. I was oblivious to this as the race rules don't allow
any form of outside communication devices other than simple VHF
radio. VHF communication is only good for about thirty-five miles in
perfect conditions, so most of the time I had the radio switched off to
save power. I needed as much juice from the batteries as I could muster
to run my automatic pilot and navigation lights. Cut off from the rest of
the world, I would not learn of the full extent of the devastation about
to hit the fleet until I reached the first stage stopover in Lanzarote,
some nine days away.

Daylight revealed a marvellous yet humbling sight. We were sailing under full gale-force conditions. The sea was rough and confused,
with large waves towering over us. At this stage we were still making
reasonable progress. I had never assumed the Mini Transat was going
to be easy, and the choice of tactics was to play an important role in
the events that followed. We were sailing into the wind and waves. The
wind was coming from the south-west, directly where we wanted to
go. I had two options: head inshore or point the bow offshore towards
the west.

I knew the right decision was to head out to the west and into the
seemingly desolate Atlantic. By heading further out to sea we would
benefit from being closer to the frontal boundary of the weather
system. The wind would eventually shift from south-westerly to a more
favourable north-westerly direction. Out to the western side of the race

track we would be closest to that shift in wind direction and feel the benefits sooner than anyone sticking close inshore in the Bay of Biscay.

Also, by heading out to sea, we would cross over the continental shelf, where the sea floor suddenly drops from being relatively shallow to thousands of metres deep. Outside the shelf on the open ocean, waves would be much less confused and more manageable for a small boat like *English Braids*. By contrast, being closer inshore, locked into the Bay of Biscay, my options would be limited and the seas would be treacherous. Heading west was the best and safest option.

I was starting to worry about the mainsail. We were sailing with just a small part of the sail hoisted but the harsh conditions were taking their toll. Some of the batten-ends, the plastic fittings that retain the stiff fibreglass battens into the sail, were obviously not up to the job in this weather. Several had broken, allowing the battens to work themselves out of the pockets. There was also damage to the trailing edge of the sail at the head. The fabric stitching was coming apart because of the continual flogging the sail had endured as almost every wave laid us over on our side.

I had spent the whole night on deck keeping *English Braids* on her feet and it was time to go below to put a fix on the soggy Admiralty chart and make a cup of well-earned tea. I hadn't ventured into the cabin during the night because of the large amount of commercial shipping in the area: visible by their navigation lights cutting through the darkness, these vessels were quite an intimidating presence. Putting an accurate fix on the chart below decks in those conditions could take up to fifteen minutes, plenty of time for a tanker to steam over the horizon and run us down.

Climbing into the cabin, it took a couple of seconds for me to take in the chaos. The violent motion of the boat had turned the cabin into a complete mess, with equipment strewn everywhere. There was several inches of water sloshing across the cabin floor too, though that's not unusual in these conditions with this type of boat. Everything was soaked, and to make matters worse my single-burner stove and kettle had been destroyed. There would be no hot food or drinks until we reached the Canaries. Just about the only thing that was intact was my Dictaphone, which I had stuck to a bulkhead with Velcro.

The view out of the companionway hatch into the cockpit looked impressive from below decks. Large waves with frothy white crests were sweeping past our little boat. It was an ideal opportunity to shoot some video and take a few photos. I knew I would be giving plenty of seminars after the race and this was just the kind of footage I needed to inspire an audience.

The noise of the hull pounding across the wave crests would amplify the drama. I pressed 'record' on the Dictaphone, and with my knees wedged on the cabin floor, set about describing the first night of the race while, putting a quick fix on the chart. We were making reasonable progress, given the circumstances, but Cap Finisterre at the southernmost tip of the Bay of Biscay seemed a long way away and was almost off the corner of the chart.

View from the cabin – menacing waves during the first leg of the Mini Transat.

We had several hundred miles to cover before we could escape the claws of Biscay. The first night had been pretty full on and I was knackered. There was nothing I could do but dig deep and suck it up, a phrase my games teacher had used at Fyling Hall during particularly tough rugby matches. "Just suck it up, lads," he would say. His words gave me inspiration.

The weather was relentless and it took more than three days to cross the ferocious Bay of Biscay. *English Braids* was responding with everything she had to climb over the now huge seas. The situation on board by day three was pretty diabolical. The constant pounding and exposure to the elements was taking its toll on both the boat and on me. Pretty much everything below was broken or saturated. The camcorder I'd used to capture some breathtaking footage had been destroyed by the violent motion and was lost in the rising amount of water in the cabin. The generator that I relied on to replenish the batteries was also swamped and would not start. I was very tired but could still feel the adrenaline pumping through my body. We still had the mast intact and were making progress, albeit slowly, towards our goal. Mentally, I felt solid as a rock. Giving up was not an option.

I hadn't seen any other boats since the first night at sea. Looking out across the huge, mind-numbing waves I could have been forgiven for thinking I was the only person left on the planet. Then, suddenly out of nowhere, I caught a glimpse of another boat. It was unmistakably a Mini. She was about a hundred yards away and crossing behind us. I only saw her for a moment as the tiny boat leapt off the top of a wave like a coiled spring. The fluorescent orange of her storm sails caught my eye, making the boat just visible in the moment she popped up on the crest. In an instant she was gone, sliding down into the trough. The waves were so huge I couldn't even see the top of her mast as she disappeared. I was not the only one caught in this cauldron of turmoil, after all.

We were way out of sight of land and off the continental shelf, but by the third day the seas were still enormous. The race rules at the time banned any kind of wind instruments, but I could tell from the sea state and the wind whistling through the rigging that the wind speed had been regularly gusting to fifty knots, severe gale force nine.

I spared a thought for anyone who had taken the inshore course option and headed into Biscay. I had no idea where the rest of the fleet was, but anyone inshore would undoubtedly be in grave danger.

The following night we rounded Cap Finisterre, hoping that the worst was behind us. I was still having problems with the generator and desperately needed a break in the weather to repair it. Otherwise, without the ability to charge the batteries we would have no instruments and no automatic pilot and we would be effectively out of the race. The thought of getting through a storm of that magnitude only to be scuppered by electrical failure was so frustrating that I shouted all kinds of obscenities into the air.

Approaching Finisterre on our fourth night at sea we were closer to the land than I had initially planned. I had wanted to pass the area with a margin of about thirty miles between us and the coast, but the storm had sucked us in to within just a few miles of the famous headland. We were close enough to easily see the beam from the lighthouse at Cap Finisterre as we navigated our way past.

My last night in Biscay was not going to be easy. We had been sailing in survival conditions for the past couple of days. I had dropped the mainsail and lashed the boom firmly to the deck. Our tiny scrap of storm jib and trysail was all the canvas I could hoist to attempt to make headway. I'd had no sleep since the start and the effects of severe sleep deprivation were manifesting themselves.

Most of the time, manually steering *English Braids* had been the only way I could be confident of getting through the worst of the storm without being rolled upside-down. The conditions were way in excess of what I could expect the autopilot to cope with. The wind was incredible, visibility had reduced dramatically during the last couple of hours and with near-horizontal rain pelting the decks the sea was white with spume and foam. *English Braids* was near her limit for making forward headway in those conditions. As each and every gust came through we would just lay over on our side, virtually flat in the water. It was all I could do to just clip on my harness to the safety lines and hang on. There was a real possibility of capsizing in those conditions and I kept running through in my head what to do if we went over, how to deal with the situation and keep my head above water.

We were slammed by a huge wave that came out of the darkness like an express train. It thumped into the side of my little boat with such ferocity the masthead was thrown down into the water. Hanging on with my arms, gripping the high side of the boat, I knew that the keel would be completely out of the water. Here we go I thought, this is the one. There was little time to think anything else, all I could do was react and rely on my survival instinct, praying the mast would hold up. I held my breath for a few moments and then she came back up. Miraculously, the mast was still intact.

That last night in Biscay was a true test of my resilience and determination. I was asking *English Braids* to punch well above her weight. In those conditions, I couldn't really have blamed her if we hadn't made it through the night.

With Finisterre finally behind us, the weather system had also passed, delivering a dramatic moderation in wind speed and direction. We had escaped the clutches of Biscay by the thinnest of margins. The rollercoaster that is the Mini Transat would deliver a brief respite before we got back to the task in hand – racing.

We had not come through the storm unscathed, however. Structurally, the boat was fine but my biggest problems now were the generator and myself. I was physically exhausted and struggling to concentrate. I had given everything to get us through the weather and desperately needed some sleep. The batteries would need re-charging soon and the generator had to be fixed to make this happen but I had nothing left to give. I knew I had several hours of current in the batteries and decided to power up the autopilot and get my head down. *English Braids* would have to sail herself for a few hours.

Awakening from a deep sleep, I was convinced we were doing badly in the overall rankings. It had taken so long to get to this point that I was sure we must have a lot of catching up to do – I couldn't know we were actually in the top five of the fleet and making great progress. The sun was warming the decks as we sailed along under a light following breeze off the Portuguese coast. It was time to tackle the generator problem and try to keep us in the race.

I'm not a mechanic but in an attempt to fix the problem I started to dismantle the generator. Out on the ocean a solo sailor has to be a jack-of-all-trades and I was starting to become accustomed to this way of life. With the machinery in pieces on the cockpit floor, the situation didn't seem very hopeful. I could hardly remember how to reassemble the damned thing, let alone pinpoint the problem. I knew it had been submerged in the cabin during the height of the storm and just hoped I could dry everything out in order to keep us racing.

Exhausted after the storm during leg 1 of the Mini Transat.

Two-stroke generators are notorious for being temperamental, so I had bought a brand-new unit just before the start of the race in the hope of eliminating the risk of such a mechanical failure. Having reassembled it all, added a new spark plug and covered everything in DW40 for good measure, I gave the pull-cord a tug. Nothing. It took several desperate pulls of the cord before our hopes and dreams finally coughed back to life. The sound of the generator buzzing away brought with it overwhelming relief and satisfaction. We soon had thirty amps running into the batteries, and life was sweet once again.

Keen to keep pushing hard rather than taking more time to recover, I hoisted the spinnaker. I was convinced we were at the back of the fleet and wanted to make up some ground and improve our position. The breeze steadily built throughout the day and it soon became clear I would once again have to manually steer *English Braids* to achieve her potential. This race was turning out to be a monumental test of character. By nightfall I was once again struggling to keep my eyes open and maintain focus. Sitting at the back of the boat holding the tiller in my hands my imagination started to play tricks on me. I remember thinking the folded up headsail on the bow was actually the Michelin man. Then I would be dragged back to reality and realise I was seeing things. It was a strange experience, and looking back, I realise I was really in a bad way. I had been warned about the effects of sleep deprivation and how hallucinations during the race can have disastrous consequences.

Inevitably, whilst steering the boat in the darkness, I lost my fight to stay awake. Head nodding, my eyes closed. I have no idea how long I was asleep for, probably seconds rather than minutes. I awoke to find myself surrounded by cold sea water but couldn't see anything in the pitch black. I was certainly wide awake now.

I had fallen asleep whilst steering and allowed *English Braids* to wander off course. We had Chinese gybed – the boom had flown across the boat and hit the backstays, pinning us down in the water on the same side as I was sitting. I was clipped on by my safety harness and struggled to climb up to the high side. The light of the moon had been obscured by the mainsail, which was almost on top of me. My heart felt like it was about to explode. I was soaked and had just endured the scariest ten seconds of my life.

I had to retrieve the spinnaker and get the boat back on her feet. Letting the halyard go, the sail inevitably ended up in the sea, somehow wrapping itself around the keel bulb. We bounced back upright and I started to wrestle with the eighty square-metre sail as it trailed in the sea off the back of the boat. I was sweating buckets and quickly running out of steam but I couldn't afford to lose the sail. It was our biggest spinnaker and one of just two sails essential for sailing with the wind behind us. If I had to buy a new sail in the Canary Islands I would receive a time penalty, which would be disastrous. I eventually retrieved the sail, but not before the sea had left a lasting impression by ripping it in two.

With just a hundred miles remaining to the first leg finish in Lanzarote, I spotted a ship in the distance, converging on our position. It was a large freighter which would pass by fairly closely. It was my first sign of outside life since spotting the other competitor in the Bay of Biscay. I had turned on my VHF radio and was debating whether to call him up and ask if he had seen us when the radio burst into life. He was calling me.

The voice came across in perfect English but it was obvious the operator was of Asian origin. I was surprised to be asked if I needed any assistance. When I replied 'no', he asked if I was part of the Mini Transat race, saying that lots of boats had set off distress beacons in the Bay of Biscay and several were unaccounted-for. I realised then that some people had been in a lot more trouble than me. The radio operator took my details, explaining he would pass them onto the race headquarters in France.

It was an unnerving intimation of the tales of disaster that would unfold. Later that afternoon, I spotted a sail on the horizon. We were reeling them in at a fair old rate. At first, I thought it was a small cruising yacht sailing southbound but I was soon in no doubt that it was a fellow competitor. The shape of his sails, clearly visible through my binoculars, told me that it was a Mini. This was good, I thought it meant we were closing in on the fleet.

We passed by about a quarter of a mile to the west. The boat was sailing very slowly with reefed sails, quite unnecessary in the fairly light wind. I was a little concerned and wondered why the skipper would have adopted that heavily-reefed approach on a near-perfect day for sailing. Three scenarios were plausible. He was most likely asleep down below, exhausted like me. A more scary thought was that he might not be on board at all. There was also a chance he was on board but unable to sail the boat for some reason. If he was sleeping I didn't want to wake him and blow my advantage, but if he was on board and hurt, I might be able to help. It was a difficult situation, but without any obvious signs of trouble and with the boat adopting a straight course through the water, presumably being steered by autopilot, I decided he must be asleep and carried on.

Half an hour later, with his sails distant on the horizon behind us I saw his spinnaker start to fly; he had indeed been asleep. We had gained an advantage that we would hold to the finish. I crossed the first leg finish line early the next morning and was greeted by two members of race organisers Pole Atlantique.

I was battered, bruised and worn out by the first leg experience. We had made it, but my hands and body had been punished by the ordeal. I was covered in salt blisters which made it excruciatingly painful just to sit down. Normally so self-sufficient, I was pleased to accept a kind offer of help from the race officials to lower my sails.

Entering the small harbour of Puerto Calero, the race officials told me I was just the sixth competitor to finish. Hardly anyone had arrived yet. This result was beyond my expectations and despite being totally exhausted I suddenly felt an overwhelming sense of achievement. It was early in the morning and the dockside was still and quiet. Nobody was around, so I took the opportunity to throw the sails onto the pontoon and lay down on top of them to get some shut-eye. Allowing myself to switch off mentally and fall asleep felt really good. It was the first time I had done so in nine days and nights.

It was several hours before I was woken by the sound of busy footsteps on the pontoon. Opening my eyes, I could see that the previously quiet dockside was now bustling with life. A couple more competitors had arrived while I was asleep. I took a moment to consider who had arrived before me and how their boats looked compared to mine. It was obvious that we had all been through hell of one kind or another.

An observer would not have to look far to see the trail of broken equipment littering the dockside. We had all had our own issues to overcome. I began to feel that English Braids looked positively upbeat tied to the pontoon, with her white hull reflecting the ripples in the water. Apart from some hefty sail damage and continuing generator problems, the boat was by and large in good shape. Unfortunately, the same could not be said for me. I later had to visit the local hospital to have treatment for my severe blisters and bruised body.

Seemingly out of nowhere, Dad and my friend John Wright turned up. They had not long stepped off a plane from England and having eventually found the marina, were both pleased as Punch to see me, although a little disappointed that I had arrived sooner than expected, as they had wanted to be on the dockside to welcome me to Lanzarote as I crossed the finish line. Dad gave me a big hug and told me how proud he was, saying that they had all been pretty worried during the storm. My poor mum was terrified, apparently. Dad knew exactly what I would have been going through. He's a sailor and had a good degree of relevant knowledge to draw upon. But my poor mum could only imagine what I was facing. For her, the unknown must have been the worst thing. Speaking to her on the phone that morning, I did my best to play down the whole episode, but I'm sure she knew the reality was different.

Dad and John were well up to speed with the destruction that had been wrought upon much of the fleet. The majority of skippers had taken the inshore option and been overwhelmed during the height of the storm. Some competitors had run for shelter and been close enough to reach a safe haven before the worst of the storm hit, but others had been caught out and had got into difficulties during the worst of the weather.

A major air-sea rescue attempt had been launched for several boats that had activated their distress beacons. People I knew – friends of mine – had been in serious, life-threatening trouble.

Tuesday 30 September 1999 would be remembered as one of the most dramatic days in the history of the Mini Transat. Six competitors had activated their EPIRBs (emergency positioning indicating radio beacon) to indicate that they were in grave and imminent danger and required rescue.

Coastguard agencies in Britain, France and Spain were coordinating multiple rescues in the atrocious conditions. Stefano Pelizza was one of the first competitors to be rescued when his keel broke away from the bottom of his boat. Talking to him after the race, his account of his experience was terrifying. He was down below, sheltering in the cabin at the moment his boat reared up over the crest of a large wave and dropped into the cavernous trough. The resulting impact was so violent that the keel effectively dropped through the bottom of the boat. His boat instantly turned upside down. After he activated his distress beacon, he was lucky that the boat stayed afloat long enough for him to be rescued.

Another friend, an experienced sailor from Australia, endured perhaps one of the most harrowing of experiences. Nick Maloney had been one of the unlucky few who had suffered a collision with another competitor at the start of the race. Having returned to Concarneau with a gaping hole in his boat Wild Colonial Boy, he made repairs and subsequently set off again only to be rolled completely upside down by a breaking wave during the height of the storm.

That capsize was a near-death experience for Nick. He had been thrown overboard, and surfaced alongside his inverted boat, attached only by the tethered lifeline. When the boat eventually righted herself, the violent motion was enough to break his arm. Nick was faced with a titanic struggle as he clambered back on board. He had no option but to retire from the race. The mast was severely damaged, but amazingly still intact. Despite his debilitated state, he eventually made it to the sanctuary of the Spanish port of Gijon without any assistance.

Another friend and fellow British competitor had been rescued from the cold waters of the Bay of Biscay. Paul Peggs, sailing his brand-new immaculately self-built boat Blue One had also been rolled upside-down. His mast had been broken, and faced with diabolical conditions near the shipping lanes off the north-west tip of Spain, he too had been in serious trouble. Paul very nearly made it round Cap Finisterre but with no mast and few options available he made the difficult decision to call for help. Having activated the distress beacon, he tied it to the back of the boat and set about preparing for rescue.

The next time Paul checked to see if the distress beacon was still working, he saw it was gone. The constant pounding of the waves had severed the securing line and the beacon had floated away. This caused plenty of confusion with the rescue services, as they were initially looking in the wrong place. A Nimrod fixed-wing aircraft had been dispatched from RAF Kinloss in Scotland with orders to pinpoint his current position and help coordinate a final evacuation.

Paul was eventually sighted by a commercial freighter called the Cape Race. The news brought great relief to his family and friends who were all climbing the walls with worry. The Cape Race stood by Paul and his stricken yacht but was unable to launch a RIB (rigid inflatable boat) to rescue him, as the conditions were just too rough. Paul was eventually airlifted to safety by a Spanish air-sea rescue helicopter, but not before having to jump from his beloved boat into the savage ocean. They had to leave the boat to its own fate. Months later, it washed up on a remote beach in France and Paul was reunited with his pride and joy.

I was thankful for the twelve-day stopover in Lanzarote. It gave me a chance to recover from my painful salt sores and prepare *English Braids* for the second leg of the race across the Atlantic to Guadeloupe. Biscay had highlighted the crucial need to be fully prepared and although the chance of seeing very rough weather like that again was remote, I knew that we needed to be in as good a shape as possible if we were to improve upon our current sixth position. The next leg would be a drag race to the finish. The stopover in Lanzarote provided an invaluable break for everyone. Of the original eighty starters, only forty-four had made it to the Canary Islands. One skipper finished just a couple of nights before the second leg start and was understandably exhausted. With no time to recover, it would be tough for him to muster the energy to continue. A hot bath and a decent meal would be all there was time for before the restart.

Sailing south between the Canary Islands was a tricky task. The fleet started the second leg under a light evening wind with a glassy sea. I was concerned about being caught in windless zones in the lee of the Islands. Picking my way through the islands and into clear waters beyond would be a challenge. From Lanzarote, the fleet had the option to pass Fuerteventura on its eastern side or pass to the west. It was a difficult decision and one which I made at the last minute, electing to stick with the bulk of the fleet as they passed to the west side of the island.

It was a good choice. Despite light winds all through the first night, we managed to keep moving and quickly settled into a routine. Clearing the islands and their influence on the local wind and weather took several days – the Canary archipelago reaches high up into the Atlantic skyline and can have a significant effect on local weather conditions.

By the morning of the second day I was once again all alone on the ocean. The fleet had dispersed and, apart from briefly sighting a sail behind in the distance, I would not see another yacht until I reached the Caribbean.

Left **The fleet tied up in Puerto Calero, Lanzarote, after leg 1.**

Below left **Calling Mum at home after the first leg of the Mini Transat to reassure her that I was OK.**

Below right **Twenty days' worth of food and water, ready for leg 2.**

It wasn't a fast start. The wind was light for several days, making progress painfully slow. We were almost becalmed several times before the Canaries were out of sight. Looking over the side into the deep ocean, I was surprised to see the fin of what looked like a shark break the surface of the glassy sea about a hundred feet away. As it drew closer it commanded my full attention. Passing right alongside the boat, I saw that it was definitely a shark and an enormous one at that, nearly as big as the boat. Fifteen feet would seem like a realistic length. I was perfectly safe sitting on the deck looking down into the ocean, but just three feet away there existed a different world. I had never seen a shark of this size in real life and would not have believed it had I not seen it with my own eyes. 'Huge' just didn't do it justice. It looked like the perfect predator, searching for its prey. Cruising by our fragile eggshell of a boat, the enormous creature soon disappeared beneath the surface. An awesome experience.

Having made the decision to head slightly further to the south instead of taking the more accepted south-westerly route, I was confident of reaching the north-east trade winds within a few days. I had taken the opportunity to talk to Lee Bruce, an expert weather router before leaving Lanzarote and felt confident of our approach. Lee's company Tactical Weather regularly routed vessels of all descriptions across the oceans of the world. His advice would prove invaluable for the first few days of this leg of the race.

Throughout the duration of the race the event organisers would transmit daily fleet rankings and weather reports via Radio Monaco on the SSB (single side band) radio. These reports would help to break up the day. Individual boat positions were not broadcast but their overall fleet rankings were. Despite not knowing where an individual competitor was, it provided a good source of weather information, although the broadcasts were mostly in French.

My daily routine consisted of being either on deck manually steering the boat for as long as I could or down in the cabin keeping on top of the daily chores. Charging the batteries twice daily was a necessary activity and together with chart work, packing sails and eating rather dubious freeze-dried food, this formed the basis of my day. Manually steering *English Braids* whilst sailing under an eighty-square-metre masthead spinnaker was always necessary to achieve our absolute maximum speed. The autopilot was good, but never as capable as a human hand responding intuitively to every wave and gust of wind.

I would grab sleep when I could, mindful of my first-leg experience when sleep deprivation had caused plenty of problems. I didn't want to make the same mistakes twice, but it was a fine line between keeping the boat at full speed and getting enough sleep to make coherent decisions. However, no matter what the conditions, sleep could only come in the form of one hour naps several times a day, mostly during daylight. I reasoned that ships would find it easier to see me during the day. Through the nights I would be on watch, mostly steering to keep up the pace. When I did sleep, I would catnap in the cockpit, curled up in a ball with one hand poised to grab the tiller should the autopilot stray off course.

We had been at sea a week before I felt comfortable enough to go below and properly close my eyes on the bunk in the cabin and even then, never for more than an hour or two at the most. The dangers from shipping in the Atlantic were just as real as in the Bay of Biscay, though perhaps not as frequent. We were doing well in the rankings, trading places within the top ten and enjoying some exciting sailing.

Blasting along under blue skies, driven by the north-east trade winds constituted perfect sailing conditions. During the day we had steady winds and, combined with a moderate swell, we were surfing towards our goal of Guadeloupe at speeds regularly exceeding twelve knots. The night hours were the most challenging. Every night the breeze would increase under stormy-looking clouds. Sometimes I didn't see them until they were upon us, so keeping an eye out for the tempestuous clouds became really important. They could regularly bring an increase of wind to near gale-force for short periods. If we

The halfway point, mid-Atlantic, over a thousand miles from anywhere.

Spray covers the decks during the second leg of the Mini Transat.

were caught out with full sail up when one hit, we could be in danger of losing the mast.

Like all Minis, *English Braids* was a capable boat, but always required the skills of the skipper to keep her on an even keel. It was a game of cat and mouse, with some nights being more intense than others. I would regularly make the decision to change from the biggest spinnaker to our smaller sail in the interests of safety. Sometimes I would change sails three or four times in one night.

I was blasting across a vast expanse of ocean on a twenty-one foot pocket rocket, racing against a fleet of seemingly invisible competitors. I felt so lucky to be living this experience and remembered my days at Fyling Hall School when I could only dream of such an adventure. Right now, alone in the middle of the Atlantic, I felt all my dreams had come

Pushing hard, mid-Atlantic.

true. I was just twenty-three years old.

Thirteen days into the race, we were approaching 50 degrees west longitude and had just seven hundred and twenty-four nautical miles to go to the finish. We had been sailing for days under spinnaker, revelling in the trade winds, but I was starting to feel pretty tired. Two weeks of round-the-clock sailing, constantly pushing my little boat to her limits without a break was exhausting and by early evening I decided to get my head down for an hour in order to be fully prepared for the night watch.

Over the previous three nights I had seen constant squall activity which had produced exciting but demanding sailing. One minute we would be sailing along with eight knots registering on the speedometer, enjoying the warm conditions, and the next a squall would roll through, pushing up the boat's speed to fourteen knots or more.

Sometimes we were right on the edge of control and it would take my best efforts to keep us from being knocked flat.

I climbed into the cabin through the hatchway and lay on the small narrow bunk. I was exhausted and knew it. It was still daylight outside, plenty of time for an hour's sleep before the sun sets, I thought. Laying my head on the folded up storm jib that also doubled up as a pillow I drifted off to sleep while keeping one ear tuned into the sound of the boat moving through the water.

Solo sailors regularly tune themselves into a routine of short catnaps, waking up after only very short periods of sleep. I normally find this routine easy and don't need an alarm clock to wake me. But this night I should have recognised the signs that my body was giving me. I slept for much longer than an hour. When I eventually opened my eyes four hours later, it was because the intense noise and motion of the boat had woken me.

I was briefly disorientated. The boat was flying through the water, surfing off into the night. The noise echoed through the cabin. *English Braids* was on the limit, I could literally feel the strain the boat was under. I could hear the autopilot struggling to keep control as we heeled over alarmingly. Looking out through the hatchway, it was dark outside, the cockpit illuminated only by the intensity of the moon. I knew we were going fast and glancing across the cabin to the speedometer I was terrified to see it reading nearly sixteen knots! That's way too quick. Any second we would wipe-out. I had never experienced the boat sailing under autopilot at these speeds and certainly not under full sail.

Fumbling around in the darkness of the cabin, I struggled to find my lifejacket. I had to get on deck to take control quickly, but didn't want to venture outside without being fully prepared. Waking from a deep sleep to jump immediately into the cockpit would be a sure-fire way of falling over the side on such a small boat. Climbing off the bunk to prepare myself, I realised it was too late. The pilot had finally lost control. Moving my body weight from the high side bunk to the middle of the cabin to grab my kit had been enough to tip the balance in favour of a big knock-down. We were over in an instant.

Equipment and kit stacked on the high side was thrown across the cabin as we went over on our starboard side. Lying on my back on the cabin floor, I felt rather like a marble rattling around a jam jar. I could only watch as my world was turned on its side. The view out from the hatchway into the cockpit didn't seem too inviting either. With the boat on her side, the normally flat cockpit floor now looked like a vertical cliff edge. I was terrified that the strain on the mast would be too much and would bring it crashing down. I would learn later that three of the top five boats would finish the race with broken masts because of this very situation.

As things steadied I clambered on deck. We were still on our side, being dragged through the water by our huge spinnaker. The wind was too strong for us to keep going under full sail and once again I found myself reaching forward to release the rope that held the sail to the top of the mast. The recovery was easier than I expected, though – by now I was well-practiced in emergency spinnaker retrieval.

Bringing *English Braids* back on course, I sat down in the cockpit with one hand firmly on the tiller. Steering into the darkness, eyes fixed on the compass, it was time to take stock and make sense of what had just happened. I had been so tired that my body had shut down and allowed me to sleep for hours. The boat had been happily sailing along until the squall had overtaken us. I felt exhilarated. This was crazy seat-of-the-pants sailing but I loved it.

We spent the remainder of the night sailing under just the mainsail at a steady twelve to fourteen knots. We were flying along, with frequent squalls strengthening throughout the night. I knew we could probably handle that amount of wind with the small spinnaker but followed an instinct to allow seamanship to overcome the desire for absolute speed.

During the final days of the race I was faced with a tough decision. Listening to the rankings on the SSB radio, I knew we were doing well. Fourth place overall was certainly possible, maybe even a podium position if I was lucky. But to achieve that we would have to keep the throttle pushed down hard all the way to the finish. I would be putting the boat under a lot of strain by sailing day and night with the big spinnaker and would be in danger of losing the mast by pushing so hard for so long. If that happened, our lead over the boats behind us would not be sufficient to allow us to limp across the finish line under a jury-rigged mast. We could end up outside the top ten in the overall rankings.

It was high-risk strategy. A fourth place really would be no different

Approaching Guadeloupe, looking for the finish line.

GBR 85
English Braids
Performance yacht ropes
English Braids
English Braids

Fooling around with the camera the day before we finished.

to a fifth placing. But a classification in the teens for this leg, having been so highly ranked on the first leg, would be disastrous, while fifth overall would be the best British placing in the twenty-year history of the race. Having weighed up the situation and its implications, I decided for the first time in the race to relinquish my attacking approach and to adopt a defensive strategy. I would let the top four boats go, accepting they were too far ahead to risk trying to catch. With the final stages of the race under our keel, I would do my best to maintain the gap between us and the boats behind, whilst keeping *English Braids* in one piece.

It was a tough decision. My natural instinct was always to go for it, but the dice had been rolled. Fifth would be a remarkable result, and enough to get the journalists back home excited.

Friday 7 November was our last night at sea. We were closing in on Guadeloupe. Sighting the flashing lighthouse on the off-lying island of la Desirade with its distinctive two white flashes every twenty seconds was confirmation that we had crossed the intimidating Atlantic ocean. We had just a few miles to run before reaching the finish line of the 1999 Mini Transat, which was set just off the harbour entrance of Basse Terre, the capital of Guadeloupe, and our final port of call for this race. The following morning, whilst sailing around the island I noticed a motor launch speeding towards me. They were flying race flags and people were waving and shouting. It was the race organisers with their welcoming party. Dad was on board and it was his voice I heard first, excited at his first sighting of his son since leaving the Canaries. He was shouting, "Go on son, keep going!"

It was a fantastic moment. *English Braids* was revelling in the warm breeze flowing off the mountains of the island. Twenty minutes later we ghosted across the finish line to claim our fifth placing out of an original 80-strong fleet. We had done it, achieving the best British result in the history of the race. As the gun fired, I could hear cheering. I almost felt like crying. Whilst battling it out during that storm in the Bay of Biscay, I had imagined this moment, but it had seemed so far away. My trusty little *English Braids* had seen me through diabolical conditions and looked after me throughout. We had succeeded where so many had failed and come through the worst to complete this epic test of endurance. As we tied up to the dockside in Basse Terre I was greeted by Dad and a barrage of well-wishers. There was just enough time for a brief but welcome hug from Dad before the race security team climbed aboard to check over the boat and make sure everything conformed to the class rules and measurements. In the Mini Transat, heavy equipment such as the life raft is sealed by a small security tag to prevent its use as movable ballast whilst sailing. These mandatory checks are standard procedure and testament to how far some competitors will go to achieve that fractional improvement in performance.

Whilst the security checks were underway, I was guided to a stage

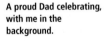

A proud Dad celebrating, with me in the background.

Crossing the finish line at
Basse Terre, Guadeloupe.

and introduced to Miss Guadeloupe, the local beauty queen. The bizarre but enjoyable ceremony involved me dancing with her whilst being paraded around in front of several hundred onlookers. High on life and enjoying the moment, I was up for it. The spokesman holding the microphone was a good public speaker and did his utmost to motivate the crowd, not that they needed any encouragement. Thrusting the microphone into my hands it was obvious he wanted me to say a few words. I made a brief speech, ending by thanking the people of Guadeloupe for their hospitality and fantastic welcome to their island.

Dad was by my side and with the spokesman rambling on in fluent French he was asked to comment too. Dad didn't have a clue what the guy was saying but as always extricated himself with his usual degree of skilful flamboyance. My first thirty minutes back on terra firma after sixteen days on the ocean had been quite surreal, though I would later realise this warm welcome was something each and every skipper received upon arrival.

Dad and me full of smiles in Guadeloupe after the Mini Transat.

10
STEVE RIGBY

The finish of the Mini Transat is a time when lots of superb craft flood onto the open market, all for sale. Having completed the race, skippers are generally keen to sell their boats ahead of the next occurrence of the event. This ritual is common within the fleet and many boats are sold by the time they arrive back into Europe. Some people even take the opportunity to grab an early bargain by purchasing a boat directly after the race. My father had been in discussion with one such skipper who was looking for a competitive boat to enter in the next race.

Steve Rigby had been monitoring my progress since the start and had contacted my father to express his interest whilst I was still at sea. The pair had arranged to meet in Basse Terre in advance of my arrival to discuss a potential deal. Steve was a lovely guy, a yachtsman with moderate experience who despite being newly-married was building the foundations for his own Mini Transat adventure.

Steve's passion for the Mini Transat equalled mine and it was clear that he was committed to competing in the next race. He wanted to give himself the best chance of success by starting his campaign early and saw the immediate acquisition of my boat as his ticket into the big time. Steve was a happy-go-lucky type of guy, the kind of man you couldn't fail to warm to. We gelled from our first introduction.

We soon agreed a deal. Steve wanted the boat with all the kit, lock, stock and barrel. Two days after my arrival, with the financial side of things completed, I took off just my sleeping bag and Mum's lucky teddy bear mascot. *English Braids* had served me well but she now had a new owner.

I spent my remaining few days in Guadeloupe with Steve, giving him an insight into the world of Mini Transat boats. I explained that the boat was not like any other yacht he would have experienced before and presented a tough challenge to master. Steve acknowledged this, and seemed grounded in his approach to the learning curve ahead of him. I suggested he take several weeks to learn the basics of sailing the boat before he set out on the 200-mile passage back to Tortola in the British Virgin Islands, which were his Caribbean base.

On the morning of my departure for the United Kingdom we said our goodbyes on the dockside next to the boat. Steve shook my hand and asked if I thought he would be alright. I thought little of it at the time, and replied, "Of course, as long as you take it easy and build up slowly, you'll be fine."

We could have had no idea of the tragedy that was to follow. Days later, back in the UK, it was close to midnight and I was sitting at my desk, engrossed in my computer screen with the television on in the background. I heard the weather presenter mention something about a tropical hurricane that was slamming through the Caribbean. Looking at the map on the television it was clear that Guadeloupe was in the path of the storm. My thoughts immediately turned to Steve and the boat. I assumed he had her securely fastened to the dockside in the marina at Basse Terre.

I was plucked from my thoughts of storms raging in faraway lands by the phone ringing. It was Julia, Steve's wife. Her voice was desperate, close to despair. Initially I struggled to understand what she was saying but it soon became clear that Steve and the boat were not in Guadeloupe, he was fighting for his life on the yacht at sea.

It transpired that rather than stay any longer, Steve had decided to set sail from Guadeloupe straight away to head to Tortola. In his haste to leave Basse Terre it seems he had neglected to obtain a suitable long-range weather forecast. At the time of his departure, warnings were already being sent out by the National Hurricane Centre. Steve was unwittingly sailing into the jaws of Tropical Hurricane Lenny. The storm was devastating, delivering lethal winds of up to one hundred and fifty knots. Lenny was the twelfth tropical hurricane of the 1999 season and would eventually be classified as a category five, the worst there is.

Poor Steve didn't stand a chance in those conditions. The details of exactly what happened are fragmentary. What we do know is that he got to within spitting distance of Tortola. His wife Julia had contacted the coastguard after he became overdue, and they consequently managed to make contact with Steve via VHF radio. The coastguards advised him to abandon the boat in favour of being rescued by the emergency services, warning that a rescue later on could not be guaranteed. The weather was gale force at the time but not extreme, and Steve wanted to carry on. He felt he could reach Tortola before the worst of the weather arrived. It was a decision that would seal his fate. By the time he sent out his Mayday distress call the hurricane was in full swing. The rescue services could no longer launch airborne support in the prevailing conditions. In a desperate attempt to rescue Steve, the coastguard dispatched a Dutch naval frigate that had volunteered to have a go but they were soon forced back to port after being nearly rolled over in the cataclysmic conditions.

Steve's desperate shouts for help were answered by another yachtsman in the area. American Carl Wake was undertaking his first solo passage of notable distance and was also caught in the hurricane. He answered Steve's desperate Mayday and it turned out the pair were only a few miles apart.

After discussing the situation over the VHF radio, a decision was made to attempt to evacuate Steve's boat in favour of the relative safety of the larger 40-foot yacht. That Carl Wake managed to even locate Steve in those conditions defies belief. We know they made the transfer successfully, an act of seamanship that deserves the highest praise. We also know the weather was hurricane force at the time. The pair made several VHF transmissions to the coastguards after that rescue but would later face the end together, when the heroic rescuer's yacht eventually succumbed to the might of the storm.

It was a tragedy and a harsh reminder of just how unforgiving the ocean can be. To my knowledge, nothing was ever found of either of the boats, but we did hear unconfirmed reports of the remains of a small yacht being washed up on a beach somewhere in the Caribbean months later. There were rumours that it might have been Steve's boat, but nothing concrete emerged. Carl Wake's body was recovered from the sea after Hurricane Lenny passed. Steve was never seen again.

Despite having only met Steve Rigby shortly before the hurricane, I can say that during those days we spent together in Guadeloupe he had become more than just the guy that bought my boat. He was my friend. I have fond memories of those warm nights sitting in the harbour-side bar that overlooked the marina where the Mini Transat fleet was moored. Steve and I would discuss his plans well into the night. He was ambitious and keen to make his mark in the racing world. I admired that, and agreed to help him with his preparations leading up to the next Mini Transat race.

We all make mistakes. The tragedy for Steve was that he had entered a world where mistakes can prove fatal. Just one seemingly insignificant decision, to leave Guadeloupe in haste with a new and unfamiliar boat, would end up costing him his life. Steve made the ultimate sacrifice in pursuit of his dreams. It was a desperately sad outcome for him, his family and the friends he left behind. Writing this chapter has brought tears to my eyes, but it highlights just how dangerous life on the ocean can be.

If there is an afterlife and you are reading this, mate, you may have left this world but you will never be forgotten.

Fair winds, Steve Rigby.

11

TEAM PHILIPS

I finally arrived at Goss Challenges to assume my new role as a full-time crew member on *Team Philips*. I was bursting to see how the build had progressed. The sheer scale of the giant catamaran is still firmly imprinted on my mind and it takes my breath away whenever I think about it. At the time, *Team Philips* was the largest carbon fibre composite structure in the world and certainly the biggest racing catamaran on the planet.

The build team had been working overtime and had virtually completed the assembly of the structure since my visit to the factory before the start of the Mini Transat. The project was quickly capturing the attention and heart of the nation thanks both to Pete's fame after his heroic Southern Ocean rescue of Raphael Dinelli and to the revolutionary design of the gigantic boat. The media and public interest were seemingly gaining momentum by the day.

Team Philips was nothing like the other multihulls that would ultimately compete in The Race. They were all around one hundred feet long. Known as G Class or Giant Class, these boats are certainly the fastest sailing yachts afloat. However, for *Team Philips*, that was where the similarities ended. She was the biggest and widest of her kind. At one hundred and twenty feet long and seventy feet wide, she dwarfed the 105-foot catamarans from France. The other boats represented a conventional step forward in terms of design evolution. They were in effect scaled-up versions of smaller tried-and-tested designs.

Team Philips, on the other hand, was a unique extreme machine.

Her twin 41-metre, high rotating wing masts and long razor-sharp bows designed to pierce through waves were revolutionary. Even the number of crew required to operate this goliath in full race mode was reduced from the accepted number of around a dozen for a conventional design to just six. However, when we set off on our fateful last voyage it was agreed that a crew of seven would be more suitable. Fewer people on board meant less weight to carry in terms of food and supplies for a two-month lap of the planet. That meant a lighter and faster boat. Adrian Thompson, *Team Philips'* designer had been given the brief from Pete to design a vessel a generation ahead of her time. To my mind, she resembled a spacecraft more than a sailboat. Nonetheless, she was a truly magnificent-looking yacht, designed for just one purpose: to circumnavigate the planet faster than anything afloat.

Her only rival in terms of sheer size was the American-flagged Playstation, owned by the late billionaire adventurer Steve Fossett. But even Playstation took a back seat when comparing the numbers. Playstation was the first of the new generation of G Class yachts to be launched and as a result would have a significant advantage over the remaining competition. She would eventually conquer many of the existing long-distance world records for speed under sail, although she did suffer a series of setbacks that would prove serious. Whilst sailing in early sea trials, she almost capsized because of a lack of adequate volume in her bow sections. Steve Fossett and Playstation's designers decided to increase the size of her bows significantly, in an effort to make the boat more seaworthy, an expensive process involving radical surgery to the front of each hull section. Such is the nature of these giant catamarans.

Looking out across the build shed from the office balcony, I could see our marvellous craft taking shape. For me, this was the pinnacle of ocean racing and at just twenty-three years old I felt I had won the lottery to be one of Pete's chosen few.

Before joining Pete Goss and the Goss Challenge team I had thought myself reasonably commercially aware, but it was Goss Challenges that really helped me to understand how to deal with the media and to organise myself. I already knew the importance of giving value to sponsors, and giving a tangible return for their investment was always in the forefront of my mind. Without commercial support, very few professional sailing projects would exist and it was Goss Challenges that helped me understand that the sport of sailing is indeed a business.

Pete and the management team were masters at the publicity game and very proactive. We had a dedicated public relations department lead by Vicky Bartholomew. Vicky was the one who initially set up interviews, liaised with the media and briefed us before any public appearance. Every interview was different, and each crew member was given responsibilities that involved talking regularly to the media. Making the most of any interview or public appearance was always essential. We were ambassadors for our sponsors as well as for our company. Vicky always made sure we were well-briefed and prepared. The operation was organised and professional. There was even a set routine for answering the telephone.

I had to learn numerous key company straplines that helped paint a clear picture to the public of the enormity of the project. 'Technology and innovation', 'pushing the boundaries of technology' and 'dare to dream' were among some of our most commonly-used catchphrases.

The facts relating to *Team Philips* were always backed up with easy-to-understand comparisons such as 'larger than the Centre Court at Wimbledon', and 'each mast is the height of ten double-decker buses stood on top of each other'. This all helped to highlight the groundbreaking path the project was taking. It was an inspiration. Despite being the youngest member of the crew, I shared equal responsibility and quickly realised that I enjoyed my media commitments almost as much as I relished the impending sailing opportunities.

We had a broad spectrum of sponsors, ranging from companies like the Danish shoe manufacturer Ecco who designed footwear specific to our requirements, to large financial sponsors like BT, Sun Microsystems and Musto clothing. Our multi-million pound title sponsor was Philips Electronics.

Initially there were just six of us who would be fortunate enough to pilot *Team Philips* around the globe. I say 'pilot' because I always felt we were more like test pilots than sailors. Pete's second-in-command on board was Andy Hindley, whom I had met during the Round Britain race, a great guy and a talented sailor. He had already completed two circumnavigations, one of which was on the British Steel Challenge yacht Hofbrau, which Pete skippered. Andy also held a degree in electronics and would play a pivotal role in selecting and installing all of the onboard electronic systems during the build.

Graham Goff, a sailmaker by trade and an experienced multihull sailor, was in charge of constructing and maintaining the huge sails that would propel *Team Philips* across the oceans at speeds of up to forty knots, nearly fifty miles per hour. Graham has a great personality and was always one to keep us laughing with his jokes and humour. On one occasion he changed the number plates on my car with a makeshift set that described in derogatory terms the state of my haircut. I drove my car to Plymouth and back before I realised. I must have looked ridiculous, but we all found it highly amusing.

Mike Calvin was the only non-professional yachtsman on board. At the time Mike was the chief sports writer with the Mail on Sunday newspaper and would be responsible for all media communications from the boat when we were at sea. Our communications sponsor British Telecom would install state-of-the-art satellite communications equipment on board. This technology would not only allow us to talk to the outside world when at sea but also give us the ability to send email and access the Internet throughout the voyage. Mike had sailed with Pete and Andy during the 1992/3 British Steel Challenge.

Paul Larsen, 'Larso' as he is known to his friends, was the fifth team member. A professional yachtsman from Australia, he had been part of French sailing legend Bruno Peyron's team which set a new Trans-Pacific record onboard the multihull Explorer. Paul is a talented and experienced multihull sailor and was tasked with the specific role of structural maintenance when at sea. He would become a good close friend.

I was responsible for supplies and provisions. It was my job to order all the food necessary for a round-the-world voyage and arrange it for easy deployment on a daily basis. At sea, food comes in the form of freeze-dried meals which have had the water content removed in order to keep everything as lightweight as possible. It needs to be high in carbohydrates, palatable and quick to prepare. Food is fuel and each of us would need to consume up to 5000 calories or more a day when racing, more than twice the daily average recommended intake for a male adult.

In addition to our specific roles, each of us would have to balance our duties with the perpetual task of keeping *Team Philips* at optimal performance hour-by-hour during the race. Pete's military background and training in the Royal Marines had given him the perfect foundation to lead, organise and delegate. Everyone at Goss Challenges from the management team right down to the person who swept the factory floor knew their responsibilities and commitments. I think it fair to say that everyone looked forward to coming into work each morning. As a team, we were a professional outfit and I for one felt not just proud but also honoured to be at the heart of it.

The project had a dedicated visitor centre called The Goss Centre of Challenge & Adventure which was manned by a small but dedicated army of volunteers. Pete's ethos of openness and accessibility captured the public's interest to the extent that hundreds of thousands of people would pour through the doors of our visitor centre throughout the life of the project. Larso and I would regularly host tours at the centre for visitors, taking them through the various aspects of the project. We would walk the groups through the life-sized mock-up of the accommodation pod aboard *Team Philips*, before finishing the tour on the viewing platform overlooking the hangar where the state-of-the-art catamaran was being assembled. There was also an online education programme. The Goss team's challenge to win The Race was big business and provided enough excitement to keep us all captivated.

My first month at Goss Challenges was a whirlwind and seemed to pass in the blink of an eye. Initially, the race crew took up residence in an old converted mill just a few miles from the factory. Crowdy Mill was local but just far enough away from the build site to offer a suitably quiet location for us to relax and gel as a team. If Goss Challenges was headquarters, then Crowdy Mill was our place of sanctuary and soon became accepted as the crew house. Being part of such an organised and committed team was a breathtaking experience and offered everything I had ever wanted. Every morning I would wake up with excitement and anticipation for what the day would bring. Pete was always around, but being the head of such a large project his responsibilities and commitments were twice as demanding as ours. However, despite the hectic schedule he would regularly find time to sit down and discuss progress.

One of Pete's main concerns was that we should all be fit enough to endure the relentless motion on board during a round-the-world passage. Squeezing the absolute best performance out of our magnificent boat day by day would be essential. Fitness was taken seriously and each crew member was issued with a Concept 2 rowing machine to help with our training. Goss Challenges also had contacts in Formula

One, and Pete, keen to improve our physical fitness as a team, arranged for the six of us to visit the Benetton Formula One Human Performance Centre at Oxford to set up our training programmes. This was a serious place for serious people, dedicated to producing the best in human performance and fitness. Very few have had the privilege to even walk through the doors, yet we had an appointment with the man in charge, Bernie Shrosbree.

Bernie is an ex-member of the elite Special Boat Service or SBS as well as the Royal Marines. In 1987, he was runner-up in the World Survival of the Fittest competition and won a bronze medal in the European Triathlon championships. As part of Benetton, Bernie was involved with training Formula One racing drivers such as Jenson Button. He is, without doubt, a serious guy and deserving of respect, but he is also super-fit and was willing to help each of us improve our personal fitness. This was an opportunity not to be missed.

Our day at the centre was a real eye-opener and highlighted the need for each of us to be at peak fitness when race day arrived. Bernie and his assistant subjected us to what can only be described as scientific hell. The evaluation seemed endless. Starting with a simple warm-up session, the programme soon developed into a full-on and exhausting test of physical endurance, pushing each of us to our limits and beyond. We were scrutinised on various machines that measured everything from our strength to our all-out cardiovascular capabilities and total lung capacity. The programme concluded with a test of our ability to focus, concentrate and react while in a state of physical exhaustion. One test I particularly enjoyed was the Batak machine. It is a wall with flashing lights that an athlete must strike when they illuminate. It starts at a comfortable pace but the machine quickly speeds up to test hand-eye coordination. I achieved what seemed like a quite high number of hits on the board. Then I was told that the average Formula One racing driver can achieve nearly twice that number of hits in the same time.

To add insult to injury, we had been followed around the facility by a journalist from the Times, intent on recording all the facts and figures relating to our endurance capability or lack of it. Even while in the gym, our project was in the public eye. A rather interesting yet demeaning picture of me at the exact moment of total exhaustion on the VO2 Max machine was published a few days later in the national newspaper.

Still, it helped to illustrate the lengths that we were going to in order to achieve the best chance of success in The Race.

Larso was the fittest of all of us and displayed an impressive level of endurance ability. He was truly fit while the rest of us received a rather disappointed glare from Bernie over our ability. I remember taking comfort in the fact that I seemed to be the strongest of the group, narrowly scraping ahead of Andy, who soon advised that I should also be the fittest due to my age.

Tired and burnt-out, we made the journey back to the West Country that evening with a long and detailed list of daily exercises specifically designed for each of us. Part of the training schedule would involve a significant length of time on the Concept rowers. I was supposed to do at least ten thousand metres a day but must confess to being regularly worn-out after about seven thousand. Larso on the other hand could go on for hours at a time and on several occasions left me wondering if the machines came with any long-term warranty on the various component parts as I was sure he would wear them out. I think one night he did about twenty thousand metres in one session and only stopped because we had to be up early the following morning and needed some sleep.

Having considered physical fitness, it was a natural progression to give proper thought to sleep deprivation, which is a common yet often overlooked condition. Lack of sleep when at sea can quickly develop into a real problem and is a situation which most offshore sailors will be confronted with at some time or another. On a 120-foot super catamaran travelling at speeds approaching forty knots, sleep deprivation becomes a real issue. A simple mistake by a crew member could make the difference between success and disaster. Again, we would take advice from an expert in the field on how best to monitor and control our sleeping patterns. Dr Claudio Stampi is one of the world leaders in the area of sleep, alertness and fatigue research and was brought in to advise how best to prepare for and combat the effects of long periods with little sleep. During our first meeting, we were introduced to the benefits of power napping throughout the day and how even short naps or periods of downtime with your eyes closed and body relaxed can help prolong alertness.

Claudio wasted no time in asking us to perform a few simple tasks to evaluate our ability to sleep during the day. Short but frequent sleeping sessions are a practical solution to combating the effects of sleep deprivation and Claudio was keen to monitor our ability to individually regulate our sleep at any given time. During one session, Pete's secretary knocked on the boardroom door, only to find six grown men asleep on the floor, tucked up in their sleeping bags like a group of nursery kids taking a nap. With Claudio sitting in the corner of the room in the dark making notes, it must have been an unusual sight. With my experience in solo sailing, I found the exercise useful albeit quite familiar, which is more than can be said for Pete's secretary Rachel, who must have thought it quite bizarre.

By December 1999, *Team Philips* was almost complete and stood magnificent in the hangar at Goss Challenges headquarters. With a few minor finishing touches outstanding, the hull structure was by and large complete, with just the cosmetics needed to finish the job. The masts and booms were a different story, however, and were proving rather more intricate and time-consuming to finish. Nonetheless, just before Christmas we had achieved our target of a completed structure. To celebrate, we held a special party at the factory for our sponsors, volunteers and staff who had all contributed so much to making the campaign a reality. It was time to give something back to them and it was a celebration to remember. We had reached a significant milestone in the project and wanted to mark the birth of a giant.

There must have been two hundred people there that night, familiar faces and some I had never met before. As crew members it was our task to pour the drinks and mingle. While the champagne flowed, I watched as people looked up, awestruck at the goliath we had created. Something about *Team Philips* sitting there, silent in the hangar made me think she was almost alive and part of the party. I felt dammed lucky to be involved in something so special.

The Christmas booze-up lasted well into the night. It was an opportunity for the whole team to let their hair down and enjoy a short but welcome break from the daily grind. The build team had been working around the clock for months, committed to achieving our goal of a completed structure by Christmas. By now they were all understandably quite exhausted yet still very much aware that our beautiful boat needed to be ready for launch in less than three months. We were on track for that, but only just and were hanging onto the schedule by the thinnest of margins. Every hour would count if we were to launch by the end of February.

By mid-January, the visitor centre at the factory had become a hive of activity and had already seen over half a million people walk through its doors. We held an open day to mark the launch of our new campaign website. The website would act as the public's window on the project. It was an instant success and regularly achieved millions of hits a week. With our popularity growing, people from across the country and beyond kept coming to the centre, hungry to learn more about the revolutionary catamaran that was making front-page news around the world. Our team of volunteer staff had their work cut out dealing with the huge increase in visitor numbers, but it was thanks to these dedicated people that the centre became such a success. Soon we added new attractions and exhibits, and one morning while walking through the centre I noticed a full-size ocean rowing boat on display. It was a new arrival and a sign that the visitor centre was now evolving into a portal for all things to do with adventure on the ocean.

The communications team at Goss Challenges was constantly developing opportunities for us to tell our story and my time was spent on a number of tasks. There was much new and essential equipment to be ordered and the necessary provisions had to be carefully calcu-lated and sourced. I was also given the responsibility of hosting talks at various events on behalf of the company and found my work load of tours in the visitor centre also on the increase. It was a hectic time but I wasn't about to complain. There was always a positive atmosphere surrounding the project and despite being a fully-paid crew member, I would have done the job for free if it meant keeping my place on board. It was that type of infectious enthusiasm that made everyone want to be part of the project.

We had taken to leading tours through the build shed, walking people underneath *Team Philips* and around the structure to give a better idea of the sheer scale of the boat. My tours would generally last about forty minutes, with my party piece and closing statement coin-ciding with our arrival at the port bow. I would grab hold of the slender tip and wiggle the hull. Seeing the bow moving people would always comment on how flexible it was and ask whether it would break off at sea. Time after time I would hear the same question and must confess to initially having the same thoughts as the public. But we had been told by the designers that the bows could flex by up to a metre when at sea and that this would be routine in certain conditions. I would later find it ironic that it was the port bow that snapped off during our sea trials; we joked that it was my fault because of all that wiggling.

The accommodation pod under construction.

With our intended launch date looming ever closer, the build team could finally see an end to the construction phase. Once *Team Philips* was launched they would effectively hand over their creation to us as a crew. It was then our job to take command and push the 'go' button, starting the work-up period and sea trials. In an ideal world, we would have scheduled a long and slow work-up period for such a new craft. However, as is the nature of sponsored sailboat projects, we had serious commitments to fulfil.

One of those commitments was an amazing privilege. Through some incredible networking, the management team at Goss Challenges was able to arrange for Her Majesty the Queen to formally name *Team Philips*. The ceremony would take place in the heart of London at St Catherine's Dock, just below Tower Bridge on the River Thames. Royal approval was the ultimate recognition for the project and this would be a huge occasion. Making sure we were ready would prove more than just a challenge, though.

For me and the lads, the volunteers, general staff and sponsors, the news was met with a flood of positive emotions, but for the build team it only added to the already huge amount of pressure they were under. An appointment with the Queen is not a date that can be rescheduled. We just had to be there and 14 March 2000 was now set in stone. The race to get to London was on.

With final preparations underway, the build centre continued to operate like a well-oiled machine. Scores of different tradesman were on site, working on the various components that make up the finished product. It was not unusual to look out from the office balcony and see upwards of sixty people swarming around the boat like bees round a honey pot. Electricians, boat builders, hydraulic engineers, canvas specialists, painters and sign-writers all shared floor space in the hangar. This was an enormous operation and Garry Venning our build manager and Keith Fennell, head of production, oversaw it all on a daily basis. These guys were very skilled and it was clear that Pete had absolute faith in their abilities; they had previously built Aqua Quorum, the yacht that Pete had sailed around the world in the Vendée Globe.

Since Christmas, the fairing team had been working day and night, preparing the final aesthetic finish to the whole structure, filling and sanding any slight imperfections in order to create a perfectly smooth, crisp finish. This type of specialist work is a time-consuming and highly labour-intensive process. Just fairing and painting the accommodation pod was a big job, as it was effectively a 50-foot yacht on its own. The fairing team went about their work with impressive dedication. They worked twenty-four hours a day with two rotating teams for weeks on end in order to keep to the now very tight schedule.

One major logistical hurdle to overcome was moving *Team Philips* out of the build shed. There was no way she could ever come out through the tiny roller shutter doors at the front of the building. From the very start of the project, Pete knew we would have to dismantle the front of the building and this alone would take a skilled team of builders several days to achieve. Even once fully out of the shed, we had to negotiate a 90-degree right turn in order to get clear of the hangar and the surrounding buildings. There would be little more than a few feet of clearance at times, and it would require some precision handling by a seriously-focused crane driver to complete the manoeuvre. Our campaign logistics manager Nick Booth took the lead in this exercise. An experienced yachtsman in his own right, Nick was used to dealing with all sorts of logistical challenges. It was his job to oversee the operation and coordinate everyone.

Despite its importance, the operation was reasonably simple in concept. The builders would systematically dismantle the front of the building and when ready, we would jack up *Team Philips* onto wheels and then slowly drag her out of the hangar using a block-and-tackle system. It would be a slow and painstaking process but eventually, inch by inch, our big blue giant would be freed. The manoeuvre went like clockwork and by late evening on Monday 28 February 2000, *Team Philips* emerged from the confines of her birthplace, looking truly glorious.

The launch was scheduled for the following day and our preparations continued late into the night. After such huge media interest in the construction, we knew the launch was going to be big news. The

Team Philips ready to come out of the build shed at Baltic Wharf.

project's accessible ethos had been a winner from the start and now people arrived in significant numbers to watch us prepare for the long-awaited moment.

As the sun came up on the morning of 29 February, the weather was less than ideal. Our team meteorologist Lee Bruce had been watching the forecast closely all week and had warned us that conditions might prove to be unfavourable. The day had arrived and there was just a slim chance that a forecast short break in the weather might allow enough time to get *Team Philips* into the water. The 200-tonne crane that would lift *Team Philips* had an upper wind speed restriction of twenty knots. Anything more and it would be a no-go for the launch.

As it happened, it was not the wind that scuppered our chances that day. Persistent heavy rain during the previous week meant the River Dart was experiencing an unusually high influx of fresh water from high up on Dartmoor. This extra water increased the tidal flow by a considerable margin. After several hours spent carefully monitoring the speed of the river, we all knew it would be too dangerous to attempt a launch and it came as no surprise when Pete announced that we would have to postpone.

It was the right call and not really a difficult decision to make. Given the swollen state of the river, it would have been foolhardy to go ahead. But another major concern was the twenty thousand or so people lining the river banks waiting to witness the launch of this marvel of modern technology. The day was in danger of becoming a PR disaster. Pete took hold of a microphone and addressed the crowd. He explained the situation and invited everyone over to the build site to have a closer look at the boat. It was an admirable quick-thinking decision, and one that proved popular.

Four days later, on 4 March with near-perfect weather conditions, *Team Philips* was finally lowered into the River Dart in front of a huge crowd. It was estimated that forty thousand people turned up for the second launch attempt. The place was packed wall-to-wall. Other than in a football stadium, I've never seen so many people in one place. I remember standing next to the boat on the quayside at Baltic Wharf, looking up the river. There were rows and rows of people as far as the eye could see. Looking up to the hills above the build shed the fields were also packed with people. There was an electric atmosphere. My parents, friends and family were all there. It felt like half the world had turned up.

In an effort to make the day more interactive for the public our sponsors set up a giant TV screen on the opposite side of the river to show interviews with the crew and key personnel in the lead-up to the moment of launch. Surrounded by an armada of journalists and their respective satellite trucks, we were at the centre of an epic moment in history. I hardly had time to catch my breath between the countless interviews and preparations for the big moment. As the crane lifted the giant 30-ton super yacht out across the river and started to lower her into the water, the crowd's silence gave way to waves of cheers. It was one of those intense moments that seemed to last a lifetime as we all waited with bated breath, although in reality the whole exercise from lifting to launching only took about five minutes.

Once *Team Philips* was afloat, the six of us stepped on board for the first time. We gave a wave to the crowd while unveiling a banner that said, "Thanks for your support. Cheers, Pete and team". It was our way of giving something back to the thousands of spectators who had quite obviously taken the project into their hearts. They were just as much a part of the project as we were. Indeed, thousands of names had been applied to the hulls as part of our fundraising programme for the campaign. The plan was to carry those names around the world – without doubt *Team Philips* was the people's boat.

In true military fashion Pete wasted no time in slicing the top off

Left **Me and the lads standing by the bow of *Team Philips*, left to right: Graham Goff, Pete Goss, Andy Hindley, Mike Calvin, Paul Larsen, me.**

Above **The giant catamaran ready for launch with over twenty thousand people lining the river bank.**

Right **A bird's eye view, *Team Philips* just moments before launch.**

a bottle of champagne with a sabre and poured the contents over the bow. It was only then that I realised what people mean when they say a moment can last a lifetime. The Sunday Independent described the moment as a 'Splash Hit', while others coined phrases such as 'launched on a sea of love and tears' and labelled the moment 'historic'. Whichever way you looked at it, the boat was already famous and it hadn't yet sailed a mile.

A long awaited moment, _Team Philips_ is finally lowered into the water.

For the trip down the river we had devised a clear and well-rehearsed plan to get _Team Philips_ safely to Dartmouth. She would be pushed along by three rigid inflatable boats (RIBs). One would be connected to the rear of each hull in an effort to create some extra manoeuvrability, while a third RIB situated between the forward hulls was used as the primary tug boat and completed the tow.

In places, she would span almost the whole width of the river. As she was a new generation of vessel, nobody knew exactly how she would handle. In an effort to keep the day running smoothly, Pete had wisely drafted in support from the Royal Marines. It was my job to join four of them in a Zodiac inflatable and speed ahead to the first bend in the river, ready to deploy an anchor ashore in case we needed to winch

Team Philips around the tight bends.

As it turned out, *Team Philips* handled like she was on rails. Pete had no problem manoeuvring her with effortless grace, even though we had installed a set of small makeshift rudders for the passage to Dartmouth. The sea-going rudders were too deep for the river and would need to be fitted once moored in the deeper waters of Dartmouth harbour.

That night, having secured *Team Philips* safely in Dartmouth, we returned to Totnes. A private informal reception had been arranged for our sponsors and friends of the project at the Steam Packet Inn, which was just a few hundred yards from the build shed. It was time to celebrate with a few well-earned beers. We were all on a natural high.

The accommodation pod on *Team Philips*.

Despite it supposedly being a private party, one or two members of the press were also invited to share the celebrations.

I learned an important lesson that night. Larso and I were sitting together at one of the tables, tucking into some grub, when a newspaper reporter who we both knew sat down and started to chat to us. Larso, like most of the others, had sunk a few beers by now and was enjoying the atmosphere as much as I was. We did however both realise that the reporter was probing for rather more information than she should have been. This was party time and everyone was off-duty. After a few minutes I noticed she was holding a small recorder in her hand below the table. I couldn't believe it, she was recording the conversation, hoping for one of us to say more than we should. Leaning across the table, I explained that the time for questions had passed and politely asked her to put the recorder away.

We had been warned about this by the press office at Goss Challenges but I now realised what lengths some journalists would go to in order to get their story. The moment passed without any embarrassment on either side, leaving Larso and me to enjoy the evening. But the incident stuck in my mind and highlighted the importance of keeping your wits about you in public. After all, we were not only ambassadors for the project but were also ambassadors for our sponsors.

Later that evening, approaching the small hours, I found myself being bundled into one of the work Land Rovers. Everyone had been invited to a party in Totnes and the consensus was that Alex would drive them. I was the only non-drinker and sober person in the group, so I was the only one who could drive. This mission was being led by a representative of one of our biggest sponsors, backed-up by a couple of others who were just as keen to keep the festivities going. Saying it wasn't a good idea wasn't really an option and not wanting to disappoint our sponsors, I reluctantly fired up the Landy as everyone piled in.

By the time we were ready to leave the pub car park it would have been an understatement to say we had a full load. Inside the car, we were definitely at double capacity, with a further ten or so people clinging to the roof outside. I couldn't help feeling this was an accident just waiting to happen. Mike Calvin was sitting in the front seat and there was a blonde I had never met before sitting between us, attempting to give directions to this party. She was smashed and was absolutely no use at all. I took a moment to consider the implications of driving down

Totnes High Street with ten drunken people hanging off the Landy. Now that really would have been a story for the newspapers. Pete would definitely kick my backside if that happened.

Larso and Andy were on the roof with one of the sponsors, keen to keep the party going. Then Mike seemed to sober up and leant over saying calmly that it would be alright. It was as if he understood the worries I was wrestling with. Stuff it, I thought, I would drive slowly. It turned out the party was only a few hundred yards up the road and after shedding some unnecessary load we arrived at the house, which could be easily identified by the thud of the bass emitting from the building. Everyone piled in to see out the night.

Back to business the next day and the pressure was still on. We had just ten days to make *Team Philips* shipshape and ready for sea. To the outside world the boat looked finished and ready but there was a lot of detail to attend to. In those ten days we had to install both masts and assemble the wishbone booms, bend on the giant sails and bring online all the electrical systems. Then we had to sail the boat along the south coast and up the Thames to London. Each of the mainsails alone required the strength of several men to just lift it off the ground. It was a tough schedule, but we were all spurred on by the excitement of the upcoming royal engagement.

From the moment *Team Philips* hit the water the six of us had taken the decision to live aboard full-time, at least until we got London out of the way. This allowed us to make the most of our time and get every-thing set up for the trip. The fitting of the masts was another major logistical challenge. They were brought by road the short distance from Totnes to Dartmouth. With the cooperation of the local authorities and police, Dartmouth's main promenade was closed to traffic to allow us to set up a huge crane on the harbour-side and lift the two 41-metre wing masts into place. As they weighed 1.5 tonnes each, this was not a simple task, but nothing about *Team Philips* ever was. The exercise again drew a huge crowd. Having brought the town of Dartmouth to a standstill, the rigs and booms were lifted into place under the eyes of hundreds of onlookers. It was a full day's operation, made all the more difficult by the tidal rise and fall. We needed to leave the town quay well before low water, which only added to the pressure the team was under. Despite the constraints, the plan went without a hitch.

The passage to London would be our maiden voyage and coming

along for the ride were several reporters and photographers as well as our logistics team. In the final days before leaving Dartmouth it became apparent that there would be very little wind if any in the English Channel. The calm weather posed a real problem, potentially thwarting our efforts to arrive in London on time for the ceremony. We decided to have the RIBs shadow us all the way from Dartmouth, along the south coast and up the Thames to Tower Bridge. When the wind died away to nothing, the RIBs would tow us and help us to keep to the now painfully tight schedule. On paper this sounded perfectly plausible, but it would take careful planning to make it a success. The RIBs were powered by turbocharged diesel engines and despite having a good range, would require several fuel stops in order to make the whole passage by sea. Further, if there was any wind above fifteen knots, *Team Philips* would be off like a rocket. Maintaining twenty knots or more on the RIBs would require a lot of diesel. Making the right choices about where and when to stop to refuel them would play a critical role in the whole operation. Nick Booth took charge of the details and rounded up several of the build team to man the RIBs. We would be

The view of *Team Philips'* deck from the end of the starboard boom.

working around the clock and it was essential we had a strong team to endure the passage ahead.

We left Dartmouth with just enough time to arrive in London on schedule but it would definitely be tight. Leaving the harbour was no easy task. The river was bursting with activity – word had spread about our impending departure and hundreds of spectator boats were out in force to witness the occasion. On the quayside it was a similar story. It was packed with people all keen to catch a glimpse of us as we left on our maiden voyage. Crowds lined the length of the Dartmouth harbour-side and in true *Team Philips* style the moment was a very public affair. The light winds presented a rare opportunity for us to hoist our sails within the confines of the harbour, something we would never have attempted if it was not for the fact the weather was so calm. Seeing us leave Dartmouth under full sail was a real treat for the crowds and in full view of the whole of the town we slipped out of the harbour under a setting sun, bound for London.

Even in the lightest zephyr of wind we found *Team Philips* to be extraordinarily efficient. That night, with just six knots of breeze and a glassy sea we slid through the darkness at more than ten knots. She was an incredible machine. The following day as we headed towards Brighton under tow, it was my turn to take a shift in one of the RIBs. We needed to refuel and Brighton Marina was the nearest port. I knew the area well because my parents used to live in the marina development. I also knew that there was a McDonalds restaurant right on the quayside and it would be a pleasant surprise to come back to the boat with burgers for the crew. Refuelled and restocked with cheeseburgers, we blasted out of Brighton Marina at high speed in search of our big blue giant.

Buying the cheeseburgers was one thing, but getting them back on board without dropping them into the sea was another matter entirely. The generally accepted method for boarding *Team Philips* whilst at sea was to approach the rear of the hulls on the RIB whilst endeavouring to match the speeds. At the opportune moment you then had to jump onto the rear hull section from the bow of the RIB. Not an easy manoeuvre at the best of times, but try doing it at twenty knots whilst togged-up in safety kit carrying a bag of cheeseburgers.

That night we picked up some wind and were approaching the Dover straits. The RIBs were following behind in convoy and again required refuelling so that they would be ready for the long haul up the Thames to Tower Bridge. Always one to enjoy a RIB ride, especially in the dark, I volunteered to take one of the boats while Nick took charge of the other. Getting onto the RIBs was tricky in the dark but we made it without too much fuss and set off into the night bound for Dover. I was having the time of my life with all the commando-style operations. It was an awesome adventure and I was determined to make the most of it.

Leaving Dover with full fuel tanks, Nick had made it quite clear that he wanted to lead us back to rendezvous with *Team Philips* and I was to follow behind. The only trouble was I was keen to put the hammers down and get there quickly and he wasn't. Also, on leaving the confines of Dover harbour, we found that the wind had picked up. In the pitch black we struggled to find *Team Philips* until her red navigation lights eventually gave her position away. In the distance, we could just make out a red light ripping along at high speed. It had to be her. Despite all the shipping in the area, nothing was travelling faster than this faint red light.

Hanging back behind Nick's boat it was clear that at our current speed we would take forever to catch up. I shouted that we should

Team Philips on her maiden voyage to London.

speed up and in what felt like a bid for freedom I opened the throttle and powered past Nick. Despite the darkness, I could see that he was not amused. There were two of us in each RIB and we were navigating our way through the Goodwin Sands between Dover and Ramsgate. This is a notorious stretch of water whose sandbanks have claimed many a vessel over the centuries and this was the reason for Nick's caution. I knew this and was familiar with the area, having sailed past the Goodwins on numerous occasions. Blasting through the narrow channels between the sandbanks at twenty-five knots under the cover of darkness was definitely my idea of excitement.

The following morning, the wind had died away to nothing and we were being towed the final miles up the Thames towards Tower Bridge and St Catherine's Dock. Time was still tight but we would just about have enough of it to secure the dock lines and grab a quick shower and shave before the show started. The rest of the Goss Challenges team, including all the build crew, were arriving by coach and would already be there to greet us when we arrived. As we passed the Millennium Dome we were all getting excited. It would soon be time to meet the Queen.

By the time Her Majesty arrived our stage was set. The team had organised the last-minute details and installed the special custom aluminium gangplank that connected *Team Philips* to the shore. This gangplank was covered in red carpet and had cost the company a small fortune to construct just for the one-off event. The Queen required a sturdy platform to walk along and our boat, despite being perfectly formed, wasn't easy to negotiate. With the platform in place the Queen would be able to walk up onto *Team Philips* and make her way around the deck area to the rear beams. There, a bottle of champagne was attached to another custom-built stainless steel gantry, ready to be broken as is customary when naming a vessel.

The bottle was rigged to hit the tip of our huge anchor, which was suspended off the rear beam. This would ensure the bottle broke on the first attempt and didn't cause any embarrassment. I remember being impressed with the team's attention to detail that day. They had thought of everything. Thousands of people were there to watch the ceremony and tens of thousands had tuned in online to watch live via our website. This was a huge media event as well and I remember the building anticipation as we waited on the platform aboard *Team Philips*. We were about to meet the Queen. It was the first time Her

Above **Her Majesty the Queen** naming *Team Philips* beneath Tower Bridge.

Right *Team Philips'* and a spectacular backdrop, moored beneath Tower Bridge, London.

Majesty had ever named a racing yacht, so once again the project was making history. Involving the Queen in any public event is always a huge deal and this occasion was no different. Dozens of people I didn't recognise swept through the boat, checking every nook and cranny to make sure the area was safe and secure for the big moment. Their

Mum and Dad meet The Queen at the naming ceremony.

Mum and Dad meet The Queen at the naming ceremony.

presence only added to the excitement.

Pete had greeted the Queen at her car as she arrived and as they negotiated the platform I suddenly wondered what to say. Let's worry about that if she talks to me, I thought. Pete skilfully played host as they walked up the red carpet and onto the boat and then it was time for introductions. Andy was first, then Mike and Graham. I was second to last before Larso and by the time it was my turn I was buzzing with excitement. My heart was racing, although I did my best not to show it, conscious that the eyes of the world were watching. When the Queen finally spoke to me, all I could think of to say was that I was the youngest member of the crew and it was an honour to meet her. Talk about stating the bleeding obvious, but it didn't matter.

The champagne christening went well, the bottle shattering on the first attempt. That must have come as a great relief to Pete as he stood beside the Queen on the platform. With the naming ceremony in the bag, we all retired to a reception ashore where the Queen was introduced to the rest of the team and the crew's families. My parents were there and were also introduced and my father struck up quite a conversation with her. For a second or two, I wondered if Her Majesty would have time to meet everyone else.

The following morning we had an early start. We were now officially moving into our sea trials period and needed to catch the tide for the journey down the Thames Estuary. Just as we were preparing to leave the dock, an embarrassed-looking girl popped her head up from the port-side mast cockpit. She had come aboard the night before and apparently had fallen asleep at the base of the mast. Interestingly, a second later Larso popped his head up from same mast cockpit and explained that she was in fact a friend from Australia. They had apparently crashed out in the early hours after some of the build team had enjoyed a few private beers on board after the festivities ashore fizzled out. Larso looked more embarrassed than the girl, who speedily scuttled across the trampoline nets and jumped ashore. We all found it most amusing and spent the rest of the morning cracking jokes at Larso's expense.

The plan was to sail back to Dartmouth, restock and then head out into the Atlantic for a short work-up before setting off on the Jules Verne record attempt around the world. The Jules Verne had always been part of the plan, but privately, Pete had made it very clear that we would have the whole of the north and south Atlantic to stretch *Team Philips*'s legs before making the decision to enter the Southern Ocean. With such a new boat, we needed to satisfy ourselves that she was up to the ultimate test. For a beast such as *Team Philips*, the north and south Atlantic oceans were her backyard. Cape Town at thirty-three degrees south would be the point of no return. If everything was in the groove and the boat had given us no reason to doubt her, we would pass south of the thirty-third parallel and head towards the Roaring Forties and ultimately the Southern Ocean. If not, we would turn around and head for home to reassess the situation.

Pete's plan to sail around the world with such a new and revolutionary vessel so soon after launching might have seemed at best a little optimistic and at worst completely crazy. But I saw method in what some might call madness. Pete is not a man who would make a decision of that gravity on a whim. We needed to train hard for The Race and what better way than to effectively walk the course several months before the actual event? As for the Jules Verne, we would have been unlikely to break the then record of seventy-one days for a non-stop circumnavigation of the planet. Although none of us said so, I think in our hearts we all knew that *Team Philips* was certainly capable of breaking the record but at that early stage we did not know the boat or her full capabilities – or ours. We needed to spend time on board to explore the boundaries of this new type of craft and walking the course or even just part of it was a good idea. It was a clear and considered plan.

Having cleared the confines of the Thames estuary, we were approaching the Dover Straits, sailing under a steady twelve knots of wind and making good progress. Pete called for a volunteer to climb the mast and check that everything aloft was functioning normally. Despite having nothing to prove I was quick to push myself forward. This turned out to be something I would regret. Harness attached, the lads quickly hoisted me aloft, forty-one metres to the masthead.

I was about three-quarters of the way up when the pitching motion became too great to hold on and my grip was wrenched from the smooth surface of the wing mast. I was instantly flicked towards to middle of the mainsail. I collided with one of the huge fibreglass stiffening battens before being thrown back towards the mast. I did my best to grab hold of something to steady myself but the pitching motion was incredible. At deck level it was hardly noticeable, but up there was a scary place to be. I was being driven into the mast and tossed around like a rag doll. Each impact was really painful. I shouted to the lads to get me down and do it quickly. They jumped into action. I could hear Pete saying something about 'bring him down steady' as they smoked the halyard and brought me back to the safety of the deck. For a moment or two I laid on the trampoline nets, looking up at the masthead, trying to get my breath back. It was a scary experience and a stark reminder of how powerful and potentially dangerous the boat could be, even in clement weather.

The turnaround in Dartmouth was swift. With fresh provisions on board the six of us set sail into the English Channel, full of hope and anticipation. The initial plan was to head towards Land's End at the south-western tip of England and conduct manoeuvres close to Mount's Bay, before poking our noses out into the Western Approaches and stretching Team Philips's legs. The first night at sea was an eye-opener indeed. Having rounded Start Point, the first significant headland from Dartmouth, we spent the remainder of the night sailing in a moderate breeze with the wind coming across our side, making a steady fifteen knots. We were making that speed without any sails hoisted at all. The windage from the twin wing masts was enough to create significant forward drive, even in moderate conditions.

Standing at the steering pedestal looking forward was such a buzz. We were finally sailing this dream machine and the fact that she was making such high speed with no sails up at all was a good start. Pete had wanted a vessel that was ahead of her time and it seemed that Adrian Thompson had achieved that goal. We were starting to think that the performance envelope of this boat would exceed our predictions. Pete was so pleased he suggested we refrain from hoisting the sails until first light the following morning. None of us was minded to suggest anything different. We were all content to sit back and enjoy the ride.

The whole of the following day was spent sailing off Mount's Bay in Cornwall. We were all keen to settle into life on board and were kept busy with manoeuvres, raising and lowering the sails and learning how to adjust and control the giant rotating wing masts. Despite being a pretty simple boat in concept, sailing *Team Philips* did require a complete understanding of the operational capabilities of the wing masts. The masts were shaped similarly to aircraft wings and capable of rotating within their sockets in order to create the most efficient angle of attack to the wind flowing across them.

In the most extreme case, the masts had been designed to rotate one hundred and eighty degrees from the centre line so that they could be fully de-powered if we needed to slow the boat down quickly. It was a great idea, and to a point, it worked. But, as we would later find out, the concept of rotating the rigs by one hundred and eighty degrees in extreme weather to fully de-power them was fundamentally flawed because the weight of the booms contributed to pushing the bow of the boat under the water. We would be more at risk of capsizing with the masts fully rotated. In those extreme conditions the boat was most comfortable with the masts centralised and sheeted-in tight, with the booms hanging over the aft hull sections rather than over the bow.

In normal sailing conditions, rotating the masts meant we could increase the efficiency of the boat and as a result she would sail faster. The concept was by no means new to the world of sailing but the sheer size and power that was generated by the masts onboard *Team Philips* made them ground-breaking. The network of blocks and cordage suspended beneath the gigantic wishbone booms was all that was required to tune and maintain the performance of the rigs.

Despite being fairly robust pieces of equipment, they did have their weaknesses and like any piece of machinery, it was essential to fully understand how to operate them in order to avoid accidental damage. Barry Noble, the masts' co-designer alongside Martyn Smith, had been quite particular about the safe operation of the rigs and had issued a special document to each of the crew so that we could gain a more complete understanding of their operation and limitations. We were all aware of the implications of making mistakes, especially in the early stages of learning how to operate everything.

Later that evening we started to adopt our watch systems. We had been at sea for forty-eight hours and it was time to establish the routine. With six of us on board we divided ourselves into three watches. Larso and Graham would take one watch, Andy and Mike another, with Pete and I pairing up for the third. Having decided to head out into the Western Approaches, we sailed throughout the night, heading for the Isles of Scilly.

The first indication of trouble came the following morning with a sudden and shockingly loud crack. Crisp and menacing, the noise vibrated through the hull structure. It was just getting light outside. *Team Philips* was sailing under a conservative amount of sail at a sedate sixteen knots in a north easterly Force 5 wind. Andy and Mike were the on watch team and had almost completed their routine checks when the first crack sounded. Larso and I were in the front section of the accommodation pod while Pete and Graham were between us and the galley. The four of us were all in our bunks when the noise came. Responding to a primeval sense of danger, Larso and I reacted instantly, jumping out of our sleeping bags. We were so eager to get on deck that we fell on top of each other, scrambling to get out of the accommodation pod. As we ran past Pete he was already getting out of his sleeping bag.

Shooting out of the pod, I saw Mike was steering and looked worried. "Fuck, did you hear that?" he said. I was still coming-to from the deep sleep I had been in moments before. I turned around to see Andy running across the trampolines toward the cockpit yelling, "It's the bow, there's a huge crack in the bow!" More cracking and splintering could be heard as Pete shot through the companionway into the cockpit. We all knew instantly that we were facing a potential disaster. The weather was reasonably calm with a fairly flat sea but despite the clement conditions it was obvious that our goliath had somehow been seriously wounded. Pete took control, giving us clear and concise commands to get rid of the sails and slow us down.

The adrenaline was pumping as we struggled to lower the giant mainsails. This was our first true test as a team working together under real pressure and what a test it was, we were well and truly in unknown trouble. With the sails stowed, *Team Philips* slowed down to about seven knots. It was time to assess the damage. Andy went below into the nav station to call up the shore team on the satellite phone while the rest of us congregated around the front beam and looked down at the port bow. There was a crack running from the waterline up the side of the hull. It was about five feet long and plainly visible just in front of the forward beam. Pete shouted into the cabin and asked Andy for an exact update of our position on the chart. "About twenty miles north west of the Scillies," came back the call.

The initial heart-stopping cracking sounds had momentarily given way to silence, giving us some calm to assess the situation. The starboard bow looked fine, with no immediate evidence of damage. It seemed the trouble was confined to the port side. It was now about 7.45 on the morning of 29 March 2000. Any dreams of undertaking a Jules Verne record attempt had been blown out of the water by that first crack. Andy surfaced from the accommodation pod and Pete went

A dazzling array of technology – the navigation station onboard *Team Philips*.

below to talk to the shore team while the rest of us set about checking the boat for any other visible damage. Andy had his doubts about whether the starboard bow was really unaffected and wanted to check the forward bow sections.

Shortly after he disappeared down the hatch, the noise of splintering carbon fibre again resonated throughout the port hull. The cracks in the bow were propagating. A few seconds later Andy came up through the starboard hatch looking as white as a sheet. The starboard hull was also delaminating, although not as spectacularly as the port side: there were cracks about fifteen feet forward of the front beam. The look on Andy's face said it all. The situation had escalated and we now had two problems to deal with. Pete called a team briefing in the cockpit. He had informed MRCC Falmouth, the local Maritime Rescue Coordination Centre. In response they had dispatched the St Mary's lifeboat which was leaving the Scillies at that very moment. Unless the situation escalated out of control they would just stand-by, ready to give assistance if required. We would head for the sanctuary of St Mary's in the Scilly Isles to get some shelter and review things there. Goss Challenges headquarters was already contacting our families to inform them of the situation and representatives of the company were on their way to the Scillies to meet us. Our crisis management plan had just kicked into action.

By the time the lifeboat arrived, the damage to the port bow had significantly increased and we were facing the very real possibility that it might snap off completely. The cracks and other noises were intense and now reverberated continuously throughout the structure. The port bow was physically being moved as the sea flowed underneath the hulls. The hull was rapidly delaminating and losing structural integrity. Whole sections were 'panting' around the cracks, opening and closing as the hull flexed. The cracks by now almost completely encircled the hull.

Pete wanted everyone sitting on the rear beam in survival suits, with the life rafts ready for deployment. We discussed what would happen if the bow severed completely and came to the unanimous conclusion that a complete capsize was very probable. The sea state had increased since the early hours of the morning and we didn't fancy our chances of staying upright if the bow separated.

By 11am we were fairly close to the relative shelter of St Mary's and had just twelve miles to go to gain some shelter from the islands. We

Above **A wave breaks over**
***Team Philips* 9 miles from**
the Scillies.

Left **29th March 2000, the**
moment the bow breaks.

were powerless to do anything and it was clear the port bow was not
going to hold together. We could only wait and watch as it systematically destroyed itself in the seaway.

Back on dry land, the media frenzy was building and very soon
we would have helicopters flying above us, all intent on catching our
stricken vessel on camera while we struggled to reach a safe haven. It
must have been one hell of a story from the media's perspective, but on
board we felt like they were vultures circling their prey.

Just nine miles from the islands and with the media watching from
above, the port bow spectacularly broke away from the main structure, exposing a huge hole in the hull. The ocean instantly poured in,
popping one of the watertight bulkheads. *Team Philips* listed heavily
over and slowed to almost a standstill. I remember watching the bow
section float out under the rear beam as we sailed over the top of it. I
braced for the capsize. We had a clear plan of action if she started to
flip – we were all ready to go over the aft beam into the sea.

Seeing a huge section of our boat tear itself apart in such a violent manner almost defied belief. Despite having had several hours to prepare for the calamity, when the moment of disaster arrived we were all still stunned to see the bow snap. During the build-up to the breakage, Pete had contacted Adrian Thompson on the satellite phone to ask if we would stay upright if the bow broke away completely. It was a difficult question to answer with any degree of certainty. Adrian quickly ran some numbers to check and called back with an inconclusive verdict. He could not be sure in the circumstances, but advised us to prepare for the worst.

It was the instant deceleration once the bow had separated that dragged me from my world of disbelief. Holding onto the rear beam I could feel the down-draft from the rotor blades of the helicopters above, they were that close. The television cameras were perfectly positioned to capture whatever happened next. I remember thinking 'what a mess, we will definitely be all over the ten o'clock news tonight'.

One minute passed, then another and despite listing significantly on her port side, *Team Philips* resisted capsizing. We realised that the boat was reasonably stable in the prevailing sea state and despite the forward motion being at almost snail's pace, we decided to keep heading for St Mary's. Even though our fears of an instant capsize had not been realised, once the bow had parted there was a constant threat that we could flip at any moment. If that did happen, it would be essential to get clear of the structure as we went over. Anyone caught underneath the trampoline nets would very probably drown. When we fitted out *Team Philips*, Pete had tasked me with sourcing small emergency air bottles with mouth regulators for each of the crew in case of a capsize at sea. I handed them out and we tied them around our waists.

When a multihull capsizes, it will always remain upside-down. If any of us were in the accommodation pod we would very likely need an air supply to give us chance to get out of the inverted and flooded cabin. *Team Philips* was a very well-equipped vessel and even had emergency waterproof lighting around the accommodation area.

The port hull was gradually settling in the water, getting lower and lower. It was clear the remaining watertight compartments aft of the mast bulkheads had also been breached and were slowly filling with water. I opened up the rear access hatch on the port side aft hull only to find the water almost level with the top of the ladders below the decks.

Initially, the St Mary's lifeboat tried to recover the broken bow section. Their intention was to tow it into St Mary's but they soon decided to abandon the 40-foot piece of wreckage so they could lend assistance to us should our situation worsen.

Being unable to recover the bow section was something we absolutely did not want to consider. It would take a lot longer to build a whole new bow than to just repair the existing one and we would then certainly miss the deadline for the start of The Race on 31 December. Behind the scenes, the crisis management team at Goss Challenges was putting the wheels in motion to locate the bow and mount a recovery attempt. Our meteorologist Lee Bruce was working out a probable drift pattern for the section in the prevailing wind and sea conditions, and Nick Booth was already preparing one of the company RIBs to take to Cornwall and launch for the search. One concern was that someone else might find it first and make a salvage claim. There was also the hazard to shipping posed by a floating piece of wreckage of that size. Losing it completely or somebody else finding it could only

Me sitting on the front beam after the bow broke off.

add to our already precarious situation.

It was six in the evening before we finally reached the safety of St Mary's and dropped anchor in the bay. We had managed to save the boat and in doing so overcome the first hurdle in what would turn out to be a very long road to recovery for the whole team. We were all knackered as the adrenaline that had kept us so focused and alert all day finally started to dissipate. With the boat secured just a few hundred yards from the shoreline, it was time to go ashore for some food and try to make sense of the ordeal. Pete, Mike, Andy, Graham and Larso were all keen to go ashore but someone needed to stay on board and maintain a lookout. I wasn't that bothered about going ashore and didn't really want to leave *Team Philips*, so I volunteered to stay behind. I didn't feel much like socialising and was more comfortable staying on board. Once everyone had gone ashore I made a cup of tea and sat down to call Mum and Dad. I needed to offload and talk about the experience.

The following day we had some difficult decisions to make. Even though we had made it to the shelter of the Scillies, we were not out of the woods yet. We could not stay in St Mary's long-term. *Team Philips* was seriously damaged and needed to return to the factory in Totnes for a full assessment. This would not be an easy task. It's about one hundred and twenty miles from St Mary's to Dartmouth and anything could happen along the way. After careful consideration we hatched a plan to get the boat back to Dartmouth. We would wait for a suitable weather window and then with calm seas we would tow *Team Philips* backwards, all the way home. Towing backwards would be necessary to allow the boat to move through the water more easily. With such a huge hole in the front of the hull, the damaged area acted like a gigantic brake and imposed an unnecessary load on the surrounding structure. Towing backwards might have looked odd but it was the most efficient mode of travelling given our changed situation.

The saga had been a cruel blow to the whole team. At the time of the incident we had all been on a high after the naming ceremony with the Queen. Failure was just not on our radar but in a strange kind of way the incident made us bond even more as a team. Pete was defiant and confident that we would get through this. It was a time to dig deep and move forward together.

During the initial crisis, Goss Challenges had been approached by a member of the public who was an avid follower of the project. John Frewer owned a small light aircraft and offered to help in the search for the bow section by taking a couple of team members out over the sea. This was an incredible act of generosity and one that proved absolutely crucial to locating the missing bow. Andy and Keith Fennell went up in the plane and within just a few hours had located it some twenty-five miles out to sea. An up-to-date positional fix was enough to guide the lads in the RIB to its position to recover it.

Whilst the bow recovery operation was underway, the rest of us set about making *Team Philips* seaworthy for the potentially hazardous trip back to Dartmouth. Firstly, we needed to attach flotation bags around the hull to support the structure and prevent her from sinking any lower into the water. With the airbags in place and with the help of the local fire service, we rigged up powerful pumps and drained the seawater from the flooded hull sections. We needed to establish whether or not the forward watertight bulkhead hatch was still in place, so I went over the side in my survival suit to swim down into the exposed hull to have a look. The sea in the Scillies was beautifully clear and despite finding it difficult to swim down to the hatch because of trapped air in my suit, I could see that the watertight emergency hatch had been blown open.

We were blessed with unusually good weather for the delivery back to Dartmouth. Conditions were near-perfect with light winds and a calm sea but we had a race against time to run for the shelter of our home port before the weather turned. It was a long and tedious journey, made all the more tiring by the painfully slow rate of progress. I remember feeling like a wounded animal running for cover. Whilst at sea, *Team Philips* was exposed and vulnerable in that state. It was essential to waste no time once we left the sanctuary of St Mary's.

We made it to Dartmouth without incident and tied up to prepare for the trip upriver. We removed the rudders, a job that required several divers in the water and a lot of coordination. Little did we know that this would not be the last time we would negotiate the confines of the river with our giant yacht. With the boat safely secured in Dartmouth, our attention turned to the recovery of the bow. Nick Booth had salvaged the huge section and towed it into a small harbour in Cornwall. We needed to transport the wreckage back to Totnes, best done by road.

Containment of the situation was always a priority and with this thought, Graham headed down to Cornwall to rendezvous with Nick and help coordinate the road trip. Meanwhile, back at Goss Challenges, Garry Venning, Keith Fennell and the rest of build team considered how best to deal with the repair. It was all very much dependent on our sponsors remaining loyal to the project.

Liaising with the sponsors was a task that rested firmly on the shoulders of Pete and the management team. He and Mark Orr called an emergency meeting to discuss the situation and explain that we were down but by no means out of the running.

At the time, the only certainty was that *Team Philips* would come back Totnes to be hauled out of the water and put back into the build shed. Whatever happened with the sponsors, we couldn't leave the boat in the water in her current state so the decision was made to organise the necessary lifting-out process. This also meant the front of the build shed that had been so elegantly reassembled not two weeks earlier would have to be taken down again.

News came that the meeting with our sponsors had gone well, given the circumstances. Pete and the steering committee, which consisted of representatives from each of our major partners, were in agreement that the project must continue and would do so with their full backing. Too much time and money had already been invested for the project to be canned just because the bow fell off.

Safe in the knowledge that our sponsors were fully behind us, we took the first step in our master plan to getting ourselves back on the water. *Team Philips* needed a full structural survey, which would be done in conjunction with an independent team of engineers. They would establish not just what went wrong, but also the full extent of the damage. With the boat and broken bow now back in the hangar the build team prepared for the required 'cut and shut' repair job.

The results from the structural survey were not good. *Team Philips* had significant structural defects running the length of each hull section. The tests had revealed areas in both hulls that had voids or gaps between the laminate layers. The hulls on *Team Philips* were constructed using a sandwich technique and we learned that the core, which was made of Nomex honeycomb (the same stuff that is used in the aerospace industry) had not adhered satisfactorily to the inner and outer skins of the carbon fibre hull, leaving voids in the laminate. Consequently, the hull sections had a dramatically lower tolerance for the huge loads generated by the ocean and failed at a fraction of their design strength.

These voids had been present from the moment the hulls were created and unknown to us, our revolutionary vessel had been riddled with serious structural flaws from the beginning. Based on the analysis that came back from the survey, it was a matter of when rather than if *Team Philips* would suffer a dramatic structural failure. This answered the question of why *Team Philips* broke apart the way she did, but did not explain how the hulls had come to be so flawed.

Prior to commencing the build, Pete and the design team had commissioned a full structural engineering programme from an independent company. They had taken on the responsibility of engineering the structure after Adrian Thompson drew up the concept design. In the world of sailing, the naval architect draws the shape and dimensions of a boat and that design is then sent to an engineering company. The engineers decide how the boat should be built so that it will withstand the rigours of its intended purpose.

It turned out that the voids in the hull had occurred as a result of the methods employed in the build process. Some said that inconsistencies on the production line contributed to the outcome while other opinions pointed towards an equal share of the responsibility resting with the structural engineering company. Either way, it was clear that *Team Philips* had touched the water with only a fraction of her design strength and as a result broke apart during her first significant trials. I thought how bad it would have been if we had seen a decent amount of wind for the trip to meet the Queen. The bow could have come apart then. Or even worse, if it the boat had been just a fraction stronger, it might have held together until we reached the Southern Ocean on the Jules Verne. Down there the incident would very likely have had a different outcome, with potentially tragic consequences. It was a chilling thought. We had perhaps had a lucky escape.

With such a high-profile and disastrous failure of the hull, the rumour mill surrounding the project had already stepped up a gear. The media were understandably looking for the inside story and seemingly everyone had a theory as to why the bow had broken off. The chat forum on the TeamPhilips.com website was inundated with various opinions. These ranged from 'I told you so' to in-depth discussions about the requirement for wire bracing to add rigidity to the bows and even a suggestion for a third forward lateral support beam. The discussion forum had certainly exploded with comment, suggestion and speculation. Sometimes of an evening Larso and I would take the time to read through the latest postings and try to gauge public opinion. It was clear that the project, even in disaster, had an overwhelmingly loyal following. If anything, for some people it made the project all the more exciting to follow. Either way, the website hits went through the roof.

As days turned into weeks, we settled into our new regime and drew up a strategy to prepare for the lead-up to The Race. It was an uphill struggle and time was short but the six of us focused on how best to get ready. The build team was making progress with the physical structural modifications to the boat. The repair would take months and involved major reinforcement of each hull. The plan was to laminate thick carbon fibre strakes into the hulls. These would run the length of *Team Philips*, acting like solid supporting girders and stiffening the hulls. The process involved cutting into each hull from the outside to remove large sections of carbon fibre, together with the Nomex foam cores. Once the cores had been removed the recess would be filled by applying new layers of carbon fibre which would act as the stiffening strakes.

On the inside of the hulls, dozens of new ring frame supports would be fitted; these would encircle the structure every few metres to complete the strengthening process. The result would be a much heavier-than-intended craft, but we hoped a bulletproof one. The work repairing the outside of the hulls was easy compared to the task of grinding carbon fibre in the dark whilst cramped in the confines of the forward hull sections. That part of the job was a tough and painstaking procedure that proved to be the most tedious of the repair. Several times a day the lads would emerge from the interior of the hulls with their white protective paper suits covered in black carbon dust. With their special breathing apparatus, some of them looked more like spacemen. It was a tough and dirty job.

As we considered how the six of us could best prepare for The Race, Pete voiced concerns about the lack of time to adequately familiarise ourselves with the boat. One of the most important aspects of sailing *Team Philips* was the efficient operation of the twin masts. We came up with the idea of inserting one of the masts into the ground at the build site so we could practice operating it. Because the masts were unstayed and rotated within a recessed socket on board, we could easily replicate this by digging a big hole in the ground and filling it with concrete to support the mast. We would not be able to sheet the sails in and load up the mast to any great degree, but the idea would certainly allow us to test the functionality and tune everything up.

The idea also created an added attraction at the visitor centre. With the boat back at the yard, the centre had seen an unexpected explosion in visitor numbers. If the volunteers in the visitor centre were busy before, it was nothing to the number of people now cascading through the doors. It was becoming the success story of the project to the extent that the management team decided to increase floor space and built a cafeteria in the roof of the building in an effort to create a more complete experience for the visiting public. In the face of adversity we were moving forward, just not in the way we had expected.

The repair job would take six long months to complete. During that time we concentrated on gaining an in-depth knowledge of the wing masts and sails, how they worked and how best to operate them. That knowledge would prove invaluable when we hit the water for the second round of trials.

One of the main issues with a prolonged period at sea for any sailboat is the chafing of ropes and hardware. On a vessel the size of *Team Philips* this problem would always be amplified, so we needed to reduce the likelihood of any downtime due to damaged ropes and equipment. Working on the masts also allowed us to regularly practice hoisting and lowering the mainsails, a task that seems insignificant until you consider the size of them. At forty-one metres tall the wing masts were already huge, but the sails attached to them were simply massive. Hoisting the state-of-the-art Carbon-Kevlar laminate sails took nearly three quarters of an hour the first time I tried it on my own. Even with two of us working side by side winching from the mast base cockpits, we still only managed to reduce the time to a little under half an hour. After several months practice we all improved our personal times. Larso held the record at eighteen minutes flat for a solo attempt while I squeezed into a comfortable second at twenty-six minutes, a result I felt pleased with, given the huge effort required. Hoisting the mainsails was more about cardiovascular fitness than just physical strength.

Team Philips was so huge and powerful that we needed to develop a strategy to best handle this monster when things started to approach the limit out on the race track. At speeds of up to forty knots we would need to be on the ball if we were to stay upright and in control. It was the innovative design of the rotating wing masts that would give us the ability to quickly de-power *Team Philips* should we ever need to do so. It was a comforting thought, especially given the fact that Playstation, one of our competitors, had nearly capsized due to being caught by a severe gust of wind. They had not been able to quickly and efficiently get rid of the power their mainsail generated whilst sailing with the wind directly behind them.

In an effort to gain a more complete understanding of how far we could push the boat on the race track, we installed special strain gauges into key areas on the masts with the purpose of monitoring the load the rigs were under at any given time. In theory, this was a precise way for us to gauge whether we had scope to push *Team Philips* harder in any particular situation or whether we should back off, if the rigs were under too much load. Andy was particularly keen to see the technology used on board and worked tirelessly to achieve a working solution with the manufacturers. Part of the calibration process involved applying a two-tonne load to the top of the mast in order to simulate testing sailing conditions and prove some degree of reliability. The test was successful and the system was installed on board.

Throughout the summer we continued our testing programme, looking at various aspects of the operation of the masts. Reefing the sails was another major consideration. A typical reefing procedure required three crew members: two of us would operate the winches in the mast cockpits while the other would position himself up in the air on the outboard end of the wishbone booms. At sea, walking out to the end of the booms brought a real kick of adrenaline. The booms were over twenty feet above the waterline and always offered a fantastic view of the boat and horizon. As we winched in the reefing lines, the ropes would gradually bring together the special custom-built titanium locking mechanisms that would hold the outboard end of the sail in place. It was the responsibility of the guy on the boom to indicate when the mechanical locks were attached so that the team winching in the cockpit could stop. On a boat the size of *Team Philips*, even a simple task like reefing required significant communication and teamwork. Each of us was issued with military-style communication devices that had an earpiece and a 'press to talk' switch integrated into our custom-made Musto lifejackets. On super-fast multihulls like *Team Philips*, wind noise and the motion of the boat through the water can often drown out voices. With these devices, we would always be able to communicate.

Our practical knowledge of the boat was growing by the day and the repairs were progressing. By June, the broken port bow section had been reattached. In another month, the build team would have the internal ring frame supports in place and eight weeks after that, *Team Philips* would finally be ready to go back to sea again.

Apart from our main commitments there was still plenty going on around the factory. Goss Challenges had various other projects running alongside our campaign, one of which was a contract to build a new Open 50 class yacht for a private client. The owner wanted a fast manageable yacht for an attempt at a solo round-the-world trip. The new design would be an updated version of Pete's famous Open 50 Aqua Quorum, the boat he sailed around the world in the Vendée Globe in 1996. Pete was keen to involve me in the project, knowing of my desire to build a new 60-foot boat for the next Vendée Globe. He suggested I take an active role in the project as it developed. This was an exciting prospect, but after several months the project was moth-balled. The project matured beyond the design phase and the moulds for the boat were built, but the client ran out of funds. The moulds lay on the factory floor underneath *Team Philips* and I kept thinking 'if only they had been designed for a ten-foot larger racing yacht' – that would have been my ticket into the next Vendée Globe.

As part of our new master plan we created a revised sailing sched-ule in order to kill two birds with one stone. We needed to put to rest any scepticism about *Team Philips* and prove her capability as an ocean-going racer by completing the required two-thousand mile passage to qualify for The Race. The sponsors also wanted some creative PR and what better way to achieve that than by sailing across the north Atlan-tic and rocking up into the heart of New York to celebrate? Our spon-sors would be there to meet us and share in our new wave of success, having fixed the gremlins that had so publicly thwarted our progress. In addition to the test of the Atlantic, we would sail back across the pond to Gibraltar and on into the Mediterranean for an official rendezvous with The Race fleet in Monaco.

Wave piercing at speed.
Team Philips doing what
she was designed to do.

Pete suggested privately that if the Atlantic test went well for boat and crew, we might consider having a crack at the transatlantic record for a west-to-east crossing. With two transatlantic crossings under our belt in a matter of weeks and a possible world record in the bag, we would be able to shrug off any element of doubt from the media. We would turn up at Barcelona with the boat's reputation intact, a proven force to be reckoned with.

By 23 September we were ready to re-launch. The master plan was agreed and sounded perfectly achievable. As *Team Philips* slipped into the water at Baltic Wharf for the second time in less than eight months, we felt confident of the future. The build team had completed a tough challenge under difficult circumstances. Within a matter of days we would be putting back to sea, energised by a shared desire to prove that *Team Philips* was the boat we had all hoped for.

Standing on the aft deck as we were leaving Dartmouth I felt a wave of emotions. I was glad to be going back to sea, but conscious that the might of the Atlantic was a danger we must face. Despite having achieved so much in the last six months, the real test had not yet been met.

Once again a big crowd had turned out to see us off. The media were also out in force, afloat and in the air, all poised to capture our triumphant departure from our home port as we set out into the Atlantic. We had already publicly announced our plans to cross the north Atlantic to New York, so it was only fitting that we motored off the marina berth with Frank Sinatra's 'New York, New York' blasting from the onboard stereo. This was Larso's idea and an excellent choice. He was standing right at the back of one of the hulls, waving to the crowds as we motored down the river towards the harbour mouth. It was obvious that he was enjoying the moment. We all were.

Hoisting the mainsails when on board didn't seem as tough as it had when the mast was in the ground at the factory. Perhaps we were much fitter after our summer of training or maybe it was our anticipation and keenness to get to sea. One thing was for sure, as we sheeted in the giant mainsails our blue goliath accelerated from a standing start like a greyhound out of the traps, leaving most of the spectator craft floundering in our wake. For the initial departure, several of the management team were on board to experience the thrill of a short but memorable sail on the boat they had worked so hard to make a reality. Pete was keen that they should be part of the action, albeit briefly. When the time came to offload the passengers the look on their faces changed from joyful euphoria to a rather intimidated and apprehensive stare. In all the excitement I don't think they realised they would have to jump from the aft hulls into the RIBs whilst *Team Philips* sliced through the water at nearly twenty knots. Getting them safely into the RIBs proved quite entertaining, but with a flat sea and a skilled RIB driver it was easier than it might have looked.

Soon the spectator craft turned for home and once again we were left to our own devices, free to head out west into the big blue and over the horizon. Under a stiff breeze we powered along the English Channel for three hours, achieving a steady twenty-plus knots under conservatively-reefed sails. It was day one of our new lease of life and Pete was concerned not to press the boat too early, a sentiment we all shared. There would be plenty of time to push *Team Philips* on the way back from New York once we had seen some weather and got plenty of distance under our keels.

It was incredible to finally experience the wave piercing technology working as Adrian Thompson had intended. The razor-sharp bows slicing through the chop of the English Channel were a sight to behold as we pushed our way westward. A lone helicopter appeared on the horizon. This time, it was one of ours, commissioned to rendezvous mid-Channel and film the action from above. Rick Tomlinson, the famous marine photographer was on board, ready to capture the action. We needed some good footage of the boat sailing offshore and although we were sailing at well below full potential, the images taken that day were spectacular.

Unfortunately, the feeling of freedom and achievement did not last. Quite soon I noticed a problem with the portside mast, which wasn't rotating smoothly in its socket. At first I couldn't be sure but something had certainly caught my eye. Climbing out of the cockpit, I walked across the trampoline nets and looked at the base of the mast where it disappeared into the socket at deck level. It was difficult to see anything obviously wrong but every now and again the mast would lose its smoothness as it rotated within the giant bearing. I had been staring at the mast base for a while when Pete asked what was wrong. "It's the mast base, its movement doesn't seem right to me," I explained. Pete took a second to consider what I had just said whilst looking at the mast from the cockpit and replied, "It looks fine to me."

At first it was difficult to spot any definite problem but within half an hour it became obvious. There was indeed an issue, and a big one. The port mast started to make a grinding noise that was impossible to ignore. You could see that it had settled into the socket by about three inches and every time the rig rotated, a horrible grinding noise echoed through the boat.

Once again we would have to take emergency action. Just a few hours into our scheduled transatlantic passage, we would be once again returning for the shelter of our home port with our tails between our legs. Pete called for the rigs to be de-powered to slow the boat right down. We shot into action, easing out the mainsheets but the feeling of déjà vu was hard to ignore. With both masts de-powered and the booms facing forwards, hanging over the bows *Team Philips* quickly slowed. The port-side mast was showing real signs of fatigue. It seemed the custom-made metal bearing had somehow pierced through the base of the mast.

At that stage there was very little we could do other than reduce sail and monitor the situation. Andy emerged from the cabin and told us the nearest point of dangerous land was Ushant, on the north-western tip of France, about three hours away at our current speed and heading. It was clear that we needed to turn about and head for home but first we had to get the situation under control. With all sail lowered on the damaged mast, we hauled in on the mainsheet to centralise the boom and secure the rig as best we could. Despite this, the rig was constantly moving inside the bearing socket because of the motion of the boat, and progressively destroying itself. It would be a race against time to get *Team Philips* to the safe confines of Dartmouth harbour before the situation escalated out of control. We could make Dartmouth on our own steam but would have to sail with a heavily-reefed mainsail on just the starboard mast to make headway in the choppy seas.

Sailing back, the mood on board plummeted. Pete went below to break the sobering news to the shore team over the satellite phone and organise our arrival plans, while the rest of us huddled around the cockpit to discuss the situation. Despite the damage I never thought we were in any danger, although Mike was concerned that the rig might break through the hull. If that did happen it would certainly catapult us into immediate peril but I was confident this was an unlikely outcome given the conditions. The weather was not rough and we were not isolated out on the high seas. As long as the mast stayed upright we should be fine.

As we closed in on Dartmouth, Andy and I discussed the immediate future. Andy was understandably subdued, suggesting that this might be the end. The sponsors had shown real commitment by sticking with us through the broken bow saga but they would be quite justified if they pulled the plug after this. They were understandably expecting great things now that the bow problems had been rectified and this was nothing short of a great failure. At least, that's how the media would portray it.

The facts were not favourable. Having spent six months in the shed being repaired after the first round of sea trials, the boat had only lasted another four hours going into the second round before something else broke. The future looked bleak and I wondered if this might be the last time we would sail our awesome boat. The future of our great project was hanging in the balance.

It turned out that the damage was confined to just the heel of the mast and was not as serious as it looked. Despite the embarrassing situation it would not be a major job to repair. It took just four weeks to sort out. The project's reputation was a different story, however, and this was the bigger casualty. It did not take long for word to spread that we had encountered yet more problems and the wonky-looking mast served as a 41-metre indicator that things had not gone well.

To me, this was the moment when the media completely lost faith in the project and began to ridicule our plans. Goss Challenges was certainly under fire, with speculation from both the media and some of the general public, not to mention the yachting fraternity. I had to ask myself some difficult questions as to whether *Team Philips* was actually the vision of the future we had all been led to believe it was. Was the risk really worth the potential gain? The Southern Ocean is the most unforgiving place on the planet, did I really want to go down there on this boat and risk my life? All the crew would have to ask themselves the same question.

For me, the answer was still an emphatic yes. I had signed up to the project when the chance presented itself. I knew the risks from day one and had made a conscious decision to accept them. My loyalty toward Pete and commitment to the project would not falter. I had spent my whole life waiting for a chance like this; there was no way I would drop the challenge when the ride started to get a little bumpy.

Mike Calvin was starting to have doubts of his own about the ultimate safety of *Team Philips*. Mike was the only non-professional sailor amongst us and despite being an excellent choice for the role of onboard communications manager he was by his own admission out of his depth when it came to the technical side of sailing the boat. Mike was all too aware of the risks involved in taking any boat into the Southern Ocean, especially an apparent maverick like *Team Philips*. He was father to four children and openly acknowledged that his loyalty ultimately – and rightly – rested with his family. His crisis of confidence with *Team Philips*, as Pete called it, would prove to be an insurmountable barrier for Mike and the mishap with the mast was the straw that broke the camel's back. Struggling with a difficult moral choice, he soon decided to resign from the team. He felt *Team Philips* was not ready and was just too much of a gamble. He couldn't risk his life in an unproven yacht, given the challenge ahead of us.

Mike's decision to leave was a sad one. We had been through so much together as a team and developed a close bond that would be difficult to replicate. We would be sorry to lose a respected member of the crew. I was particularly fond of Mike, who had always been a source of wisdom when I needed it. But I respected his decision and admired his ability to stand up and say 'sorry boys, I'm out of my depth'. His leaving the team would have implications both public and personal. If we didn't handle the delicate situation correctly, the media would have a field day with the news.

Pete and Mike's friendship was also on the ropes. Their relationship of some ten years' standing went way beyond this project; Mike had even asked Pete to be godfather to his youngest son. They were colleagues in business and friends in private. They had ignited the fires of the *Team Philips* project together, building the huge media interest in the project over the last three years. Mike's decision to leave, especially now, threatened that friendship. The stakes were high for all of us.

It must have been a particularly difficult time for Pete and the management team. They once again had to explain the situation to our sponsors and once again, Pete would have to use all of his charm and negotiating skills to keep the project going. For the rest of us, once the masts were safely back at the factory there was very little we could do other than hide our frustration and keep our composure.

As I arrived at the factory on the morning of 29 October, Pete was visibly furious as he walked past me into his office. He certainly had more than the usual on his mind. There was an atmosphere I had not encountered before. Pete's assistant Rachel handed me a newspaper, saying "Mike has written a damming report about the project in the Mail on Sunday." Pete was livid.

The title said it all: 'I'm no coward... but Pete Goss's plans are madness. That's why I'm leaving his crew'. Explaining the rationale behind Mike's decision to leave and how the moral dilemma had rocked the foundations of their friendship, the article also highlighted Mike's concerns that the project was profoundly unprepared for the rigours of the Southern Ocean. It was an interesting article and apart from the eye-grabbing headline I didn't think it was that bad. At best the article was a fair interpretation of the facts and at worst a betrayal of friendship.

The problem was that as well as being a crew member Mike has a commitment to his newspaper. The minute he resigned from the project he came under pressure to spill the beans on *Team Philips*. I think he resisted that pressure and retained as much loyalty to our camp as could be expected under the circumstances. My opinion was unimportant, however, it was Pete who came under scrutiny and it was clear he was taking it as a personal betrayal of trust. Not only did we now have to find Mike's replacement but the project also had to bear the weight of the very public resignation of one of the crew.

Finding Mike's replacement would be tricky. There was no shortage of professional sailors wanting to sign up but Pete wanted a known quantity, someone with specific character and ability. The logical choice would be someone we all knew, someone with a vast experience of ocean sailing and the kind of person that could understand the stakes and shoehorn themselves into our framework, working as part of the team from the outset.

The logical choice was Richard Tudor. A 41-year-old professional with two circumnavigations under his belt, Richard had skippered the yacht British Steel 2 in the 1992 British Steel Challenge and Nuclear Electric in the 1996 BT Global Challenge. He had first-hand knowledge of our project and had known Pete and Andy for a number of years.

Richard was the steady, experienced figure Pete was looking for and immediately accepted Pete's offer to join the team.

It was a good decision. In just over a week Pete had managed to take solid and decisive action and appoint the perfect candidate to not only replace our lost crew mate but also increase our strength as an experienced team, something I had always been concerned about. Sailing a beast like *Team Philips* around the globe with just six people was always a worry to me and I had voiced this concern during my initial crew interview. Pete had obviously been giving this some serious thought too, and it came as no great surprise that just a few days before we set off on our fateful last voyage we had a meeting in the boardroom to discuss the possibility of a seventh crew member for The Race. It was decided that we would suck it and see, a familiar phrase from Pete. We would however offer a place on board to one of the build team for the delivery to Barcelona. That way if we felt we needed a seventh man by the time we reached the race start we would have one of our own ready to join up.

A competent sailor and talented composite craftsman, Phil Aikenhead was given the nod and wasted no time in accepting the once-in-a-lifetime offer. Phil was a sensible choice, having been heavily involved in the physical construction of the boat, and he had a good working relationship with the rest of us. A round-the-world passage at that stage was not guaranteed for Phil but once invited on board for the delivery, his chances were good.

By 14 November we were once again back on the water and preparing to go to sea. This was our last chance to prove that *Team Philips* was ready for The Race. We were running out of time. Pete had spoken privately to the sponsors and it had been agreed there should be no pressure to actually compete, should we feel the boat was unprepared for the trip around the world. If we pulled out of the event the pressure would be off and we could concentrate on a longer work-up period while satisfying a revised promotional programme for our sponsors – a situation none of us wanted to accept. The whole point of the project had been to compete in this grand event, a celebration of the new millennium. But if the boat really wasn't up to the job, it would be crazy to attempt it anyway. Pete knew this and always displayed a clear and grounded approach to the decision. There was no way he was going to lead the team into the desolate Southern Ocean on a wing and a prayer. *Team Philips* had just one last chance to prove herself, otherwise The Race was off.

This was the last opportunity for us to complete the mandatory qualification passage. The latest in the long line of revised plans was to sail anticlockwise around the British Isles before heading out into the Atlantic towards Gibraltar. We would then sail into the Mediterranean and on to Barcelona. This was effectively an extended delivery passage and would pass enough ocean under our keels to satisfy the qualification requirements. It would also give us enough of a blast to confidently gauge whether *Team Philips* was up to the job. Even then, Pete made it clear that if we started The Race we would rigorously monitor progress until Cape Town in South Africa and make a final decision then before entering the Southern Ocean.

Repairing the mast had been a pretty straightforward affair although in the final moments before we refitted the twin 41-metre sections, one of them slipped off its cradle whilst being wheeled out of the shed and nearly crushed one of the build team's legs. Keith Fennell was lucky to walk away from the incident and the mast had sustained some superficial damage to the fairing and took another three days to be repaired. It was an accident, but was it also a bad omen?

We knew we would see some rough weather on this trip. It was December and the north Atlantic in December is no joke. But *Team Philips*, like other giant multihulls, was fast enough to outrun the most dangerous weather systems and keep herself out of trouble. Unlike monohulls, the multis don't need very strong winds to propel themselves at top speed. Full speed potential is achieved in around twenty-five knots of wind and anything above that generally just produces more probability of gear failure, despite any extra performance. This was a comforting thought, but on this trip we needed to see rough weather and test our boat. And rough weather was precisely what we would get.

We left a sleepy Dartmouth harbour on 2 December and enjoyed perfect sailing conditions as we charged along the English Channel toward Dover. Our first real test of weather came as we turned northwards and sped along the east coast. Rattling along at a sustained twenty-seven knots, *Team Philips* was finally able to stretch her legs and deliver some of the awesome performance potential we had been promised. She was amazing and genuinely handled like she was on rails. The wave-piercing technology seemed to be doing its stuff, slicing though big green waves like hot knives cutting though butter. The Thames Estuary, The Wash and the Humber River all passed by in just a few hours. Emotions were on the crest of a wave and the memories of hard work and bitter disappointment were quickly ebbing away as we powered northwards on our big blue giant.

As we passed into Scottish waters we were experiencing our first gale. Conditions had deteriorated as we approached the north-eastern tip of Scotland and while the seas were rough, progress remained rapid as *Team Philips* negotiated the stormy weather with ease. We were still adopting a cautious approach but the performance of the boat was nothing short of amazing. We started to feel that she was finally over her teething problems. That's not to say we hadn't seen any issues. During our passage along the east coast of England one of the two diesel engines used to power *Team Philips* in and out of harbour and replenish our electrical supply at sea had suffered problems and would not start. This wasn't initially a significant problem, but later the disabled engine would have a significant role to play.

"All hands on deck, lads," came the call from Pete. We were rapidly approaching the Scottish shoreline and needed to change our course by gybing away from the land. With gale-force conditions outside we were all togged-up in our wet weather gear and poised for action. The wind generators on the front and rear beams used to top up our electricity supply howled as their rotor blades spun around at high speed. This screaming noise certainly helped to amplify the high octane drama. This was the real thing, a racing situation under real pressure. It was essential to work together to complete the manoeuvre and clear the mainland ahead.

The months of training and preparation kicked in as Larso and I made a quick dash across the trampoline nets to the port side mast cockpit. Throwing ourselves over the cockpit edge we landed on our backs on the floor before helping each other to our feet, the motion of the boat was so intense. Regaining our footing, we started to adjust the rotation of the mast while the team in the central pod winched in the mainsheets. Two other guys were in the starboard mast cockpits doing exactly the same manoeuvre and Pete was on the helm. Visibility was poor, spray and spume were blowing across the boat as we careered across the ocean at nearly thirty knots. Together with that howling noise from the wind generators it was an exhilarating environment. The land had just popped into view through the mist and at this speed we would be on the hard stuff in a matter of minutes unless we could pull off a perfect manoeuvre. Pete gave the call over the radio headsets. It would have been impossible to communicate by shouting, the noise was too intense.

Larso and I stayed in the mast cockpit throughout the gybe. I could see the guys in the central pod preparing to ease out the mainsheets once the wind came around. As Pete steered away from the wind we experienced a momentary calm as the wind speed decreased and *Team Philips* slowed down. Then as the booms flicked across to the new side and filled with wind we accelerated away in spectacular fashion. Pete brought the boat onto her new course and steadily the awesome power came back as we shot off, away from the danger of the coastline. It went like clockwork and the memory of that ballsy manoeuvre in such testing conditions is fixed firmly in my mind as one of the defining moments of the project. That one experience alone was worth all the effort.

Having successfully weathered our first significant gale and passed to the north of the Orkney Islands our faith in the boat was building as we headed west into the Atlantic. Soon however, we were losing the wind. It wasn't long before we lay totally starved of breeze, becalmed and floating on a glassy sea. We were miles offshore, out of sight of land and had to wait impatiently for new breeze to breathe life into our sails. We needed to head south and start our descent through the parallels of latitude towards the warmer climate of the Mediterranean. Being becalmed so far north at that time of year really didn't sit well with any of us. We knew we were exposed on the west side of the British Isles but without wind we were going nowhere. If a big storm came through we would have little option but to head even farther away from civilisation. We were all nervous for a while as *Team Philips* wallowed on the ocean.

Our proposed route around the UK at that time of year always had the potential to put us in the path of some severe weather. However, in the days leading up to our departure from Dartmouth the direct route from the UK to the Straits of Gibraltar had been blocked by a series of apparently unending depressions, bringing strong south or south-westerly headwinds. It would have been foolhardy to have set out into the teeth of bad weather whilst trying to cross the Bay of Biscay. Trapped in that area, we would have had very few options if the weather deteriorated. It was a far better plan to head north and gain some necessary sea miles by sailing around the UK. Once around the top of the British Isles, the strong north-westerly winds on the western side of the depression would propel us in exactly the right direction towards the Mediterranean. The timing was a little on the tight side, but achievable nonetheless.

Our meteorologist Lee Bruce was thousands of miles away in America, sitting in his office evaluating the situation. Despite not being physically on board, Lee played a pivotal role as our weather advisor. He was in constant contact with the boat via our satellite communications equipment and would regularly send through updated weather faxes and digital weather files or maps called Grib files. We could then overlay the information onto our onboard computers and keep abreast of the constantly changing weather. In this respect we were using the trip as a training session for The Race.

Lee was also a little concerned with our current lack of progress. He advised that a weather report from a ship just twenty miles to the south of us reported a solid wind from the north-north-west of about twenty knots. At sea, many commercial ships are equipped with facilities to monitor weather conditions and transmit this information over the satellite network for others to use. If we could get into that zone, we would be off and able to make best speed south. The trouble was we had no real way of propelling *Team Philips* into that position. There was literally no wind and we didn't have the option of motoring because of the ongoing problems with the engines. One of the diesel engines had packed up due to sea water ingress and the other just failed to start. We would just have to wait and sit it out.

We drifted for almost twenty-four hours. When the wind eventually arrived, we made best speed but it soon became clear that we had missed the corridor of favourable north-westerly winds on the back edge of the low. We would have to head west and sail further out into the Atlantic. Now, we were faced with an altogether different situation and the prospect of a new approaching depression that threatened to block our path southwards with its severe gales.

During the following days we rattled across the ocean at high speed, trying to forge a path to the south. We were enjoying a sensational ride. It was clear that the performance envelope of this boat was significant. As the hours ticked by, we were settling into a more relaxed regime on board. But the clock was ticking and we could no longer be liberal with our time. We had to start heading for Gibraltar if we were to get to the start of The Race on schedule, but the possibility of a low pressure weather system blocking our path was now starting to turn into reality. Having skirted over the top of one weather system, we were now hundreds of miles west of Ireland, truly in the middle of the north Atlantic and right in the firing line for any approaching bad weather.

That evening, we were treated to some fantastic sailing. I remember standing behind the aft beam in the cockpit, steering into the darkness. Our progress was rapid. I was coming to the end of my watch and we had been slicing through the ocean at thirty knots for a while. Pete was constantly monitoring the situation, allowing us to gradually wind up the performance of the boat. Our speed had been steadily increasing all day. We were still way off full potential for the conditions but nonetheless just moments before I relinquished the helm to Andy for the change of watch, the boat speed indicator registered thirty-four knots. Everyone was excited. It was a new record for the boat, but what made it so incredible was at the time I had been talking to Andy whilst steering with one hand and holding a can of cola with the other. *Team Philips* was undoubtedly an easy boat to control, a testament to the design philosophy of Adrian Thompson.

The record-setting pace was actually not that big a number for the type of boat we were sailing. It was super-fast, but not extreme. As I stepped into the cabin and walked through the galley to the forward sleeping quarters I wondered how long it would be before one of the lads got us that little bit closer to the 40-knot barrier. Before I had time to sit down and take off my boots, an ecstatic Andy shouted, "Thirty-seven knots!" We were all smiles and cheers that night. It had been an exciting day for all, and I could see that Pete was quietly pleased with our progress.

As the sun came up the following day, so did the sea state. Lee had sent through a new update describing some particularly nasty weather coming off the Grand Banks of Newfoundland. The developing low-pressure system was in its infancy but would soon move into a position to potentially block our path south, bringing with it rough weather. With limited options and having discussed at length the situation with Lee we decided to face the weather and continue towards the approaching low. The plan was to initially sail into the northern side of the weather front, which would deliver strong easterly gales. Then later, whilst passing into the southern side of the front we would face west-south-westerly winds. All this translated into a less than ideal set of circumstances given our current position so far west in the Atlantic. Heading north away from the worst of the weather was really not an option at that stage, as it would only prolong the inevitable. Eventually we would have to face bad weather in order to make progress south and so with that in mind, we prepared for rough but not extreme conditions.

The approaching bad weather meant we would eventually be sailing into the wind and waves under gale-force conditions, something none of us was particularly looking forward to. That situation is less than ideal on any giant multihull. Sailing into the wind and waves is never favourable on these craft. Their sheer size and the power they generate make life onboard very debilitating, as the motion becomes increasingly violent for the crew as the boat punches headlong into the sea and wind. It shakes and rattles the fillings in your teeth to the point of physical exhaustion. In those conditions, it's easy to feel like your brain is a marble, rolling around inside your head.

That type of sailing also places a high level of stress on the boat and equipment and despite wanting to test *Team Philips*, there were better ways to learn the capabilities of our new boat than exposing her to that kind of weather. But now we had no choice.

We had now settled into our watch systems and sitting in the companionway at the entrance to the accommodation pod Andy and I were preparing for the changeover of watch when I noticed the oval door frame looked like it was flexing. Andy noticed it too. Every time the boat burst through a wave, we could see the companionway door frame distorting slightly under the load. The movement was very subtle but it was definitely happening. There wasn't much we could do about it, and after a few moments' deliberation, we decided to put it on the list of things to monitor. However, it was an early indication of the trouble to come.

The following afternoon I was lying in my bunk listening to the noise of *Team Philips* bursting through the ocean. I was off watch and enjoying some shut-eye while considering the big picture. The last twelve months had been such a rollercoaster ride. The feeling of being at sea on this awesome machine was just incredible. I was so lucky to be part of the action and as I lay in my bunk I felt exhilarated at the thought of the impending trip around the world. Larso was also off watch and asleep in the bunk opposite, while Graham was recovering in his bunk from a debilitating bout of seasickness. Outside the lads on deck were in full control and making the most of the fresh breeze. I could feel the boat really starting to stretch her legs. Happy days.

Suddenly and without warning, there was a loud cracking noise. Déjà vu, but this time the noise didn't originate from the bows. Instead it was right near my feet, at the end of my bunk at the forward end of the accommodation pod. "Bloody hell, Larso, did you hear that?" "Yeah mate," came the reply in his understated Aussie accent. Everyone heard it. The chilling sound ripping through the boat had the unmistakable acoustic signature of splintering carbon fibre. We shot out of our bunks, not bothering to get togged-up. Conditions outside were far more aggressive than the calm conditions when the bow fell off. Anything major would happen fast.

Running through the galley, we could hear Pete's voice. Once again he gave the order to rotate the rigs and slow us down. By now an all-too-familiar action, the lads were already easing out the mainsheets before he had finished saying what he wanted. Looking around on deck it didn't take long to spot the damage. There was a significant crack along the front of the accommodation pod where it joined the forward beam, right where my feet had been at the end of the bunk. Considering what had just happened, we came up with two possibilities. Either it was just the fairing on the front of the pod that had split as a result of the boat flexing across its structure. That would not be a major problem. Or it was an early sign that the boat was once again starting to come apart. That would be a major problem.

This time we did not have the shelter of a nearby port to run for. We were on the high seas, way out west in the middle of the Atlantic and well and truly on our own. Having completed a check of the remaining deck area, we carried on cautiously while Pete talked over the sat phone with the team back on dry land. At that point, other than the ugly crack in the front of the pod, there was no sign of damage, but this incident was enough to send us all into a state of high alert.

As we sheeted in the sails and urged *Team Philips* to gather some momentum I noticed that Pete was visibly burdened by it. He carried the ultimate weight of not just the project on his shoulders, but also of our lives. I felt my heart sink as I realised the implications of what had just happened. Having been in the position of decision-maker on many other yachts I knew it was now only a matter of time before Pete announced that our fight to get *Team Philips* to the start of The Race was over. That crack could not be ignored. One of the lads muttered, "No way is this boat going into the Southern Ocean now". In that moment we all knew that our fight to get to The Race was over.

The sea state had been building all day and was becoming quite confused. It was not the usual uniform set of waves that one might expect so far out on the deep ocean. With the weather on the decline, Lee called on the sat phone with an update, confirming that conditions were indeed going to deteriorate further.

As we approached the frontal boundary of the weather system, conditions were diabolical with the sea more like a boiling cauldron than anything I had seen before. To make matters worse, the situation on board had also taken a downward spiral. The accommodation pod was showing further signs of fatigue. Having been battered by the rough sea, multiple stress cracks were developing around the structure. Further cracks were evident on the left-hand aft beam where it connected to the hull. *Team Philips* was starting to fall apart and this time we were completely isolated.

This was a potentially life-threatening situation and Pete was faced with a difficult decision. Given the fragile state of the boat, should we turn around and run north-west, away from the worst of the weather and try to remain in the relatively calmer conditions until the low weakened or should we continue on our current course and try to ride out the worst of the weather, staying within reach of the shipping lanes in case we needed to call in the cavalry? We were too far offshore for any kind of airborne rescue so only possible support would come from a nearby ship. It was an impossible decision with so many variables. The lesser of two evils was to keep heading into the storm and so the decision was made.

Within a couple of hours, the barometer started to drop at an almost unprecedented rate, well beyond what the forecasts had suggested and it wasn't long before we were experiencing solid Storm

Looking towards the bow, a giant wave hits with destructive force during the early part of the storm.

Force Ten conditions. It was obvious that there was a great deal more to this storm than we had anticipated. It transpired that there was a secondary low forming very close to our position and with that secondary system there was a deepening storm of epic proportions. At this point we were already sailing under bare poles with no sails set, in anticipation of the big winds kicking in. When they arrived there would be very little time to react, so we wanted to be ready. The next move would be to deploy the drogue, a kind of parachute device that acts as a sea anchor. This would help to slow *Team Philips* down as she surfed on the waves at great speed, and would be our last line of defence should the storm reach the next level .

No one on board could believe what they were seeing on the weather charts. Lee had just called the boat and briefed Andy on the rapidly changing situation. He was very concerned about our proximity to the new secondary low and given the structural problems, Lee was understandably very worried. Pete gave us a quick debrief. We were about to be slapped by hurricane-force winds that would drive the already large sea state through the roof. It was just about the worst-case scenario. Pete suggested we all call home on the satellite phone and speak to our families while we still had the chance. Nobody actually said it, but we all realised that Pete had just told us to call home and tell our families we loved them just in case we didn't get through this. That was the moment when the magnitude of the situation hit me like a freight train. This could really be it. I suddenly felt an overwhelming

The view from the starboard aft hull: huge waves approaching during the storm.

sense of guilt. What had I done to my family, my poor parents? If we didn't get through this how would they get over it? God, what had I done?

Pete went below into the navigation station to contact MRCC Falmouth and update them on our plight. Outside the ocean was alive with energy. The seas were really starting to build and as *Team Philips* rode high up on the crests we were treated to the most amazing view. The sea was white with spray and spume. Despite the terrible sea state, *Team Philips* was riding the waves reasonably comfortably and we were all still going about our business on board despite the now-numerous cracks opening up around the accommodation pod.

Andy shouted out that it was my turn to call home. For the first time in my life I didn't know what to say. As I dialled the number I prayed that Dad would answer the phone. I just couldn't face it if my mum picked up the call. I knew she would be distraught. The call connected and it was Dad who answered. They both knew what was happening. Mark Orr at Goss Challenges had been in constant contact,

Severe cracks starting
to appear in the
accommodation pod.

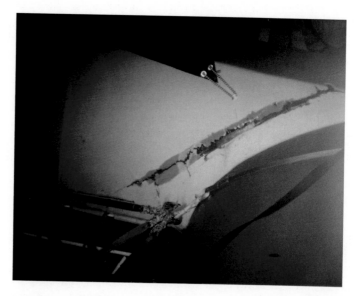

keeping them updated. They both knew the severity of the situation. Before I could speak, my father shouted out, "Don't give up son, keep fighting!" I felt terrible. I could accept my fate, whatever it was to be. I had known the risks from the beginning and had chosen to accept them. But my poor parents...

Our conversation was pretty brief. Dad could hear the noise in the background. He knew that was the sound of the boat breaking up around us. We were in a world of shit and my parents both knew it. All I could do was say I loved them and I would be back soon, although I wasn't convinced I would be. It was such an emotional phone call and I struggled to keep my composure.

Back on deck, the storm was approaching the next level. *Team Philips* was really taking off as she surfed down the now gigantic waves. As the wind speed started to touch Beaufort Force 11 we realised we needed to start slowing the boat down. Conditions on deck were becoming too dangerous for us to be out there without good reason and so the decision was made to deploy the drogue. We had already prepared it earlier so all that was left was to slowly lower it off the rear beam and into the sea whilst easing out the six hundred feet or so of rope attached to it. Paying out the twenty millimetre-thick rope was not as easy as it sounds and was quite a dangerous task. With all of it let out and every mooring line onboard also streaming off the rear beam in order to create as much friction on the surface of the water as possible we were managing to limit our speed to a steady and comfortable fifteen knots.

Because of the rapidly declining state of the accommodation pod, we discussed the implications if it were to come apart completely and break away from the main structure. It would be a nightmare, but could we still maintain control? Pete asked Phil if it would affect the steering. Phil had been heavily involved in the build of the boat and was best qualified to answer. Phil knew the answer was yes. If the pod came apart completely, it would take out not just the steering but also our ability to communicate with the outside world. The moment the pod separated from the boat *Team Philips* would become nothing more than a raft afloat on the ocean. We would have no ability to steer or control anything and if we didn't capsize before that, we would most certainly do so then.

With the boat still under some degree of control, Pete gave the order for everyone except Andy to take refuge in the starboard aft hull. Andy was needed in the pod to keep a continuous line of communication open with the outside world while Pete assumed control of the boat and steered. One of our biggest concerns was capsize. In that gigantic sea state there was a real danger of us flipping over as we surfed down one of the huge liquid mountains moving under us. If that happened, the end would probably be upon us. Pete and Andy would definitely come off worse, being immersed underwater. I couldn't see a route out for them. For the rest of us, survival in the short term would very much depend on how violent the impact was during the capsize. After that, who knew what would happen?

Grabbing some essential supplies, food and a little water, together with our emergency grab-bag we all took up shelter in the hull. The noise of rushing water down there combined with the haunting sound of the wind howling across the decks was incredible. It was dark in the hull and this only added to the tension. Everyone huddled together in the lower section by the engines, apart from Graham who was sitting on the top level just below the decks. He was still fighting the debitating effects of terrible seasickness and had to dig deep to summon the strength just to vacate the accommodation pod. I was worried about him and mentioned my concerns quietly to Larso, who sat next to me in the dark. We agreed to help him first if the worst happened.

Entombed in the dark dungeon-like hull we could tell that conditions were declining further. Outside, the storm was raging well above Hurricane Force 12 and was so bad that without a lifeline attached to the deck any of us would easily have been blown off the boat or washed away by the many breaking waves that swept across the decks. The noise in the hull was intense and getting louder as time passed. Pete and Andy kept in contact via our personal radios. It was clear that Pete was literally steering for our lives although the calmness in his voice would not have suggested it.

Our speed through the water had been steadily increasing hour by hour: eighteen, twenty, twenty-five and now regular speeds of thirty knots were being registered as we careered into oblivion. This was without doubt the ultimate rollercoaster ride and I remember thinking if it was my time, then this was an awesome way to go, smashing through the pearly gates on a 120-foot supercat. I was pretty scared, though.

There was nothing any of us could do but hold on and mentally prepare for the seemingly inevitable crash. We were all togged-up in our yellow Musto survival suits and physically as prepared as we could be. Discussing the situation again with Larso, we considered our options. Looking around the hull by torchlight it suddenly occurred to me that if we capsized our place of sanctuary would very likely fill with seawater. The rear beam that connected both hulls together was partly hollow. Large conduits run through it for cables and electrical wires leading through to the central pod. Upside down, the beams would fill with water and eventually would very probably flood the entire compartment. If we did go over, the only safe place would be the aft sections of the hull. This space was even more cramped, but it was the only option. The access hatch was a small round waterproof door situated about a foot off the floor. But if we were upside-down, the hatch would be well above our heads, about ten feet up in the air and we would have a desperate struggle to reach it. The question of how best to get through that hatch in the event of us flipping over weighed heavily on my mind.

I had decided to check on Graham again when Pete's voice came over the radios. He wanted a volunteer to go aft and check the steering linkages. Phil immediately answered the call and stepped up. He went aft as I climbed the ladder to the top level to check on Graham, who was coping remarkably well but still wanted to remain up there instead of climbing down into our black dungeon, despite my warnings that we needed to be prepared in case we went over.

God, it sounded wild outside. The wind noise was haunting. I just had to have a look and see it for myself. Looking though the clear Perspex hatch didn't reveal much, so I decided to open it and check that Pete was still at the helm. Timing my moment as best I could, I popped my head out above deck level. The environment was a mixture of grey and pure white. The seas were so enormous that I couldn't tell horizon from ocean. This was nature at her most pure and ferocious. I felt momentarily humbled. Very few people on Earth get to experience this sort of thing first hand and survive, yet here we were, immersed in an environment of pure energy. The wind speed was now a steady seventy-five knots.

I had just enough time to catch a glimpse of Pete, still at the helm. He was fine and definitely in the zone and totally focused. Looking aft, I could see a massive wave approaching. It lifted our stern high out of the water before we started to surf, an awesome sight. Even with the drogue and six hundred feet of rope hanging off the rear beam, we were still doing thirty knots. I was transfixed as Team Philips surfed down the waves in this boiling cauldron of energy. The wave-piercing bows were certainly having the test of their lives now. As they both disappeared into the bottom of the wave I caught a glimpse of the front beam bursting through white water and I dived back into the relative shelter of the hull, locking the hatch behind me. This was one kick-ass ride. Water covered the hatch where my head had been. The mast cockpits must have been engulfed completely by that one.

Back in the depths of the hull the lads were concerned by loud noises emanating from the rear beam. Could all the weight of the drogue hanging off the rear beam be contributing to that structure coming apart too? There was certainly nothing we could do if it was. It seemed our world was rapidly falling apart around us and we were helpless to do anything about it. Again the subject of worst-case scenario was broached. Richard suggested sending one of the life rafts to the back of the hull so that we could deploy it once we had capsized, but this was quickly dismissed as the raft would have been unlikely to fit through the small watertight hatches. It was a desperate situation, one of those moments when you look into the eyes of your teammates and really see the measure of the men around you. Despite the bleak outlook, everyone kept their composure.

The constant battering had taken its toll on the pod. Large holes were appearing around the connections to the aft beam and it was inevitable that the pod would come off. *Team Philips's* days were certainly numbered. The only question now was could she hold together long enough to weather the storm in one piece? Our situation had become desperate and the time had come to make a decision.

Pete declared we would abandon the boat at the first available opportunity and went into the accommodation pod to issue the Mayday distress call. We were now officially asking for outside help and it was MRCC Falmouth that put the wheels in motion, coordinating our rescue. Getting off the boat, even with a ship standing-by, would not be easy. In any case, there was no chance of any rescue until we had weathered the storm, we simply could not slow *Team Philips* down enough.

None of us wanted to leave our magnificent boat. She represented the hopes and dreams of so many people. But events had conspired against us. Here we were in the middle of the north Atlantic in December with major structural problems and hurricane-force winds. The decision had to be based on the lives and the safety of the crew. Deciding to abandon *Team Philips* was heart-wrenching but it was the right decision.

News came through that the emergency services were coordinating a rescue effort. They were diverting a ship to rescue us. We endured several more hours down in the hull before conditions improved enough for us to rejoin Pete and Andy on deck.

When we did venture out, the environment was still very hostile. With the wind down to just storm force we set about preparing for the rescue. Giant breaking waves surrounded us and I wondered just how we would make the transfer from our boat to the ship. How would they even find us in these conditions? *Team Philips*, despite the obvious structural problems, had put up a gallant fight. She'd ridden out the worst of the weather and kept us all alive so far.

Andy reappeared from the pod to give us an update. The worst of the weather had passed for now but there was still another fast-moving 50-knot severe gale closing in. There would be a short break in the weather before it arrived. We hoped that when that break in the weather occurred we would be in a position to make our move to get off the boat.

The wait for the ship seemed to last a lifetime. Then from the clouds above burst the sound of engines. It was a RAF Nimrod aircraft, dispatched from RAF Kinloss and was a most welcome sight. They switched on their landing lights as they buzzed overhead. Word came through that a freighter, the *Hoechst Express*, was en route to our position and would reach us shortly. The Nimrod was there to help coordinate our rendezvous and monitor the situation from the air.

Not long after the plane's arrival, we caught sight of the freighter. Despite it being a 53,000-tonne container ship, the sea state was so enormous it dwarfed both our vessels. Even when the *Hoechst Express* was just half a mile away we regularly lost sight of her navigation lights in the darkness as she disappeared into the troughs of waves.

In anticipation of rescue we had prepared for the final moments on board *Team Philips*. The drogue had been recovered and stowed on deck although the ropes and mooring lines were still trailing off the rear beam. Amazingly, we had also managed to start one of the engines in anticipation of manoeuvring into position once the ship came alongside.

With the ship drawing closer, Pete had established VHF radio contact with the German captain. All seven of us were huddled together in the confines of the cockpit area when the captain suggested over the radio that we should prepare the life rafts and deploy them before the ship made the transfer. We unanimously and simultaneously agreed that was not an option. Personally, if that was the only choice, I would rather have taken my chances onboard *Team Philips*. There was no way we could have deployed both rafts and safely got into them in those seas, especially when the only place for deployment on a multihull like ours was the rear hulls. We would have been swept off the deck before we had a chance to get into the bloody raft!

Pete was rather more tactful when he explained to the captain why this was not an option and it was agreed that a ship-to-ship rescue was the only way forward. The *Hoechst Express* would provide as much shelter as it could while drifting down onto our position. Once contact had been established, ropes would be thrown down to us so we could tie ourselves alongside. Then, rope ladders would be positioned for us to climb up to safety. It all sounded reasonable, given the circumstances.

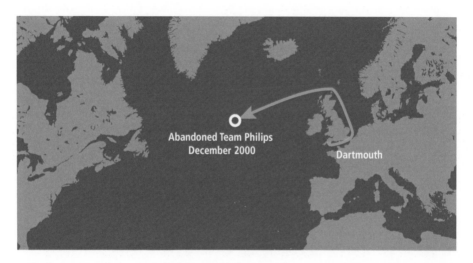

Abandoned Team Philips
December 2000

Dartmouth

The final voyage of 'Team Philips".

As the two vessels drew together we formulated our plan to evacuate. I would be third to climb the ladder, behind Phil and Graham, with the other lads following closely behind. Pete would be last off, he made that quite clear. With less than a boat-length separating us and the ship we realised the transfer was going to be messy. Huge rolling waves were passing underneath the ship. One minute we would be looking at the waterline of the freighter and the next we would be eyeballing the captain on the deck of the bridge. That must have been at least fifty feet above the ship's waterline.

The second we came alongside, all hell broke loose. The port bow was the first point of contact. As we came together, the bow took a heavy glancing blow before the mast cockpits took the full force of the collision. It was like crashing into land. Carbon fibre could be heard splintering as we bounced down the side of this huge ship. Pete did his best to bring us to a halt using the engine. The port mast was being smashed to pieces as it crashed into the steel hull. Because *Team Philips*'s masts were mounted on each hull the port-side mast took the full force of the impact every time we crashed up alongside. The noise was horrendous as the mast's aerofoil sections were pierced by the edges of the stacked containers on the ship's deck. 'If the mast knocks one of those containers off the side and it lands on us, it will all be over,' I thought.

The deckhands were leaning over the side of the ship and began throwing lines down to us. We ran up to the forward beam to attach them. Andy tied the first one onto a super strong padeye on the front beam that was used to lift *Team Philips* into the water when we launched her back in Totnes. Taking up the strain, the rope instantly pulled the stainless steel loop of the padeye out of its base on the deck like it was a plastic toy. There was no time to consider securing ourselves alongside. We knew getting off our boat would be difficult, but this was horrendous.

Down came the rope ladders, with commotion going on above and all around us. Pete made it quite clear that each of us must individually decide when to jump for the ladder. Phil made it without too much trouble and quickly scuttled up the ladder to the safety of the ship's intermediate deck. Next was Graham. I was worried about him because of the seasickness. It was clear he was pretty debilitated and dangerously low on energy. He knew the next five minutes would be the most dangerous and important of his life. Getting up that ladder meant seeing his family again and we all made sure he knew that.

With Andy crouched down by the forward daggerboard, Graham tied a rope around his waist, paused momentarily and then jumped for the ladder. I was in the central pod cockpit at the time standing alongside Pete and the other lads. Just as Graham grabbed the ladder, our boat rose up on a wave and lurched forward, bringing the portside mast perilously close to him. It was the only time I ever heard Pete sound anything other than super-cool. The tension was so evident you could have cut the air with a knife. Realising this was his only chance, Graham clawed his way up the ladder and disappeared over the deck edge rail.

Andy shouted that it was my turn. Pete looked at me and said something to the effect of 'only jump when you're ready, mate'. He was looking me straight in the eye. I knew what he was saying. If I got the timing wrong and jumped too early, the boat could crush me as she rode up on the waves. That's what had nearly happened to Graham.

Just before making first contact alongside the ship I had prepared my small rucksack with some personal belongings and put it on my back. Now, seeing the environment in front of me, I realised I would need every ounce of strength for the climb and was already quite restricted by my survival suit and lifejacket. It was time to get rid of anything that wasn't essential. I threw the rucksack back onto the cockpit floor and ran across the trampolines towards Andy.

Talking of essential items, just before Graham had climbed up the ladder I suddenly realised I hadn't grabbed my lucky teddy bear that Mum had given me years before. That bear goes everywhere with me and there was no way I was going to leave him. He had been in the pod, tied up in the galley area as one of our mascots. Despite the pod being in a pretty fragile state, I ran into the cabin and cut him free, then stuffed him into my survival suit before running back through the pod and into the cockpit.

By the time I reached Andy at the forward daggerboard I was seriously pumped up on adrenaline. A combination of the hostile environment and the approaching climb had me fully charged. I knew this was a one-shot deal for each of us, and now that it was my turn I was ready. Andy handed me the safety rope and I tied it around my waist. Looking at the rope ladder lying flush to the side of the ship's steel hull, I chose my moment and jumped for my life.

I remember slamming into the side of the ship and grabbing hold of the ladder, but after that I have no memory of the climb to safety. My next memories are of lying on my back on the deck of the ship looking at a group of faces I didn't recognise, before seeing Phil and Graham. Clambering to my feet I suddenly caught an awe-inspiring view of our beautiful yacht some 50 feet below being smashed to oblivion as Pete did his best to keep the giant super cat in position so the others could climb up to safety. That view will stay with me for the rest of my life.

When Andy finally flopped over the deck edge rail his presence meant that Pete was the last remaining team member on board *Team Philips*. Up on deck we grouped together to form a chain and threw down a security rope for Pete to tie himself to. For Pete, his job was far more difficult. There was no one to keep *Team Philips* in position while he made his preparations to jump. We watched our skipper leave the steering pedestal for the very last time, climb out of the cockpit and run across the trampolines to the forward daggerboard. As soon as he had secured the line around his body the six of us, aided by the deckhands, heaved on the line and within seconds Pete flew over the deck rail and landed in a heap on the floor. I don't think he even touched the ladder.

We were all safe and uninjured. We had just survived the most extraordinary experience and come through it unscathed. Unfortunately the same could not be said of our magnificent boat which by now had sustained a terminal battering. As we stood on the ship's deck we took a final glance at our battered warhorse. *Team Philips* slowly slipped down the side of the ship into the darkness. Andy, reaching out to touch the mast for the very last time muttered the words, "Bye bye, baby." We were all pretty much in tears. Everything that so many had worked so hard for over the past three years had just disappeared into the clutches of the darkness. That was the last time we saw *Team Philips* in one piece.

We were all professionals but it was Pete's exemplary seamanship and leadership qualities that had seen us through the most diabolical circumstances I have ever experienced at sea. It had been a near-death experience. It was Pete who had the last word on whether to abandon *Team Philips*. We would all have stayed on board to face our fate if he had made a different decision. Under impossible circumstances he made the right decision at the right time. Abandoning the boat meant the end of a long-coveted personal dream as well as the realisation of impending financial ruin. Our three-million-pound super catamaran was not insured. With all of this in his mind as he considered our options, Pete came through for the crew, putting our needs before any personal goals or likely penalties. We looked to him for leadership and received it. He will always have my utmost respect and gratitude for that.

We'd survived one major storm but another one of an altogether different kind was gathering force back on dry land. The media were going crazy. For them our plight was a major news story. News reports were being aired on most of the major networks. It soon became clear our terrible ordeal would be subjected to the full scrutiny of both the media and public. In all of the commotion during the past couple of days we had been so focused on staying alive that we had not given any thought to the media fall-out. Now, having lost our giant catamaran and escaped with our lives by the thinnest of margins, our project was once again headline news, just for all the wrong reasons.

The captain and crew of the *Hoechst Express* were the perfect hosts and went out of their way to make us comfortable. From their point of view, we were men of the sea just like them. We'd lost our boat and nearly our lives and they understood perhaps more than most the meaning of what had just happened. The *Hoechst Express* had responded to our calls for help and skilfully snatched us from certain doom. They had acted on an often-accepted yet rarely spoken rule of responding to the calls of those in peril on the high seas. They had diverted a significant distance from their original schedule, something that would undoubtedly have cost the shipping line time and money. Now that we were all safe on board, the captain gave the order for the huge ship to resume her original course for Halifax, Nova Scotia.

I remember lying on the bunk in one of the cabins on the second night. We were approaching the Grand Banks of Newfoundland. The weather was still atrocious and blowing close to force ten. The motion on board was quite alarming, with the ship rolling from side to side and pitching up at high angles. For the second time in less than forty-eight hours, I had an uneasy feeling about the surrounding environment and wondered if we were entirely safe. The rolling action was uncomfortable, not like on a small yacht but much slower, a long sweeping rolling from one side to the other. It was rather like the motion on a cross channel ferry in rough weather, only much worse. I wondered whether it was possible for one of these ships to roll over completely. Eventually, feeling a little nauseous, I decided to venture up to the bridge to see if everything was OK. Graham was up there too, presumably also thinking the same thing while intently staring through the plate glass windows into the night. We stayed there until morning, enjoying some banter with the officers on watch.

It took four days for the *Hoechst Express* to reach Halifax. Pete had been in regular contact with the team back at Totnes although the media had been told we were mostly out of reach for the duration of the passage. Pete and the PR team at Goss Challenges had been busy formulating a plan of how best to handle the inevitable media scrum once we landed. Team HQ had warned us there would be a large contingent awaiting our arrival, but their warnings did nothing to prepare us for the turmoil that ensued.

Halifax was shrouded in darkness as we steamed up the channel leading into the harbour. We had made it. Before leaving the ship and saying our goodbyes there was the usual customs and immigration formalities to deal with then we met up with some friendly faces for an initial private debrief. Representatives of our sponsors had travelled out to Nova Scotia to help coordinate the press conference. The plan was to take a taxi to a nearby hotel. The world's media were there eagerly awaiting our arrival. They had questions that demanded answers and people were keen to hear our story.

We had just enough time to change into some clean clothes before jumping into the taxi for the short ride to the hotel. As we pulled up outside we could see a large rabble of reporters through the blacked-out windows of our car. They were gathering on the hotel steps, virtually fighting each other for the best position, cameras at the ready, pushing and shoving each other out of the way. It was quite incredible. Pete was in the front seat and turning around to face us he warned again to think before we said anything to anyone. Before leaving the port authority we had been briefed about this moment. Once we got out of the taxi we were not to stop walking, just follow Pete who in turn was following Vanessa, a representative from British Telecom, one of our sponsors. She would lead the way into the conference room.

As the car door opened, we were greeted by a barrage of flashing cameras. The ground was covered in thick snow. I was surprised by how aggressive the mood was, not particularly towards us but more amongst the press themselves. The media swarming around the hotel steps were all fighting for the prefect shot and shouting questions randomly in the hope we would stop walking and start talking. One guy holding a big television camera on his shoulder fell over on his backside, presumably losing his footing on the icy stairs. He was still holding the camera when he hit the deck. 'Good on him,' I thought.

As we walked into the room I could tell that our arrival in Halifax was a big deal. There were dozens of television cameras all positioned around a small table with seven chairs at the far end of the room. Literally hundreds of electrical wires and cables were strewn across the floor connected to a mind-boggling array of technical equipment. It was clear these people had been awaiting our arrival for some time.

Pete took a deep breath, sat down and started proceedings. Talking directly to the audience he explained how the press conference would run. He would give an account of the facts, then there would be an opportunity for five minutes of questions and that was it. I was surprised by his unusually stern approach but I had to admire him. A lot of these people were out for the story of the century. Someone was going to take charge and he wasn't going to allow it to be the media. Pete was in no mood to waste time on pleasantries; he was polite, but to the point. Everyone knew where they stood.

Looking around the room, I caught a glimpse of our old teammate

Mike Calvin. We had been told that Mike would be there but I hadn't seen him until now. Mike was standing in the corner of the room, leaning against the wall, patiently waiting to hear our story. I gave him a smile and he nodded his head in recognition. Despite looking pleased and relieved to see us I could tell he felt slightly uncomfortable being there in his official capacity as journalist rather than shipmate. Mike's presence definitely didn't sit entirely comfortably with Pete. Although both of them managed a civilised conversation afterwards you could tell the emotion of Mike's resignation weeks earlier still ran high for Pete.

With the cameras rolling, the whole room fell silent as Pete gave an emotional account of the events of the past two weeks. For those that know him we could tell reliving the loss of *Team Philips* was difficult, but he never faltered and executed the account with admirable confidence and resolve. Accepting defeat in front of the eyes of the world was an incredibly difficult thing for all of us, but none more so than for Pete.

The emotion in the room was undeniable. Pete acknowledged that as a mariner, any decision at sea is based on survival and the safety of the crew. He explained how the severe damage to the accommodation pod had been the main factor in forcing a decision to abandon *Team Philips* and with it our dreams.

The atmosphere was intense as questions from journalists flew across the room: would the sponsors stay with us, what did the future hold, was there any possibility of salvaging the giant catamaran? That last question had been in all of our minds and was yet to be publicly addressed. Behind the scenes, a last desperate attempt to locate and salvage the boat was being considered. *Team Philips* at that time was still emitting a signal from the emergency beacon, which was being tracked by satellite.

We all had our chance to answer the torrent of questions but I felt relieved when it was time to get up and leave the room. It was all over fairly quickly but throughout the conference all I could think about was calling Mum and Dad to tell them I was OK. We hadn't spoken since that horrible phone call from the boat when we all thought my days were numbered. They knew I was safe but I wanted to hear their voices and reassure them. Pete, still retaining his sense of humour as we walked out of the room, pulled a toothbrush and tube of toothpaste out of his jacket pocket. He showed it to a television camera and smiled. Even in defeat, he managed to remain upbeat though I'm pretty sure that inside he was devastated, as we all were.

Our stay in Halifax was brief. The press remained for the duration and constantly updated the various news channels and newspapers, following the story. While most of the press respected our requests for a little space, some of them relentlessly tried to corner us for further comment and a more personal view of the saga. They were only doing their job, but the intrusive hassling didn't do much for our morale.

A couple of days after our arrival we flew home to the UK. Tired and subdued, we landed at Heathrow airport for an emotional reunion with our families and yet another round of questions from the media. A final photo-call signified the end of our commitments, for that day at least. With just a few days remaining before Christmas we all took the opportunity to enjoy some family time and reflect on the enormity of what had just happened. Meanwhile, out on the ocean, *Team Philips* remained adrift nearly eight hundred miles to the west of Ireland.

Despite the disaster, one issue we were able to finally address was the speculation as to whether the design concept of *Team Philips* had actually worked. There had always been plenty of scepticism and while on the face of it the boat seemed to have failed, what I witnessed suggests otherwise. During the press conference, Pete said that as a result of those eight days at sea we were all left with no doubt that she was fantastic. Having seen her perform in the harshest of conditions, I can certainly support that statement.

The wave-piercing hulls and twin rotating masts were indeed a revelation and certainly worked. It is important to understand that *Team Philips* was a prototype, a vision of what the future of performance sailboat design might look like. Unlike a plane or a car, we didn't have dozens of prototypes tested to destruction before the designers completed the finished article. *Team Philips* in one respect was no different to any other sailboat in that she was expected to be perfect from day one. But when pushing the boundaries of technology and innovation to that degree and having made such a radical departure from accepted design thinking, it was always going to be unrealistic to expect her to perform straight out of the box. That said, she shouldn't have experienced the catastrophic structural failures that contributed to her demise.

As a result, *Team Philips* was seen as a bit of a maverick. Some might call her a wacky design while others would suggest more of an outright flop, given the all the problems we encountered. But the truth is far removed from that.

What Pete Goss set out to do was create a vessel a generation ahead of her time, a radical departure from existing design philosophy. The fundamental idea was to design a 120-foot wave-piercing catamaran that could reach speeds of up to forty knots. *Team Philips* achieved that and did what she was designed to do. She was an absolute credit to her designers, especially Adrian Thompson who unfairly took a big chunk of the public blame when things started to go wrong.

The very slender bows certainly minimised the deceleration effects of bursting into waves and the twin rotating wing masts worked with a high degree of efficiency. She really had huge performance potential and at the time of her loss we had barely scratched the surface.

However, due to the teething problems with the hulls and the subsequent rebuilding of the boat she ended up much heavier than had been intended. That was an unfortunate by-product of radical surgery after her initial design and construction. Had she made it to the start of The Race and been structurally sound, I have no doubt she would have put in a credible performance. But could she have won? That's a very difficult question to answer.

The French-designed Giles Ollier catamarans were slightly smaller but significantly lighter than *Team Philips* and were better suited to the varied conditions you're likely to encounter on a round-the-world race. They would have had the advantage in light winds. After all, such a race is often won or lost in the north and south Atlantic Oceans where wind conditions are on average much lighter than you might think. *Team Philips* would surely have been dominant in rough and windy conditions, where her sheer size and power would have allowed us to push her harder than the more conventional designs. The frustrating thing is that we will never know.

Sometimes I think about all that happened and wonder what might have been had Pete chosen a more conventional design from the outset and taken the fight to the opposition on equal terms. Would Goss Challenges still be in business today? Given the team behind us, their expertise and commitment to our cause, we would most likely have successfully completed The Race and still captured the heart of our nation in the process. At that time, the new breed of Giant Class multihull yachts being constructed around the world were an inspiration to anyone who came into contact with them. I think the British public would have connected with even the most conventional of designs and still given us their full support.

With hindsight I think that we really didn't need such a radical design to secure success in The Race. But who knows? Decisions are always easier with the benefit of hindsight. In Pete's words, 'We dared to dream'.

THE TRANSAT JACQUES VABRE

The loss of *Team Philips* would bring devastating financial consequences for Pete and his company Goss Challenges, although initially everything continued as normal at the factory in Totnes. The various arms of Pete's subsidiary companies were still active in their respective roles. The composite facility that originally constructed the super catamaran had secured a contract to build a 77-foot cruising yacht, a significant achievement, and that project was well underway.

During the Christmas break both Larso and I had been contacted by another syndicate that was due to compete in The Race. They were already in Barcelona and were looking for two crew members to join their campaign. With less than a week to go before the 31 December start date, we found ourselves flying out to Barcelona with a new opportunity and revived hope of competing in this once-in-a-lifetime event.

Larso arrived a day before me and warned me that the state of preparation was not at the same level as we had enjoyed with Goss Challenges. The atmosphere in the race village was second to none, however. Several of the world's largest racing multihulls were secured to the dockside. Tens of thousands of people were milling around the race village, awestruck by the sheer size and presence of these giants. I was ecstatic to be there but both Larso and I agreed there was a definite feeling that something was missing. It would certainly have been some sight to have had *Team Philips* tied up to that dock. Despite the sad lack of our special boat, this was one awesome extravaganza.

Some of the great names in ocean racing were present and it was here, whilst waiting in a lift to go to the press office, that I met the late billionaire adventurer Steve Fossett for the first time. His boat Play-station was registered to compete and was one of the favourites. I couldn't know at the time that four years later I would be at the helm of his boat, racing through the desolate Southern Ocean.

Larso and I met up later that day. As we sat on the dockside soaking up the atmosphere, we discussed our options and spared a thought for the rest of the lads from the *Team Philips* crew who were not here to experience the event. On the face of it, this was the opportunity both of us had always wanted. This was what we lived for, a chance to race around the world. But scratch the surface, and beneath it we both felt that the boat which was now supposed to take us on this high-stakes adventure was ill-prepared for the rigours of a lap of the planet and certainly not ready for the Southern Ocean. We had both spoken to the crew and met the whole team. Understandably, we were now being pressed for a decision.

Larso had also been holding out for a possible place on another yacht but had seen that possibility dissolve away to nothing. I could see he was seriously considering taking up this one while it was still available. He said he would go if I would.

It was a surprisingly difficult decision. This project had gained its financial backing very late in the day and as a result was struggling to achieve any real state of preparation. The amount of freeze-dried food required to keep twelve guys fuelled during a round-the-world race is significant and theirs lay in the middle of the dockside team tent, seemingly untouched. Piled up high, it looked as if it had been delivered by a JCB and just dumped there. It needed to be sorted into day ration packs, labelled and packed aboard. It was little things like this that worried me the most. If attention to detail was lacking here, I wondered what other more significant problems were waiting to surface. We had had the food organised and signed off a month ago with the *Team Philips* project. The crew was also a concern. Despite being mostly yachtsmen with good experience, no one had spent significant time together working as a team and only a couple of the guys had any real sailing time aboard this particular yacht.

Even the mandatory qualification passage required to gain entry into the event had not yet been completed. The boats were now not allowed to leave the confines of the harbour until race day, but the team had somehow secured an eleventh-hour reprieve from the race committee. They would be allowed to start the race but would then have to immediately complete a 300-mile, non-stop passage then return to the starting area off the Barcelona shoreline to re-cross the start line. It was a bizarre arrangement, no doubt born out of the race organiser's keenness to see as many of these goliaths compete as possible whilst still satisfying their legal requirements and responsibilities.

This was not just some jolly across the English Channel or even a transatlantic race. This was a marathon, an example of the ultimate in sporting events. It was a race around the world for the fastest and most powerful sail-powered racing machines to ever navigate the oceans.

Given the apparent state of the last-minute preparations I voiced my concerns to Larso, who was also wrestling heart against head to make a decision. We both wanted a round-the-world race so much. It represents the absolute pinnacle of achievement in our area of the sport. The Southern Ocean and Cape Horn are our Everest and had been the stuff of legend for both of us since we were children. Despite growing up on different sides of the planet, we both held the same ambition. Now here we were with the opportunity just waiting to be seized.

Sometimes in life people reach a crossroads where they are presented with a choice. It could be in business or in private life, an opportunity for adventure, an invitation to risk all and take the gamble in pursuit of achieving our dreams. Some of us go for it and some of us let the chance pass by. For Larso, I think this was his crossroads. He had made the long trip from Australia the year before on a hope and a prayer that he might become involved with the sailing elite and take part in this very race, a celebration of a new millennium. He truly had the skill and talent.

Having been through the *Team Philips* saga together we both knew the implications of making a rash decision. For me, despite feeling the pull of the ocean on an almost uncontrollable scale, I had something else to turn to. For months we had been in discussions with a potential sponsor who was interested in supporting a project to build a state-of-the-art Open 60 yacht for the next solo around-the-world race, the Vendée Globe. Goss Challenges was to take on the management of the project with me at the helm of the new boat. It was conceivable that I could compete in The Race and then come back to start on the new campaign but I just didn't feel comfortable setting sail in such a state of unprepared chaos and so with a heavy heart I declined the offer and returned to the UK to start on the new project. For Larso however, the gamble was worth the risk. He signed up and assumed his new role on board. They got around the course and he achieved his goal, but not without their fair share of drama.

The short time I had been away was enough for me to accept that *Team Philips* had been lost at sea. However, shortly into the new year a small glimmer of hope emerged as the emergency beacon I had left behind in one of the aft winch cockpits started to transmit a position. Back from the dead, *Team Philips* it seemed had not given up her own fight for survival. The beacon, despite transmitting a position, did not indicate her overall condition although the activation of the device did allow us to draw some important conclusions.

This type of beacon could only be activated by either manually flicking the switch or by being immersed in water for a sustained period. The only way for this beacon to have activated was if the boat had capsized and it was in the water, attached to the boat. The beacon had a finite battery life and so a recovery plan was quickly set in motion. The sponsors, despite having no real option other than to pull out of the project once the boat had been lost, had previously agreed in principle to support a salvage effort, should the boat be found in one piece. With that in mind Pete, Andy and several key sponsors chartered a plane and went in search of *Team Philips*.

Their arrival back at the Totnes factory the following day brought with it the realisation that the project truly had reached its natural conclusion. They had not found the boat, nor any indication of wreckage, despite undertaking a significant search of the area where the beacon had been transmitting. That was it. There would be no further attempts at locating the boat. A line had been drawn in the sand. But I often wonder 'what if..?' What if they had found the boat but she had been in such a bad state that she was beyond salvage? The sponsors could have taken the view it was a better option to allow the ocean to swallow her up for good. Either way, we shall never know. The night we looked down at our dream machine from the decks of the *Hoechst Express*, *Team Philips*' fate was sealed. In our hearts, I think we all knew that then.

With no future for the race crew, we all went our separate ways. Paul would soon be entering the Roaring Forties on his adrenaline-fuelled adventure around the planet. Phil went back to boat building, Graham initially returned to his sailmaking business but would soon decide that life was too short and take up a new career as a long-distance truck driver, something he had always wanted to experience. Richard went back to his life in Wales while Andy was quickly head-hunted by the Volvo Ocean Race management team.

My future seemed certain under the guidance of Goss Challenges. My project to build a new 60-foot yacht for the next Vendée Globe would go ahead. The project would have an environmental aspect with a big emphasis on sustainability and recycling. The boat itself would be made from a high percentage of recycled materials. I was tasked with researching opportunities to incorporate recycled products into the build of the new yacht. Pete even had me looking into the possibility of using recycled material such as compact discs as part of the non-slip finish on the deck. It was an exciting project and quickly became my sole focus.

Walking into the office one cold April morning, I could tell something bad had happened. The sombre mood was infectious. Pete walked into the office and rounded us all up to break some shocking news. We knew the company had been struggling with significant debts since the loss of *Team Philips*. Everyone had been working tirelessly to drag the company out of the quicksand but despite making significant headway, everyone's efforts had been in vain. The loss of the uninsured super catamaran and subsequent withdrawal of financial support by the sponsors had severely damaged the company's financial foundations. In the end, the factory landlord who owned the building in Totnes called in the debt and that was that. On top of the implications for Pete and everyone employed at the factory, any hopes of our new project coming of age went up in smoke the minute the liquidators walked through the front door.

With the dust barely settled, out of the ashes came an opportunity. Goss Challenges was in liquidation and the company assets were being sold off. One of those assets was Aqua Quorum, the Open 50 yacht that Pete had famously sailed in the Vendée Globe. Pete was keen to see me purchase the boat, suggesting that given the circumstances, it would be an ideal opportunity for me to further my career. Furthermore, the boat would be sold off by the liquidators at well below her true value. The boat had corporate hospitality bookings for that summer and there was a chance I could pick up that business too if I secured the boat. It was a good opportunity. The only problem was that I wasn't the only one who had eyes for her.

I really liked the idea and set about raising the money to secure the boat. Time was tight and I needed to act quickly if I were to be successful. In the short term, my only real avenue was to borrow the money from my family, who recognised there was a potential business opportunity and had offered to loan me the funds. The following two weeks were intense, not knowing if we had secured the boat or not. Aqua Quorum represented both a business and my best route into either the Vendée Globe or the Around Alone Race, both solo around-the-world races.

Eventually the call came through with the news that the boat was ours, but there was little time for celebration. Aqua Quorum, soon to be renamed *One Dream One Mission* on account of my aspirations to sail around the world, was in France in La Trinité-sur-Mer. She had been out on charter competing in the Vendée Globe and had not long returned. The charter period had been and gone but she was still in the care of the charterer who had also wanted to purchase her. I had to go down there, reclaim the boat and sail her home without delay. This meant rounding up a crew, hiring a big van and taking the ferry over to France before driving down to La Trinité.

When we eventually arrived we couldn't get on board. She was secured to a mooring alongside several other similar yachts just off the harbour wall. Having tried without success to contact the charterer, we eventually managed to paddle out to the boat in our inflatable dinghy. There was much to organise if we were to be ready for our scheduled departure the following evening.

I had not long fired-up the diesel engine with the intention of charging the batteries when a guy started shouting loudly in French from the quayside. He was a well known French yachtsman and I recognised him straightaway. He was the one who had chartered the boat. I replied in English, trying to explain I was the new owner and had come to collect the boat. The man's French turned into broken English and he accused me of being a thief and stealing the boat. He was obviously not happy. Doing my best to calm him down, I explained we had just purchased the boat and that I used to work with Pete Goss. My efforts however were in vain. Looking back, the fact that I had the engine running probably only added fuel to the fire. We must have looked as if we were about to leave the harbour.

It turned out that the liquidators had not informed the charterer that the boat had been sold, despite agreeing they would do so. He was convinced we were trying to steal the boat and ran off down the quay, claiming to have called the police. It was clear something was about to happen. I asked one of the lads to go ashore to keep out of the way and just observe whatever happened next. Being in a foreign country and taking charge of a boat from someone who knew nothing of our arrival or ownership looked like causing trouble and I wanted one of us ashore so they could call home and raise the alarm if necessary.

Not long after, the French guy returned, this time in a dinghy with four French police officers. They were pretty intimidating with their side-arms clipped to their belts. The guy had convinced them that we were thieves and should be arrested. The situation was delicate but the gendarmes were calm enough to allow me to explain my side of the story. I said while I understood etiquette required us to inform the charterer of our intentions, we hadn't been able to get hold of him. I was quite firm that I was the new legal owner and that she was a British-registered vessel. They asked for paperwork to prove it so with my mobile phone set to speaker I called my father and asked him to contact the liquidators and get them to send a copy of the bill of sale to the local police station.

Things calmed down when an urgent fax arrived. The police were satisfied, and left me and the lads to iron out our differences with the French sailor. It turned out that he was mostly concerned about a couple of sails on board which he apparently owned. In an attempt to defuse the situation further, I persuaded him that the sails were no use to him now and that I would be willing to purchase them if the price was right. We were soon shaking hands and exchanging smiles. Despite the shaky start everything was now under control.

The following evening, with a high tide under our keel we slipped our lines and ventured from the marina under a blanket of stars. It was a beautiful night and the lads on board were all keen to experience the thrill of sailing such a thoroughbred of the seas. The sense of responsibility for both boat and crew was enough to keep me focused as we hoisted the sails and set a course for home waters.

The plan for the upcoming season revolved around a mixture of competitive racing and bill-paying corporate hospitality. The grand finale would be in November, the four thousand-mile Transat Jacques Vabre ocean race from Le Havre to Salvador in Brazil. At the time the TJV was the biggest two-handed race in the world and certainly one of the most fiercely contested. It is also one of the most respected events on the ocean racing calendar. We would be up against some serious competition and would need the whole of the approaching summer to prepare for the gruelling challenge. Joining me in this adventure would be my old friend David Barden, who was very keen to be involved. Despite having a full-time job working as a yacht rigger, he was certain he could negotiate the time off work and join in the adventure.

Our bill-paying corporate programme was starting to take shape. Shane Dickson, a friend and former colleague from Goss Challenges, had expressed an interest in joining my new business venture. Shane had been the company secretary at Goss Challenges and originally Pete's bank manager back in the days before the building of Aqua Quorum. Shane had demonstrated incredible kindness and faith in me by fronting up the cash to pay the VAT liability on the boat when I purchased it from the liquidator. Shane was keen to join forces, and soon started on the tricky task of retaining the corporate hospitality bookings that had originally been taken though Pete's company. In just a few weeks, a phoenix had risen from the ashes. I had a new boat, a new business venture and a clear path into the big time. Things were looking great.

The first event of the season was a two-handed race from Brixham on the south Devon coast across the Bay of Biscay to Santander in northern Spain. It provided the perfect training platform for the TJV and I knew the course, having competed in the race a few years earlier. With the entry fee paid, our place in the event was assured but my co-skipper's presence was not. Dave could not make the start, blaming it on problems with getting time off work. I asked whether he would actually be able to honour his commitment for the big event but he assured me he had everything under control.

With that in mind I rounded up Chris, another friend from my days sailing on the Mini circuit, and together we were ready to take on the fleet. The race was a great success. Despite being the last boat to sail out of the bay, we soon took the lead and finished the race in first place, a whole twenty-four hours ahead of the next competitor and smashing the course record in the process. It was a great result.

The trip across the Bay of Biscay had been a fast, adrenaline-fuelled ride. *One Dream One Mission* had shown us a great adventure, or so I thought. As we sat on the veranda at the Real Club Nautico in Santander sipping cold drinks in the evening sun, my co-skipper told me that the trip that I thought had been such an exciting blast had for him been a pretty scary ordeal. Conditions had been a little rough, but I had no idea he had been so terrified. The delivery back to the UK was just not going to be an option for him and he told me he would be flying home instead. We had a good laugh about it and I certainly didn't mind sailing the boat back to the UK on my own, indeed I was looking forward to it. The trip home would be my first opportunity to sail the boat alone. I remember the feelings of freedom and anticipation as I sailed out of the harbour, the bow pointing north towards England. I remember thinking life was good.

I hardly had time to catch my breath once I arrived back into British waters. Our corporate hospitality programme was upon us and I had to get the boat up to Southampton for our first round of day sailing trips. The busy corporate schedule kept my focus during the day while my nights were spent writing letters to companies in the perpetual search for sponsorship for the approaching race to Brazil. It was around this time that I was introduced to the owner of a sports management and marketing company based in London.

Judith had an apparently successful agency and expressed an interest in the project. She had learned of my plans to compete in this exciting sporting event and knew I was looking for a financial sponsor. Ever the savvy businesswoman, Judith saw an opportunity and suggested she could find us the money and would be willing to act on my behalf as my manager. Furthermore, she was so confident that she could find a suitable sponsor she would bankroll the operation until a suitable commercial partner was found. She would then take her percentage and everyone was a winner.

It was a sweet deal and an opportunity I quickly agreed to, although at the time I wondered whether Judith's company was the success it appeared to be. Judith wanted a formal contract in place, so she drew up a document which I passed on to a colleague I had met earlier that year. Malcolm Dickinson is now the managing partner at a successful law firm in Exeter. He had booked a corporate event on board the boat for later that year and had expressed an interest in supporting the project by helping with any contractual work, should the need arise. Malcolm is a keen sailor and was well aware of my ambitions. He had also been an avid follower of the *Team Philips* project. Should I ever need the skills of a legal team, he was willing to help. It was an amazingly kind gesture, and little did I know that it would lead to the start of a great friendship.

One Dream One Mission sailing along Southampton Water.

The Michelmores legal team scrutinised the contract and briefed me on exactly what I was signing up for. The contract was given the all-clear and Judith came down to Exeter to close the deal. With an open mind and an agreed plan I signed up and looked forward to the future. With the backing of a management company I soon found myself being shuffled around the city of London and being introduced to all manner of people in the search for the ever-elusive hard cash. Judith seemed to be well-connected, or at least skilled at opening doors. At one stage she even scored me a cheeky job with a modelling agency, an opportunity that I was less than convinced was my thing. But that photo shoot led to an invitation to work on a television commercial with boxing legend Frank Bruno. My friends and family all found it highly amusing when the commercial was eventually aired on national television.

It was a bizarre yet exciting time but, apart from enjoying the opportunity to meet some real characters, I started to wonder just what this new-found lifestyle was actually doing for my sailing career. Judith was confident that this was the right path toward securing our much-needed funding and remained adamant that our moving and shaking would get us in front of the right kind of decision makers, a sentiment I didn't entirely share. By the middle of the summer, despite enjoying the high life, the parties and boardroom meetings in the heart of the city, we had still not secured that all-important sponsorship deal. That's not to say we didn't have any leads. Judith's ability to hype-up the project had been sufficient to whet the appetites of several potential candidates but as yet no one had taken the essential leap of faith and signed on the dotted line.

The corporate hospitality calendar was by now in full swing. Cowes Week, arguably the UK's premier sailing regatta, was just around the corner. *One Dream One Mission* was fully booked for the whole week. There was huge interest in this year's event, fuelled in part by the cele-brations of the America's Cup Jubilee, so we had chartered a second fifty-foot racing yacht. Business was good. There was no shortage of people wanting to sample the fizz-bang champagne atmosphere that Cowes Week provides. After all, it's the ultimate corporate sailing experience. The busy daily schedule proved to be exhausting but by the end of the week we knew we had enough funds in the kitty to secure not only our entry into the TJV should Judith not come through, but also and more importantly, to pay the bills.

Meanwhile back in the city, Judith was busy exploring various avenues of opportunity in the hope of nailing us a commercial partner. As much as I liked Judith, I was starting to get the feeling that her initial desire for the campaign was beginning to dwindle. Certainly the promises of a clear line of funding leading up to the start of the TJV were starting to dry up. The monthly salary we had initially agreed on was now struggling to find its way into my bank account. I could tell Judith had more on her mind than just our project. People's facial expressions often paint a much clearer picture of the facts than what is conveyed through speech. I figured she had problems, I just wasn't sure what kind. I guessed it was money.

Ploughing on, we eventually received a call from a communications company we had previously pitched the project to. They were very keen and wanted to run with the project for the TJV leading into real commitment for the solo round-the-world race. It was just the kind of news we had been looking for. At the time I was sailing around Start Point off the South Devon coast, enjoying a day of corporate sailing with the Michelmores legal team. Malcolm was on board and he grinned as I looked across the cockpit from the aft deck, giving him the thumbs-up. What a result.

That was early September 2001. A week later, the events of 9/11 changed everything. Just days after the twin towers came down, our miracle sponsor pulled out of the deal. They had had business interests in the World Trade Centre.

In the end, our funding for the Transat Jacques Vabre did come through but it was through a private donation from an individual I had met through our hospitality programme rather than any big sponsorship deal. This person, who wished to remain anonymous, was a keen sailor who just wanted to see the project succeed. He knew of my aspiration to sail the boat around the world and was inspired by our dreams. The TJV was the natural stepping-stone to achieving that goal and he wanted to help.

The summer was drawing to an end. It was time to undertake the three hundred-mile qualification passage necessary to gain entry into the TJV. *One Dream One Mission* was back on her mooring in Plymouth and I was busy putting the final kit aboard in preparation for our departure to sea. Dave and I had planned the qualifier months before and he was due to arrive at any minute for the off. It was a Friday evening and soon we would be blasting out one hundred and fifty miles into the Western Approaches before turning around and heading back to Plymouth to complete the trip.

I had everything ready. All the kit was stowed below, food and water prepped, spare clothes packed and the diesel running to charge the batteries. Even the red and green navigation lights were on, illuminating the dockside ready for imminent departure into the night. With the stereo blasting out some inspiring Rolling Stones, I felt on top of the world and excited to be going to sea with my best mate. The upcoming race was a great opportunity to show the world what we could achieve and I felt confident we would do well. With just four weeks to go before the start of the race the qualifier represented the final step before the big one.

Nine o'clock came and went. Minutes turned into an hour before Dave finally arrived. I had the feeling something was up the instant I caught a glimpse of him walking along the pontoon. Head down, seemingly walking with a heavy heart. He looked devastated. We looked at each other, waiting for one of us to say something. Struggling to look me in the eye and almost unable to speak the words, Dave delivered a sledgehammer blow that literally knocked the wind out of my sails. He couldn't come on the race, his boss wouldn't give him the time off work.

I was stunned. Talk about last-minute issues! We had everything prepared. Apparently Dave had known for weeks about his boss's reluctance to grant him the time away from work and had been struggling with both making a decision and with breaking the news to me. Dave's mum was in tears as we stood on the dockside, the three of us staring at each other. I couldn't believe what I was hearing but it was clear no amount of persuasion was going to change the situation. Dave, his mum and his boss had made the decision and that was that.

I was livid. We had been planning this race all year. We had talked about his work commitments and Dave had been convincing about his dedication. This was no ordinary race, not some local regatta that you could take part in some other time. This was the Transat Jacques Vabre and an opportunity to compete in one of the all-time great events. I suggested he chuck the job and pick up the gauntlet. Dave couldn't do it and we parted company that night less than the best of friends.

I felt betrayed and angry. Not so much angry with Dave for dropping me in it, but angry that he couldn't see the real opportunity in front of him. And his boss had known about the race for some time and was well aware we had been preparing for the event all summer. Leaning on Dave in that way just wasn't fair.

Current affairs had suddenly thrown me into a world of turbulence. With no co-skipper the campaign was left floating in limbo. Thoroughly pissed-off, I decided to lock the boat down for the night and headed home to sleep on it. Things always look better after a decent night's sleep. There was a chance I could contact the race committee and ask for permission to change my co-skipper. It was pretty late in the day for that, but entirely probable that they would grant dispensation, given the situation. However, the question of who should be Dave's replacement was a difficult one.

The only real option was my friend Larso from *Team Philips* days but at this late stage he would probably already be committed to another project. Larso was the obvious choice if the project was to have the best chance of race success, so I made the call. Tracking him down was not that easy but eventually, after a little answerphone ping-pong, I managed to make contact. His reaction was everything I could have hoped for. He was back in Australia but just said he'd be on a plane the next morning and with me in forty-eight hours. It was great news. With the two of us together we had the best chance of a good result. Above all else, we were still great mates and I knew it would be a real adventure.

Forty-eight hours later, a slightly jetlagged Larso rocked up to the boat, bags packed, ready and willing. Many people in life tell a good tale but fewer are actually up for the moment. Larso is one of those solid gold characters that make life happen. We soon secured dispensation from the race committee for the change of co-skipper and with that headache out of the way, the show was well and truly back on the road. We polished off the qualifier the following weekend and then spent the remaining few weeks preparing the boat. The official photo shoot for the race crews in Paris signified that the start of the epic race was just around the corner. With the two of us confident of success we returned to Plymouth to prepare for the delivery to Le Havre.

A mix of friends, family, well-wishers and press loitered around the pontoon the morning of our departure from Plymouth. It was only a

Fooling around on the bow during the qualifier trip. Larso was at the end of the bowsprit with the camera.

short sail across the English Channel to the race start but we had a tight deadline and needed to get the boat over to the race village in Le Havre a full week in advance to satisfy the race requirements. In France, the TJV is another one of those major sporting events and the race village attracts a simply colossal number of spectators in the week preceding the race. Race week is something special for the French, an opportunity for the general public to stroll along the dockside and get

up close and personal with the amazing yachts. Global brands bran-dish their logos along the sides of multi-million-pound state-of-the-art boats. It's also a chance for people to meet the teams and pose for the cameras alongside the skippers that compete in this distinguished race.

The skippers gather at the official press launch in Paris.

Larso and I were overwhelmed when we turned up with our trusty yellow steed. The atmosphere was pumping as we motored into the sheltered Paul Vatine dock and tied up to our allocated space on the pontoon. People were swarming around like ants. Everyone seemed to be holding handfuls of promotional literature and glossy posters of the various competitors. It wasn't long before we were being asked to give autographs and pose for the cameras ourselves.

There was a certain amount of showmanship and muscle-flexing amongst some of the competitors during the seven days before the race start. We were competing in the Open 50 Class, a division for fifty-foot yachts. Several of our direct competitors made no secret of the fact they had brand-new high-tech sails and hoisted them in the dock in full view of the whole race village. They looked fabulous as the sunlight glinted off them in the windless basin. We realised that these boys were playing mind games, trying to gain a psychological advantage.

Our sails were certainly not new. They had already endured a round-the-world voyage and were starting to show their age. *One Dream One Mission* was seemingly surrounded by a flock of mean-looking war birds all out for our blood. It was evident that victory in this race would not be easy. Nevertheless, both Larso and I told each other that we didn't give toss about the others, we knew we were prepared. We were determined not to be fazed by bravado. While they hoisted their new and unblemished sails, we confidently attached adhesive patches to repair the holes in ours.

Our faithful yellow boat was certainly not the prettiest girl in the park compared to the new high-tech big-budget speed machines, but what she lacked in aesthetics she more than made up for with her performance and reputation. The question was whether *One Dream One Mission* could compete with the newer boat designs. The pundits acknowledged the significance of my and Larso's racing experience but didn't seem to rate our chances too highly. My father obviously fancied his son's chances though, and was keen to place a bet on us to win at a high street bookmakers. Despite his best efforts, they declined the bet.

The night before race day I chose to sleep on board. It's become something of a ritual for me. I always like to be with the boat the night before the start of a big race. It helps me to focus, although that night I should have known better. The noise of thumping music and chatter could be heard throughout the race village until the early hours and kept me awake longer than I wanted. Nonetheless, as I sat in my bunk snuggled up in my sleeping bag listening to the sound of a party raging in one of the tents at the end of the race village I felt excited. Tomorrow would be the start of yet another great adventure.

Larso arrived at the boat early the next morning as agreed. We had scheduled a telephone conversation with our weather router Lee. He had the latest information and it was time to talk tactics and decide on a plan for the first few days of the race.

Time passed quickly on the morning of the start. After some teary-eyed goodbyes, we cast off the lines and left the pontoon to rapturous applause. The short trip out of the Paul Vatine dock, through the lock gates and into the outer harbour is legendary. Thousands of people line the harbour-side to cheer the teams as they venture out to sea. It was a great spectacle and an experience I was keen to share with my parents as a small way of saying thank you for all of their unceasing support, both emotional and financial. I knew Mum would not set foot on board. She just doesn't get on with boats and felt safer on land, despite being on the quayside to wave her son goodbye. A quick nod to Dad was all that was needed to entice him aboard. With our ex-military friend John Wright and Shane as well as a handful of friends we motored towards the harbour entrance. I looked over my shoulder for a last glimpse of Mum. She blew me a kiss and did her best to hold back the tears. I will always be her little boy no matter how old I am. Dozens of racing yachts ghosted back and forth across the starting area, weav-

Signing autographs before the start of the Jacques Vabre.

Larso and me discussing tactics before the start.

Final preparations before the start with Mum on the pontoon lending a hand.

ing their way through the myriad of spectator boats gathered to watch the start. Choosing the best route through spectator craft is always a difficult task. Often, your manoeuvrability is very restricted as everyone is tightly bunched together after crossing the starting line. Marshalls usually patrol the area and clear a path for competitors as we head out into the open ocean.

The route for this edition of the race was a real test of endurance and tactical skill. We would sail west along the English Channel towards Ushant on the north-western tip of the French Atlantic coast. From there we would head south across the notorious Bay of Biscay before passing Cap Finisterre and the Portuguese coast. Madeira and the Canary Islands would be directly in our path and would present their own tactical challenges. Decisions would be have to be made about which side to pass the islands – get it wrong and you could lose the wind.

After the Cape Verde islands comes the tedious crossing of the Doldrums, a stretch of ocean close to the equator where the strong trade winds nearly always die away to nothing. The Doldrums are a significant obstacle for any ocean race that crosses from one hemisphere to another. It is often here that these great races are won or lost. Luck can be a significant factor, as teams struggle with conditions ranging from flat calms to short, aggressive bursts of strong and sometimes destructive wind. Downdrafts delivered by threatening, black thunderhead

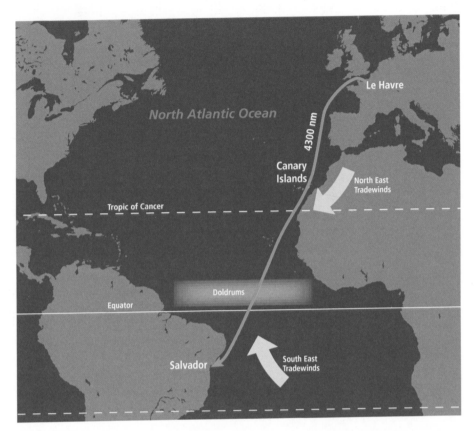

The Transat Jacques Vabre race route.

clouds piled high into the atmosphere bring with them torrential rain. Pass on the wrong side of one of these giant cloud formations and you will be left drifting for hours with a confused sea that knocks even the slightest whisper of wind from your sails. In this situation the boat struggles to make any significant headway and you are left watching the clock, wondering if your competition is knocking off the miles in a steady breeze. It's sailboat racers' hell.

Blue skies and cumulus clouds delivering a solid breeze from the south-east signal the escape from the clutches of equatorial doom. From here, the southern hemisphere awaits and with it a generally reliable wind field, until the final stages of the race and the approach to the Brazilian coastline. In the closing stages, tired sailors must decide whether to sail close to the Brazilian coast or take a more offshore

Leaving the dock in Le Havre at the start of the Jacques Vabre.

route in the hope of enjoying better wind conditions. Once you've sighted the cluster of skyscrapers overlooking Salvador harbour, your arrival at the long-awaited finish line is imminent and with it the end of an epic race.

Larso called 'Ten seconds to go'. He had been timing the countdown sequence as we made our final approach to the starting line. Yachts were zooming around and coming in from all directions in the attempt to gain an optimum starting position. Larso shouted over again, asking whether I'd seen the boat underneath our sail. Suddenly, the splendid bow of a sixty-foot yacht appeared. Sailing directly along the starting line with the wind flowing from right to left across her decks, she had the right of way according to the racing rules of sailing. Even if we had been the stand-on vessel, she was much bigger and discretion is always the better part of valour in these situations. An aggressive pull on the tiller was enough to clear her stern quarter by little more than inches. A close one.

The start of the race was not perfect for us, but it didn't really matter. We were right up there, in amongst the pack. It was 3 November 2001 and the fight to claim victory in the Transat Jacques Vabre had just begun.

Approaching Ushant, the first significant mark of the course, weather conditions were steadily building to a solid Force 6 and we were doing well. Slightly further offshore we saw two yachts, suggesting we were fighting it out for the lead. A quick look through the binoculars revealed their identities. *Saving* and *Tredici* were brand-new, latest technology designs that had been constructed especially for events like the TJV. They were both competitors in our division. We knew that these two boats more than any others posed the biggest threat to our success. We were all in a line, riding the wind and waves as the building crisp northerly breeze propelled us along at smile-inducing speed. This was where the race really started, the entrance to the Bay of Biscay.

From the start, Larso and I knew that the only way we could compete with these new-generation boats was to have the confidence to push hard when the conditions were harsh. In light winds, the new boats would undoubtedly have a significant advantage. Our weather router Lee Bruce had been forecasting very strong northerly winds in Biscay and it was here that we knew we had to pile on the pressure. Any gains we could make now would set us up for the latter stages of the race where the new designs would be better-suited to the lighter wind conditions. We knew we simply had to out-sail them. As we passed Ushant we set course south and without hesitation hoisted our colourful spinnaker. With sails set, *One Dream One Mission* blasted off on the crest of a wave. The rollercoaster ride had just begun. Looking out to sea it was clear we were not the only ones unfazed by the strong conditions; both *Tredici* and *Saving* hoisted in similar fashion, with equal confidence.

In the end, memories are all we have. For me, it's these moments at sea when I feel most alive. The adrenaline is pumping, the boat feels alive with the forces of nature running through her structure. The sight of a silent but formidable adversary on the horizon is what makes life so worth living, the pure spirit of competition. I have been so privileged to have had these experiences. They are fantastic memories that will stay with me forever. If you share the same passion for your dreams you will understand.

One Dream One Mission was really smoking. By the fourth day, despite blowing apart our small spinnaker and having no option but to hoist our giant pure white spinnaker, nicknamed the 'womper' on account of its size, we had secured a healthy lead of forty-five miles over the fleet. The uncharacteristic heavy northerly winds were propelling us across the Bay of Biscay at breathtaking speed. We agreed that the best course of action was to push close to the limit until the winds lightened. Then, hoping to have established a commanding lead, we would adopt a more normal watch system and grab some proper sleep.

Staying on deck for so long while fending off the vice like grip of sleep deprivation was dangerous so early on in the race. Burning-out prematurely was a real possibility but one that we both accepted was worth the risk. At the front edge of the cockpit we had a canvas hammock-style seat, next to the instruments. We would each take turns catnapping for twenty minutes while the high-octane conditions prevailed.

In the meantime we continued to pile on the pressure and keep our biggest sails set. This decision certainly wasn't taken lightly. Pushing *One Dream One Mission* this hard for so long was really high-stakes sailing. If any piece of equipment let go now – the mast, the sails, anything major – that would spell the end of our race, bringing instant failure. We were well aware of the risks but if you want to win, you have to go fast.

Blasting across oceans on these modern racing yachts often has potentially dangerous consequences. The chance of colliding with objects at sea is a real problem. Whales and other sea mammals, together with general flotsam are the biggest threats. Hit anything like that at speed and it could sink you. Something we had not prepared ourselves for, however, was a sudden attack from jellyfish. With Larso at the helm guiding *One Dream One Mission* through the waves, the boat ploughed into a trough, sending water sweeping right back to the cockpit. As the water flowed across the deck we could see that we had scooped up a number of small jellyfish. They littered the decks, stinging Larso's hands in the process. It was most bizarre.

That night, the phosphorescence formed by the stimulation of plankton in the sea as we raced along was a sight to behold. Under autopilot we were consistently sailing at twenty-five knots down the faces of huge rolling waves. It was pitch black and on deck you couldn't see past the front of the boat. I remember standing at the chart table inside the small cabin next to Larso as we discussed tactics. Soon the rollercoaster ride would slow to a more sedate pace as the wind moderated, but for now, as we looked at the charts and discussed options in the cabin, *One Dream One Mission* continued at breathtaking speed into the night.

Solid water covers the
decks as we thunder
across the Bay of Biscay.

Twenty-five, twenty-seven, twenty-nine knots then a prolonged surf just nudged us into the elusive 30-knot territory. For a monohull, this kind of white-knuckle performance was just insane. The sound of the water rushing under our keel was intense. Pete Goss had once told us of a time in the Southern Ocean when the boat hit thirty knots. We now knew what that felt like. This was beyond the limit, all Larso and I could do was stare at the speedometer, hold onto the chart table and hope she would ride it out. The tension gave way to nervous cheers and laughter as we realised everything was OK. It was an awesome night of sailing.

Having ridden-out the big winds and built a considerable lead on the fleet we were faced with some tough decisions as we approached the Canary Islands. We now had to choose the best route through the cluster of islands. A ridge of high pressure with little or no wind had

One Dream One Mission surfs down a huge wave with Larso on the bow.

blocked the direct path south. Hoping to have skirted around that by keeping closer to the coast of Morocco for more favourable wind, we would make our way between Lanzarote and Tenerife.

As we approached the northern tip of the islands we discussed our plans. The big push in the first three days as we crossed Biscay had taken its toll. Yes, we were in the lead but we were close to the wall of exhaustion. We decided to get through the islands then each take our turn for some serious sleep. The passage would be negotiated under the cover of darkness and once again *One Dream One Mission* was leading a charge. We were constantly debating whether we should drop the light wind spinnaker well before the areas of known wind acceleration between the islands. These acceleration zones are always problematic for yachts. At night, fatigued to the degree we were, it could be difficult to get a spinnaker lowered and stowed safely if the wind piled on the pressure. But the conservative option of dropping the sail early would undoubtedly lose us time to our competitors. That was a thought we didn't relish so the decision was made to push on.

We had passed the mid-way point through the islands before the wind kicked in but when it did, we suddenly had a big problem to deal with, tired or not. We were powering along on a flat sea, pressed to the max with a wall of sail hoisted. We were certainly clocking up the miles, but we knew we had to get the big sail down. The wind speed was close to thirty knots as we stood in the cockpit looking up at the sail. We agreed it was time to get the canvas off.

We quickly formulated a plan. Larso would go onto the foredeck ready to douse the spinnaker by pulling on the ropes attached to the sock at the mast head. I would stay in the cockpit and deal with the steering and when ready, release the controlling sheet of the sail from the winch.

At that instant, a vicious gust of wind hit the boat. Our trusty steed groaned under the pressure on the sails and equipment. Suddenly there was a bang followed by a tearing sound. The spinnaker had blown. There was nothing we could do, all hell had just broken loose. Things were definitely going a bit crazy as Larso clambered out of the cockpit and made his way onto the foredeck. Huge amounts of spray and seawater were shooting out from the side of the hull as *One Dream One Mission* powered on into the night, heeling over under the strain.

The Dyneema sheet connected to the spinnaker was under so

much pressure that it felt more like solid steel than a piece of synthetic cord. I prepared to change our course and set up for the drop manoeuvre. Larso had reached the foredeck and shouted that he was ready. I pressed the automatic pilot control buttons for a thirty-degree change of course and quickly eased out a large chunk of mainsheet to relieve the pressure on the boat. The rope smoked off the winch drum with a vengeance the second I released my grip. The trusty autopilot pulled on the rudder and slowly *One Dream One Mission* came onto her new heading. With the wind coming from directly behind us I shouted into the darkness that I was ready. Larso yelled, "OK mate, smoke it!" He wanted me to completely let go of the spinnaker sheet control line. Instantly, the sail began to whip and crack as it flogged. The sail had already blown out so we thought any further damage was pretty unlikely.

Larso was struggling to pull down the retrieval line connected to

Me concentrating on trimming the headsail during the Jacques Vabre.

the sock. I could see him pulling on the line for all he was worth but the strain was too great. I clambered up onto the pitching foredeck and did my best to help. Even with both of us pulling as hard as we could the recovery sock just wouldn't come down. We struggled for what seemed like an eternity, trying to douse the sail. The spinnaker, already torn to shreds, started to wrap itself around the forestay, creating an even bigger mess. It was a nightmare situation to find ourselves in. The only good news was that even with the blown-out sail we were still hitting serious speeds.

It must have been over an hour before our desperate wrestling with the sail eventually came to an end. We managed to recover what little was left and regained some semblance of control. The spinnaker had been completely destroyed and had mostly ended up in the sea, leaving us with just the corners of the sail connected to the boat. I later presented my father with those two corners of spinnaker when we finished the race. They have pride of place hanging on a wall in my parents' house as a reminder of our epic fight through the Canary Islands.

A rare view from the end of the boom as we blast across the ocean.

The prolonged explosion of activity had worn both of us out and

with literally nothing left to give, we decided to leave the boat sailing under autopilot and both hit the sack below decks. The Canary Islands were by now fading astern in our wake. The thought that neither of us would be on deck to keep watch didn't seem a priority as we clambered into our bunks. We were both completely spent. As I closed my eyes and drifted off to sleep I could hear the sound of water passing under the hull. Even with all that noise it didn't take long for me to drift off.

By 12 November we were well and truly in the north-east trade winds and revelling in the strong conditions. At one stage our lead over the fleet had been reduced to just seventeen miles as we struggled in

the light winds south of the Canary Islands. But now, with a little less than two thousand three hundred nautical miles to the finish line in Salvador, we were enjoying being sixty-five miles out in front, confident that our unrelenting fight for the top slot was paying off. We were in our element. With the Rolling Stones blasting out from our speakers and flying fish bombarding the decks, our spirits were high.

As we approached the Doldrums, the light winds and notorious thunderstorms were taking shape all around us. For days we had been in discussion with our weather router, working out which was the best angle to take through them. Now that our latitude was just ten degrees north of the equator we could only hope that our passage through would be less compromising than that of our competitors. The yacht *Saving* that had been sparring with us since the start of the race now seemed to have finally reeled us in. The latest position reports revealed they were just two miles behind. The now-constant light winds had reduced our performance considerably. For the first time in the race it seemed our lead was under serious threat. Everything was still to play for, but if we weren't first out of the Doldrums we were done for.

Later that day, *Saving* eased ahead. Having chosen a more westerly course they were now enjoying slightly stronger wind. For the next two days we played a private high-tension game of cat and mouse. They weren't visible on the horizon but the constantly updated position reports we received over the satellite comms showed we were regularly trading places for the top slot. All Larso and I could do was battle with one thundercloud after another, hoping the passing of each would bring evidence that the Doldrums had released their grasp. When it finally happened, we were treated to a splendid sight. We had just popped out of a huge grey squall and bang, there it was. Blue skies and a crisp building south-easterly breeze. We had done it, we were through. Welcome to the superhighway that is the south-east trade winds.

The passage thorough the Doldrums had been pretty tense for everyone with all those thunderstorms and fickle winds. The competition that had been breathing down our necks had reeled us in from a long way back and even started to look as though they would sail off over the horizon. But we had been the first into the zone and with a little luck shining on our sails we were the first out. We soon started clocking up the miles and within just a few hours had restored our lead to a comfort-

Fast sailing in the North East Trade winds.

Right **Menacing storm clouds build as we cross the Doldrums.**

Below **A big wave rolls down the deck, I'm just visible on the bow about to be engulfed.**

able margin. The nearest competitor, *Saving*, remained wallowing in the no-wind zone for several hours before eventually breaking free themselves but by then it was too late. We were on the superhighway, fully stacked and racked. Everything was piled up on the high side of the boat in an effort to maximise even the slightest ounce of extra performance. Boat speed was great and so were expectations. Our crossing of the equator brought with it celebration and sacrifice. As has been tradition for mariners over the centuries, an offering to King Neptune from first-timers during their passage of the equator is always seen as a good idea. It's a superstitious tradition that many offshore sailors still respect and for us it would be no different. Since the start I had been aware that Larso might be planning something and sure enough, as we passed into the southern hemisphere he emerged from the confines of the cabin dressed in full regalia as King Neptune himself.

Neptune was holding a cooking pan full of a disgusting-looking mixture of mashed potato, sausages and beans, although I'm sure the ingredients included more than just those. I would have to endure the humiliation of being bombarded by this ugly-looking mixture while eating the rest as an offering to the wind gods. To make matters worse, Neptune was armed with Larso's camera and seemed intent on documenting the occasion for future reference. Needless to say, I was soon completely covered in the stuff. Neptune found the occasion amusing

Me taking a salt water shower in the tropics.

and for a few minutes we completely forgot about our intense battle for the lead. Laughter turned into hysterics as great chunks of food flew across the cockpit in my direction.

Covered in food, the offering to Neptune as we crossed the Equator.

The remaining six hundred miles became a simple drag race to the finish. Despite *Saving* being theoretically the faster boat, we were confident we could hold them to the end. Just like a thoroughbred racehorse approaching the final furlong, *One Dream One Mission* was being pushed to within an inch of her life.

In an effort to keep in a consistent corridor of wind we elected to stay twenty miles or so offshore in the final stages of the approach to Salvador. It was a important tactical decision and one made all the more difficult by the fact that the weather forecasters were predicting a high probability of no wind for the closing stages. If that happened, it was entirely probable that *Saving* could hunt us down in just a few hours, if they stayed in favourable wind. So the race was not yet won, and it looked like it would go down to the wire.

As it turned out, our worst fears did not materialise. Under the cover of darkness *One Dream One Mission* sailed into the wide expanse of Salvador harbour triumphant. With just five miles left to run we sighted the bright lights of Salvador and realised we had arrived victorious. Out of the night the first spectator boat emerged. The thirty-foot boat was packed with people. Dad was on board. He and John had travelled from the UK the day before, determined to meet us as we arrived. Good old Dad, he's always there at the race finishes. I knew it was him, he was shouting into the night, "That's my son! Go on, boys!" No doubt it was a proud moment for him.

With all the activity and bright lights beaming down on the boat we couldn't see where we were going. The finish line was marked by a

Lighting the victory flare at the end of the Jacques Vabre.

small inflatable buoy located directly off the entrance to the small yacht harbour some three miles away. Concerned we might miss the finish line, I shouted for the support boat to clear off and give us some space to get over the line. It might have seemed a bit rude but we had been completely blinded by the lights and couldn't see a thing. Dad could see we needed some space and instructed the driver to ease back.

These were the final minutes of this spectacular sporting event, *One Dream One Mission* was graciously gliding toward the finish line and to put the icing on the cake, my dad was there to see it. I was bursting to light the red hand flares and hold them up with Larso for the traditional victory shot. Bugger it, I couldn't wait. I had seen so many images in yachting magazines of winning sailors holding up flares and now it was our turn. We were just a few hundred yards from the line, so with a quick twist and push I ignited a red flare and held it up high, illuminating the back of the boat. We had already contacted race control via our VHF radio to inform them of our imminent arrival, as we entered the harbour approaches. Seeing the premature ignition of the flare a softly-spoken Frenchwoman's voice came over the radio: "Alex, you have not finished yet, don't you think you should wait until you have won?"

We didn't care. It was as much a release of adrenaline as it was a statement of victory. Seconds later we crossed the line. We had been at sea for eighteen days, sixteen hours, thirty-four minutes and those all-important forty-five seconds. The long-awaited blast from the gun roared into the night, accompanied by a splendid display of fireworks. Dreams had just turned into reality. Larso and I shook hands and hugged. Against the odds, we were victors and the Transat Jacques Vabre was ours. Not only that, but we had broken the course record for the four thousand five hundred-mile race. We were now the new record-holders. We felt like heroes. Life just doesn't taste any sweeter than this, I thought. I was just twenty five years old.

13 HERO TO ZERO

Our stay in Salvador was a real eye-opener. Armed guards brandished automatic weapons as they maintained a reassuring watch over the small marina village where the race fleet had gathered. Several crews had been robbed and in one incident a crew had even been held up at gunpoint. It was becoming increasingly obvious that Brazil, despite being a beautiful place, was also a very dangerous one. Every night when the guards changed shifts they would walk into the marina café for a quick coffee before heading home. We nicknamed one of them Robocop on account of his striking resemblance to the character from the film. Togged-up in what looked like flak jackets and armed to the teeth, they certainly had the right kit.

Rest and relaxation was top of everyone's agenda. Having sailed four-and-a-half thousand miles across the north and south Atlantic, we were all keen to take some time to just chill. With the impressive parties and festivities in full swing I started thinking about the upcoming trip home. Larso was flying back, while I would sail *One Dream One Mission* solo to the UK in order to qualify for the Around Alone race the following year.

With the media spotlight on our win I had taken the opportunity to formally announce my entry into the Around Alone race. High on my success, Judith and her team back in England had organised a meeting with a representative of the event who had come to Salvador to promote the race. It was agreed there and then that I would enter the prestigious race. The solo passage home would more than satisfy the legal requirements for my entry into the race and would also give me valuable training time.

Before the boat and I were ready to go back to sea I first had to overcome a nasty bout of food poisoning. A lot of the food I had been eating, particularly the salads, had been washed in tap water which contained bacteria that didn't agree with my stomach at all. The bug was completely debilitating. I remember the night the illness kicked in. It was coming out of both ends and I lost a lot of fluid. Dad was in the apartment, considering my symptoms and wondering if he should call for a doctor. I was so thirsty, the temperature in the apartment felt unbearable, despite the air conditioning.

I'd cleaned out the fridge of anything worth drinking and Dad was just about to walk into town and get some more water. It was nearly midnight and I was all too aware of what had happened to the other sailors who had been mugged walking though the area just days before. That was the last thing I wanted to happen. I pleaded with him not to go outside at that time of night. Despite needing fresh water, I was prepared to wait until morning.

Dad wasn't having any of it. He could see I desperately needed fluids and wasn't fazed by the fifteen-minute walk through potentially dangerous territory to get it. My father is the type of man that faces life head on and doesn't need a chaperone. He grew up in a tough area of west London, rubbing shoulders with household names of the London underworld. Without doubt he knows how to look after himself, but this was a foreign land and a long way from home. Salvador was an environment we didn't know at all. Lying in my bed with my head spinning and my throat starting to feel like the driest desert, I was all too aware of that. If he must go I insisted he wait until John came back to the apartment and so they could go together for safety in numbers.

I was more concerned for anyone stupid enough to try it on with them. All hell would have broken out and we certainly didn't need that. I could see my pathetic pleas were falling on deaf ears but at that moment, much to my relief, the apartment door opened. It was Larso, returning from the marina. He walked into the room with two bottles of cold water. Dad relieved him of them and poured me a glass, using the other one to cool my forehead. Problem solved, although not for poor Larso.

The bug had completely knocked me off my feet and kept me bedridden for several days. It was a nasty experience but I learnt a lesson. Next time we were in a foreign country we would book into a hotel rather than hire an apartment. That way, if one of us became ill, we could just call reception and get a doctor, pronto. Not to mention room service. My dad once told me that everyone makes mistakes, but only an idiot makes the same mistake twice.

Once back on my feet it was time to prepare *One Dream One Mission* for the delivery home. One problem we had to deal with was replenishing the gas supply used for cooking on board. The Brazilian gas canisters were different to the ones we use in the UK and wouldn't connect to the stove. After hours of searching for a gas supplier, we decided to give up and just buy a new smaller camping stove. Even that was not as straightforward as it sounded. We bought and returned three stoves before we found one that actually worked. The poor shopkeeper, who didn't speak a word of English, was obviously going out of his way to be accommodating but he must have thought we were crazy. On the third trip back to return yet another defective stove he obviously couldn't believe that all of them had been faulty. It turned out he was right, and after a quick demonstration and a lot of waving hands in the air he showed us the error of our ways. There had been nothing wrong with any of the stoves, it was just user error. We hadn't removed the small blanking cap used to protect the connector that attaches to the gas bottles. Dad and I couldn't help but burst out laughing. The shopkeeper must have thought we were insane. In an effort to make up for the cock-up we purchased a huge number of gas bottles, enough to more than cover me for the trip home.

Food and water were also obvious requirements. We needed enough of both to keep me fed and watered for at least twenty-five days at sea. The decision to take a taxi ride to the local hypermarket was a good one. The distance had been rather underestimated by some of the locals at the marina café, who said it was well within walking distance. So was Canada, if we had put our minds to it.

We filled a couple of shopping trolleys with some essential provisions and hailed another taxi to take us back to the marina. The language barrier again reared its head but with the aid of a pencil and paper and a few skilfully-drawn images of sailboats we were on the same wavelength. The poor car was almost riding on its backside with four adults and half a ton of provisions piled up inside. We certainly had our money's worth that day.

As we pulled up outside the marina and started to unload, Dad walked across the road to a nearby shop. We needed about two hundred litres of fresh water for the trip home and we had noticed that the shop across the road had a plentiful supply. Just as Dad was wondering how to transport this not-insignificant amount of water across the road and down to the boat the shopkeeper raised his hand and clicked his fingers.

Seemingly from nowhere, four barefoot street kids wearing little more than rags pitched up and offered their services. On the surface they seemed happy enough but you could tell they had tough lives. The armed guard on the marina gate recognised us and did his best to shoo the kids away. He spoke good English and advised us they were homeless kids and not to be trusted. Dad, impressed by the initiative of these young entrepreneurs, said it was alright and instructed the guard to let them through. The guard reluctantly agreed but not before giving the kids an aggressive dressing-down, no doubt warning them to toe the line or else. They seemed to take it seriously.

The four of them were fast workers. In no time they had all the water and provisions piled up on board the boat. Dad gave them a few Reals and told them to split the cash equally between the four of them. It was just a few quid, nothing really. Before Dad had finished speaking, the youngest kid leaned forward and grabbed the cash. Then he high-tailed it along the quayside like lightning, leaving the others with nothing. Dad looked at me and said, "You see that kid? He will go far." I never found out if he got away from the older lads but his behaviour highlighted just how different a world he lived in. The following day we saw the same kid clambering on top of a big rubbish heap, using a metal pole to fish out old aluminium drinking cans. He had quite a pile stacking up. The guard on the gate told us they sell the cans for recycling.

With *One Dream One Mission* prepared for sea it was time to say my goodbyes to Dad and John. They were due to fly back to England later that night. Larso was due to leave the following evening and had agreed to see me off. I felt relaxed and jubilant. I was ready to wave goodbye to Salvador, so I stayed on board that night, keen to get back into the swing of things.

The following morning with a light breeze wafting through the marina village, Larso helped me slip the lines and waved me off as I motored out of the small marina. There had been just enough time for one last slap on the back and a quick handshake before I left. Many of the race fleet were still tied up as I motored out, no doubt awaiting the arrival of their delivery crews. I felt the journey home was the threshold of even greater things to come for me and *One Dream One Mission*.

The passage north along the Brazilian coast was not particularly easy. Within twenty-four hours we were sailing into the wind and waves, fighting against the teeth of an uncharacteristic north-easterly near gale-force wind. Clearing the north-eastern tip of Brazil was proving to be tough going. For nearly three days we forced our way northwards, making slow but acceptable progress. We weren't racing, so I took a rare opportunity to relax and tried to enjoy the ride despite the bumpy motion. Even the laptop that a private benefactor had kindly given to me prior to the start of the race was having problems displaying the various DVD movies that Dad had brought over from the UK. The violent motion was too much for the computer's DVD drive and the movies kept jumping out of sequence.

The second night out proved to be particularly rough. A number of the fresh water bottles we had bought in Salvador burst with the heavy pounding as *One Dream One Mission* launched off the crests of particularly short and steep waves. I was helpless to prevent it but managed to save more than I lost, exhausting my generous stash of duct tape by taping up the damaged bottles as they split. The plastic bottles were much thinner than the ones we have in the UK and didn't seem as robust. In an effort to save as much water as possible, I even resorted to scooping up water from the cabin floor and decanting it into other spare containers that I had lying around the cabin. I would keep that stuff for absolute emergencies. It was a bit of a mess but I soon had everything under control. Drinking water is vital at sea and I didn't want to waste any more than I absolutely had to. However, I knew I would be able to replenish my supplies as we negotiated the Doldrums. Those gigantic roaming thunderheads would deliver more than enough fresh rainwater. I could easily catch large quantities by attaching a bucket at the inboard end of the boom. As the rainwater ran down the sails it would fill the bucket and hey presto! It's a useful technique and one I had learned from reading all those books by the pioneers of solo ocean sailing when I was a child.

The testing weather had finally abated and we were now enjoying a warm stiff breeze from the south-east, classic trade winds sailing.

Progress was excellent as we edged past Fernando de Noronha, a small archipelago of islands and rocky outcrops roughly two hundred miles from the north-east coast of Brazil. The islands form the tip of a giant underwater volcanic formation. In years gone by this isolated cluster of granite rocks must have posed a significant threat to the unsuspecting mariner. Their foreboding appearance made me wonder just how many vessels had come to grief on them over the centuries. However, closer inspection reveals that these islands are a beautiful natural haven for wildlife with numerous sandy beaches, a real paradise.

Enjoying life at sea during the trip home to the UK.

As we drew ever closer to the equator, I was in my element. We were blasting along crystal blue seas under a hot sun. The memories of the tough first few days were starting to fade and I remember thinking how awesome an adventure I was having. Most people my age would see a night out on the tiles as an adventure. But out here, this was how to really live life.

Something that had been causing me concern for the last couple of days was a strange clicking sound coming from the keel box area in the cabin. It was hard to pinpoint but sounded like a problem with one of the two hydraulic keel rams. Boats like *One Dream One Mission* have long slender keel fins constructed from welded steel plates, incorporating a heavy torpedo-shaped lead bulb attached to the bottom. Unlike conventional yacht keels, these swivel by about forty degrees either side of the boat's centreline. They are normally controlled by two giant hydraulic rams connected to each side of the hull inside the cabin.

When sailing, the keel is swung or canted to the high side in order to make the boat more efficient. These canting keels significantly increase the speed of the boat through the water. The downside is that they are subjected to huge loads and as a result the keels are both very expensive to manufacture and also have a limited lifespan.

The keel and ancillary equipment on *One Dream One Mission* had already seen two round-the-world voyages as well as countless transatlantic crossings. The gear was tired and would need replacing before I started the Around Alone race the following year. The keel hydraulics were now struggling to hold the fifteen-foot steel keel fully canted. Every now and again the keel would slip back towards the centreline. The hydraulics would then kick in and try to pump the keel back up to its fully canted position. Under certain circumstances, this action provided a failsafe mechanism, employed if the boat fell off a particularly large wave. The keel could be dropped on a pressure release valve and then instantly be pumped back to full deployment. But that would only happen in exceptional circumstances during rough weather. The fact that the keel system was regularly doing it now set off alarm bells in my mind.

It was an early sign of problems to come. Further inspection revealed that one of the rams had become completely severed from its fixings on the side of the hull. It was just lying on the floor of the keel box, unattached. This was not necessarily a major problem, we still had

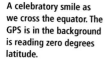

A celebratory smile as we cross the equator. The GPS is in the background is reading zero degrees latitude.

One Dream One Mission is becalmed as we cross the Doldrums.

one ram that was operational. Intent on gaining a fuller understanding of the problem, I used the sat phone to call up the engineer who designed the system. It seemed that we could continue heading home on just one ram. I had just crossed the equator at the time, normally a positive point in any voyage but this time I was preoccupied, wondering what would happen if the second ram broke too. I was well and truly in the middle of the Atlantic but as long as we took it easy the consensus was that we should be fine.

The following five days delivered some fabulous sailing. The clutches of the Doldrums proved to be an almost non-event, slowing us down just for a few hours rather than the several days that I had been expecting. Accompanied by schools of dolphins playing in the wake of the keel and rudders, my trusty *One Dream One Mission* effortlessly glided across a flat turquoise ocean at ten knots while I sat on the aft deck, remote control in hand, shuffling tracks on the CD player. The music was pumping and life on board felt simply superb. I had no idea my 50-foot bubble was about to burst.

As we reached the 15th parallel north we were once again sailing pretty much into the wind and waves. I was starting to feel the effects of the north-east trade winds. The same warm, constant winds that had propelled Larso and me towards our victory were now proving to be more of a challenge as we punched headlong into them. Nearly a thousand miles from land, the feeling of true freedom was exhilarating. I hadn't seen another boat or any sign of the outside world since leaving Salvador. Despite the isolation, life on board was never dull. I had a set routine that revolved around balancing the perpetual daily tasks essential for the smooth operation of the boat with looking after myself and keeping everything pointing in the right direction. I was hoping to be home for Christmas. I knew Mum would love it if I was present at the dining table on Christmas Day.

My daily chores were numerous and varied. They included checking the voltage of the batteries, inspecting the mast and rigging for signs of fatigue and crawling through the whole boat in an effort to keep my eye on everything else. The navigation was pretty straightforward and the evening meal became the highlight of the day, despite my average culinary skills. Every evening I would sit under the cuddy on the canvas chair at the front of the cockpit and enjoy dinner while looking out across the ocean as we glided along in our own private world. The wildlife was incredible: on this voyage I had already spotted dolphins and turtles and now clearly visible just a hundred yards away was a pod of whales. It was a magical sight. I was completely isolated from the hustle and bustle of normal life and here within my world of solitude another species appeared from the abyss. They were huge creatures, one seemed to be almost the length of the boat. Its big blow hole shot torrents of water several metres into the air. We were travelling in opposite directions but they were very close and looked so graceful. I had to remind myself that something so beautiful was also a potential hazard for the boat. Whales have been known on occasion to flick their tail fins into small sailing yachts, causing significant damage. Nonetheless, I was both captivated by their beauty and humbled by their presence.

Three days later, my life changed forever. I had once again reached the latitude of the Canary Islands, only this time I was five hundred miles west of them. It was dark and *One Dream One Mission* was sailing due north, powered by a stiff breeze from the west. All day we had been sailing through a series of squalls that brought with them heavy rain and gusts to over gale-force. We would soon be fighting the first of a series of expected storms as we edged closer to the UK. The day before I had noticed that an incredible swell was building from the west, further out in the Atlantic. It was the first sign of bad weather approaching and given the size of the swell, I knew we would soon see some serious action. A telephone call from Lee confirmed that we would see our first storm of the trip within thirty-six hours. Later that evening I saw a target on the radar screen, a big ship travelling at speed heading due south.

The VHF radio crackled into life. The ship was hailing me: "Vessel on my port bow, this is Warship one. Warship one over". The radio operator had an American accent. I called back and it turned out it was an American naval vessel. They wanted to know who I was and why I was out there on the high seas. I explained I was a solo sailor heading for the UK and gave them some official details about the boat and our home port and they were kind enough to share some weather information before we parted company. They were heading south to avoid the worst of the approaching storm and advised that I do the same.

Despite the tempestuous conditions, *One Dream One Mission* was handling the weather with ease while making a steady twelve to fifteen knots. The following evening I had just made dinner and was sitting in my usual spot under the cockpit cuddy when a whopper of a squall hit us. I could see it coming. The clouds were visible even at night and the thick outline of cumulonimbus was a certain indication of a squall approaching. As the wind speed increased to gale-force I felt *One Dream One Mission* heel over under the pressure. Mindful of the keel problems, I leaned forward and pressed the buttons on the automatic pilot to change our angle to the wind and relieve the pressure on everything. We accelerated into the night. Unconcerned, I continued eating my pasta.

Then, out of nowhere, it happened. A loud crisp bang was instantly recognisable as the second keel ram giving up the ghost. The boat was violently pitched up on her side, dipping the masthead into the sea. I was thrown out of the cuddy chair, across the cockpit to the opposite side guard wires which by now were underwater. The next second I felt excruciating pain as my left arm collided with the primary winch. It was the winch that stopped me from going over the side. Before the incident, despite the wind and rain, the weather had been extremely warm and I was wearing just a t-shirt and shorts and no safety harness.

Looking into the darkness at the high side of the cockpit it seemed as if the boat was going to capsize. I was immersed in water up to my waist, my legs dangling over the side deck. Something serious had obviously just let go with the keel but in that moment I couldn't be sure what. Instinct took over: I pulled myself out of the water and climbed up on to the highest point of the cockpit to look over the side. I couldn't really see anything in the pitch black and certainly couldn't see the keel. *One Dream One Mission* had rounded up broadside to the waves and was now lying virtually flat in the water, the seas breaking over the boat. I knew I was in trouble but all I could do was just hold on to see what happened next. If the keel had gone completely, the boat would quickly capsize. If the keel was still attached, things could be expected to remain as they were.

I was soaking wet and my arm was starting to throb like hell. At first I thought it was broken but it later turned out that it was just badly bruised. I decided to release the sails and see if she would come upright. This was no easy task. I had to relinquish my perch on the high side of the hull and slip down into the cockpit which at this stage more resembled a cliff than the deck of a yacht. Then I had to release the mainsheet and jib sheet from their winches before climbing back to the other side in order to haul in on the jib furling line so the sail could roll itself away. It was exhausting work but gradually she started to come upright. Only when the sails had been dropped could I get below and assess the situation properly. The boat was rolling wildly from side to side as I entered the cabin and I could feel the keel swinging violently as the boat drifted.

I could hear horrible grinding noises from the keel head area. I needed to have a look, which meant unbolting two large carbon fibre access covers on top of the keel box. Hardly a quick task when the covers were held in place by more than twenty bolts but I had no choice, I had to see the damage. Scrambling around the cabin I eventually found the toolkit and set about unbolting the retaining nuts. Half an hour passed before I released the final nut and removed the covers. There was significant damage. Both hydraulic rams had indeed broken away from the keel. The pressure on the keel as it dropped from one side to the other had been considerable and the motion had taken out two lateral bulkheads in the process. I had no idea whether the keel would stay connected or not. My immediate thought was to try and rig up some kind of system to lash it with ropes but this proved to be more difficult than I thought.

We were constantly being knocked down as the seas thumped into the hull. They were not ideal conditions outside, for sure. My struggle to secure the keel continued for another couple of hours without success. The approaching storm was very much in my mind. Things were tough now with just moderate seas, but in less than twenty-four hours we would be fighting full-on gale-force conditions. My options were limited – the boat had serious keel problems and significant damage. Realising I needed help, I picked up the sat phone and called my folks. Dad answered and knew by the sound of my voice that I had a serious problem. Listening intently, he took down my position and asked me what I wanted to do. We have a set routine in place for when I am at sea: I always give my position first whenever I call in. That way, if I'm calling to report a problem and don't get the whole message through at least the chances are they would have my current position. Dad suggested he call MRCC Falmouth and advise them of the situation. I made it clear that I didn't want to leave the boat but accepted it was a good idea to let the relevant authorities know I was in trouble.

I was facing an awful dilemma. Despite my best efforts I couldn't steady the keel. With the fast-approaching stormy weather due to strike in a matter of hours, the question was could I ride out the storm and get the boat to a safe port? I was over five hundred miles from one of those and that would take at least three days to reach with the current problems, and probably a lot longer. I couldn't believe it – almost a year to the day from the *Team Philips* saga I was faced with another heart-wrenching decision to stay aboard or to abandon ship. I knew that in the circumstances I really had to get off. But I just couldn't bring myself to say the words.

Given clement conditions I knew I could reach a safe port and save the boat, but the threat of storms had changed everything. We were being knocked down as wave after wave broke over the boat. With no way to stabilise the keel, life would be very difficult, not to mention perilous. It wouldn't take much for the keel to turn into a fifteen-foot crowbar, intent on ripping the boat apart. I spent another hour trying to stabilise it before I conceded defeat.

As I considered my options I suddenly recalled that I had seen the lights of a ship shortly before disaster struck. It was heading in the opposite direction, but given the sea state it might still be in range of the VHF radio. I had to make a decision. Whatever I decided would have a massive impact on my future. This was obviously my crossroads, but I had to take the only safe option and save myself. I had my hand on the VHF transmitter when the sat phone burst into life. It was the Falmouth coastguard. Dad had contacted them to let them know I might need help. With the situation uncontrollable, I explained I was issuing a Mayday and required assistance.

The gravity of that phone call was crushing. As I spoke to the coastguard I looked around the cabin, holding on as best I could. I realised all my dreams and hard work were about to end. It was a cruel twist of fate, and one I was left to contemplate while the coastguard coordinated a rescue plan. In the meantime, I did my best to raise the ship whose lights I had seen distant on the horizon three hours earlier. Initially my calls for help seemed to fall on deaf ears but several minutes later, while I was struggling to get into my survival suit and prepare for the worst, I heard a voice on the radio.

Apparently the officer on watch had heard the call but decided to wake the ship's captain before he answered. They recorded my position and had just received the distress relay that Falmouth coastguard had issued over the satellite network. Amazingly, the *EWL Central America*, a one hundred and forty seven-metre cargo vessel, was not that far away. I quickly plotted their position as I scribbled down the coordinates. The mark on the chart confirmed we were just twenty miles apart, give or take a few. The captain wanted to know if I was officially asking for assistance. I replied 'yes' and was told to stand-by.

The seconds of silence felt like an eternity as I waited for an answer. Moments later, the radio operator was back and confirmed that they were turning around and would be with me in about an hour and a half. Within minutes of making my decision to abandon, a rescue plan had kicked into effect and the cavalry was on its way. I was thankful for living in this wonderful age of modern technology.

But there was no time to be emotional. Help was on its way but I had to get organised for when it arrived. The unmistakable tone of the sat phone ringing cut through the noise in the cabin. It was the coastguard, calling to let me know that a ship had turned around and was coming to my aid. I explained that we were already in VHF radio contact and I was preparing for the rescue. I was lucky, the *EWL Central America* was the only commercial vessel for over a hundred miles. Without them I would have had to endure the approaching storm.

By the time I sighted the *EWL Central America*, I was prepared for another hazardous climb up the side of a ship. Her lights looming low on the horizon were a sign of both rescue and of personal defeat. Until now, emotions had been set aside by the need to plan my survival. As the ship steamed over the horizon and into view, poised to pluck me from the hand of disaster, emotion was suddenly all I could feel. I stood in the cockpit, braced against the entrance to the cabin and realised that tears were flooding down my face. Not because I was scared, but because I was about to leave behind my reason for breathing. I had been so sure of my future before I left Salvador. I knew I could win the Around Alone and I knew I would have my chance. I had had the world in the palm of my hand. Now everything had changed.

This was the second time in twelve months I was faced with a life and death situation that would end up with me precariously hanging off a rope ladder over the side of a ship in the middle of the Atlantic. I remember thinking at the time this story would make a good book someday. Slowly the ship drew closer. It was agreed that they would take up a position just off my portside then, with the aid of the engine, I would motor alongside and jump for the rope ladder. The captain asked if I wanted to consider a dry run of the manoeuvre before the actual event. I declined, telling him I had done this before and knew the drill.

I had my essential kit lashed in the cockpit ready to leave. The survival container was packed with an emergency beacon and flares just in case I ended up in the water. I stuffed my passport down the waterproof neck seal of my survival suit. Again, this was just in case I didn't make it. If I was lost at sea during the transfer at least whoever found me would know who I was. The teddy bear, who had already endured the whole *Team Philips* rescue, was safely stashed in the pocket of my survival suit ready for another adventure. I fired up the diesel and waited for the call to say they were ready for me to make my move. *One Dream One Mission* was still being battered by waves when the time came to motor alongside the ship. The *EWL Central America* was significantly smaller than the ship that rescued us from *Team Philips*. Her decks were a lot lower in the water, something I remember thinking was a bonus as I closed in. With lower decks, my climb up the rope ladder would be a little less hazardous.

As we came alongside I heard the crunching of fibreglass as my beautiful boat bounced off the side of the ship. I knocked the diesel into neutral and watched as the giant wall of steel edged near enough to touch with my hand. Just as before, lines came crashing down onto the deck. I tied my kit to one and tied the other around my waist. At first I couldn't see the rope ladder. As I looked up I could see the deckhands shouting and pointing towards the front of the ship. The ladder was further forward, about twenty feet. I engaged the diesel, giving it a short final burst to propel us forward. The ladder came into view and there was just enough time for a last-minute glance into the cabin which was illuminated by the inviting glow of the instrument lights above the chart table. I took a deep breath, cleared my head and went for the ladder.

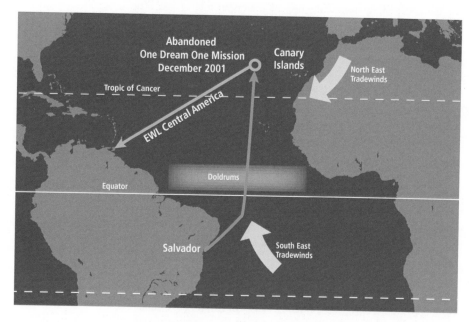

Accepting the consequences of your actions is all part of the journey of life. I already knew this, but abandoning my boat was difficult to stomach. When it came down to it, however, my life was worth more than the boat. The risk to my life if I had stayed on board was high enough to warrant abandoning. I knew I had made the right choice but that didn't help to relieve the feeling of total devastation. As I stood on the deck of the *EWL Central America*, surrounded by people, I had never felt so alone. The emotion was overwhelming.

Just three weeks before, I had won the biggest two-handed race in the world. Surely this couldn't be happening to me. As I stared into the night I could see my fabulous boat drifting away and I was power-less to do anything about it. The engine was still running as I climbed on board the ship. With a nearly-full tank it would run for days before finally falling silent as the fuel lines delivered their final drop of diesel. The batteries would retain enough power to keep the lights on for probably another forty-eight hours before running flat, a symbol of certain death for my once-proud boat. Strangely enough, this was the time I also realised that I had forgotten to bring with me my collection of CDs. They were still stowed in the chart table and represented virtu-ally the whole of my music collection, all the good stuff, at least. The empty CD covers stacked neatly on my shelf at home would serve as a cold reminder of this devastating night for years to come.

I stood on the ship's side deck tightly gripping the guard rails, watching the boat drift away into the night. I had been here before but this time it felt that much more personal. I could feel the adrenaline pumping though my veins, or was it raw emotion? The deckhands were buzzing around, keen to usher me up to the bridge to see the captain. They had plucked a total stranger from the desolate ocean and the ship's master understandably wanted to talk to him.

The climb up the narrow stairwell to the bridge was awkward. I felt rather clumsy with all my survival kit on. I must have looked a real sight as I burst onto the bridge wearing a one-piece survival suit, lifejacket and emergency beacon with just one box that contained what was left of my worldly possessions. The captain, a German seafarer in his mid fifties, walked forward and shook my hand. He immediately asked if I was OK and I could sense the compassion in his voice. I replied 'yes' but the truth was 'far from it'. Physically, apart from my badly-bruised arm, I was fine. Inside I was wrestling with all kinds of demons. The captain was quick to offer me their hospitality but a hot cup of tea was all I needed. I remember thinking I probably wasn't the first crazy yachts-man he had plucked from the ocean over the years. He looked like the kind of man who had plenty of seafaring experience. I explained the events as they had unfolded and he seemed genuinely moved by my story. I briefly mentioned the *Team Philips* saga the previous year and pointed out that it was virtually a year to the day since that rescue had taken place. How the cards of fate are dealt.

I asked where they were headed. 'Trinidad,' was the reply. Bloody hell, I thought. Why couldn't they have been headed for somewhere in Europe? Steaming to Trinidad meant at least six days on board. I decided to get my head down and see what tomorrow would bring. Pete Goss had often said that the sun will always rise in the morning, no matter how desperate things may seem. I was physically knackered and emotionally drained. It was apparent that I needed some time to gather my thoughts and get some sleep, and I was shown the way to a spare cabin and told I could rest there for as long as I needed. Breakfast and dinner times were mentioned, although I didn't take in everything that was being said. Some clean clothes from the ship's crew were the icing on the cake, though. That was really generous, I thought. They could see I had come away with literally just the clothes I was standing in.

I felt I was coping with the situation right up to the moment I closed that cabin door behind me. Suddenly, alone in the small room, I couldn't hold my composure any longer. Feeling a flood of emotions, I fell to my knees and cried my eyes out. My world had just fallen apart.

The journey across the Atlantic to Trinidad felt like a slow one although we were steaming at a steady eighteen knots for much of the time. Entombed in my little cabin I had plenty of time to consider the past and my future. At least the boat was insured; thank God that was all taken care of. Judith had arranged the insurance before the race start. At least I could repay the considerable debt to my family and somehow start to move on.

The following day I managed to get a brief call though to Dad using the ship's satellite phone. My parents had been informed of my

The view from my cabin window – containers stacked on the ship's deck.

Me in a sombre mood, reflecting on the nightmare that just happened.

safe rescue by Falmouth coastguard and by now everyone had learned of my rescue. They also knew the boat had been lost. Apparently Mum and Dad had received hundreds of emails and phone calls from well-wishers expressing their sympathy at the news. People they didn't even know were emailing them to pass on their support. The rescue had also made the news, at least in regional television and newspapers. They had been running the story since the BBC had learned of the rescue, presumably through the coastguard in Falmouth. Dad said the local news channel was keen to contact me for an exclusive but I couldn't do it. I was in no frame of mind for any of that, not yet. Until then I had never declined an interview, but this time it was different.

I talked it all through with Dad, mentioning that we should contact the insurers to prepare the claim. Then the real bombshell dropped. Dad had already contacted Judith to get the ball rolling with the insurers but she had told him that the boat was not fully insured. Apparently the insurance premium had been so high that she had elected to insure the boat for a fraction of its real value in an effort to reduce the premium and had not told me. To top it all, her company had just gone bust. I couldn't believe it. We would see some money from the insurers, but it would be a drop in the ocean compared to what I had borrowed from my family to buy the boat. This is the kind of news you never want to receive. I felt completely beaten.

My unexpected arrival onboard the *EWL Central America* gave me the opportunity to meet a different type of seafarer than I would ordinarily have encountered. Different characters from different parts of the world certainly have their own stories to tell. Despite feeling desperately low, I made the effort to meet the crew and thank them for their part in rescuing me. There was a young Ukrainian officer who was an interesting guy. He had been studying for years to become a qualified seaman and had worked his way up the ladder to the admirable position of watch leader. In his homeland, despite being just in his mid-twenties, he was a man of great distinction. His modest monthly salary kept the whole family, including both his parents and his wife's financially secure. He was saving furiously to buy an apartment he could call his own. He reckoned on another five years of saving. They would then have enough cash to make an outright purchase, something that was apparently a rare privilege where they came from.

Then there was the captain. I liked him too, but I had been warned of his love affair with the Second World War. Apparently it was his favourite topic of conversation. As we sat together at the head of the dinner table he did not disappoint. His stories used to make me laugh. For days he would be banging on about the war and how the German fleet had had superior naval vessels. Gradually I would challenge his statements, while remaining mindful that it was a German ship that had rescued me. What he didn't know was that my grandfather served on board the ship that eventually found the pride of the German fleet, the *Bismarck*. My grandfather's ship, the *Suffolk*, a County Class heavy cruiser, was too small to engage the mighty German battleship. However this didn't stop her shadowing the *Bismarck* while reporting her whereabouts.

A few days earlier, the *Bismarck* had sunk the pride of the British fleet, the *Hood*. Sir Winston Churchill was outraged and ordered all available resources to hunt down and sink the mighty German ship. Thanks in part to Granddad and his shipmates, the *Bismarck* was located and eventually sent to the bottom of the Atlantic. I kept this part of my family history to myself until the final night on board when I could take the proclamations of superior German firepower no longer. The captain took it pretty well and we had a good laugh about it.

The following day we tied up to the dockside in Trinidad and while the many containers began to be unloaded I patiently waited for the local customs to arrive and book me in. The shipping line went out of their way to help me and even arranged for a local representative to drop me at the airport, something I thought was a real act of kindness. With a flight booked in my name I said my goodbyes to the crew and thanked them for their hospitality.

The following day I arrived back in England carrying only my grab bag, survival suit and the few pieces of equipment I had managed to salvage from the boat. Mum and Dad were faithfully waiting at the airport arrival gates as I walked though. I had my equipment in one hand and a heavy heart in the other. Even the clothes I was wearing were not mine. I had lost virtually everything.

It was a long ride home from London to Devon and there was plenty of time to share the story with my parents. I remember sitting in the back of the Land Rover staring out of the window and contemplating my future. Now I was home what would I do, how would I earn a living? My sailing qualifications meant I could work anywhere in the world but working for a charter company or teaching sailing or even going back to delivering sailboats across the oceans just didn't hold the same appeal for me as competitive ocean racing. I was all set for racing around the world. Now those dreams had been taken away I didn't have a clue what I was going to do.

The following weeks were emotionally pretty tough. I felt a huge void had suddenly opened up in my life. I was taking the loss of the boat pretty hard and struggling to come to terms with what had happened. Time and purpose had no meaning. I ended up taking sanctuary in my apartment, locked away from the outside world in an effort to deal with everything. They were dark days, filled with feelings of deep regret. 'If only' became a recurring refrain in my mind: if only I had been closer to land; if only I had been able to lash the keel; if only there hadn't have been a storm on its way. Those thoughts haunted me for a long time. Even now I wonder what the outcome would have been, had any of those things been different.

It was January 2002 and I had various commitments still in place. I made a reluctant trip to the London International Boat Show at Earl's Court for a round of interviews as well as a couple of public appearances I needed to honour. The Around Alone race was holding a press conference and despite not having a boat, I was still a registered entrant. The media wanted to spin it up and I even had an interview scheduled with BBC Radio 4. The thought of reliving the whole saga on national radio wasn't something I was particularly looking forward to but I didn't want to let people down. I had to dig deep to muster a positive attitude. I knew it was important not to come across as being negative, even if that was how I really felt inside.

As the days dragged by, I came to realise that self-pity was not a long-term option. It was hard, but I knew I was the only person who could drag myself out of the turmoil. My deal with Judith had reached a natural conclusion. I had spoken to her the night I arrived back in the UK. It was a pretty frosty conversation and it was clear she was financially busted. The money had run out and despite having a contract the whole saga amounted to little more than fresh air. There wasn't any point chasing her for anything, she had her own world of trouble to deal with. I just had to accept the gloomy situation for what it was – a bloody nightmare. I knew I couldn't stay cooped up in the apartment for ever. I had to come up with a plan to pick myself up off the floor and get back into the land of the living.

A month after abandoning the boat I received a phone call. It was from a ship captain who had apparently seen her. *One Dream One Mission* was still afloat. They had passed by close enough to read my website logos which were on the side of the hull. At that stage she was still upright, although listing heavily. The captain had been concerned that someone might be aboard which was the reason for his call. The thought that she was still afloat gave me hope that we might still find her. That night I had a dinner engagement with Shane and one of our private benefactors in Southampton. The dinner had been arranged for some time and had originally been planned as a celebration of the result in the TJV. Winning such a prestigious race seemed to have fallen into insignificance for me what with the events of the past month. Later on that evening, I told the story of what had happened. There was about ten of us and everyone was keen to hear about the win and subsequent disaster.

Towards the end of dinner I mentioned that the boat had been sighted earlier that morning. Her position was not all that far from where I had originally abandoned her. One of the men who had already generously supported the project immediately offered to bankroll a salvage operation. I was stunned and explained that this type of operation would have a substantial cost. He wasn't fazed and asked if I thought a salvage attempt was possible. My reply was a simple yes, assuming we could find her. He suggested I waste no time and start my preparations.

In the time it took to order our desserts I had been given the support needed to go and get my boat back. As we sat around the table I hastily called my friend John Wright and arranged a flight to the Canary Islands. John literally dropped everything and within the hour was packed and driving down from Cambridge to rendezvous at Shane's house in Southampton. The plan was for me and John to fly to the Canaries the following morning, where we would try to hire a private plane to go in search of the boat. Shane would follow the day after with some money to help with the logistics.

If we managed to find her, we would mark her position and then charter a suitable boat to take us the several hundred miles to her location. The same plane would then fly out again once we were in the area to help pinpoint *One Dream One Mission* as we arrived at the last known position. I would board the boat and sail back to the islands in convoy. Simple enough in principle, but success relied on a number of factors outside of my control – finding a suitable plane, actually finding the boat and then locating her again several days after we had left the islands on the salvage boat.

Finding a pilot willing to fly that far into the Atlantic was quite difficult. Most of the private aircraft registered in the islands were single-engine affairs. The owners were understandably not that keen to fly so far away from land without the back-up of a second engine. I was so fired up about finding the boat that I was prepared to accept the risks but, despite my waving some serious cash in front of them, the pilots didn't share my enthusiasm. One of the few interested parties was a commercial aircraft operator who had expressed some interest but lack of availability scuppered that plan. The price was also a mind-blowing amount for just one day's hire.

While John and I concentrated on securing floating transport, Shane dealt with the airborne side of things. We had asked around and spoken to several locals before we were given the name of an ex-military guy who was also an expat, living in Tenerife. A quick phone call was made and a meeting was hastily arranged. That night, John and I met up with the guy and explained the situation. Time was running out, as several days had now passed since the ship had sighted *One Dream One Mission*.

We met the guy at a local bar in the small resort of Playa de Las Americas. He was a well-built character, about six feet tall and obviously a man who spent significant time working-out. He listened intently as I explained our predicament. He soon had serious questions and point blank asked if there were drugs on board. I hadn't seen that coming but on reflection I suppose the situation must have looked a bit dodgy to an outsider – two guys looking to recruit help with locating a lost yacht on the ocean. His reservations were understandable. I did my best to reassure him that I was a professional sailor and no drugs baron. I felt under pressure and soon tired of his over-cautious behaviour. The man wanted our passports so he could supposedly check us out and try to corroborate our story. This was ridiculous, no way was I going to give up my passport to a complete stranger. I suggested he either took the situation for what it was or he walked away. Either way we didn't have the luxury of time.

John's experience in the forces helped them find some common ground and eventually we had a possible plan. The guy explained he knew of a pilot who might be willing to fly out that far in search of the boat, although his approach to the recovery differed considerably to mine. If we sighted the boat his suggestion involved the two of us jumping out of the plane and parachuting into the water before clambering aboard so I could sail us back. The plane could drop necessary supplies and then a chartered boat would intercept, to guide us home. This proposal made the most of the time available but also sent the stakes through the roof. The guy suggested I piggybacked him on the parachute drop to minimise the risk. Minimise risk! I decided he must be nuts.

I had had no parachute training and we would be limited in the equipment we could take with us as we jumped out of the plane. There was also no guarantee we would be able to reach the boat once we landed in the sea. That far out on the ocean if something went wrong we would be dead. It was a bold plan. Stuff it, I was up for it. What an awesome story it would be if we actually made it.

Unfortunately nothing ever came of that meeting. The guy just couldn't convince his pilot friend to fly the several hundred miles across the ocean, so the plan was off. This left us with just one option. We would charter a boat and go in search ourselves. The chances of finding *One Dream One Mission* without airborne support were small but I felt compelled to try. It didn't take long to find a suitable yacht and by mid-morning we had secured the services of a seventy-two-foot ketch that was tied up to a dock in Tenerife. The crew consisted of a young first mate and his girlfriend who was the cook.

The skipper didn't fill me with confidence, however. He was a little older than me, in his late twenties, and stank of booze. His cavalier attitude towards life was a little disconcerting and I wondered whether this was just another accident waiting to happen. I had my reservations but conceded this was never going to be a perfect scenario. With a deal done for cash, we paid half upfront and agreed to pay the balance when we returned to the islands. The first mate and his girlfriend were keen sailors and knew me by reputation. They had read an article in a yachting magazine about the loss of the boat and were excited about the adventure.

The following morning, with fresh supplies loaded we slipped the mooring and set a course west. The yacht's owner had heard about the unusual charter request and had also jumped aboard for the ride. A pleasant guy in his forties with little sailing experience, he had purchased the yacht as a new business venture the previous year. His plan had been to establish a day charter business, taking paying holidaymakers around the beautiful islands. He was intrigued by our adventure and was keen to hear my story. It would take nearly three days of sailing before we reached the last known position of the boat, so there was plenty of time to keep everyone fuelled with tales of adventures on the high seas. The skipper who had given a good impression of an accident waiting to happen proved to be better than anticipated. Once sober he turned into a totally different person and was quite competent.

We searched for several days, without success. The last known position revealed nothing other than an empty ocean. For hours upon hours we searched the horizon following the general direction of the ocean currents. But after two days I conceded the search was over, it was time to turn around and head back. We returned to the UK disappointed that our efforts had drawn a blank. It would be another three months before I would hear from the boat again.

When I eventually did receive another call it was to inform me that my trusty yellow boat had been salvaged by a Brazilian fisherman who apparently had found her about six hundred miles off the north-eastern coast of Brazil. In just a few months the boat had travelled nearly eighteen hundred miles from the point where I had abandoned her five hundred miles to the west of the Canary Islands. I was amazed she had travelled so far. The fisherman spoke reasonable English, enough to hold a conversation. It became clear the boat was in a bad way. The guy was keen to make a deal and was offering the boat back in return for payment.

The news that the boat had been found brought with it a flood of emotions. By now I had accepted that she had most likely succumbed to the might of the ocean. I was both surprised and excited to hear that she had been found. The fisherman sent me some pictures and it was clear that it was my boat. Within hours, John and I were once again sitting on a plane in search of the boat.

The boat was lying in Fortaleza, a commercial port on the north-eastern tip of Brazil and it would be a long and tiring journey to get there. After flying into Recife airport John and I swapped planes and boarded a scheduled internal flight to Fortaleza before travelling the final miles by coach. We arrived at the sun-drenched port mid-afternoon, tired and hungry. We knew the boat was somewhere in the harbour and so wasted no time in starting our search. Half an hour later we were presented with a very sorry sight. Standing on a small dockside on the opposite side of the bay from the yacht marina we spotted my stricken *One Dream One Mission*. She was in a terrible state, barely afloat. The bow was sunken beneath the surface of the water and the main cabin was almost completely flooded. The mast had long since broken away, leaving just a small stump sticking up from the deck, while the hull was showing signs of serious structural damage along each side. The boat had certainly been through hell, yet despite now resembling little more than a hulk, she had remained afloat.

We couldn't climb on board. She was tied up to a fishing boat which was secured to a mooring buoy about sixty feet from the shore-line. There was little else to do other than set off in search of the fisherman. Following the directions the fisherman had given me we soon found ourselves walking through a pretty run-down area on the outskirts of town. The road was covered in a thick layer of dust and dirt and several dead animals lay by the roadside. This was definitely a poor part of town. A hundred yards ahead we could see a building surrounded by tall white-washed walls with solid wooden gates. I just knew this was the address where the fisherman would be. We knocked on the doors and I introduced myself as the owner of the boat.

As the huge wooden gates opened it looked to me like there was more than just fishing going on there. Behind the gates was a driveway with several top-of-the-range Mercedes and an impressive looking house. Two well-built men showed us into a smoke-filled office area where the boss was waiting. I noticed the solid gold Rolex on his wrist the minute I walked through the door. He was leaning back in a chair near the back of the room smoking a fat cigar.

The two heavies stayed by the doorway. Two women in their late thirties sat behind separate desks. They didn't seem to speak any English and I was later told they were family members. Whatever this guy was into, it was clear he was a businessman. He offered us coffee and explained the situation. They had found the boat and were willing to give it back in exchange for a hundred thousand dollars. I nearly fell of my chair. At this point the fisherman's son, who had been sitting quietly in a corner of the room joined in the conversation. He explained they were aware that the boat had just won a big race to Brazil and that they knew it was very valuable. They had obviously done their homework.

I tried to tell them that as the boat was now little more than a wreck it was pretty much worthless. As I sat in the smoke-filled room, the reality of the situation dawned on me. Even if they had given the boat back for free, it would have cost a small fortune to ship her back to the UK. In such a terrible condition it would make better financial sense to build a new boat than to repair her. Her delicate state was such that there was no way we could even think about sailing her back. The situation seemed hopeless.

I knew before travelling to Brazil that the people who salvaged the boat would be entitled to some kind of remuneration under the conditions of maritime law but my budget was limited to a maximum of just a few thousand pounds. Perhaps I was rather naive but I was hoping they would understand my position and accept what I had to offer. I did my best to broker a deal but it was clear that the figures on the table were light years apart. This was an awful situation, the man and his son were adamant that I would either pay their price or that was that. In their eyes, the price for the boat's freedom was not up for negotiation. I accepted they had a legitimate claim for some kind of fair remuneration but told them that I didn't think their price was remotely realistic. I could see John was looking less than comfortable sitting in his chair. My comments weren't going down well and while the boss man seemed to accept what I was saying, the others in the room were less than impressed. I almost felt lucky to walk out of the room with my life, it was that intimidating a situation.

Later that afternoon John and I were taken out to the wreck and I clambered aboard. The once-proud boat looked even worse up close. Everything of any value had been looted when she arrived in the port. The cabin area was submerged and almost everything that had been bolted to the deck was now missing. What remained was no more than a lost cause.

Later that day I approached the fisherman. He and his entourage had come down to the port to see what we were up to. He was quite hospitable but remained steadfast in his request for serious cash. His son suggested I must be a millionaire to own such a boat and a that hundred thousand dollars was a small price to pay to get it back. I admired their optimism, but the whole affair felt more like a ransom demand than a simple request for a salvage fee. I declined their offer. I was once again devastated to leave my boat behind but I knew I really had no option.

I felt devastated as we left the wreck of *One Dream One Mission* in Fortaleza.

14

SAILING TO SELLING

I had hit rock bottom but could now see a way out of the mess. Seeing the wreck of *One Dream One Mission* in Fortaleza had somehow given me the sense of closure I needed. It was clear I was facing radical change in my life but the loss of the boat had not changed my view of competitive ocean racing. The high stakes, high-risk winner-takes-all environment is one of the main attractions for me. I like being on the edge and believe sailing across an ocean at full tilt is what life is all about. The fires fuelled by the passion to compete on the ocean were still burning in my heart. But with no money and no boat I had to consider a future without the one thing that gives me a reason to get up in the morning, at least for the short term.

For weeks I had stared out of my apartment window thinking of what I wanted to do. After the Mini Transat my sponsor English Braids had hinted there would always be a job for me within their sales team should I want it. My direct experience of using their products on the race track would be an ideal foundation for actually selling the stuff to the marine industry. While this was a good opportunity, I had declined it at the time. My passion lay in professional ocean racing and even now it was my mission to eventually get back in the game. I knew I would somehow one day return to the circuit. Taking a mainstream job would mean a permanent departure from that way of life. I didn't want that and my soul is not the kind that fits well into a desk job.

When considering my future I kept coming back to one thing, the motor trade. 'Always stick to what you know in life' was one of the first things my father taught me. Sailing and selling cars are the two things I really know about. My apprenticeship in the family car business before

I turned professional had given me a great grounding and was something I always enjoyed, even though I had left that life behind when I moved to Devon and joined Pete Goss on the *Team Philips* project. I have always had a passion for cars so it made sense to consider a new path that lead towards familiar territory.

One idea I had had years before was importing vehicles from other countries to the UK for re-sale. While I had been working at Goss Challenges I had noticed the imported car trade was starting to grow. A leisurely Sunday afternoon read of the local motoring magazine highlighted the rising demand. I had thought then that it might be a profitable market but at the time I was far too busy. Now I had nothing but time, so I took the opportunity to research the market.

It was spring 2002 and I had a new project to re-energise myself and get back onto my feet, at least in the financial sense. I decided to target a specific area of the motor trade that was enjoying a particularly exciting revival. The nation's hunger for the ever-popular sports car was where I would direct my focus, in particular the Japanese import market and the Mazda MX-5. This iconic two-seater roadster had earned the title as the world's best selling sports car, no doubt because of its legendary reliability and superb handling ability. The little MX-5 punches well above its weight and as a result the lovable sports car is adored by tens of thousands of people around the world.

I knew I could buy these cars in Japan and then ship them over to the UK to sell to enthusiasts in England. The benefits of buying the cars from the other side of the world were fourfold: I would be selling second-hand examples around ten years old. In Japan the climate is such that they don't use salt on their roads in winter. As a result, the cars are less likely to display the signs of rust and stand the test of time far better than the average British equivalent. There is a different mindset in Japan which demands a much higher specification, so the Japanese cars all have power steering and air conditioning as standard. Also, Japanese cars tend to have a lower mileage year-on-year in comparison to their British counterparts.

Lastly and crucially, Japan was in a recession at the time and had been for a while. The Japanese Yen was weak and the British pound went a very long way. This was the icing on the cake. I could buy the cars cheaply enough to warrant shipping them back to the UK and still make a worthwhile profit even after dealing with the various customs charges and import taxes levied on them as they arrived on British soil.

It was a great idea. My only problem was a lack of money to get the business up and running. My financial position meant that I had to cut my cloth accordingly. Initially I would buy the cars in the UK either privately by travelling around the country, picking up the odd bargain from the maze of online internet advertisements or I would purchase them directly on the docks at Southampton as they arrived fresh off the boat from Japan.

My parents' devotion was astonishing – they were willing to help me get started. But the recent huge financial loss of the boat weighed heavy on my mind. I was reluctant to borrow any more cash than was absolutely necessary to start things off. I think they were just pleased I was pulling myself together and moving forward. I also had my credit card and so, with the intention of breaking every personal rule that I held dear, I walked into my bank and borrowed five grand in cash. This was high stakes alright. As I walked out of the bank I could almost feel the clock ticking. I had set myself a target of repaying the money within the month. Thirty days of credit. If I could do that the bank was working for me but if I missed the deadline the interest rate would be outrageous. Sometimes you have to have the confidence of your convictions. I have never had a problem trusting my own judgement and I knew the cash would be enough to buy two cars. That would get me started but I knew I had better make the right choice and they had better return a profit or I would slip further into the quagmire.

I already had my first two deals lined up before I took out the credit card loan. I had verbally agreed a deal for a car from a trader in London who imported regular shipments from Japan. I would be paying more to buy from him but there was still a profit to be squeezed. In any case, in order to buy direct from the source in Japan, I would need to be well-funded and most likely would need to buy in bulk. The second deal was with a private individual in Sheffield who sounded to me like he needed the money. The first day of my new life was underway and I felt good for making a positive step forward.

I travelled to London first and tied up the deal with the trader. The drive back from London was fantastic. The sun was shining and the little sports car was a pleasure to drive. I took advantage of the soft-top roof and enjoyed the wind in my hair as I left the capital behind me in the rear view mirror. Stereo on, blasting down the home stretch on the

A38 near Exeter I knew the little roadster was a safe bet. She didn't miss a beat and I soon had the car parked on Mum and Dad's driveway awaiting a much needed clean and polish. My parents had agreed to let me keep the cars at their place while I set everything up. Twenty-four hours later, having made a successful trip to Sheffield, both cars had been cleaned to within an inch of their lives. Their paintwork was now gleaming in the sunlight, telling me they were ready for their new owners.

The following Friday I impatiently waited for the local motoring magazine with my adverts to go on sale. I received my first call by lunchtime and by six that evening I had sold the first one for a profit. Before the weekend was out I had sold the other one and was soon glued to the computer in the search for new stock. Things were certainly looking up. I bought and sold another two cars that month before walking into the bank and repaying the cash I had borrowed. Two days later I withdrew further funds and the process started all over again. I travelled the length and breadth of the country hunting down cars. In the space of three months I had established myself and had a good routine for sourcing the metal. They were selling like hotcakes and poor Mum would regularly have to park her Land Rover on the road because the driveway was completely stacked with sporty little Mazdas. It was clear I needed to expand but that meant taking on new premises and a serious financial commitment.

This was my first big decision for the new business. Selling a few cars from the driveway was one thing, but taking on a lease for a commercial building was a totally different matter. I talked it over with Dad. I had no realistic alternative, storing the cars at my parent's house was only ever going to be a short term solution. Once the business found its footing I knew I would need a suitable storage facility. I decided to err on the side of caution and soon found a small but tidy lockup on an industrial estate in the heart of Torquay, just five minutes from my apartment. It was perfect and had enough scope for the business to grow while keeping the overheads to a minimum.

A recent trip to Southampton docks had uncovered some good trade contacts. My father had come along for a day out as we wanted to check out a new trade-only import auction that had just opened. The promise of a healthy supply of cars fresh from Japan seemed a better option than my weekly escapades across the country in search of the odd bargain.

Like all car auctions, you had to have your head screwed on to sort the wheat from the chaff. But amongst the forest of Japanese cars there were always a number of little gems waiting to be discovered. This type of auction is always fast and furious. Hundreds of cars drove through the hall while the auctioneer skilfully strived to achieve the best price. This was a professional arena and most knew their business. I could easily spot those that didn't.

Hands in the air, sign language, the subtle nod of the head, the flick of a clenched hand holding a rolled-up auction programme; everyone has their own preferred method of signalling their bid. When you walk into the arena of a car auction you are walking into a different world, one where knowledge and quick thinking are just two of the essential skills required to navigate your way through the murky world of second-hand cars. Understanding the game is critical – make a mistake and you could end up with a pup. Even if the car you are bidding on is a good one, there is no guarantee you won't pay over the odds for it. The general perception is that auctions are great places to grab a bargain, but this is not always the case. It takes just seconds for each car to go from first being introduced to being sold. It's you against everyone in the room, including the auctioneer. I prefer to do my homework a couple of hours before auctions kick off. I always get there early and check out the cars before things get underway. I know the cars I want and set a maximum price. A penny more and I let it go. An auction room is no place for emotion.

I soon discovered that the newly-established auction house was a great source for my kind of cars. I became a regular there and they quickly got to know me on first-name terms. This side of the motor trade is where you can experience the business in its rawest form. People from all walks of life come together to effectively do battle on the auction room floor. The shorts and sandals brigade rub shoulders with the suits wearing gold Rolex watches, while the overweight fifty-something traders stand to the side eating greasy bacon sandwiches. It all goes with the territory.

Despite attractive prices, I knew there was an opportunity to get these cars at an even better discounted rate if I could make contacts in Japan. Buying at source had been my goal from the start. I had managed to set up a contact in Japan that I had discovered on the internet. The company offered cheap cars direct from the trade centres. They had a clearing agent based in the UK who was willing to deal with the financial transactions and was pleased to act as a kind of broker on my behalf, for a small fee. The business looked potentially risky. I had a feeling they must either be buying the cars so cheaply that they made money from me at the point of purchase as well as taking an agreed fee, or they were just one of the many internet-based companies out there looking to scam people out of their hard-earned cash. Either way, there was no real way of knowing unless I gave it a go. There were obvious benefits from having contacts in the heart of the Japanese motor industry. I knew I had to work my way into a position where I could eventually cut out the middlemen.

I decided the risk was worth it. I would roll the dice and gamble a few pounds and have a go at purchasing a car. I would buy an older model in order to limit the potential risk. My dad always says 'only gamble with what you can afford to lose', so with that in mind, I contacted the agent and brokered a deal for a ten year old MX-5. The process seemed simple. They would give me access to a website that showed all the available cars and I would pick one that was coming up for auction. The broker, a Japanese guy who spoke good English, would then call me as the car came up in the auction house and I would make any last-minute changes to my bid while leaving him to do his best to secure the car. I would need to place a holding deposit with the UK agent before they would do anything and then twenty-four hours after confirmation of a successful bid I had to pay for the car in full. Plenty of opportunity for them to run off with my cash, I thought.

Eight weeks after receiving a phone call in the early hours of the morning informing me of a successful purchase, I received another, this time from the agent in England. The little car had arrived and was waiting for collection at Southampton docks. I couldn't believe it – the car had actually arrived? Having had weeks to convince myself the venture would probably go sour I was pleasantly surprised. My thoughts then turned to whether it would turn out to be a complete dog. I couldn't just send it back to Japan and ask for a refund. Whatever was waiting for me in Southampton, I was stuck with it.

Anxious to dive in, I rounded up my father, who was also intrigued to see what was waiting for us, and the two of us shot off to Southampton with low expectations. Three hours later, we were staring at the long-awaited package. We couldn't believe it. Not only had the car arrived, it was a cracker. The car was immaculate, not just around the bodywork but also underneath. It was as clean as a whistle, a real gem.

Less than ten days later, with the car fully prepared, I had agreed a sale and I watched as the bright little roadster pulled off the driveway with the new owners smiling from cheek to cheek. It was a very satisfying experience.

Our first sports car from Japan.

Hungry for more, I was back on the road and headed for the auction in Southampton. It was here on one particular Tuesday that my dad and I got talking to a guy from Japan. Steve was actually an Australian who had come over to the UK to drum up new business for his company. Along with his brother Wayne, who was married to a Japanese girl, Steve ran a modest import-export business from their offices in Nagoya, Japan.

We were standing at the back of the auction hall checking out a couple of cars when Steve walked up to us. In an unmistakable Australian accent he said hello. "G'day mate, you'se looking to buy some cars from Japan?" Steve's laid-back approach was probably not the best sales pitch in the world but something about his character was intriguing. His question sparked my interest and we listened to what he had to say. Steve was offering to supply used cars direct from Japan and to help with the administration up to the point of loading onto a UK-bound ship. This was certainly a good proposition although I was initially a little sceptical as to how I would limit any potential financial risk. After all, I only just met the bloke and had no idea whether he was a straight-shooter or a con man. As it turned out Steve and his brother Wayne are stand-up guys and completely genuine, although I would not realise this until after my first trip to Japan.

Our chat next to the burger van inside the noisy auction hall turned into a lengthy conversation. I remember drinking plenty of coffee that day as the three of us worked through the possibilities, only pausing when my focus momentarily shifted as cars I had been interested in came up for sale. We discussed how such a venture would work for both parties and agreed on some basic principles there and then. I would fly out to Japan and with the aid of Steve and Wayne I would buy my first batch of stock. It would be a short trip and I would purchase just a couple of cars to test the waters. Despite the allure of significantly lower-priced vehicles available directly from the trade-only Japanese auction houses, I would take it slowly and hedge my bets. On the one hand this was the opportunity I had been looking for, a chance to get to the trade centres in Japan, but on the other it could easily end up in disaster, with me losing the shirt off my back.

The key to the deal was the fact that apart from a small cash deposit to show good faith, the lads didn't want full payment for the cars until the vehicles were on a ship headed for the UK. Once they supplied an original Bill of Lading I would send the monies through. This was a sweet deal and provided my financial security.

Seven days later, I was sitting on a plane headed for the land of the rising sun. One of the interesting things about the motor industry in Japan is that you can't just rock up to an auction and start buying cars like you can in England. There, the auction process is both more technologically advanced and also more regulated. Only bona-fide registered trade individuals can gain access and the process to become registered is very complicated if you don't live in the country. Steve and Wayne were fully-fledged members with several of the major auction groups and so had access to pretty much all the cars you could want.

The lads greeted me at Narita airport and the following morning we took a drive to sample my first Japanese auction in Toyota City. The difference between the Japanese and English auction houses struck me as soon as I walked through the front doors. This was a clean modern building with what can only be described as an auditorium filled with row upon row of comfortable seats and small desks. In front of the seats, way up high, there were four giant computer screens, colour-coded to correspond with the four push button devices on the desks. I wondered how they drove the cars through the auction hall but soon realised that this was a whole new take on the auction process. With nearly a thousand vehicles to get through in just one day, the cars were not driven anywhere. Instead, their images appeared on the giant screens. Wayne explained that as the cars appeared we would place our bids by clicking the relevant button. The auction house would know who placed the highest bid because we had to insert a special member's card into a machine on the desk to identify ourselves. This was high-tech stuff, with not a whisper of anyone shouting the bids out loud as in the British way.

We'd done our homework on the cars the night before and I had identified several that appealed. When it was time to look the cars over, we went outside. The vast area was littered with hundreds of them. It required all my navigational skills just to find the ones I wanted. Back in the auditorium, the auction was a breathtakingly efficient process and once underway it was a captivating experience. I watched as all four screens flashed up dozens of cars every few minutes. The system was quite simple. The bids increased by a set amount and you repeatedly pushed the button while watching the value of the car rapidly increase until you either reached your limit or the car sold. It was certainly frantic with an array of flashing lights and funny noises all signalling various bits of information. When the red light turned to green that particular car was selling, while a beep at our table signified our bid had been successful. It was an amazing experience and I must confess to wanting to buy the whole lot. I felt like a young boy with his hand in the cookie jar.

I bought four cars on my first trip and I realised that my gut feeling had been right about the other firm. They had been buying the cars and making a extra margin on the cost of the cars in addition to taking the agreed broker's fee. I didn't mind, that was just business, but I had wanted to cut out the middle men and now I had done so. Steve and Wayne had proved to be the genuine article, as well as great guys. After taking in some of the local sights, my short trip was over and I returned to the UK both jubilant and excited. The Japanese connection was set up, all I had to do was wait. The four cars wouldn't arrive for six weeks but when they did I was positive I would make a killing.

A year and several excursions to Japan later, I had quite a production line going. The Southampton auction house that had initially provided me with a source of stock was now selling my cars. I was making regular trips to Japan in the search of quality vehicles. I was buying in bulk and regularly had shipments of thirty or more vehicles arriving at any one time. I would select the cream of the bunch for the retail side of the business in the West Country, while sending the rest through the auction on the docks.

I remember standing outside the auction one summer's day. The sun was shining as I waited for my batch of cars to go through the block. I could see the sails of yachts ghosting along Southampton Water, powered by a light gentle breeze. I recognised one particular yacht as it sailed by. The skipper was a professional sailor and a guy I knew well. I couldn't quite see the boat, it was masked by the dockside buildings, but I could read the sponsors' logos on the mainsail. I looked at my new world inside the auction hall and thought how strange life can be. Eighteen months earlier that would have been me out there chasing the dream. Now I had a new life, at least for the time being. I vowed there and then to get back into the game. When the time was right I would return.

Right now I was completely off the grid. I had plenty of offers to go sailing but I needed to focus on my new business. I didn't even pick up a sailing magazine for over a year. I think I would have found it too difficult to read about the action while knowing I wasn't part of it. For now, my twenty-four/seven diet of buying and selling cars was enough to both keep my focus and to put food on the table.

BACK TO BASICS

A phone call that came out of the blue proved to be the ideal cata-
lyst for the events that brought me back into the world of sailing.
The call was from a guy who was training for a race around the
British Isles. He was looking for advice on how best to prepare for the
event and had been given my number by a third party who suggested
I might be able to help. The guy had chartered a purpose-built fifty-
footer and was having problems with some technical aspects of the
boat. The yacht was an out-and-out racer, very similar to *One Dream
One Mission*, and was proving quite a handful. He was keen for some
coaching and support leading up to the start of his race.

Ifor Pedley is a father of two and a professional who works in the
printing industry and had just turned forty when he contacted me.
Ifor had learnt his business from ground up, having joined the printing world after leaving school. He had steadily worked his way up the
ladder and now enjoyed a position of seniority within his business. At
the time, he worked for a well-known national publishing company
responsible for printing national newspapers. He had discovered
competitive sailing only relatively recently but was a fast learner and
already more than just a competent yachtsman. He is a qualified Yacht
Master and a great guy with a lovely temperament. He has a big heart
and an admirable character. From our first meeting I could tell he was
an ambitious man who liked a challenge and adventure. We quickly hit
it off and I agreed to help prepare him for his race.

By the end of the year we had become good friends and he
suggested we sail together the following season. Ifor had secured a
modest budget through some corporate sponsorship. The money paid

the bills and enabled him to undertake the kind of challenges many people can only read about. Admirably, Ifor was using his sailing adventures to help raise money for the Printer's Charitable Corporation. Ifor is always up for some excitement so it didn't come as a surprise when I received a phone call explaining that he had just agreed a deal to charter a very fast and highly-strung forty-three-foot trimaran for the summer. He wanted us to take part in the AZAB race, a double-handed event from Falmouth to the Azores and back. Furthermore, he had the budget to make it happen. Naturally I was keen to be involved and so with an agreement in place we travelled up to Amble on the north-east coast to collect the boat and sail her home to Dartmouth where we would base our campaign.

The delivery to Dartmouth was an uneventful one. My grandparents were delighted to receive the customary telephone call as we sailed past the entrance to Whitby harbour, my childhood home. Whenever I pass the area by sea I call them to say hello. Granddad is always particularly excited to hear about his grandson's modern-day high seas adventures and would no doubt love to join me if he were a few years younger.

Despite being an uneventful passage, the three-day delivery had highlighted a breathtakingly long job list. Time was tight before the start of the race so I decided to draft in one of the volunteers who had originally worked at Goss Challenges during *Team Philips* days. Mike Shand is a keen sailor and retired ex-Royal Air Force mechanic. He had been one of the many invaluable unpaid workers who gave their precious time to the project. He had also leant a hand with some of our preparations for the assault on the Transat Jacques Vabre. Mike had already expressed a willingness to be involved with any future campaigns so I gave him a call and asked if he wanted to be part of the action. He jumped at the chance and quickly became an indispensable member of our support crew. Neither of us knew at the time but this project would be the start of a journey which would see both me and Mike achieve lifelong ambitions.

My friendship with Ifor and his willingness to help with my sailing aspirations led to a chance meeting with the head of a major corporate brand that could turn my dreams into reality. Ifor had mentioned my plans and Fujifilm were interested enough to meet up and hear what I had to say. We scheduled a meeting at the Royal Castle Hotel in Dartmouth and whilst discussing present and future sailing projects, I outlined my plans.

They were certainly keen but I could sense a cautious attitude as well. Keith Dalton and Graham Leeson both hold high positions and are decision-makers in the group. They could see the value of such a business proposition but wanted to test the water before committing to a serious project. I suggested the Mini circuit. Financially it would be more conservative than a campaign with a bigger boat. It was also familiar territory for me, I knew the circuit and the prospect of another crack at the Mini Transat was certainly appealing. I had very nearly achieved a podium place before and this time, with more experience under my belt, I would have a real shot at the top slot. Most importantly, the Mini circuit would give Fujifilm an insight into the world of ocean racing without committing serious cash. The project would inevitably have a price tag attached to it, but would also highlight the further opportunities while showing a good return for their investment. Should they want to commit to a bigger project in the future, the Mini campaign would serve as a good basis to make an informed decision.

Our pitch was successful and they agreed to sign up. I was ecstatic. Thanks to Ifor's support we had just secured the backing of a major player. Our budget was modest but more than enough to mount a serious and competitive campaign on the Mini circuit. The new twenty-one foot long boat would bear the name *Fujifilm* and be colour-coded to match the distinctive green corporate identity. I would report to the graphics division although in effect our campaign represented the whole Fujifilm brand. The graphics team was particularly keen to explore the photographic opportunities associated with a project such as this. Having a boat completely colour-coded with their branding slapped all over it was an opportunity not to be missed. From a marketing point of view, a white sail on a blue sea was perfect for some stunning photography. It was the start of a great partnership and from that moment I knew I was well and truly back.

The search for a suitable boat didn't take long. One of the best boats on the circuit was on the market and for sale locally in Plymouth. The owner was a friend of mine. He was keen to sell and more importantly, I knew the boat and her pedigree. *Reality* was several years old but had been designed by Groupe Finot, one of the most famous naval architects in the sailing world. I knew her original owner and was also aware that she had been built by one of the best builders in the business, with a big budget. *Reality* was a boat to aspire to and, in little more than the time it took to make the phone call, we agreed on a price and a deal was done. By the end of the week, I had taken delivery of the new boat and towed her by road to Baltic Wharf. We wasted no time in starting a rigorous refit programme in preparation for the upcoming season. *Reality* was all white and the rebranding exercise meant we had to unbolt and remove every piece of deck hardware before rubbing down the whole surface of the boat in preparation for the new bright green Fujifilm livery to be painted on. The process was pretty labour-intensive as well as time-consuming but it would produce the best overall finish. I was adamant the boat must look the business. After all, we were ambassadors for our new partners. What good was a boat that looked anything less than exceptional?

The plan was to compete on the Mini circuit in France. We would focus on securing an entry into the epic four thousand-mile single-handed Mini Transat race at the end of the season. Things had changed since 1999 when I had last taken part in the race. The qualification process was now far stricter and more hotly contested. Thanks to my participation in the 1999 event I was exempt from the thousand-mile solo qualification passage but would still need to satisfy the remaining requirements for qualification and complete several events in the Mini calendar.

There were a couple of single-handed events while the majority were double-handed races and for those, Ifor would join me as my co-skipper. We had already agreed we would sail together if Fuji gave the go-ahead. Without his introduction, we both knew I wouldn't have their name splashed along the side of the boat. It was a form of reward in recognition of Ifor's kind support although I would have asked him anyway. We had become good friends and I enjoyed our sailing together.

Our commitments to Fujifilm were not just limited to races. We would undertake a dedicated photography programme where the colour-coded boat with all her branding would take centre stage. From a marketing perspective the boat represented a floating promotional billboard while internally the graphics division would use the images to promote their activities throughout the Fujifilm group. I particularly liked this idea as internal buy-in from the other divisions of the company would be a key factor if they were to consider supporting a more ambitious project in the future. Last but not least, corporate hospitality would form a small but important part of the contract. We would take a select group of clients on board the little boat as part of a hospitality sailing programme. This last obligation was a little worrying because the boat was so small and didn't lend herself well to entertaining passengers. Ifor and I agreed that our pocket rocket was far more likely to scare the living daylights out of anyone other than a competent sailor. I explained we would have to pick our weather, but nonetheless was pleased to agree to the schedule and looked forward to getting back to basics.

As a rookie in the stormy 1999 event I had achieved a more-than-creditable result and nearly reached the podium. This time I knew I had the ability and confidence to achieve that top result but there was much work to do first. With the refit underway, I had more than enough on my plate. I was juggling my commitments at the car yard and the sailing project. The car business was a success and by now had become very much a family affair. My father, who had retired early, had enjoyed helping me out as the business established itself and finding that retired life was not all it was cracked up to be, Dad was now part of the infrastructure. Of course, where my dad goes, so does my mum.

By now I was very much aware that the professional sailing world is a difficult career for anyone solely reliant on corporate sponsorship. Some of the top names in the sport have other business interests that keep them going in between the sponsorship deals. In this game, you are only as good as your last contract and I was determined to keep both the car yard and my sailing business running in parallel. That way, when the contract eventually drew to a close I would have something established to fall back on.

My time was initially split between hands-on work in the boatyard and being on the phone trying to encourage some of my previous marine partners to join the project. I drew up a list of all my previous supporters and contacted each of them to inform them of my return. Several were interested and before the refit had been completed we had plenty of support. Raymarine, a major marine electronics company, agreed to supply all of my onboard instruments and most importantly, would provide two of their new state-of-the-art autopilot systems. Essential for single-handed sailing, the autopilot is one of the most valuable pieces of equipment for any solo racer. Without one you quickly lose any competitive edge.

My long-term cordage sponsor English Braids was also keen to be part of the action. Their title sponsorship for my 1999 Mini campaign had been a real success for both parties and one of the most successful branding exercises they had ever embarked upon. Their continued support was equally appreciated. They were quick to sign up as a partner and agreed to supply the mountain of cordage required to equip one of these boats. We also managed to convince Peter Earp to loan their company helicopter for one of our photo shoots as part of the

deal. This saved the project essential funds and also provided a degree of flexibility when choosing the perfect day for the shoot. Fujifilm were especially pleased and it was agreed that any business partners would benefit from royalty-free access to our campaign image library for use in their own marketing campaigns. It was a good move and one that could only benefit everyone, especially our title sponsor. With the business side of the project taking shape, all that was left was to announce our new partnerships to the media and hope that they would tell the world.

The Fujifilm team, left to right: Ifor Pedley, Graham Leeson, me and Keith Dalton.

When the boat came out of the paint shed what stood in front of us looked a completely different beast to the boat I had purchased a few weeks earlier. I had commissioned the services of a local car sprayer who was also a keen sailor. Richard Hatton had first been introduced to me during the TJV project and had repainted some of our equipment and travelled to France to watch the start of the race. After the loss of the boat, I had kept in touch with him and sent the odd car to his body shop for remedial work. Richard is a quiet, unassuming chap who, unknown to most of his clients, has a significant amount of small boat ocean mileage under his belt. More importantly, he was someone I trusted to do a good job.

Richard's workmanship was excellent and our pocket rocket looked awesome in her new all-green livery. I watched with quiet satisfaction as the white sponsor's logos were skilfully applied by the signwriters. It was a proud moment. I sat perched on a set of scaffolding overlooking the boat, relishing the feeling of achievement.

Despite being meticulous in our preparations the sailing season did not go exactly according to plan. For the 2004 season the Mini class organisers lifted a long-held ban on carbon fibre masts. Previously all masts were required to be standard aluminium sections which were heavy and sometimes susceptible to collapsing under the pressure of the giant unrestricted sail plans permitted by the class rules. With the new rules, significant savings in weight and an increase in strength and reliability could be achieved by choosing a carbon mast instead of a standard aluminium one. Ifor and I had decided at the beginning that we would order a new carbon mast and had placed an order with a local company that was already established within the industry and keen to break into the Mini fleet. I had been quite specific in detailing my requirements. I wasn't particularly concerned with having the lightest mast in the fleet but did want, above all else, a reliable product.

When I received a phone call saying the mast was ready for inspection I was excited and wasted no time in driving to Plymouth to take a look. The finished article looked aesthetically superb but I instantly had the worrying feeling that it was rather too delicate and lightweight for the task. The manufacturer was adamant he had done all the necessary calculations and seemed proud to have created a product that was nearly half the weight of the standard aluminium masts. At the time it was difficult to accept his claims and ignore my gut instinct, but they were supposed to be the experts, so I put my faith in them and hoped my concerns would prove unfounded.

The first race of the season proved to be a tough one, as if any events within the Mini circuit are ever anything but. I led the fleet out of the bay of Pornichet and enjoyed some typical close racing throughout the night and into the following morning. The wind progressively built all night and with deteriorating weather conditions, I suffered a string of annoying problems. A persistent leak coming from the onboard water ballast system kept flooding the cabin area but more importantly, an electrical short had knocked out my electrics, leaving me with no option but to hand-steer the boat. It was feasible to complete the course but with nothing to prove, I decided to head back to Pornichet and deal with the problems. It was early in the season and I wasn't too concerned with ducking out of the first race because of a few niggling issues. I had established the most important factor, our competitive ability, and that was encouraging.

Our second event was more successful with a second place in the 500-mile Mini Cup, a solo race from Dieppe to Douarnenez. Having taken an early lead I enjoyed a fantastic close-quarters battle against a razor-sharp fleet as we negotiated our way along the Cherbourg peninsula. Under failing daylight and foul tide the whole fleet bunched together, with just yards separating the first ten boats. Only one competitor had managed to scrape around the headland before the tide turned, leaving the rest of us with a frantic battle to defend our positions.

That night under the big spinnaker I had an intense and nail-biting ride as I picked my way through the Channel Islands. I had managed to steal a charge on the fleet off Cap de la Hague, the westernmost tip of the Cherbourg peninsula, and decided to pass close to the south of the island of Alderney through the Alderney Race, a notorious stretch of water between the island and the French mainland. Here there are some of the fiercest tides in Europe. The tidal race can reach phenomenal speeds as it squeezes through the relatively narrow gap between the two shorelines. I was desperate to defend my position and knew I might gain a considerable margin by pushing my luck through the islands rather than adopting a more cautious offshore approach to the north. I knew I wasn't the only one with this idea, having noticed the faint glow of several navigation lights in the distance behind me as I passed between the rocky islands of Herm and Sark.

I managed to hold on to my second place and had a convincing lead over the remaining fleet as I crossed the finish line in the bay of Douarnenez. It was a great result and I remember feeling an overwhelming sensation of satisfaction as I relaxed in the Winches Club bar waiting for the rest of the fleet to arrive.

Unfortunately our run of good luck was not to last. The first double-handed race of the season and one of the highlights in the Mini calendar was the classic seven hundred-mile Mini Fastnet race. A huge fleet had gathered for this event. Ifor and I were in the top five as we rounded the first of a number of turning marks on the course. We were sailing into the wind and waves heading north toward the Chenal Du Four, one of several narrow channels separating the mainland from Ushant off the north-western tip of the French coast. We were in the thick of it, going head-to-head with a number of competitors. The chase was on and we were both in our element. Ifor was sitting on the deck with his legs over the side, counting down the puffs of wind as they approached. His enthusiastic running commentary on our performance against the rest of the fleet kept me both entertained and informed. I was steering, doing my best to keep us in the groove and sailing fast.

Suddenly the mast took on an alarming shape. I looked up towards the masthead and saw that the supporting spreader, which was normally attached to the side of the mast and used to support the mast laterally, had sheared away. We couldn't believe it. We were right in the thick of the action at the front of the fleet and only two hours into the race. This kind of damage is a real problem at sea and meant an immediate exit from the race. We returned to Douarnenez deflated but were lucky not to have lost the mast over the side. Both Ifor and I were bitterly disappointed, a situation made worse by knowing that

Left **Action stations, Ifor and me putting *Fujifilm* through her paces.**

Below left **Ifor and me enjoying fresh conditions.**

A big wave curls up over the transom, making for some exciting sailing.

our boat had been right on the pace. We were a formidable team and had had a realistic chance of taking the podium.

By the time we reached the dock it was pretty late in the evening. We had cautiously sailed back to port in an effort to save the mast. We were tired and pissed-off and went in search of the nearest establishment that could provide food for me and beer for Ifor. The following morning I called the mast supplier and described what had happened. To my mind, it was obviously a defective component. It was an easy item to replace but my call was met with a less-than-enthusiastic response. I had expressed my concern about the flimsy-looking mast before it was installed in the boat. Now my worries looked to be warranted. After a frustrating amount of negotiation and huffing and puffing they reluctantly agreed to replace the broken component but would not replace the mast. The mast supplier intimated that I must have knocked the spreader at some point during our travels to France and that had resulted in the component failing. This argument just didn't hold water – the broken spreader showed no signs of damage other than to the area where it had sheared away from the mast and no signs of damage

were present during our pre-race routine inspections. His claims only heightened the tension in the discussion.

With just two weeks before the next event, we had an uphill struggle to get the replacement carbon fibre spreader in time for the start. I began to wonder whether it had been a smart move to commission the new rig in the first place.

The next event, called the Demi Clé after the race sponsor, turned out to be our final event for that season despite there being two more races on the schedule. We had overcome the apparent teething problems with the mast and installed the replacement component with just two days to spare before the race start. Nearly sixty boats had gathered for the popular event, in which some nine hundred miles of racing are split over three stages. The Demi Cle provides an excellent balance of razor-sharp big fleet racing and the spirited onshore festivities that are so typical of the Mini community. We were determined to put the problems behind us and get out there and enjoy the thrill of the chase.

The race started well and once again we were amongst the tightly-packed top ten boats as we forged our way along the French coastline towards Ushant. At daybreak the following morning, we were just clearing the northern end of the Chanel Du Four and entering the English Channel. Our change in direction toward the north-east had been an eagerly anticipated event. The wind was up to a challenging twenty knots and combined with a healthy seaway we were looking forward to a sleigh ride along the English Channel towards the finish in St Quay Portrieux. By now the fleet had dispersed but we had two competitors in sight as Ifor purposefully hauled the big white spinnaker to the masthead. *Fujifilm* began to surf down the face of waves and we were all smiles as we watched a fantastic sunrise on the horizon. We were doing well, certainly in the top five, and making ground on the two boats that had been just yards ahead of us before the spinnaker hoist.

Two hours later and the fast and furious pace was still continuing. Ifor and I were confident we had broken into the top three. There were plenty of miles left to go before we reached the first stage stopover but our rapid pace had boosted our confidence. By now we were well out into the English Channel. No one in the fleet behind us was visible and just a solitary sail could be seen on the horizon ahead. Things were looking good. I was just about to call for some grub when a loud bang brought the mast crashing down to the ocean. Everything happened in an instant. One second we were surfing along at double digit speed and the next I watched the bow thunder over the top of the spinnaker as we ploughed into the wreckage of the broken mast before coming to an abrupt halt.

It was a dramatic wipe-out. The mast had broken in three places. With everything hanging over the side Ifor was the first to leap into action. He didn't need any direction from me, he knew our race was over. Our primary concern shifted swiftly from race performance to staying afloat. The exciting seaway that had moments before been propelling *Fujifilm* along at a comfortable speed was now doing its utmost to piledrive the broken mast through the side of our flimsy hull. In the click of a finger there was destruction everywhere. Ifor disappeared below to grab some kit and I shouted for the hacksaw and toolbox.

The rock-steady motion moments before the incident had now given way to an unsteady feeling. *Fujifilm* rolled uncomfortably as Ifor and I worked to cut the rigging away from the deck. We tried to gather as many of the broken mast sections as possible; I wanted some evidence for when we confronted the mast manufacturer. My fears about the flimsy-looking rig had proved well-founded. Although the sea state made a complete recovery of all the parts impossible, we did manage to save one of the three broken sections, together with the boom. We also recovered the spinnaker from the sea without damage, something I was surprised but pleased to see, given the cost of replacing the sail. The rest of the rig, including the brand new mainsail, was confined to a watery grave at the bottom of the English Channel.

We breathed a big sigh of relief as we cut the final stainless steel rigging rods and watched the threatening wreckage disappear beneath the waves. Roughly ten thousand pounds' worth of kit had just gone over the side, but the immediate danger was over. We were well out of sight of land and had about fifty miles to sail before reaching a safe haven. Above all, we were both furious. For the second time in as many weeks that bloody mast had brought our race to a premature end. With no engine on board we set about rigging up a jury rig so we could sail to St Quay Portreiux under our own steam. Now that the broken mast was gone, it wasn't a big deal from a safety point of view and we soon arranged a workable system for hoisting some sail. With the bowsprit and remaining stump of mast we cobbled together a make-shift rig, lashed it fore and aft, then hoisted the storm jib and storm trysail. It was quite an effective system, and we both managed a wry smile at our achievement as we pottered along at a sedate three knots.

All day we could only watch as the trailing fleet appeared on the horizon. Without proper sails set, even the back markers who had been miles behind quickly reeled us in. I managed to hail one of them and asked the crew to relay our position to race headquarters. Our VHF antenna had gone over the side with the mast and even with our makeshift emergency antenna attached to the top of the jury-rigged pole, we had little more than a few miles of transmission range. The other boat had a better range and could radio the race organisers to advise that we would be overdue but were fine and making way under our own steam.

Those fifty miles to St Quay made for a long and slow journey. We didn't arrive until the early daylight hours of the following day. Licking our wounds as we ghosted into the harbour on a light morning breeze we could see the whole fleet rafted up together. They had all arrived long ago. The dockside was still and you could have heard a pin drop around the marina. There didn't seem to be anyone awake but we could see we weren't the only ones who had experienced problems. Another competitor had also lost part of his mast, a casualty of war just like us. I remember experiencing feelings of empathy as we tied up to the dock. Rather like a racing car driver when the engine blows, you have to just take it on the chin and move on. It's frustrating but that's yacht racing. We were both knackered and furious but it was time to get our heads down. The clean-up operation would have to wait for a couple of hours at least.

The phone call to the mast supplier later that day didn't go well. The guy flatly refused to accept that what had happened had been a result of inferior craftsmanship. To make matters worse, he suggested I had pushed the boat beyond her limits and claimed it was therefore my fault. He hung up the phone before I had chance to explain the full story. If I was furious before, I was ready to commit murder now. It was a horrible situation and my thoughts turned to our sponsors and how I would break the news to them. This wasn't just an inconvenient setback, it was a serious problem. Without a mast and mainsail there was no chance we could finish the remaining two stages of the race and complete the qualification process for the Transat.

With just one decent result to show for the season I returned to Devon less than pleased. I was worried that our efforts would be seen as inadequate in the eyes of our title sponsor. A meeting with the mast manufacturer several days later proved no more helpful than when he hung up on me in France. They were not prepared to meet any kind of warranty claim and offered no solution to help resolve the problem. Any kind of support or acceptance of responsibility would have brought the frustrating situation to an amicable conclusion but they weren't having any of it and their response to my assertions remained unchanged. I had pushed the boat too hard. It was a ridiculous claim and one I took as a personal insult, despite being fully aware they were clutching at straws.

Our exciting sailing season had come to a premature conclusion but my concerns about my sponsors being unimpressed were unfounded. The project had been a great success from a publicity point of view and we had captured some stunning images from our photo shoots. Even with the best organisation and intentions, things don't always go according to plan. The real measure of success is not necessarily the race result. It can often be how well any unforeseen circumstances are handled. I chose not to tell them that Ifor and I had considered tying the mast supplier to a chair while poking him with a sharp stick until he coughed up our cash for the troublesome mast. The problem had cost me a second crack at the Mini Transat but fortunately it had not cost me my sponsor.

AROUND THE WORLD –
THE 2005 ORYX QUEST

he Mini circuit had been a real blast and although things hadn't
turned out quite the way we had hoped, I had really enjoyed the
adventure. There was always the option of a second season within
the fleet and I had given serious consideration to it, although it was the
transatlantic race that I really wanted to take part in and the next event
was two seasons away. It was Christmas 2004 and I had plenty of time
to make a decision. Fujifilm seemed keen to continue their support in
one way or another and were pretty relaxed about everything.

The day after Boxing Day, Dad and I went down to the marina to
check on his boat. We were sitting on board enjoying a cup of tea
while gazing out across the still waters of the marina. The diesel heater
made the cabin warm and inviting but outside it was still the depths of
winter and a thick layer of frost covered the decks.

Suddenly my phone burst into life. It was Claire, a good friend and
former girlfriend. Claire is a very talented sailor and a qualified senior
doctor. She's an adventurous woman and is one of the rare people you
can call a real friend. Her call brought an opportunity that was hard to
ignore. She was involved with a syndicate who were putting together
an experienced team of professionals to compete in the Oryx Quest, a
yacht race around the world.

The boat in question was owned by none other than billionaire
adventurer Steve Fossett. *Cheyenne* was the monstrous one hundred
and twenty-foot beast that had competed in The Race several years
earlier under the name *Playstation*. Claire's partner, David Scully, was
the skipper and they were inviting me to join the team for the voyage
around the world. I knew Dave by reputation but we had never met.

Claire got straight to the point. They had been aiming to compete in the race for a while but commercial funding, as with all these campaigns, had been the limiting factor. *Cheyenne*'s skeleton crew had quietly done what they could to keep the boat as prepared as possible over the summer months but a firm ticket into the race had been far from a certainty.

This was the kind of opportunity that people like me live for. A flood of questions filled my mind. As far as I knew, the race was scheduled to start in just a couple of months. It was starting in the Gulf state of Qatar and *Cheyenne* was based in England. I knew there was not enough time to sail her to the Middle East in readiness for the race start.

Claire was quick to admit that time was tight, so tight that she needed to know if I was interested there and then. The team had only received confirmation of their funding the day before and, given that the race started on 5 February, time was very much of the essence. David and Claire were selecting a crew and I knew there would be no shortage of takers. My commitment to the car yard weighed on my mind and I asked Claire if the money was definitely in place. Her reply was enough to reassure me that this project was indeed happening. Putting aside the immediate time constraints and last-minute crew placement issues, this boat was destined for the Southern Ocean and the infamous Cape Horn. Everyone on board would be of a professional standard. If I wanted it, this was my chance to achieve one of my lifelong ambitions, to sail the Southern Ocean and tackle Cape Horn. Yes, hell yes, I was up for it! We agreed to meet at Claire's house the following evening to discuss everything in more detail.

I hung up the phone and turned to my Dad. I could see from the look on his face that given the risks, he didn't share my enthusiasm. There was also the small question of who would look after the car yard while I was away. These thoughts started flowing through my mind and seemed to hit me with the force of a tidal wave. I attempted to explain the scale of the opportunity to Dad but quickly realised that no amount of reasoning at this point would calm the situation down. Attempting to do so would only escalate the discussion into an argument. Claire's phone call had ruined the tranquility of the father and son moment we had been sharing. But it had also presented the opportunity of a lifetime.

My father's less-than-enthusiastic reaction to the prospect of me flying off into the desolate Southern Ocean was born of fear and the knowledge that this type of sailing is very high-risk. My parents had lived through the whole *Team Philips* saga when my final satellite call from the boat had presented them with the prospect they might never see their son again. Then, almost a year to the day later, when my calls for help from the stricken *One Dream One Mission* came through, they had been forced to relive those terrible moments all over again. I realised then that I hadn't really appreciated just how traumatic that experience had been for them. Despite not wanting to stand in my way, they were now worried that a last-minute decision to embark on such a serious undertaking without a lengthy period of training might result in another calamity. If disaster struck in the depths of the Southern Ocean I might not come back at all. Dad was also quick to point out my commitments to the car yard and while I accepted this, I did my best to explain what the opportunity meant to me.

Our frank discussion left me feeling burdened with guilt. I have always been very close to my parents and I felt very bad for subjecting them to any unnecessary worry or heartache. However, this was my life and ultimately it had to be my decision whether to stay or to go.

My mother talked to me again later that day to explain their feelings. From their viewpoint, I had been lucky to return home safely after two very real life-threatening disasters at sea. They just couldn't comprehend why I would want to take up the gauntlet once again and take on the Southern Ocean. In my folks' eyes it was madness, but in mine the Southern Ocean was my Everest, something I had spent my life waiting to conquer.

The following evening I met up with Claire and David. As we sat around the wooden table in Claire's kitchen we discussed the project and I felt excited at the prospect of the adventure ahead. It turned out that the campaign was privately funded by Steve Fossett who had agreed to bankroll our entry. There were rumours of a two million-dollar payout for competitors from the race organisers as a sweetener to just turn up. Steve Fossett would not join *Cheyenne* for the race but had given the green light for David to take command and put a team together.

The Oryx Quest had been billed as the most exciting round-the-world race to date and was the brainchild of round-the-world sailor and celebrity yachtswoman Tracy Edwards. Tracy had publicly announced the race to the world's media more than a year earlier. Her rumoured thirty-seven million dollar budget and cool one million dollar prize money for the eventual winner had been a revelation within the sport. That kind of cash was big news and Tracy's tireless commitment in negotiating with the Arabs had seemingly paid off big time. It wasn't known at the time, but Tracy had put her neck on the line and borrowed millions of pounds to bring this incredible sporting event to Qatar. The race was big news and it was the first time a global yacht race would start from that part of the world. Plagued by the rumour mill, Tracy's race was soon under the spotlight when the media learned that the money had apparently been slow in coming from her sponsors. The build-up to the event had caused considerable speculation as to whether the race would even happen. The race was happening however, and on the start line would be four of the biggest racing multihulls on the planet.

Just like The Race, this was an event exclusively reserved for goliaths of the sailing world. Tony 'the bulldog' Bullimore had signed up and was sailing his durable but aging catamaran that he had sailed around the world in The Race in 2001. Now renamed *Daedalus*, she had several of my friends fresh from the Mini circuit on board. They were all keen to get a sniff of the action and make their mark. There was also the eccentric Olivier du Kersauson, a household name in France whose boat *Geronimo* was the only trimaran in the race and represented a formidable entry. Together with *Doha 2006*, which was owned by Tracy's company and skippered by British yachtsman Brian Thompson, making it in effect the race organiser's own entry, *Cheyenne* was the fourth and final competitor on the list.

Our campaign was short on time but certainly well-organised. Preparation work on board was already underway. *Cheyenne* was berthed locally in Plymouth and was due to be sailed to Antwerp the following weekend. The shore team had arranged for the boat to be lifted onto a container ship and taken as freight to the Middle East, where she would be re-rigged and sailed around to Qatar in time for the start. During the delivery from Antwerp two team members would travel on board the ship and carry out essential preparation work which would save valuable time later. The sail to Antwerp would serve as a crew selection process, although Claire made it quite clear that both she and David wanted me on board.

I seized the moment. Declaring my commitment was easy, although I still had to face the fallout from my family and somehow persuade them to look after the car yard while I was away. If I wasn't success-ful in that, the only option would be to close for eight weeks and pick up the reins on my return. The situation was made all the more difficult because we had just expanded the car business and taken on bigger premises, meaning a bigger financial and personal commitment on my part. Jet-setting off around the world and asking my folks to keep the plates spinning while I had the adventure of a lifetime was a pretty selfish move and a big ask. Closing the business for the best part of three months was not a desirable alternative but as a last resort it was certainly feasible. This kind of opportunity doesn't come around very often and there was just no way I could refuse it. Not this time. I couldn't live the rest of my life knowing I had passed up such an adventure.

The delivery to Antwerp gave a short but exciting preview of the action that would unfold during the race. The weather had been fairly light as we left Plymouth but *Cheyenne* is an awesome machine and like other G Class multihulls didn't require much wind to deliver impressive performance. The trip along the English Channel reminded me of the short-lived sailing aboard *Team Philips*. Until you sail one of these boats you can never really appreciate just how powerful they are. I knew that the race and particularly the Southern Ocean would deliver the ultimate experience. Putting all second thoughts aside, I was ready to embrace the challenge.

Trying to persuade my parents to support my decision caused major friction. It wasn't until I told them of my decision to go regardless that things started to improve, albeit only marginally. Their reservations were understandable, they were just worried parents. My mother was the first to reluctantly accept that they should not stand in my way. She eventually convinced my father to view the situation through my eyes. Reluctantly, they both agreed to hold the fort at the car yard until my return. I felt immense guilt for subjecting them to this kind of worry but I couldn't say no to the chance of a lifetime and end up having to live with the regret. Once again, I had arrived at a crossroads.

I joked that it was a good job I was sailing a G Class yacht instead of anything else. I explained to my mother that being the fastest type of yacht on the planet, it would bring me home quicker than if I was sailing on any other type of boat. My parents laughed in an unconvinced and nervous way. But it was the fact that I was sailing on a G Class that had created all the fuss in the first place. A monohull would have been a safer bet in my father's eyes. When things go wrong, a monohull can be knocked down and will generally pop back up again. If a catamaran flips, that's the end of it.

I arrived at Doha International Airport a couple of weeks later. It was 1 February, my bags were packed and I was full of anticipation. The newly-recruited team was flying in from different parts of the world and we had been told to meet at the Sheraton hotel in Doha. Perched on the waterfront, this impressive luxury hotel resembles a full-scale replica of an Egyptian pyramid. I called ahead to let Claire and David know of my imminent arrival. The taxi ride from the airport revealed a city that looked like it had been built pretty much on the edge of the desert. The number of high-rise buildings and luxury cars that passed the taxi window pointed to significant wealth within the community. No doubt a by-product of the oil and gas industry, I thought.

As I pulled up outside the hotel I could see the mast of Daedalus. The boat was rather precariously tied to a makeshift set of plastic pontoons opposite the hotel. A tented area vaguely resembling a race village was built along the promenade. As I walked into the hotel I wondered where the other boats – including *Cheyenne* – were. Claire and David came down to reception and explained that everyone had expressed concerns about the lack of provisions made for the boats. Skippers were understandably worried about berthing their multimillion dollar super yachts against what resembled little more than an exposed makeshift harbour wall. The majority of the fleet had decided to berth safely on the other side of the bay in dedicated marinas. With only one of the expected four giants present, the public could have been forgiven for thinking that the dedicated race village was a ghost town.

The following day we took a ride down to the marina to help out with final preparations. Most of the crew had arrived and the others were due at any moment. Claire was pretty excited as we walked along the pontoon. We could see *Cheyenne* berthed at the end of the dock; her massive presence was undeniable. It was thrilling to be part of the party and I remember whispering a quiet 'thank you' to Claire as we approached the boat; it was thanks to her that I was here and I wanted to express my appreciation. The boat was a hive of activity, with a small army of people swarming over the decks. Riggers, shore team members, race crew and local hired help were everywhere. I wasn't sure who was crew and who wasn't.

As we stood next to the starboard hull and looked up from the pontoon, David introduced me to one of the guys. I recognised him although we didn't actually know each other. Gordon Maguire's reputation preceded him. He is a long-time pro yachtsman and veteran of the Whitbread Round the World Race. An immensely experienced and talented yachtsman, to say he knew his stuff would be a gross understatement. The man has competed on some of the most impressive racing machines afloat. He had already done the Southern Ocean several times and is a living legend. As I stretched out my arm to shake hands I could tell that sailing with Gordon would be a great experience.

Doha 2006, the eventual race winner.

Moored just behind us was *Doha 2006*, another competitor and

the race favourite. Looking sleek and mean, the boat was slightly smaller than *Cheyenne* yet an equally potent weapon. A familiar face was on board, my good friend Larso. He hadn't realised I had signed up with *Cheyenne* but as we bumped into each other on the dockside we took a moment out from the purposeful commotion to share some light banter. While shaking hands and wishing each other good luck we joked about who would be the first to Cape Horn.

Shortly before breakfast the following morning, David took the opportunity to call our first crew meeting. His confident words set the tone for the trip. The crew was now all present and a room on the ground floor of the hotel provided the perfect meeting place. It was the first time we had all been gathered together and I could see everyone was keen to get acquainted. I remember thinking there was some serious talent in the room. Some people I had already met and some I didn't know at all but we were drawn together by a common factor. Everyone here brought significant experience to the table; this was a race where there would be no passengers.

Take Hervé for instance. He is from the French school of sailing with almost a quarter of a million ocean sailing miles under his belt. Hervé is a serial circumnavigator who specialises in big powerful multihulls. Then there were the Volvo Ocean Race guys, Dingo from New Zealand, Jim from Australia and another Hervé who was also from France. These lads are great blokes and hardcore professionals. They had not done that much multihull sailing but they had already sailed around the world, knew their stuff and their credentials spoke for themselves. Another French yachtsman, Gérard, was a past world champion in Formula 18 dinghies and a perfect candidate for the white-knuckle ride ahead.

One familiar face was Mark Featherstone. He was the boat's onboard engineer and general Mister Fixit. Mark – 'Feathers' to his friends – is a past volunteer crew member with the RNLI. He had been part of the original crew that Steve Fossett put together and had sailed on several record-breaking voyages, including a successful round-the-world record attempt. Despite having limited racing experience, Mark brought an altogether more important quality to the table. He probably knew *Cheyenne* better than anyone else and together with his natural ability to fix things, he was an indispensible member of the team as well as being a likable guy that I particularly gelled with from the start.

Our navigator was a young Dutch guy called Wouter, also a round-the-world veteran sailor and together with Greg and Anders, both talented 18-foot skiff sailors, they completed the line up.

It was the Frenchmen who were the most experienced with big multihulls. Those guys are definitely from a different mould. I realised this when we were sailing deep in the Southern Ocean, with the nearest land over a thousand miles away. Our watch system was in force and constantly we were either on watch, on standby fully togged-up or in our bunks trying to sleep. It was always the French who would have the boat on the limit, day and night, sailing like it was a tiny Hobie Cat dinghy. I'm always the last person to back off the speed button when the racing starts and I pride myself on my ability to push harder than the next guy, but sailing with these people changes your view of where the limit is. They have a mixture of huge experience with this type of high-octane multihull sailing and a fearless attitude towards the consequences if something goes wrong. They didn't seem at all worried about screwing up as the 120-foot maxi catamaran was perpetually pressed to the limit in the deepest darkest realms of the big, bad and frequently very ugly Southern Ocean. Time after time as we eagerly awaited the changeover of watches we would sit in the cabin on the narrow bench at the foot of the companionway steps. You could both hear and feel the powerful blend of vibration, noise and violent motion as the rock stars on deck flogged the boat to within an inch of her life. I loved it and had rarely experienced that kind of natural high.

You just haven't seen the limit until you have taken a G Class close to the edge. I realised this one night half way across the Southern Ocean when the call came through for all hands on deck. The rock stars had overcooked it. We were out of control, blasting through iceberg territory close to the forty-knot barrier with a wall of sail up. But that's a story for later.

The race route for the Oryx Quest posed a challenge for the race teams in terms of predicting the weather. Given the location of the start port, this race imposed a significantly different route to the accepted norm. These kinds of events usually start somewhere in Europe. A traditional route then takes competitors through the north Atlantic and across the equator, before passing into the southern hemisphere. It then continues south beyond the latitude of the Cape of Good Hope before eventually entering the notorious Roaring Forties, the area between forty and fifty degrees south. As the action really starts to hot up, the temperatures start to plummet. The route heads east into the Southern Ocean along the bottom of the planet, towards Australia. Eventually, having effectively looped around Antarctica it reaches Cape Horn at the southernmost extremity of South America and then re-enters the south Atlantic before heading north back to the start.

The Oryx Quest was an entirely different race course. This race started and finished in Qatar. The fleet would sail down the Gulf of Oman with the shores of Iran on our left and to our right the coastlines of the United Arab Emirates and Oman, which would provide uncertain meteorological challenges. Once clear of the Strait of Hormuz we would make our way south into the Arabian Sea, passing close to the low-lying Maldive Islands before continuing all the way to Australia and beyond. Having passed south of the southernmost extremity of New Zealand we would change course and head east, deep into the freezing Southern Ocean towards the Horn. Having rounded the notorious stretch of water that passes the rocky coastline of Chile, the fleet would then make best speed northwards, passing the Falkland Islands, sailing towards a predetermined waypoint in the mouth of the River Plate in Uruguay. From there an abrupt change of course would send everyone charging back toward the Cape of Good Hope and briefly into the Roaring Forties before heading roughly north-east back toward the Gulf of Oman and on to the finish.

The start of the race was soon upon us. The whole team had worked tirelessly to get the boat shipshape and our hard work had paid off. *Cheyenne* looked as ready as she could be in the timeframe. Claire and I had volunteered to take care of the food stocks for the voyage and had made the necessary preparations. Together, we laid out all the food on the hotel floor and did our best to reduce the overall weight by removing any unnecessary packaging. We then allocated the correct amounts into easy-to-use day ration packs to keep everything simple. Even after meticulously going through everything to make sure we had just the correct amount for the expected duration at sea, there was still an amazing quantity.

The food was stowed under the cockpit floors toward the rear of the boat in each hull. Just reaching the food stocks was a big task, a process that involved lifting up the companionway steps and climb-

A team shot prior to the start of the Oryx Quest.

Claire sitting on the mountain of food bags that we prepared for the race.

ing though the narrow hatch that provides access to the aft compartments. Dragging the food out would always be hard work but the purpose-made bags made this essential daily task less of a grind, as everything we needed was contained in each day bag, ready to be brought into the galley for use. It was a good system and I remember feeling quietly satisfied with our work as I watched Claire climb on top of the mountain of fluorescent orange bags that we had piled several feet high in the hotel corridor. Just lugging them down to the boat would be exhausting.

Come race day, the team felt ready, although the promised complete new set of rigging had not materialised. I thought we were probably pushing our luck a little with the current setup. Most of the rigging holding the very expensive giant wing mast together had already completed at least one furious lap of the planet – surely priority should have been given to having all of it replaced? I gave a momentary thought to the consequences of losing the mast deep in the Southern Ocean before deliberately shifting my thoughts to brighter prospects. It was too late to worry about things like that now.

The starting area off Doha was a long and unobstructed line with two committee boats marking each end. Plenty of spectator craft had pitched up for the spectacle and there were hovering helicopters and speed boats zooming around with journalists and camera crews. The atmosphere was intoxicating. Everyone got off to a clean start. With so much at stake it was clear that the fleet was adopting a pretty cautious approach. There was no merit in risking a collision with other competitors just to cross the starting line first. These are very big but surprisingly delicate boats that require plenty of space to manoeuvre, as even the slightest bump could result in serious damage. Our approach provided a good clean exit from the starting area. We crossed the line with a heavily-reefed mainsail and jib. It was perhaps a little conservative, but with a fresh breeze blowing, the small sail area certainly made manoeuvring before the start far more manageable than if we had had everything flying free. Once we had crossed the line, though, our lack of sail area clearly showed against the fleet. Barely minutes into the race as we approached open water, David gave the call to shake a reef out of the mainsail and unleash the beast. We leaped forward toward the winches at the base of the mast. The game was on.

Before the start, all the competitors had been given the customary race briefing that outlined various aspects of the route. One of the things it had been quite specific about was passing along the coast of Iran. It was strongly suggested that we all keep well clear of the coastline as the authorities didn't like foreign vessels entering their waters and were liable to shoot first and ask questions later. The idea that the Iranians had rocket-propelled grenades didn't do much for morale.

That first night was fast and furious as we blasted over the horizon and along the Strait of Hormuz. The fleet had soon dispersed and it wasn't long before we lost sight of all the other competitors. There was some speculation about what direction to take as we forged our way into the night. Regardless of the race committee's warnings about the Iranian coast, our weather router was keen to send us closer inshore than we would have liked. The general consensus was that a more favourable wind could be found close to the shoreline, although that opinion was clearly not shared by our competition, who had elected to stay in the middle of the Gulf.

I remember coming off watch and lying on my bunk, listening to the sound of *Cheyenne* as we thundered into the darkness. We were blasting along steadily at close to twenty-five knots. On deck the guys were focused but relaxed. Seventy feet away in the opposite hull our navigator was busy keeping a watchful eye on the situation ahead. I couldn't get to sleep. I wasn't particularly tired and the environment was just too exciting. I lay on the bunk and closed my eyes, appreciating the moment. I could hear the sound of rushing water passing under the hull. The enormous strain of highly-loaded ropes echoed through the boat as the constant trimming of sails kept us at full speed.

Forty-five minutes later, a huge bang coupled with a violent impact sent shockwaves through the cabin. I had eventually drifted off to sleep but the force of the collision woke me instantly. Everyone heard it. We all piled up the narrow companionway steps and poured onto deck. I could see silhouettes of bodies entering the cockpit on the opposite hull. What the hell was that? As we all looked around I could see we were still smoking along at twenty-plus knots, so it wasn't the mast. We must have hit something with one of the daggerboards. It was a massive impact and there would definitely be some damage to the daggerboard blade, but there was little we could do at night other than check for any obvious signs of damage to the hull or water ingress. The lads on deck still had full control and a check of each hull revealed no obvious problems. We thought we had slammed into some kind of sea mammal, perhaps a whale, or a very big fish. Either way, we would have to wait until daylight to investigate further.

As the sun came up the following morning we had other things to worry about. Our rapid progress through the night had drawn us right up on the Iranian coast, so close in fact that we could see a sandy beach just a mile away and behind it a dramatic backdrop of mountains reaching high into the sky. The favourable wind we had enjoyed during the night had now disappeared. We were right in the place that we had been warned was a no-go zone. Our plan had been to close the coast under cover of darkness and then before daybreak change course back out to sea before the wind died, but things had not turned out that way and we were now practically becalmed.

As we looked at the shore one of the lads cracked a joke about our mainsail having USA written in big letters across the top and how much of a sitting duck we must have looked. The thought contributed to a rather uneasy feeling as we ghosted along, desperately trying to point the bows offshore and get away from this potentially hostile but spectacular coast. The sun was shining and under beautiful blue skies a small lone fishing boat could be seen heading out from the beach towards us. Any thoughts of racing were momentarily forgotten. All our attention was now directed towards the approaching fishing boat. Was this trouble approaching? I could feel the tension amongst the crew. We were indeed a sitting duck for anyone with ill intentions. Luckily for us, the solo fisherman was exactly what he seemed. He was curious about who we were but had no ill intent. No doubt he had never seen such a space-age racing machine as *Cheyenne* and we soon realised he didn't pose any threat.

The arrival of a gentle breeze spelled an end to our apparent vulnerability and with all of us working together with new purpose, *Cheyenne* rapidly accelerated away from the shore and towards the horizon. That wind couldn't have come quickly enough. With the exception of the Maldives, the imposing Iranian coastline would be the last landmass we would see until reaching Cape Horn at the tip of Chile.

Later that afternoon we inspected the daggerboard. Our checks revealed significant damage to the very tip of the carbon fibre blade. A fishy skin-like residue covered the large indentation on the forward edge. The fact that the damage was limited to the tip of the daggerboard indicated it had been both a glancing blow and a lucky one, although not for the fish! But such a large area of damage couldn't be just ignored. The collision had ruined the profile of the blade, which left alone would cause extra friction and significant drag which would ultimately slow us down. A running repair was necessary but in order to do so we had to completely remove the massive daggerboard from its housing in the deck, a difficult manoeuvre at sea. The daggerboard was huge and very heavy. When fully hoisted from its socket it dwarfed the crew. The clement conditions were forecast to continue for several hours so we decided to give it a go while we had chance.

The hot sun and light winds continued to keep a lid on progress as the fleet gradually broke free from the Gulf of Oman and crawled south into the Arabian Sea. *Doha 2006* had taken an early lead and remained ahead. Our escapade losing the wind along the Iranian coastline had cost us some time but we were still in contention, enjoying the fight for second place. As we approached the beautiful Maldives, we

Hoisting the giant daggerboard from its housing was a tricky task.

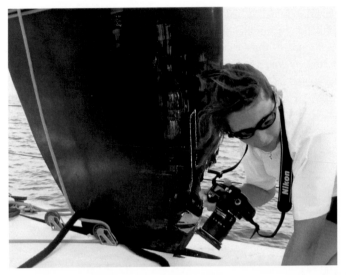

Left **Claire inspecting the damage to the daggerboard.**

Below **Sailing through the Arabian Gulf, view from the end of the boom.**

noticed an increasing amount of debris floating in the water. Straw-built structures, clothing and an apparently infinite number of trees littered the area. The sea by now had turned crystal blue and *Cheyenne* blasted across the waves, creating a feeling of superiority. With all that floating debris, we had resorted to having a couple of guys positioned on the bow to keep a lookout for dangerous flotsam. Bursting though the ocean at twenty knots, the larger areas of flotsam posed a real threat to the integrity of the boat. The guys on the bow used arm signals to direct the helmsman safely through the worst patches. It wasn't long before we realised that the debris was from the devastating tsunami that had struck Indonesia the month before. The Maldives had been directly hit too and were almost wiped out. We were sailing though what was left of people's homes and possessions that had been washed out to sea. It was a sobering experience and brought a tear to the eye.

Life on board had by now settled into a routine. Apart from a minor foot infection with one of the crew and some niggling but potentially serious generator problems that Feathers had finally managed to sort out, everything was going well. We operated a revolving three-watch system consisting of three hours on deck, three off for sleep and three on standby. The on-deck team concentrated on performance, driving *Cheyenne* across the waves at best speed while the standby crew remained below ready to come on deck at a moment's notice should the need arise. The off-watch group would only be called up to help if things got hairy outside.

By 26 February we were about seventy miles to the west of the Auckland Islands, a remote volcanic archipelago south west of New Zealand. The light-to-moderate conditions we had experienced in the first two weeks had developed into something far more furious. Now we were punching into the teeth of a gale, sailing into the wind and waves. The motion on board was very violent, and the whole fleet was getting a real pasting. *Cheyenne* shook and groaned under the strain as we speared though an uncomfortable sea, making disappointingly slow progress. Everyone was finding the rough motion hard going but none more so than Claire. She was feeling the effects of seasickness and had been knocked off her feet for several days. She looked as white as a sheet and had taken refuge in the starboard cockpit cuddy, preferring to stay there rather than seek shelter in the cabin. I had been keeping my eye on her for a while and was starting to get quite concerned. She hadn't eaten for days and was quite unwilling to drink anything either. The relentless pitching motion was no doubt the cause of her debilitating sickness. Being on deck was bad enough, but down below, the claustrophobic cabin areas accentuated the motion. We were all feeling the strain but with no end in sight we had to just grin and bear it.

Completing simple daily tasks such as cooking became amazingly difficult. Just walking through the hulls was a hazardous affair. The motion was akin to a fairground rollercoaster ride only much more intense. Despite the tough conditions we were doing well, holding onto second place but still locked head-to-head with Du Kersauson's trimaran. Claire was a member of our watch and with her out of commission for now that left just Gordon, Feathers and me to keep everything on an even keel during our watches.

The following day we had news from race HQ. The rough conditions had taken their toll on Du Kersauson's trimaran. They had suffered some structural problems and had taken the decision to retire from the race. The giant boat had turned around and was heading for Australia. Their departure came as sad news but also helped to relieve some of the pressure on us. Tony Bullimore and his team onboard Daedalus were by now far enough behind not to pose any immediate threat, which left us to concentrate on catching Doha 2006.

Eventually the harsh headwinds abated, bringing a much-welcomed but short-lived respite, allowing life on board to improve. Claire arose from her zombie-like state and emerged from the cuddy rejuvenated. We were now starting to feel the effects of our extreme southerly latitude. The temperature on deck was steadily dropping and the wind seemed to be settling down to a more expected direction from behind. This was what I had been so eagerly awaiting. Australia was behind us and to the north. This was the Southern Ocean and beyond, several thousand miles away, was Cape Horn. No turning back now.

With favourable winds, Cheyenne was now eating up the miles as we forged our way further into the Southern Ocean and away from civilisation. The boat speed indicator regularly registered speeds in excess of thirty knots and the excitement really started to kick in. For days our fast and furious pace provided plenty of action to keep us completely focused. Regular sail changes, physically steering the boat and the perpetual revolving watch system was enough to keep everyone on their toes. The night watches were the most dramatic. At times *Cheyenne* felt like she was being pushed completely to the limit. I recall sitting below decks, watching the speed indicator inexorably rise into the mid thirty-knot range and at that pace the noise below was thunderous. Right next to the seat at the bottom of the companionway steps there was a clear Perspex escape hatch which provided a way out should the boat ever capsize. Night after night, I would sit on the seat and shine my torch out of the emergency hatch window. Ferocious white water rushed past the window at breathtaking speed. In those conditions just steering a boat the size of *Cheyenne* is a demanding task and requires the absolute concentration of the helmsman. This really was high-octane stuff and I felt both exhilarated and awestruck at our performance.

The view from the port cockpit as we blast through a rough Southern Ocean sea.

One particular night stands out in my mind. Things were really starting to get turbo. It was getting pretty windy outside and I was off watch down below in my bunk trying to get some sleep. We had been on a charge most of the day and the French rock stars were on deck flogging the boat to extract every last knot of performance. Suddenly I felt *Cheyenne* really start to take off. I could tell that some big breeze had just rolled though. The boat was groaning under the strain and I remember thinking 'flipping hell, things are surely starting to get out of control'. Less than a minute later I heard the call for all hands on deck. I could tell we were in trouble from the tone of the guy's voice as he shouted into the cabin, "Everyone get their arses topside!" Those of us below didn't need any further explanation, the motion and the knowledge that we were flying one of our biggest sails provided enough clues.

I knew with that amount of sail up in these conditions there was a serious risk that we could capsize if we became too overpowered. As I jumped out of the bunk I could feel the adrenaline kicking in. There was no time for wet weather gear. I was wearing just a pair of thermal base layer trousers and they would have to do. Everyone shot up and jumped into action; this was a situation in which every second counts. I was one of the first to climb the stairs and get into the cockpit. As I looked around toward the instrument cluster I was greeted by white water and spray everywhere. The environment was powerful and intimidating. It felt like I had just stared straight into the jet of a fire hydrant. The helmsman and remaining on-watch crew were all huddled together in the windward cockpit on the opposite side of the boat. My heart was racing as I looked across to see the helmsman struggling to keep us on an even keel. I didn't have time to focus my eyes on the instruments to see just how fast we were going but it must have been close to forty knots. I could hear people shouting orders as we prepared to get the gennaker down. David was already on deck and people were climbing out of the other cockpit and making their way to the mast base to man the big winches.

Running across the trampoline nets was dangerous. You had to pick your moment otherwise you would be slammed by a wall of water as the nets dipped through waves. This was a scary moment indeed. As I ran across the nets I could feel the windward hull lifting under the pressure from the wind in the sails. The lads had already blown off the hydraulic release for the mainsail but *Cheyenne* was still hitting crazy speeds. I'm sure that if we had had wings that night the boat would have taken off.

Each of us flicked the switch to link all of the winches so they would work as one. I gripped the handles of the nearest coffee-grinder winch and paired up with Feathers. Our eyes met through the dark and I could tell we were thinking the same thing as we started grinding to help get rid of the big sail: we were facing twenty minutes of non-stop strenuous activity. As we winched like there was no tomorrow I could see the port side bow slicing through the waves out of the corner of my eye. This was intense stuff, our heart rates must have been through the roof. I certainly remember gasping for air as the furious winching action started to take its toll. After ten minutes of relentless work everyone was starting to feel the effects of fatigue. Our initial aggressive approach had now given way to a steadier but equally determined rate of progress. A couple of the lads started to shout aloud in an effort to keep the pressure on. "Come on lads, keep it going!" As if anyone was proposing to stop for a break. A couple more voices cut through the night with purpose. I decided it was a good idea too and loudly contributed my own words of encouragement: "Come on, come on!" I was really trying to spur myself on as much as anyone else, as I was knackered.

Taming this huge and powerful sail under such extreme conditions was an epic feat even with the muscle of eight men but, deep into the Southern Ocean, approaching iceberg territory and over a thousand miles from civilisation, if we didn't succeed *Cheyenne* would certainly capsize and we would all be dead. Eventually we brought the situation under control and the sail was secured on the deck. The wild unsettling motion had given way to a more comfortable and controllable one. We were all soaked from a mixture of salt spray and sweat. With *Cheyenne* out of the danger zone our exhausted team collapsed on the trampoline nets and took some time to catch our breath and allow the adrenaline to dissipate. That was both one of the scariest and most exhilarating moments of my life at sea. Each of us was thankful the boat was still the right way up and back under control.

Two days later, a change in wind direction presented us with a difficult tactical decision. Until now we had been heading pretty much directly for Cape Horn, several thousand miles away. The change in the wind's direction, albeit only for a matter of hours, meant we needed to position ourselves further to the south in order to capitalise on a better angle to the new breeze once an expected wind shift occurred. We were already at the 58th parallel where the risk of encountering icebergs was high. In an effort to make a tactical gain we would be sailing even further into the wastes of the Southern Ocean. Antarctica was the nearest landmass and it would soon be a whole lot closer than we would have liked.

As we coaxed *Cheyenne* onto her new southerly heading and started to pull in the enormous sheets that controlled the sails, the mood on board seemed to plummet at the same rate as the boat speed increased. No one liked the idea of sailing closer to Antarctica than we already were. Passing beyond 58 degrees south really wasn't the best exercise in seamanship . The likelihood of encountering icebergs increases dramatically but it was a necessary risk in order to make gains on the race track. The view from on deck had not changed from the day before or the day before that or indeed the week before that. The grey wastelands of ocean that blended into the horizon without clear definition were exactly the same. With our feelings of isolation and anxiety about our recent change of course, the surroundings seemed to take on a more menacing aspect.

That night as we struggled to keep warm in the confines of the hulls we were faced with an altogether more serious problem. Because *Cheyenne* is a catamaran with two hulls, there is accommodation in both. On the port side hull there is the galley and sleeping quarters. Beyond the bunks there is a marine toilet far up in the bow area and beyond that, empty space for storage. In the right-hand hull the navigation station occupies a prominent position at the bottom of the companionway steps leading down from the cockpit. Ahead of the nav area there are further bunks for the crew with a second toilet and stowage area in the bow. Each hull has a diesel heater to keep the cabin areas warm and relatively dry. We also use the heater to dry wet clothing from time to time.

The addition of a heater on board was a new experience for me but I had quickly grown used to its benefits once the outside temperature started to drop. It's amazing how the little things make such a difference at sea. When the heater in our hull failed on one particularly cold night the effects were instantly noticeable. Feathers, Claire, Gordon and I were sitting at the bottom of the companionway steps in the port-side hull waiting for the call to change watches. We had been the standby watch for a while and Feathers had been fiddling around with the heater for hours in an effort to convince it to kick into life. On deck the usual noise of spray and the grinding of winches gave a good indication that it was business as usual. Feathers and I had become good mates and as we climbed out into the cockpit he whispered that he had a plan to get the heater working again. Claire

and Gordon were residents of the starboard hull. In their neighbourhood the heater worked perfectly. Three hours later, at the end of our
watch we ventured below tired and soaked to find our cabin warm
and homely. Strangely though, Claire and Gordon's side had seemingly suffered a similar problem to ours and the heater had stopped
working. What a coincidence. Everyone in the starboard hull smelled a
rat. Feathers, our faithful engineer, had indeed liberated some essential
parts from what we deemed the 'spare' unit and replaced them with
our broken ones. Problem solved.

The following morning David announced it was time to change
course and head back towards the land of the living. It was a welcome
decision and everyone breathed a sigh of relief as the compass needle
started to point directly towards Cape Horn. By now, meal times had
become a focal point of the day. Everyone took turns to cook the different daily rations of freeze-dried food. The galley onboard Cheyenne,
like all racing yachts, is basic but nonetheless built to cater for more
than a dozen people and supply enough daily hot sustenance. As we
ventured beyond the halfway point in the Southern Ocean our plentiful
supply of Tabasco had started to run dry. Our freeze-dried food while
well-balanced with the necessary nutritional and calorific requirements,
sometimes tasted a little bland on its own. Additives such as Tabasco or
even tomato sauce do wonders to spice up the flavour and had become

an essential supplement to each portion as it was served out to the crew.

As the contents of the last bottle disappeared there were disappointed grunts and murmurs as the news worked its way around the crew. Claire and I had packed a plentiful supply into the ration packs but not one in each bag. Two days later, the moaning about the lack of Tabasco could be endured no longer. I mentioned to Feathers that Claire and I were sure there was a stash of the stuff somewhere in the numerous food bags stowed onboard, we just had to find it. As *Cheyenne* drew ever closer to the Horn, Feathers and I decided to boost morale and went in search of the elusive Tabasco. As we squeezed though the narrow watertight hatchway under the cockpit we could see the ration packs hanging up. Somewhere amongst the dozens of bags was what everyone wanted.

A hasty rummage through the first two bags revealed nothing, but forty-five minutes later, having rifled though the contents of the remaining ration packs in the portside hull, our search had triumphantly turned up two bottles. We had enough to last for a while if we used it sparingly. The next evening meal tasted really good. Everyone seemed satisfied with the new found discovery and, with smiles all round, it was clear that order was once again restored.

Left **Food time – me enjoying some hot noodles.**

Right **Enjoying a hot brew before we go on watch. Left to right: Gordon, Claire and me.**

The seventh of March was the day before rounding the Horn and we were charging along at speed, making great progress. *Doha 2006* had rounded a couple of days before but we were catching them and had narrowed their lead to just seven hundred miles as the most significant milestone of the race approached.

Throughout the whole of the Southern Ocean passage I had managed to keep my base layer clothing dry, apart from the terrifying episode with the large gennaker a week earlier. Keeping yourself and your kit dry is an important task at sea and I had been careful to make sure I achieved it. That last night in the Southern Ocean was marked by two memorable events. Earlier in the day I had stripped off my kit to get into my bunk. My mid-layer thermals that I had placed over the edge of the bunk bed had dropped into the bilge while I undressed. This momentary lapse of judgement had left me with soaking wet clothes. With no spare mid-layer thermals I had two options: either pull on my trousers and try to ignore the cold wet feeling as the water-logged thermals soaked my skin or I could sit in front of the tiny air ducts of the heater for an hour and a half and slowly dry my clothes. I decided on the latter and while I sat and stewed over my bad luck I was grateful that the incident had occurred at the end of my watch and not at the beginning, otherwise I would have had a wet backside for three hours before I could do anything about it.

Later that night I returned to the bunk after a particularly tiring session of flat-out helming on deck. I was still miffed at what had happened earlier in the day but this time I made sure I didn't make the same mistake and successfully clambered into bed, tired and annoyed. The events that followed helped to instantly dispel any grumpiness on my part and highlighted the important truth that when you're having a bad day there is always someone having a worse one.

I had been in bed for about half an hour and was just starting to drift off to sleep when I sensed one of the lads clamber past the bunk. It was Gérard, one of our French rock stars. He was obviously heading to the toilet which was just forward of the bunk in front of mine. A carbon fibre bulkhead separated the two compartments but the distance between the two was no more than ten feet. I was half asleep at the time and thought nothing of it. A minute or two later I could hear the noise of the suction pump as Gérard pulled the handle up and down to flush the toilet. All of a sudden there was a loud pop reminiscent of a pressurised pipe exploding from a socket. "Merde, merde!" I could hear Gérard cursing from within the cramped and enclosed compartment. By now I was wide awake, it would be hard not to be woken by that kind of noise. By the sound of it the toilet waste disposal pipe had exploded off the housing and blown excrement all over the toilet area. Poor Gérard!

Seconds later, a thick French accent cut through the air and I could hear my name. "Alex, Alex, there is shit everywhere! Are you awake?" Gérard obviously wanted some help. I was giggling like a small child under the covers of my sleeping bag and remember holding my breath as I heard him call out my name. There was no way I was getting involved and while I felt slightly guilty, I did my best to pretend I was asleep and quietly pulled the sleeping bag zip over my head. We were teammates but this was above and beyond the call of duty.

Two-and-a-half hours later one of the lads shook my sleeping bag and woke me up. It was time to get back on deck for another round of action. Gérard was still kneeling on the toilet floor, cleaning up the mess. As I climbed out of the bunk we looked at each other and in an effort to conceal my deception I asked what he was doing. My attempts to pretend this was all news to me obviously left Gérard wondering whether I had indeed been asleep. "Alex, did you not hear me calling? There was shit everywhere." I burst out laughing, but remember thinking that I was probably the only one of us that found the situation funny. Later I was told that the lads on deck had been in stitches for the past two-and-a-half hours.

The next morning under the cover of darkness the faint outline of Cape Horn came into view. We were about a mile off the rocky shoreline but even in the dark the imposing Chilean landmark was impressive. For hundreds of years sailors have endured extreme hardship and frequently perished in the attempt to round this famous place. It was 8 March 2005. Many of the crew had seen Cape Horn before and to them it was a symbol of our imminent departure from the freezing wastes of the Southern Ocean. For me and Claire this was a real milestone. I had waited all my life to be looking up at this lump of granite. Ever since I was a small boy I knew that one day I would lay eyes upon the famous Cape.

I had read the books by the pioneers of solo ocean racing as well as countless other nautical publications of tales of adventure on the high seas. They all cite Cape Horn as the mariner's Everest and now it was my turn to experience the feeling of achievement and join what some might call the elite club of the few who have sailed past the area. It was a magical moment and one that I was keen to share with my parents. I had always promised to call Mum and Dad when we rounded the Cape and now, with the coastline in sight, I pushed the buttons on the satellite phone.

Having rounded the most significant mark of the race, our course now changed towards the north. We would soon be entering the south Atlantic and ahead were the Falkland Islands. A welcome stiff breeze swept the decks and provided near-perfect conditions. For several days *Cheyenne* enjoyed consistent high speed sailing, propelled by an excellent conveyor belt of breeze as we charged northwards. *Doha 2006* was still ahead and also enjoying favourable conditions but we were closing the gap. Tony Bullimore and his crew onboard the reliable Daedalus was bringing up the rear. They were fighting their own battles and trying to escape one last onslaught from a particularly nasty Southern Ocean storm. We spared a thought and prayer for them as we knew they were in for a real pasting.

Gordon and I had shared the helming duties on our watch from the beginning of the race. Down in the Southern Ocean, even during moderate times, the concentration and physical strength needed to keep the boat not only on the pace but more importantly safe had become quite a tall order. When you take the wheel of such a formula one machine as a maxi catamaran you are effectively taking responsibility for the lives of everyone on board, especially when you're in the Furious Fifties. With just the two of us working as the drivers on our watch the work rate had been very demanding.

The sun was shining and we were blessed with near-perfect conditions as we blasted along on port tack at close to thirty-four knots. The windward hull was just beginning to lift free of the water and life felt great. I had been on the helm for the best part of an hour. Gordon stood relaxed next to the steering pedestal and I could see that Claire was keen to sample the thrill of helming a beast such as *Cheyenne* at least once during this adventure. The fact that Claire had not previously been allowed to take a stint at the wheel had obviously frustrated her, although she didn't openly voice any opinion on the matter. She is an excellent sailor and I knew she had the competence and strength to take charge of the boat in moderate conditions.

Due to our rapid progress we had been keeping in touch with David and the navigator down below via the onboard radio mikes which were positioned at each steering pedestal. On board any boat communication is essential but nowhere more so than a monster such as *Cheyenne*. David and Woulter were both sitting at the chart table in the opposite hull, monitoring the situation. Visibility on deck was excellent and with a virtually flat sea and no land in sight we were enjoying a rare but exciting rollercoaster ride. David agreed that Claire could take the wheel and despite enjoying the steering I was pleased to take a half-hour break and hand over. *Cheyenne* felt solid, stable and furiously fast as we thundered along under the invisible power of the wind. In these conditions, even at this speed, with a flat sea and stiff breeze the stability and performance of these craft is nothing short of amazing. However, all the fun was about to come crashing to an abrupt halt.

Claire had been hands-on at the helm for about fifteen minutes and was competently guiding us on course. The breeze had started to increase steadily and we were getting close to the point where a sail change was approaching. I was standing in front of the steering binnacle and Gordon was standing behind Claire, ready to take the wheel should she need any extra muscle. It's a standard procedure when things start to get a little twitchy. As the breeze increased so did the boat speed and things were getting very rapid as we closed on forty knots. Thirty-eight knots registered on the speedometer, a sure sign that we were close to the max. We made a quick call to the nav station informing them that we were still in control and we received a calm reply to keep the pressure on, *Cheyenne* felt in the groove.

If needed, a quick ease of the mainsail sheet and a decisive right-hand turn of the steering wheel would have taken the pressure off should we have become overpowered at any time. We were ready for that – Feathers stood by on the mainsail hydraulic release and I was poised to blow off the headsail sheet should the need arise.

In an instant it was all over. Without warning, one of the main supporting shrouds that held the mast in place failed, sending the whole rig over the side. Everything happened so quickly but it was the rapid deceleration that firmly sticks in my mind. We went from nearly forty knots to zero in just a couple of seconds. As the carbon fibre wing mast crashed into the ocean *Cheyenne* stopped with the force of a car crash. There was no time to react and we were all thrown violently forwards. Claire was nearly thrown right over the top of the steering pedestal while Gordon piled into the back of her. Feathers and I were catapulted towards the forward end of the cockpit, my rapid progress halting only as my face smashed into the coffee grinder winch. The impact bloody well hurt and split my nose open. I remember the claret added to the drama of the situation as everyone checked that everyone else was OK. As we dragged ourselves to our feet we were all visibly in shock. There was chaos everywhere. Gordon, calm as ever, attempted to lighten the situation, cracking a joke that it must have been Claire's fault as she was the one driving at the time. I think for a second or two she believed him until I shouted, "He's joking!"

The mast was down and lay in the water over the starboard side. The forward longitudinal supporting beam where the forestay wires attached had completely shattered and as a result the forward trampoline nets had gaping great holes torn in them. The boat was a real mess. Nearly all of the winches surrounding the mast base had been crushed as the mast fell down. To make matters worse, the boom and mainsail were obstructing the entrance to the cabin where most of the lads were sleeping. It took a while before everyone could assemble on deck to check the damage. In a split second our race was over and the chance to claim a share of that million dollar prize money was gone.

Clearing up the mess after being dismasted.

The broken mast, still attached to the boat. The clean-up took hours.

While the rest of us started on the clean-up job, David went below to use the sat phone to contact race HQ. We were out of the race but the priority now was to work out how we were going to get out of this mess. We had no onboard engines as all the competitors had removed their diesel engines prior to the race start in an effort to save weight. Constructing a jury rig that was big enough to propel this thirty-tonne monster anywhere would be difficult with limited resources. These thoughts occupied our capable skipper's mind as the rest of us proceeded to cut away the debris and hack through half a million pounds' worth of mast and sails. It would all end up at the bottom of the ocean now. In an instant, our priorities shifted from performance to making the decks safe and securing the boat. We were about two hundred and twenty-five nautical miles off the Argentinean coast but closer to the northern tip of the Falkland Islands.

Cutting away the huge broken mast and rigging was not easy and it was several hours before we had the debris cleared. Our situation, while not in any way life-threatening, certainly presented us with a bit of a challenge. Now that the mast and sails had sunk to the bottom of the south Atlantic we were adrift on the ocean with no way of making headway toward a safe port. We needed a tow and quickly.

David seemed glued to the sat phone as the rest of us congregated on deck to discuss our options. Outside assistance was the only real way out of this mess. Before the Oryx Quest, as part of her medical career, Claire had worked for the Royal Navy. Being so close to the Falklands, she was keen to make contact to see if they would be willing to help. The Navy's response was positive. They were willing, but within hours of the mast breaking we had drifted into Argentinean waters and it was actually the Argentinean navy who eventually came to our rescue.

David had explained our predicament to Steve Fossett and with the support of the Oryx Quest race organisers they speedily coordinated a plan of assistance. Whoever came to our aid this far out on the ocean, it would not be a cheap exercise. As the boat owner, Steve would ultimately have to foot the bill. Admirably, he wasted no time in instructing David to use any means necessary to get us home quickly and safely. David later emerged from the cabin and told everyone that help was on its way and for now all we could do was to wait. The Argentineans were coming.

The Argentinians on the horizon, a welcome sight.

During our passage through the Southern Ocean I had coincidentally come across a book that had been discarded in the navigation station. The book was about the Falklands War and had been written by an ex-SAS serviceman who had fought in the conflict. The book lay unclaimed on the chart table for several days so one night I decided to read a few pages when I was off-watch. By the time the mast went over the side I was really into the book and was three quarters of the way through.

Later that evening, just as the sun was settling below the horizon, we sighted a vessel in the distance. As the ship drew closer we weren't sure whether it was the Argies or not. The vessel looked old and was painted grey but it looked more like a relic from the Second World War than a vessel that ought to be in service today. I was sitting in the port-side cockpit as the Argentinean navy arrived. Feathers emerged from the cabin and started running around in a fluster. He was doing his best to single-handedly get everything ready for the tow when he noticed I was reading the book. Realising what the book was about, in a moment of madness he grabbed it out of my hands and threw it over the side. "What the hell are you doing?" I asked. "Alex, we can't have that book about the Falklands conflict on board. What if the Argies come aboard and find it?" It was a ridiculous statement. I was just getting to the good part and now I would never know how it finished.

Under normal circumstances I think I might have blown a fuse but something about the panicked look on his face made the situation amusing. Our new-found friends were about a hundred yards away when they launched a small rigid inflatable with three guys aboard. They motored over to us and we welcomed them on board. They were nice guys and offered to take some of us across to their vessel for some decent food and a hot shower. Of course everyone was keen to go but in the end just a couple of the lads went as the rest of us were needed on board *Cheyenne*.

The following morning with light winds and the aid of daylight we hooked up the lines and our long slow tow to civilisation began. There had been much speculation amongst the crew as to where we would eventually pitch up but in the end David and the Navy captain made that decision between themselves. We were heading for Comodoro Rivadavia, a southern Argentinean city port in the Patagonian province of Chubut, about two hundred and twenty-five nautical miles away. Until now I had never heard of Comodoro Rivadavia but looking at the charts it was the logical choice, being the nearest commercial port which could cater for a boat as large as ours. There was also a small airport close by, which would be useful as some of the guys were already talking about flying home and I was having thoughts about getting back to the car yard now that the racing action was definitely behind us. Progress under tow was constant but certainly not quick. The journey took two long days before we finally caught sight of the sandy shores of that far away land.

Life on board since the mast break had taken on a different meaning. Everyone was disappointed that the race had reached a premature end but while I shared the weight of disappointment, I was pleased we had successfully endured the might of the Southern Ocean and rounded Cape Horn. *Cheyenne* and the Oryx Quest had enabled me to achieve two important lifelong ambitions. I looked at the result as an achievement rather than a disappointment, although I'm sure it would have been nice to have taken a share of that elusive million dollar prize.

I think everyone was pleased when the spectacular calm shores of southern Argentina came into view. Comodoro would only be a pit stop, a chance to prepare *Cheyenne* for the long haul under tow back

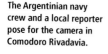

The Argentinian navy crew and a local reporter pose for the camera in Comodoro Rivadavia.

to the United States. Only a skeleton crew would be required to stay with the boat for that journey so Steve had already instructed David to make the necessary arrangements to fly the rest of the team back home once we had secured the boat and sorted ourselves out.

As we entered the harbour we could see this was a commercial port. Several large but rusty-looking ships and a handful of deep sea fishing boats were tied to the dockside. There was a gap between two of them just large enough for us to fit into. As we began securing *Cheyenne* to the harbour wall a small group of intrigued locals gathered around. They soon turned into a large crowd of onlookers and within twenty minutes we got the feeling that the whole town had come for a look. Even a reporter from the local newspaper turned up and started snapping pictures. She spoke passable English and soon started talking to each of us. We were splashed all over the local newspapers that night and apparently had created quite a stir amongst the local community who had never seen such an amazing craft tie up to their quayside.

That night, having booked into a nearby hotel and bought some new clothes from a local store, we all gathered for a final meal together and tucked into some of the biggest steaks I have ever seen. Two days later, the team shook hands and each of us went our separate ways. It was time to fly home and return to normal life – at least for a while.

BUILDING A DREAM

After the tremendous experience of the Oryx Quest I returned home to focus my energies on the car business. Settling back into a more normal way of life after such an extraordinary adventure is never easy and it wasn't long before the draw of the ocean started to make my imagination run riot. Barely a month after I had come home I was hatching new plans that would get me back to the big blue.

The summer passed quickly. I had been working hard at the car yard and had made several trips to Japan to replenish our stock. Life was good but the prospect of another project had become a dominant thought in my mind. I had learned about an exciting new breed of offshore racing yacht that had recently been introduced to the market. This new class of monohull was quickly becoming big news within the yachting community and was designed to strike a balance between affordability and practicality without the usual sacrifice of sailing performance. Class 40, as the association is called, brings big fleet offshore racing to a wider audience of sailor, allowing both professionals and amateurs to compete together. At forty feet in length, the boats are big enough to be seriously capable machines and also powerful enough to make the racing exciting and above all physically challenging.

The Class 40 organisation was in its embryonic stage but with nearly a dozen new boats already on the water it was clear that the vision had all the right things in the mix to become a successful racing class. Class 40 provides the perfect route into some of the great short-handed ocean races and for me would become my route into arguably the most famous of them all, the solo transatlantic race known as the

OSTAR. This race had been on my hit list since I was a schoolboy. After the round-the-world race I had decided to make sure I would be on the start line for the next OSTAR. For that to happen I needed a new boat and Class 40 was the logical choice. The only trouble was being such a new fleet, there were no second-hand yachts on the market. If I was determined to get to the start of the race in two years' time and be at the helm of one of these boats I would just have to build one from scratch.

The prospect of building a state-of-the-art racing yacht from the drawing board up didn't faze me. Other people do it, so why shouldn't I? But if I were to do this, I knew that I would need help. The project was a huge undertaking and would only be as successful as the people who surrounded it. The race across the Atlantic might be solo, but it would be a whole team of people who would make that dream a reality. At that time, the conventional route of approaching a professional boatyard to commission the building of such a yacht was out of the question. I had no sponsor and the costs involved would have been completely unaffordable. If I was going to do this I would have to start with a blank piece of paper and bring the project together myself. It would be a longer road that way but certainly a cheaper one if I could pull it off.

It must be said that my talent and experience weren't centred on any personal boatbuilding skills but more related to project management. I was under no illusions – if this project was to be a success I needed to pull together a team who shared my vision, people who had the necessary skills to tackle the various specialist areas of such a project. I knew I had the experience to bring everything together but equally accepted that I would need to hire the services of numerous specialists such as naval architects, structural engineers, electricians and sailmakers, not to mention skilled boat-builders.

I mulled it over for months, thinking about the various aspects of the build, trying to decide what was feasible and what wasn't. I had a clear vision, but without corporate sponsorship I knew it was unlikely I would be able to complete the boat. For an individual with limited funds, such a project is a huge undertaking. If I took this on, it would be by far the biggest project of my life. If I wasn't careful and completely realistic it could financially ruin me. From the moment I gave full commitment the clock would be ticking. Not only must we successfully build a state-of-the-art boat, I would also have to find a sponsor before my own funds ran out. There was a lot of risk attached, both financial and physical. But above all else, whatever we created, once it hit the water, the weight would solely rest on my shoulders. I would need to have the strength of my convictions to sail the thing across an ocean single-handed. And not just any ocean but the mighty North Atlantic, against the prevailing winds and currents.

Many people across the world dream of building their own yacht, whether it be a cruising boat or an out-and-out racer. But for whatever reason so many people don't see their dreams evolve beyond the initial ideal in their minds. There are those who take the plunge and embark on their dream, determined to make it happen. For some it's a success, but for others their ambition quickly turns into a nightmare. I had seen this all before. Was I just another dreamer, someone with big ideas but the kind of guy who didn't have the means, either technical or financial, to pull it off? I knew I had the necessary commitment but was that enough, would I be biting off more than I could chew? For months I quietly researched the project and wrestled with these thoughts.

Financially, I was just getting back on my feet from the whole *One Dream One Mission* saga. Did I really want to put my neck on the block again and take the full risk for a second time? I gave this some very serious thought.

To follow your dreams you sometimes have to take a chance. I finally decided to push the button and go for it. I had enough savings to get the project underway and commission a pedigree design. We could perhaps get half-way through the build of the hull before running out of cash. At that point if a sponsor hadn't surfaced, ready to sign on the dotted line, I would have to admit defeat. There was no way I was going to remortgage my house and risk the roof over my head but I knew that as a last resort with a pedigree design under construction it was likely I could sell the boat as a half-built going concern. I viewed it as a simple business decision, risk versus reward. It was worth it. If it failed I would have the comfort of knowing that I had given it my best shot. I would rather deal with the reality of failure than the feelings of regret because of inaction. Life is just too short for that.

When you first decide to design a racing yacht on a blank piece of paper you are presented with an infinite range of possibilities. Virtually anything is possible and the only constraints are those of time, imagination, budget and the racing rules of sailing. For my boat there was a lot to consider beyond just budget and time. Every boat is different, even though some might look the same. Custom racing yachts are a bespoke reflection of both their owners' desires and their practical requirements.

Different keel configurations, different sail plans, the size and shape of the cockpit to suit an owner's requirements, the layout of equipment on deck together with the type of sails carried on board, all make a difference to the specification of the finished product. Fortunately I knew exactly what I wanted. Not something extreme that would excel on just one point of sail but rather a good all-rounder. A boat that would perform admirably in varying wind and sea conditions, a lightweight and well-designed boat but ultimately a safe one. For months after the loss of *One Dream One Mission* I had experienced vivid recurring dreams of the events that unfolded that night out on the high seas. I was determined the new boat would adhere primarily to an ethos of safety.

In an effort to gain a complete understanding of the various options available I approached several naval architects with a view to hearing their ideas and opinions pertaining to the ideal Class 40 yacht. There was however really only one design house that could ultimately secure my signature on a contract. Merfyn Owen and Alan Clarke are the core of Owen Clarke Design, a company that enjoys an excellent reputation within the world of race boat design, and for many reasons they were the right choice for me.

Merf was the same guy who had trusted me with their potent thirty-footer Maverick when I had been a young rookie just starting out. As naval architects their name is synonymous with quality and they already had two latest-generation Class 40 prototypes under construction in South Africa. They were willing to listen to what I wanted as a sailor but most importantly prepared to work closely with me throughout the evolution of the project. After a preliminary meeting where we discussed everything from budgets to expectations I felt energised and determined to go ahead. The computer-generated image showing the basic attributes of my boat was all that occupied my thoughts, and I couldn't wait to turn it into reality.

The question of who I would appoint as the build manager had also been on my mind. This was a major decision. I knew plenty of people who had the necessary experience to undertake such a responsibility but after serious consideration it was a close friend who eventually got the job. My friend Martin Boulter had gained a degree in yacht manufacture and surveying at Southampton Institute and had been working for a specialist boat-building company based in the south coast town of Lymington for years. As part of his job, Martin had travelled all over Europe, working in the construction of high-tech America's Cup yachts as well as specialist custom-built carbon fibre racing yachts for the Volvo Ocean Race. Most recently he had been part of a skilled team which built lifeboats for the RNLI. Despite being a couple of years younger than me, Martin had gained a huge amount of practical experience and knowledge. He had reached the stage where he wanted to set up his own enterprise within the boat-building world and this project was a step towards that. We had always spoken about the possibility of building a boat together, so now I had set the wheels in motion we arranged a meeting at the car yard to discuss the prospect seriously.

I could see that Martin was keen; this was just the opportunity he had been looking for and my plans couldn't have come at a better time. We soon settled on a mutually-beneficial agreement and shook hands on the deal. Martin had just become my new build manager and I was his first client. Despite being good friends, we both agreed to keep things completely professional as after all this was business. He would deal directly with the day-to-day aspects of the physical construction of the boat while I worried about the overall management of the project. The following day I asked Malcolm Dickinson if he would draw up a contract. My loyal friend at Michelmores Solicitors has supported my adventures for nearly ten years and the firm always looked after the legal side of things.

With the naval architecture underway and a build manager sorted my thoughts naturally turned to finding a suitable place to build the boat. Due to the nature of the project I knew I would be hands-on, so I wanted to find a facility close to the car yard in order to make life easier when I needed to pop down to the boat to check progress. During early discussions both Martin and I had covered all the options. We even considered places abroad as far afield as Thailand. This was actually a viable option because of the incredibly low labour rates. Your money goes a long way out there, but this venture would need my eyes on the project pretty well every day. Basing the project away from the county of Devon let alone abroad just wasn't going to work.

The search for a warehouse or similar suitable site began. Baltic Wharf boatyard in Totnes was just a couple of miles down the road, but they didn't have spare undercover space big enough to make it viable. What we needed was a large dry barn that we could easily heat through the winter once the hull laminating process started. As I sat in my office at the car yard I looked out of the window across the rolling green fields that sandwich the site and experienced a moment of blinding clarity. The answer had been staring me in the face. Just along the lane at the bottom of the hill there was a group of agricultural barns. Two of them were brand new and huge, big enough to build not just a forty-foot yacht but a boat twice the size. They would be ideal.

The barns were owned by a local farmer whom I knew and luckily enough, one of them was practically empty apart from a few lonely-looking hay bales. The farmer seemed a little perplexed as I explained our intentions. I suppose the thought of someone constructing a state-of-the-art racing yacht in one of his barns seemed a bit strange to him, but the mention of money and my willingness to pay for three months rent upfront soon helped to clarify his thoughts. I called Martin to arrange a visit. To my mind, the place was perfect but he was the one who needed to have the final say on whether it was really a suitable venue. A couple of days later the two of us walked around the dusty barn and planned the future. Martin agreed that it was perfect. The solid, level concrete floor was particularly useful and despite it having no front doors yet, we agreed that we had just found our build site. The farmer was keen and agreed to get some doors fitted, everyone was happy and things felt like they were falling into place. Best of all, the build shed was perfectly placed within sight of the car yard. I could pop down any time and check on progress.

Within days, Martin arrived with a van load of equipment and together we started preparing the site. It would take a couple of weeks to set everything up before we could start work properly. There was also the minor point of hiring some extra help. That was really Martin's area but one person that I was particularly keen to bring into the team was my faithful friend Mike Shand. I had already spoken to Mike about the impending project and he was busting a gut to be part of the action. His practical engineering skills would be a real asset as the build evolved. I knew I could trust his hand on the project, especially when I mentioned that he would be part of the delivery team once the boat was finished. I was well aware that Mike had dreams of sailing the Atlantic Ocean. Once the boat had completed the solo transatlantic race, I planned to make that ambition a reality by giving him a well-deserved place on board for the trip home. We had a lot of hard work ahead of us before we got to that stage but I knew he would jump at the chance to be part of the crew that would sail the boat back from America to England. For Mike such a chance was his Everest.

Left **The hay barn before we turned it into a boat-building facility.**

Right **Martin sweeping the barn floor before we started the build.**

It was August 2006 and the project had taken its first step on the ladder of success. In just a few days I would make the call to order the materials and from then on there would be no turning back. We all felt beyond excited.

From the moment I had committed to the design of the boat Owen Clarke had been busy preparing the myriad technical drawings that accompany the design of a modern racing boat. My boat was subjected to a comprehensive structural engineering programme and Alan and Merf looked after the details. Virtually all the construction drawings came in digital format on a disk, requiring a specialist computer program just to view them. There were drawings and specifications for just about every component on board, from the big items like the hull, deck and keel support structures to intricate sketches for the complicated spider's web of internal stringers, fibreglass strengthening beams that make the whole structure rigid and safe. There were even drawings illustrating how to construct the twin tillers used to steer the boat. One of the most important documents was a detailed bill of materials or BOM. This printed document was supplied by the structural engineers and was a comprehensive list of everything required to construct the new boat. The BOM listed specific materials and quantities: epoxy resin, different types of fibreglass and various quantities of high-density foam together with a vast array of consumable items were just some of the many things we had to acquire. The BOM listed it all in black and white and it was my job to source the various products in time for when Martin needed them.

Not everything came from one source. Some components, like the high density foam cores used to form the centre of the hull and deck laminates, would be sourced from as far afield as Canada. There was a time delay for those and only one supplier who could fulfil the order, so there was a real need to be organised. Martin drew up a timeline for the project, showing the various build stages and expected dates for the commencement of each phase. This was an invaluable source of information and helped me to get organised early on.

Having studied the materials list and checked the prices from various suppliers, something that kept me desk-bound for days at a time, I decided to order all the big items such as the resin, foam cores and various consumables in one go from just one supplier. That way I was able to negotiate a deal and get a better price. Some items I knew I could secure through sponsorship, while others I realised would only arrive in exchange for hard cash. There were always deals to be done and it was my job to nail the best prices. Having identified exactly what we wanted, I set about contacting the various manufacturers to order the rest of the kit.

There are numerous methods available to construct a modern racing yacht but generally each process revolves around the requirement to make a set of moulds prior to building the real thing. Our chosen construction route was by and large the same, although we had decided to build the boat using female moulds, which is considered the best method to save on overall weight. A boat made from female moulds usually requires less filler to be applied to the hull and deck to create the final cosmetic finish. This route would be more costly but we would end up with a lighter boat which is always a bonus in the competitive world of ocean racing.

The first stage of the build would include the construction of a wooden plug. This mock-up structure, while not actually part of the finished boat, forms an essential part of the build process. The pin-point accurate structure is built from precision laser-cut wooden frames that slot together rather like a jigsaw puzzle to form the shape of the hull. These frames are then attached to a plywood structure called the strong back which is raised about two feet off the floor and bolted to the ground to keep everything rigid. Once all the frames are erected onto the strong back they are then joined together by a process of battening with thin strips of flexible wood before being covered over with several layers of thin plywood sheet to create the desired hull shape. That shape is then covered by a layer of fibreglass before the final stage completes the process, a long, slow procedure of filling and fairing to remove any imperfections to create a perfectly smooth finish. This stage is real back-breaking work and would take four guys more than a month to complete. Time and care spent here pays dividends in the finished article. Once the plug was finished we would use that shape to create the female mould which would then be used to make the real boat. Building the plug was the first stage of our journey so it was essential that we covered all the bases and checked our measurements twice over.

Martin and Mike set to work with unity of purpose the minute the frames and timber arrived. By the end of the first week I could see the familiar outline of a boat starting to take shape. It was amazing to stand at the end of the build shed and watch as the frames were slowly lowered into place. The worry of the past months as to whether I should embark on such a huge undertaking dissipated as I watched the lads get down to business. I felt satisfied that I had made the right decision.

Martin was thorough in his attention to detail and continuously checked his measurements with the aid of a special laser tool to ensure that his work perfectly mirrored the drawings supplied by Owen Clarke. I remember feeling impressed with both his skill and his knowledge as the plug started to take shape. While the lads in the boatyard got stuck in to stage one, I was kept more than busy with the management side of things. This alone was a full-time job and that was before taking into account my daily responsibilities of running the car yard with my father. It was a very busy time.

There was so much to organise, but nothing occupied my time more than the endless task of pursuing that ever-so-elusive sponsor to take the title of the project. I constantly approached companies and chased down leads in an effort to nail the support the project so desperately needed. Unlike some campaigns, ours had started with me injecting my own cash. I believed this to be the strongest declaration of our commitment. I reminded myself every day that this project was happening and was already a reality. Confidence is the name of the game. How can you expect anyone to believe in you if you don't first believe in yourself? My father had taught me that. We would get there, one way or another. Just walk into the boatyard and see the boat being born – the excitement was infectious. If I could get a potential sponsor to walk through the doors I knew we could inspire them, I was sure of it.

Now that we were spending serious money on materials the pressure was on Martin to get the plug to a stage where I could pass it off as a boat well under construction. We needed good quality images of the plug so that I could take them to potential sponsors. I had a couple of warm leads but wanted my pitch to pack a real punch. A picture is worth a thousand words and I planned to use ours to demonstrate our commitment, to help us stand out from the crowd as a project with a future. At least that's how I viewed it. One of the problems when you go on the sponsorship hunt, just as in an ocean race or in business when competing for a contract, is the competition. There are so many other projects out there from all types of sport – sailing, horse racing, motor racing, extreme sports, mountaineering, probably even tiddlywinks, the list is endless – and we all share a common goal. Everyone needs the cash. It's a competitive arena and frequently only the most impressive and closely-tailored pitches see success.

The words of my first big sponsor have stayed in my mind to this

Left **The laser-cut frames secured to the strong back. You can already start to see the outline of a boat.**

Right **Martin and Mike busy laying the wooden battens to the plug with a long way to go yet.**

day. Peter Earp from English Braids had wanted to know why his company should sponsor me, and so would others. I knew that if we were to attract serious support we needed more than just words, we needed something that was real, something a sponsor could grab hold of. Something that is happening today, something that is already a work-in-progress. The plug was my party piece, our proof of commitment. Walking into a boardroom with a project already underway and beating its own path would be the X-factor that made us stand out from the crowd.

The days of a logo on the side of a boat and a quick 'cheers' in exchange for cold cash are long gone. Those types of deals did nothing

Martin engrossed in his work, checking his measurements with the laser.

but give sailing sponsorship a bad name. Investors are looking for real tangible returns on their investments no matter how small their financial commitment, and nowadays creativity is the key. Thirteen years of boardroom pitches and sponsorship hunting has made me realise this. In this business, cold-calling and letter writing although important rarely lead to hard cash. Introductions, motivational talks, corporate events, hard work and sometimes just being in the right place at the right time make the difference between sink or swim for a project. This is the world of no replies, disappointing declinations and uninspired boardroom decision-makers who struggle to see 'opportunity' unless it jumps up and slaps them across the face. It is the world of the sponsor-ship hunter and I love it.

Product support was not so much of a problem and much of the equipment or material we required was generously exchanged for some prominent advertising space on the boat and campaign website. Many companies associated with the marine industry were receptive to my calls and had no difficulty seeing the benefits of being associated with our ambitious project.

When it comes to sponsorship, it's a buyer's market to a certain degree and professional ocean racing is one of those sports that some-times lags behind in areas like consistent television coverage, one of the all important 'pull' factors when negotiating with potential spon-sors. In our sport we have to be a little more creative than the more mainstream sporting industries in order to attract the TV cameras. For a project such as ours national television coverage is possible but is rare and infrequent. Local television coverage, on the other hand, was probable and this is where we would build the foundations for promot-ing our project. Every campaign looking for a sponsor needs media coverage and our project had reached the stage where we needed to start proactively promoting it. The local guy competing on an interna-tional stage with a home-grown product, built in the West Country by local people, that's where we would start. I knew that was enough to spark interest, and that we could achieve excellent support from the regional media if we took the right approach. Previous campaigns had helped to build some good working relationships, which are invaluable in this game.

By now the invoices for materials were starting to flow though my letterbox in giant tidal waves. My calculator became both the most useful and most hated instrument on my desk. Adding up all the bills took more courage than I had needed to sail solo across the Atlantic. I started to seriously consider how far we could get before the money-pit soaked up the last of my cash. I didn't burden Martin and Mike with those concerns as they were making excellent progress with the plug and now that the filling and fairing had started Martin had taken on some extra staff to keep up the pace. Everyone had a routine and mine consisted of getting into work at around 7.30am, opening up and cracking on with paperwork while I waited for Dad to arrive. I would then walk down the lane to the build shed for a cup of tea with

Martin to discuss progress and the objectives for the day.

I was keen to get the photographs of the plug for a pitch that was coming up with one of my past sponsors, Fujifilm Graphic Systems. I had kept them informed of our plans for the new project and now that we were going full steam ahead they were keen to hear more. Fujifilm had proposed a meeting but in the interests of having the images of the plug to hand, I had stalled them for as long as I could. I desperately needed those pictures but the plug wasn't finished and certainly wasn't painted. The trouble was it looked less than inspiring unless you were standing next to it. Martin and I discussed the problem the following morning over a cuppa. There was only one thing for it, I suggested – we should paint it all one colour. That would look better for the photographs. The plug was a long way from requiring a layer of top-coat paint, but a quick flash over of base coat primer wouldn't do any harm and would provide the basis for a decent photo opportunity. It worked. The following day we had the pictures I wanted. The plug looked the business, so I phoned Fujifilm to arrange the meeting.

By the end of the week I received a phone call from the suppliers.

The plug half way to completion.

The major materials we had ordered were due to arrive any day. It was exciting news but posed a bit of a problem. The farmer who owned the build shed had experienced delays with the installation of the electric roller shutter doors and until now the build shed had remained essentially an open site. Every night we had to pack up all the tools and lock them away in Martin's container. The lack of security had been a constant worry for me. We were out in the countryside and hidden away from the main road but the arrival of thousands of pounds' worth of materials would be a red rag to a bull for any would-be thieves who spotted it unattended. Until the farmer completed the installation of the doors we couldn't leave that amount of material on offer in the shed. The plug was a worry too – the effects of vandalism would be catastrophic if anything like that occurred. It was a less than ideal situation, although one that I had been aware of from the outset.

I had just twenty-four hours to find a solution. The only one I could come up with was to commandeer one of the small buildings at the car yard. If I moved a couple of cars from our valeting shed I could store the materials in there. It was dry and secure and provided a perfect solution, being so close to the build site.

The following day I was sitting in my office with Dad when he noticed a huge truck struggling to negotiate the narrow lane leading to the build shed. It was our delivery but the truck was huge and literally blocked the whole lane. An hour and a half later and with the help of the farmer's fork-lift truck and some muscle from Martin and the lads we had a giant pile of kit safely stashed in the valeting shed. Several large barrels of epoxy resin and a massive tower of high-density Corecell foam almost touched the roof of the building as we pilled everything into the corner. It was literally a shedload of material. As my father walked in to have a look he asked if we were really going to make a forty-foot racing yacht from the pile of materials in front of us. I didn't say anything, but the grin on my face must have said it all.

In the days preceding the meeting with Fujifilm I had spent a significant amount of time preparing a dedicated computer-based presentation to introduce the project and help illustrate the various aspects and opportunities available. The images of the plug looked fantastic and together with a small selection of pictures showing the team working around it I felt the slideshow was ready for scrutiny. My plan revolved around a short but factual presentation highlighting the aspirations of the project, the key facts and timelines as well as the associated opportunities for a potential partner. I had initially been torn on how best to deliver the presentation but eventually decided upon a plain but I hoped high quality approach: no flashy PR rubbish with bells and whistles, just the facts, plain and simple.

I had been expecting to deliver the presentation in a boardroom with a large projector screen that would give the slideshow real punch. Unfortunately the reality was quite different and instead I had to make do with the small screen of my laptop, a cramped restaurant table and a noisy background. In my desire to create the ideal big-screen presentation I had completely overlooked the possibility that the meeting might be informal. It didn't matter, and despite the self-inflicted confusion the pitch went well and they seemed pleased. They promised to get back to me within a week with a decision. We shook hands and I drove home feeling pleased but unsure if I had done enough to light the fires in their hearts.

My arrival home coincided with an altogether different problem. Local people were starting to notice the activity surrounding the build shed and were becoming increasingly inquisitive as to what we were up to. Apparently, there was no formal planning permission for the barn to permit its use for anything other than agricultural activity. The farmer hadn't given much thought to it at the time, but now that locals were starting to notice all the activity difficult questions were being asked and he was getting itchy feet. The lack of doors at the front of the building had done little to help the situation, but this new development was potentially a big problem. The build of the plug was well underway and the whole structure was bolted to the floor. There was no way we could just move it. I reiterated my worries to the farmer who also shared my concern. He had warmed to the project and its ambitious aspirations. He would regularly bring his young children into the barn to have a look at progress and he didn't want to see the project suffer from red tape. There is nearly always a solution or compromise, so it was up to us to work together to find it.

We agreed that until the doors were installed, the farmer would block up the entrance with a fifteen-foot wall of hay bales which he hoped would help to divert attention away from the barn and conceal the fact that a state-of-the-art boat was being built inside. My immediate thought was of the fire risk but what else could we do? If the

council got wind of what we were doing before official permission was granted for the use of the building we would be done-for. The farmer agreed to pursue the relevant legal permissions and with a plea for us to keep the noise to a minimum we had a way forward, although I couldn't help but worry that the project was skating on thin ice. In a funny way, the fact that the boat was now hidden behind a huge wall of hay bales made the project all the more interesting. A couple of days later, I walked into the build shed only to be confronted by a wall of hay. There was so much of it that it took a few moments to find my way through the cunningly-concealed entrance. I could hear the lads working away but just couldn't see anything.

Mike working contentedly on the plug. Note the hay bales in the background.

By late October the plug was finished and the project had reached its first milestone. Not only that but Fujifilm had been back in touch and after a second meeting, this time at the build shed, they formally agreed to partner with the project as title sponsor. This was simply fantastic news and it couldn't have come at a better time. Fujifilm's commitment was such that it allowed all of us to continue our work unburdened by the worry that our dedication might be in vain. Their support ensured that the boat would be completed and from that moment I knew my entry into the single-handed transatlantic race was as assured as it could be. The project had just found its wings and developed a new identity, we were now representing a global brand and as the head of the project I was an ambassador for Fujifilm wherever I went. Again, the boat would be branded in their distinctive green corporate colour and would brandish the name *Fujifilm* along each side of the hull in bold white lettering. A custom computer-generated graphic of what the boat would look like was quickly created and my vision was well and truly on its way to becoming reality. I remember thinking that life couldn't feel much sweeter than this.

The only drawback with sponsorship is that once you sign up, everything takes on a more serious nature. Before, if a deadline was missed it wasn't too big a deal, a decision to change the plan or schedule could be made on the spot without much regard to the consequences. Now that we answered to a commercial partner the requirement to raise our game was apparent. Deadlines and timeframes suddenly take on new meanings. They can't be missed or just pushed back, or least not without consultation. The race was on, as was the pressure of expectation. Now more than ever we had to get the boat in the water for our intended launch date of April 2007. That would be a whole year before the start of the transatlantic race and would allow plenty of time to not

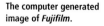

The computer generated image of *Fujifilm*.

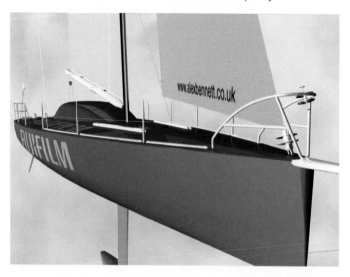

only work the boat up but more importantly to prove that she was up to the job of tackling the tough North Atlantic route to America.

I had a clear plan mapped out for when we entered the sea trials phase and felt it imperative that we should experience varying wind and sea conditions, including sustained gale-force weather, before we crossed the start line. This boat was going to take me across the Atlantic and there would be times when I would push *Fujifilm* to her limits. We would undoubtedly see severe weather and huge seas. This was something I impressed on the team regularly throughout the build – ultimately they had my life in their hands. I trusted each of them to keep it safe and I wanted them to know that.

Having built the plug, the team progressed on to the second stage of the build, constructing the hull mould. This initial process was a relatively straightforward procedure which involved covering the plug with layers of wax. This is used to create a slippery barrier so that the mould would not stick to the plug and could be released once complete. After applying a layer of gel coat to create a near-perfect mirror-like finish to the inside of the mould, the lads applied layer after layer of fibreglass.

The last layers of fibreglass were applied between Christmas 2006 and 1 January 2007 and we were finally ready to prise the two structures apart and lift the mould away from the soon-to-be-redundant wooden plug. While the lads had been tirelessly forging ahead at the build site, I had been concentrating on sourcing the various component parts that would eventually make up the finished vessel. The keel, mast, diesel engine, navigational systems, sails and deck hardware, right down to the stainless steel bolts that attach the winches to the deck were just some of the multitude of components that required sourcing. The question of which manufacturers to use required timely decisions. Researching all the possibilities and hammering out the best deals was not only a full-time job but also a rewarding one. Because we were building this race boat from scratch, virtually everything required bespoke manufacture. If we couldn't build it ourselves the job needed to be outsourced and that's where my expertise came into play. Hardly a day went by without some kind of equipment or materials arriving; it was not uncommon to have three or four separate deliveries a day.

The arrival of delivery trucks became so frequent that I decided to divert the deliveries to the car yard in order to reduce the pressure on the lads. Every time a delivery arrived one of the build team would have to down tools to deal with it. For all but the bulkiest of arrivals it was more productive for me to take the deliveries from the car yard so that the guys could keep the pace on.

With Christmas and New Year a distant memory the lads returned to work from a well-earned but short break. A crucial stage of the build was upon us. It was time to turn the mould and place it the right side up. This was a daunting process that involved lifting it with the use of special chain blocks and suspending it precariously from the roof of the building while the guys removed the now-redundant plug from underneath. Once clear, the giant forty-foot mould was lowered to the ground and rotated until completely upright. The whole process took two hours but it was the longest two hours of my life. Two of the four laminated chain plates where the hoisting blocks connected to the mould broke apart during the lift. There were men underneath at the time and I have a vivid memory of everyone running like rats fleeing a sinking ship the instant we heard the bang. Time seemed temporarily on hold as we looked up to see our precious creation hanging by what

Turning the mould, a nail-biting process.

seemed a hope and a prayer. Martin and I momentarily looked at each other wondering if it was going to come crashing to the floor. If that happened it would spell disaster for the project.

The mould was dangling at least ten feet off the floor so with the finesse of bomb disposal experts we gently pulled on the chain blocks and inch by inch slowly lowered the delicate structure to the floor. It had been a tense operation and I could see the lads were pretty shaken-up, not to mention knackered. It had been a long day, so with the mould safely resting the right way up on the barn floor we called time and locked up for the night. Tomorrow was another day.

The project had become the preeminent focus in my life. I had made a conscious decision to give my absolute commitment throughout the duration of the build. Little else mattered at that time, and I was happy to live, eat and sleep the project for almost a year. The same could be said for Martin too as one of his priorities once the build of our boat became public knowledge was to secure further orders from similar clients looking to build bespoke race boats. This had always been part of our agreement and one of the main reasons in addition to my own requirements why we had chosen the more costly route of building a female mould. This method of construction allowed the flexibility to reuse the tooling to make other boats.

My boat was a showcase for Martin, and once it was built he was free to build another boat or indeed several more, should there be sufficient demand. Part of our agreement involved me handing over ownership of the moulds once *Fujifilm* was completed, which in theory would be a lucrative proposition for him. Although the two of us had discussed it, I wasn't interested in a boat-building business. I had enough on my plate already. But now the world was aware that we had secured the support of a big sponsor, *Fujifilm* acted as an endorsement for Martin, and people soon started to knock on his door.

It was the depths of winter in the UK and not really the best time to build a composite structure. In an ideal world you would build a boat like ours during the summer months when the ambient temperature is higher. Heat is an essential ingredient when working with composites so as the hull laminating began we were faced with the job of keeping the build shed as warm as possible – no easy task when you have a five thousand square-foot building to heat! In an effort to avoid the cost of heating the whole building, we decided to build a temporary lightweight bubble around the boat. This way we could confidently regulate the surface temperature of the mould as we applied the various layers of fibreglass. I was particularly pleased with this solution as the amount of gas and electricity we were going through at the time was staggering, not to mention financially unsustainable.

The hull lay-up itself was not a process that could be done in one go. There are numerous key stages but perhaps the best way to describe it in simple terms is to think of a cheese salad sandwich. You have two slices of bread which represent the inner and outer skins of the hull and in the middle are the high density foam cores which are the filling in the sandwich.

The first layer of the outer hull skin was a worryingly thin piece of fibreglass just millimetres thick, something my lawyer friend Malcolm Dickinson was quick to point out during a visit to the boat. I explained that the material was just one of several heavier weight layers that would be applied before the outer skin was considered to be complete. The look on his face said it all and I remember trying to soothe his concerns by explaining the wonders of modern composite technology. His reply was sceptical and he asked if I had forgotten my experience with *Team Philips*. Malcolm was only thinking of my best interests and while we stood looking at the mould I gave a brief thought to the past. That project had been a completely different scenario. *Fujifilm*, while a state-of-the-art design, was not pushing any boundaries in composite engineering like *Team Philips* was. The Class 40 rules specifically banned anything like that. In fact, because of my experiences with *Team Philips* and *One Dream One Mission*, safety at sea had been my primary design focus and my boat would be one of the safest Class 40s afloat. The race rules required two watertight bulkheads to be installed to slow the process of sinking should the hull be breached at sea, but Fuji had been designed with four watertight compartments, making her safe in even the worst foreseeable circumstances.

A chance introduction to an innovative Turkish company called Metyx Composites had led to a recent sponsorship deal that ensured no shortage of quality material for the build. Once the material arrived direct from the factory in Turkey the lads had the green light to start building the hull.

As per our planning one of the first components we installed on board was the diesel engine. Alongside the original materials the engine had been one of the first items I had ordered, partly because we needed it and partly because I wanted to learn how the thing was put together. Understanding how your equipment works is another essential consideration for the solo sailor. Out on the ocean there is no one else to help you, so you have to be completely self-sufficient in all aspects, not just sailing. The list of requisite skills includes diesel engine maintenance, electronics, sail repair and first aid amongst others. Those who are the most resourceful and have the best understanding of the equipment that constitutes their environment will have the advantage when everything starts to fall apart, as it inevitably will.

The diesel engine had to be installed before the hull and deck were bonded together. If we waited until afterwards we would have had to completely dismantle the engine to fit it through the narrow hatchway to the cabin. The construction planning for this project was critical; every task required forethought and this was where Martin's experience really came into play. He knew exactly what needed to be done and when.

As the build team expanded, someone I was keen to see join the project was a local guy called Rick Powell. We had been introduced by a mutual friend who knew that Martin and I were looking to recruit some extra help. I could see Rick was keen to join the team as soon as he walked into the build shed. His eyes seemed to light up as Martin and I gave him the guided tour. Rick is a quiet, unassuming character with an instantly likeable disposition and it took less than five minutes for me to feel completely comfortable with his presence. Rick is a sailor who already worked within the marine industry and is especially competent with all things mechanical. His particular area of expertise is the installation and maintenance of marine diesel engines, so he was the ideal man to oversee the installation of ours. We offered him a place there and then and he quickly settled in with the lads and became an invaluable member of the team.

For technical reasons, Martin had decided to carry out the application of the outer hull layers in one go which in theory was a good idea. In practice though, the procedure required everyone's focus and planning was key. It would be a very long day because once the lads started mixing the resin and applying the Metyx fibres into the mould there was no stopping. This was demanding physical work. No one could stand in the mould during the procedure for fear of damaging the wet fibreglass as it lay on the surface, so we erected scaffolding that spanned the boat to allow complete access to the mould surface while suspended from above. A guy hanging off a narrow ledge whilst suspended across the middle of the mould, holding a long pole with a roller stuck on the end certainly looked rather strange but it was the best way to approach the job. Contamination was also a major consideration. It was essential to keep the area clean and as a result the dress code for the day was white paper suits and special blue plastic covers for everyone's feet.

The preparation for the big day took most of the week to organise. All of us pitched in, under Martin's expert direction. Each layer of fibreglass would be applied in sections about 1.5 metres wide, spanning the entire width of the boat. The sections of fibreglass matting required pre-cutting and labelling before being rolled up and placed on the work benches in order so that everything went smoothly. Cutting the various sections to length was a really laborious job, but essential if the whole process was to be a success. At this stage we could ill-afford any cock-ups; Martin made that quite clear and he was thorough in his preparations.

When the day arrived, everyone turned up early and gathered around the kettle for Martin's briefing on how the day would progress. We had chosen to do this on a Friday, the idea being that once this stage was complete we would leave the fibreglass over the weekend to cure and go rock solid. Everyone was given a specific task. Mike and Chris were the laminators and they would get stuck in with the rollers applying the fibres to the hull. Chris's son Dan who had only recently joined the team was one of the runners. He was responsible for bringing each section of material to the guys and would take away the empty containers of epoxy resin, replacing them with new ones as the job progressed. Martin mixed the epoxy resin, making sure the two-part mixtures were accurate and then helped with the more tricky areas of laminating while keeping an eye on everything else. Rick was due to arrive later in the day and would pitch in with the laminating crew. My role was chief bottle-washer, general runner and of course the all-essential teaboy. Keeping the lads fuelled with tea and snacks throughout the day I felt was an important role and while I was keen to get down and dirty with the laminators I was conscious that this was Martin's show and it was important to let him run the operation his way. I would be on hand for when the unexpected occurred.

Milestone moments became a regular occurrence as the build progressed. These milestones always represented points of significant achievement for the team and were celebrated as such. As each phase of the build was successfully completed, the boat seemed to take on her own personality. The day the first hull layers were applied, the day the foam cores were bonded into place, the day the final bulkheads were glued in position, all were milestone moments. Perhaps one of the most memorable and significant stages of the build was the day we released the boat from the mould. It had been a long-anticipated event and a lot was at stake. If the lads had not applied enough releasing agent prior to laying-up the hull the boat would be glued to the mould and impossible to prise apart. Once again the success of the project completely rested on Martin's knowledge and ability to apply his skills. It was 15 April 2007.

From the early days of the project publicity had been a major consideration for me. We live in a commercial world and we were proactive in our quest for media attention, in order to give our sponsors a consistent return. We had enlisted support from the media to build interest and help increase our profile. Our regular progress reports had been well-received and for many the campaign website provided a window on the project, achieving thousands of hits a month. It was clear that our story had found a significant audience. People were naturally intrigued when they learned of our plans and I regularly received emails of encouragement from total strangers who were following our progress. The media too were genuinely fascinated. For them the project represented an adventurous story of one man who had decided to stick his neck on the line and make his dream a reality. It struck the right chords.

Local interest had always surrounded the project, even in the early days before we started construction. So as we approached the most significant stage of the build to date, it came as no surprise that some local journalists wanted to capture the moment on camera and asked to be present as we prised the boat free from the mould. I had my reservations, wondering whether it was wise to have the media there in case the procedure didn't go according to plan. I shared my concerns with Martin and we both agreed that we didn't really want anyone around for the procedure other than our own team. It was better for us to break the boat free without any added pressure from the outside world. In the interests of keeping everyone happy and gaining some vital column-inches we agreed to leave the boat in the mould overnight for a staged release the following morning. This way we could be sure that any unexpected problems were not subjected to the full scrutiny of anyone reading the newspapers.

As the end of May approached, the hull and deck lay alongside

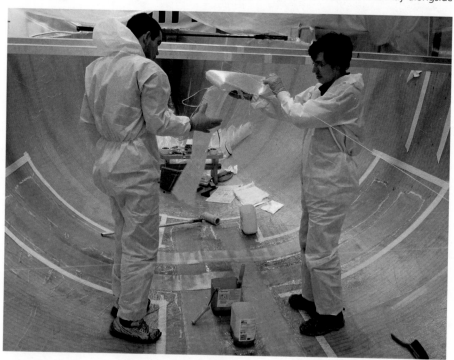

The lads busy applying layers of fibreglass to the keel area.

each other on the factory floor, waiting to be bonded together. The build shed had become a place of intense activity and the sound of power drills and orbital sanders could be heard almost continuously as I made my one hundred-yard daily commute along the lane from the car yard. The barns had recently been given official permission to be used as a build site so the extra noise being emitted from the shed was now of little concern. The lads' focus was admirable. They were busy installing the major internal structure to my boat while pushing forwards with a second near-identical yacht for an American client that Martin

Above **Applying the foam cores to the hull.**

Left **A milestone moment, releasing the hull from the mould.**

had recently signed. Martin had been approached by the American, who was in the market for a new racing yacht, keen to commission a design with Owen Clarke and knew of our project building *Fujifilm*. At a visit to the build site to inspect the progress of my boat he had been suitably impressed and appointed Martin as the builder. This was just the break Martin was hoping for and as a result even more staff were brought in to cater for the increased production demand. In just a few months, the uninspiring agricultural barn had been transformed from an empty space into a full-on production line with two state-of-the-art racing yachts in build alongside each other.

Although progress in the build shed was good we had suffered a bit from delays in the arrival of essential equipment during the winter months. These delays were unforeseen and could not be helped, but as a result we had missed our intended completion date of April. In hindsight, I think an April launch was always a little ambitious. As the deadline had loomed ever closer I liaised with the sponsors to keep them up to speed with progress. They knew we were struggling to meet the deadline so it had been agreed to push the schedule back to a more achievable date. Fujifilm had been very understanding and were keen to not impose any extra pressure that would put further obstacles in our path. With a revised schedule we were now working to a much more realistic timetable, targeting completion for the end of July.

Despite the reprieve, it was important not to become complacent. Time was still tight and the weight of expectation was heavy on my shoulders. Our commitments with Fuji ran deeper than just brand promotion through ocean racing. Corporate hospitality was an equal part of the deal and we had made a pledge to have the new boat sailing and ready to accept their guests in time for the annual Cowes Week regatta on the Solent during the first week of August.

Over the past months we had managed to forge ahead when outside influences had threatened progress but having changed the launch date once, I was determined not to move the goalposts again. The new schedule was real and a definite stake in the ground, and was the final target the build team would have to meet before handing the finished boat over to me for sea trials. We had slightly less than two months to finish the boat and get it launched. Now more than ever the project required the support of the whole team. Everyone would have to burn the candle at both ends and push that extra mile for success.

The trouble was I could see the lads were exhausted and already giving it their best.

By now most of the major components had arrived. The keel, which I had commissioned from a local company in Cornwall, had been delivered and was lying next to the bow of the boat at the front of the factory. When it arrived, even the muscle of the farmer's forklift truck had not been sufficient to lift it off the trailer. We had to suspend extra blocks and tackle from the building roof to counterbalance the weight. The two-ton keel and lead torpedo bulb looked imposing, and I can still recall the look on Chris's face when the overweight alarms started to scream from the cab of the forklift as he lifted the load. The 4x4 and its trailer rose about a foot when the keel slid off the back and onto the ground. "Blimey, it's heavy, what a beast!" someone said. I remember thinking it certainly was impressive.

The serious task of selecting and sourcing the various electrical components and essential navigational equipment had also been completed. Thanks to a sensational sponsorship deal with marine electronics giant Raymarine we had been supplied with an excellent array of state-of-the-art equipment which was just waiting to be installed on board. This was one deal that I had considered essential to secure. The onboard automatic pilot systems would play an essential role during the race across the Atlantic. I wanted *Fujifilm* to benefit from two independent pilot systems to create as much redundancy as possible. If a system failed you could bet your bottom dollar it would happen under the cover of darkness at 2am, while surfing down huge waves with the big spinnaker up. Solo ocean racing is not at all the same as sailing with a team around you. With other people on board such an event would not even be considered an issue, but when you are on your own it's a whole different ball game.

I had experienced exactly this problem before and was adamant that in the event of a problem, I should have the ability to just turn a switch at no more than arm's length from the steering position in the cockpit and switch over to a backup autopilot. Without the ability to steer the boat under autopilot a solo ocean racer just can't operate at sea. The automatic pilot is your best friend and I needed a system that was not only reliable but also easy to operate. Having used Raymarine products for most of my sailing life I was familiar with the equipment, but most importantly, I trusted them. I think the clincher for the deal

Me standing in the cabin before the deck was fitted, halfway through the build.

came during my presentation to the marketing team in which I flat broke told them that I needed their systems on board even if I had to pay for them myself. I think they liked that because it was the truth.

A very welcome delivery of impressive-looking equipment soon arrived, sparking an altogether bigger question – who would install it? Raymarine had been pleased to partner with the project and supply the equipment but we had to cover the cost of installation. Of course, their team of technical support experts was on hand continuously at the end of a telephone for any kind of advice but beyond that it was down to us. I had given this some serious consideration and while I knew we could easily install everything on board and get the equipment working ourselves, what I really wanted was to find a specialist with the necessary skills and time to undertake a custom installation. A saltwater environment coupled with the constant vibration delivered by the continual slamming motion as the boat pounds through waves is certainly not the best combination for anything electrical, yet the continuous functioning of the kit was something I would depend on at sea. There is no point in having the best equipment money can buy only to be let down by an average installation job. The task demanded the attention of a professional.

As it turned out, despite knowing several local companies who were more than capable of taking on the work, the right man for the job just happened to walk onto the car lot and purchase a little sports car. It was a chance opportunity and one that only came to light when the guy mentioned what he did for a living. As a retired Raymarine installation technician, Frank Rees had more than twenty-five years' experience with exactly this kind of work. As soon as I mentioned the project and my requirement for someone with his skills the conversation abruptly shifted from a pleasant chat about sports cars and Sunday afternoon driving to the far more interesting subject of boat electrics, and more specifically how best to tackle the challenge of installing the mountain of electrical equipment that was currently blocking up my hallway.

The final push was upon us. With just weeks remaining before the deadline everyone rose to the challenge. The team was working near twenty-hour days in the attempt to bring the boat together in time. All of the interior structure was now in place and the bonding of the hull and deck had been a real red-letter day. For the first time as the deck rested on top of the hull we could see the real proportions of this superb machine. As the lads buzzed around the boat like bees around a honey pot, I could see that *Fujifilm* was starting to become the fabulous vision I had hoped for.

Throughout the build, long after the guys had gone home for the night I would often sneak into the shed for some quiet time with the boat and my thoughts. One particular night I spent a couple of hours just looking around, sitting in the cockpit and visualising how things would be once we reached open ocean. This project had always been about a journey, one that had started with humble beginnings but had ambitious aspirations. Until now, the thought of sailing this boat solo across the mighty North Atlantic had always seemed way off, but sitting in the cockpit with my hand on the tiller, the realisation that I would soon be setting sail for far beyond the horizon really set in.

I imagined how the boat would handle as we surfed down waves at over twenty knots. Just the thought of the adventure ahead sparked emotion, I was filled with so much excitement and anticipation. Building this boat was truly one of the most liberating and emotional experiences of my life. Those private moments in the build shed during the small hours gave me a real sense of achievement.

As the days ticked by, the cosmetic preparations became the dominant focus. The final paint job was now the priority, a responsibility that had been strictly reserved for the trusted hands of my old friend Richard Hatton. Having done such a good job with the first Fujifilm boat it made sense to offer him the job of putting the new boat into her eye-catching livery. As he pitched up to the build shed with his equipment I could see he was keen to get started. Like the other guys, Richard was driven by a real sense of commitment to get the boat finished and launched. Apart from anything else, as an experienced yachtsman and friend of the project, Richard knew that he was on the list to come sailing during the sea trials. What he didn't know was that I was considering offering him command of the boat for the delivery back across the Atlantic after the transatlantic race. He had the necessary sailing experience, having already crossed the Atlantic himself four times, and I knew he would keep the boat and crew safe.

Finding the correct shade of green to match the Fujifilm corporate colours had been an unexpected challenge. The distinctive Fujifilm green had been slightly revised since we had painted the last boat. I had spent weeks trying to find a company who could mix the exact colour but despite having a decent swatch showing the correct shade of green I had so far drawn a blank. I knew it was essential to get this element of the project right so after speaking to the team at Fujifilm Graphic Systems they pulled out the stops to get hold of the exact paint codes. Once I had these it was easy. I contacted a leading automotive paint manufacturer and went direct to the head guy who was delighted to help. Less than a week after my initial phone call I received a sample, and after passing scrutiny at Fuji that turned into three large tins of shiny green paint, more than enough to transform our boat into an eye-catching masterpiece. Job done.

Back at the build shed, our small but dedicated team of professionals continued to sand and fill any remaining imperfections in preparation for the final paint job. Now that Martin and the lads had finished the major interior work, Frank was keen to start the electrical installation before the boat was taken out of the shed. Frank and I knew that once *Fujifilm* was transported down to Baltic Wharf ready for launch there would be a real push to install the keel, deck hardware and remaining equipment. Everyone would be in his way, falling over each

The completed structure. *Fujifilm* awaits her distinctive green livery.

other's feet and making the job more difficult. The more he could cross off the list now the easier it would be later. Frank didn't just have to install the electronics; he would also have to explain virtually every step of the job to me so that I gained a better understanding of how everything was put together. This kind of tutorial process would be a source of invaluable knowledge if anything malfunctioned on the race track.

As the distinctive green paint was applied I was preoccupied with taking care of the final details. There was a mountain of things to take care of. The arrangements for the boat to be transported the two miles from the build shed to the banks of the river Dart required finalising. Months earlier I had spoken to a local company specialising in the transport of boats over land. The owner of the firm had come to the build shed to discuss the logistics and settle on a price. We agreed that I would call two weeks before we were ready for their help. It was now time to make that call.

The various brightwork or custom-made stainless steel fittings that come together to finish the boat were also arriving thick and fast. Everything from the safety guard wires that encompass the deck edge down to the solid stainless steel chain plates that connect the rigging to the deck required ticking off the list for the final fit-out. The chain plates had to be machine-cut from a single billet of solid steel and then polished to look aesthetically pleasing, which was not a cheap process. Even a custom-built cradle for the boat had to be fabricated. These jobs, amongst others, had been given to a local guy based in Plymouth whose company Anything Steel does exactly that.

Robbie had done a great job with all the brightwork and had been closely involved from the early days. He would always make the thirty-mile drive up from Plymouth to drop in to the office and price a job as and when I needed it. I enjoyed our chats, especially the light-hearted banter about the budget. He would give me a price and I would say, "How much?!", then he would spend half an hour explaining how difficult and intricate the job was in an effort to justify the cost. He always looked after me on price and we both knew it, but more importantly, Robbie always delivered the kit on time when we really needed it. Robbie is old-school and just laughed when Martin presented him with a computer file containing all the drawings and measurements for the kit we wanted him to make. Robbie wanted paper drawings, not some flashy new-age computer-generated file. Robbie said he didn't even own a computer. We all had a good laugh about that.

The jobs list that I had started at the very beginning of the project had evolved from a simple numbered sketch on a piece of paper into a never-ending list of jobs compiled in order of their priority. As soon as something was ticked off, several more would be added. That was only to be expected, such is the nature of yacht building. Most of the time boats become ready but rarely does the job list ever get fully signed-off. It didn't matter, most of the important jobs had been dealt with and *Fujifilm* was nearing completion. With just a couple of weeks to the deadline the boat looked stunning in her new livery .

As far as I could tell, everything was in place. The signwriters had been in and applied the logos. The carbon fibre mast had arrived from France and looked a million dollars. Even the sails, which had been another seriously important consideration, had now arrived. The sails are the engine of the yacht. The difference between a good set of sails and a bad set is instantly noticeable the minute you move into a competitive environment. Again, the requirements for the solo sailor will be different to those on board the same boat with a larger crew. For me, durability and functionality were the key factors. But the wish list didn't stop there. There are many considerations to take into account: the rules only allow a maximum of eight sails to be carried on board a Class 40, so deciding what sail material to use, how big to make certain sails and their precise shapes were also of great importance. Handling one hundred and eighty square metres of spinnaker on your own in twenty-five knots of wind while standing on the edge of a pitching deck is a serious challenge.

For a significant amount of time the boat would sail at speed under autopilot and the cut of the sails, especially the spinnakers, would play an important role in the autopilot's ability to control the boat when I was asleep below decks. That's not all, either. Consider for a moment the world of the solo ocean racer: it's two in the morning and dark. The boat is overpowered and struggling on her feet. You're on deck trying to reef the mainsail to bring the boat under control. Without crew, the whole procedure takes twice as long and for a good length of time the sail is flogging itself to pieces, flying like a flag in the wind as you do your best to tighten all the ropes and complete the manoeuvre. The sails are subjected to this kind of treatment day after day during a race. A good sailmaker would appreciate this and build the sails differently to the norm because a solo sailor has slightly different requirements to those of a boat set up for racing with a crew. The choice of whom to trust with this essential aspect of the project had been a difficult decision.

Thanks to a word from my old friend Graham Goff from *Team Philips* days I was introduced to a firm called Halsey Lidgard. A guy called John Brinkers was the owner of the Southampton-based sail loft. They were part of a bigger worldwide franchise and together with the American arm of the company they agreed to support the project and work closely with me to produce the right sails at the right price. I was impressed with John's willingness to listen. I could see the bottom line with this company wasn't just about the profit margin. They were genuinely driven to produce the best results for their clients, a refreshing attitude that certainly got my vote.

The day the transport company arrived to collect our beloved boat for the short journey to the water's edge the weather had decided to give us a taste of things to come. It was bucketing down and the boat looked so stunning it was almost a shame to drag her out into the rain. In the lead-up to the transporters arriving we had spent a lot of time considering how to lift the boat off the ground and onto the delivery truck. The only real option was to use the metal supporting beams in the roof of the building to take the weight of the boat while we lifted her off the cradle using the chain blocks. The only trouble was that the boat was now in the centre of the building and as a completed structure weighed more than two-and-a-half tons. Adding that load to the middle of the roof beams seemed a good way to literally bring the roof down. The idea had been the subject of much debate amongst the lads and I had that worrying feeling myself. What if we dropped the boat? Not to mention the effects of pulling the roof of the building down on top of everyone. That would be a bad day.

Unexpectedly, a discussion with the farmer helped to dispel some of the concerns. I had taken a rather meandering path to broaching the tricky subject of hoisting the boat from the beams of his building and was just getting to the point of the conversation when he mentioned that the roof had been designed to withstand over seventy tons of pressure from snow. We had been worrying about nothing, although when the day was finally upon us I was filled with last-minute reservations. In an effort to reduce the risk of any problems and allay our fears we stationed a couple of the guys at the base of each supporting beam to watch for any distortion or noise as we slowly hoisted *Fujifilm* off the ground.

The journey to Baltic Wharf had been in the planning for months and we had even measured the width of the lane to ensure the boat would fit, something that was done before we had committed to using the barn. But on the day, as soon as *Fujifilm* was secured onto the truck and coaxed out of the narrow entrance of the build shed everything happened quickly. The lads all jumped into their cars and followed in tight procession as we headed up the lane towards the main road. Dad was cheering as *Fujifilm* passed by the car yard while one of the lads drove ahead to stop the traffic on the main road .

We hadn't realised until then but our journey to Baltic Wharf coincided with the annual Totnes and District Agricultural Show, one of the largest one-day events in the country. Thousands of people flock to the area and road traffic is always a nightmare. Nonetheless, I was deter-

Above **Hoisting *Fujifilm*** onto the truck. Another nerve wracking moment.

Left ***Fujifilm*** coming out of the build shed.

mined that neither hell nor high water would to stop us. As the convoy passed by the entrance to the show grounds the local police, who were directing the congested traffic into the show, seemed shocked to see the massive truck spanning almost the width of the road. To say our magnificent boat turned heads would be an understatement. The two police officers sprung into action as they clearly had no option but to stop all the traffic and wave us through.

Just seven days later, after a mammoth last-minute push to install all the deck hardware *Fujifilm* sat in her cradle on the banks of the river Dart ready for launch. The lads had done it, in the final weeks everyone had worked their socks off to keep to the schedule and complete this stunning boat. The culmination of eleven months and over five thousand man-hours of hard work, blood, sweat and tears could be seen by all. Even the boatyard staff at Baltic Wharf had gone out of their way to help us, providing the full support of their crane as we fitted the keel. The yard manager Dave Sharp, an experienced boat builder in his own right,

Feeling proud of ourselves, Martin and I stand in front of *Fujifilm* at Baltic Wharf.

A perfect fit, as the boat is lowered onto the keel for the first time.

spared the time to lend a hand with the final touches and his experience and expertise were a real asset as we prepared to install the keel. The intricate process of drilling the ten holes for the keel securing bolts and the checking of measurements took nearly two days before Martin was entirely happy to tighten the bolts for the last time.

Finally it was time to lift the eighteen-metre carbon fibre mast into place, the last significant job before we launched. But as the impressive looking rig was slowly lowered into position problems with the rigging became evident. The manufacturers had inadvertently supplied an incorrect component for the rigging and to make matters worse, the shrouds that support the mast laterally and stop the whole thing falling over the side were too long. We were just days away from the start of Cowes week, what was I to tell Fujifilm? Our sponsors were expecting our presence for some important corporate hospitality on the Solent in just a few days' time. Yet here we were with a rig that effectively didn't fit. Without the time constraints, our new-found problem wouldn't have been much of a setback. But given the timeframe and the fact that the vital part of the rigging originated from a factory in the Netherlands which was now closed for the holiday period, that posed a huge problem. The whole team had moved mountains to keep to the deadline and now in the final hours we were facing defeat through no fault of our own.

The rigging could easily be shortened, but the custom-made fitting was a real problem. A phone call to the rigging company did little to improve the now-desperate situation. They readily accepted responsibility for the cock-up, but despite being very apologetic and full of understanding were unable to offer a solution that could get us sailing within the following seventy-two hours. The factory was closed and nothing could be done for a week. I was fuming but sometimes you have to just accept a situation. After several hours of pacing up and down the boatyard trying to find a solution, the reality was staring me in the face. I had to break the bad news to Fujifilm.

I felt terrible. I had promised our sponsors we would be at Cowes Week. Arrangements had been made on my word and now I was about to break that commitment. As the head of the project the responsibility rested firmly on my shoulders even when it wasn't my fault. As it was, Fuji took it better than I had expected. We were a team and our partners had been well aware of the hours everyone was putting in to complete the boat. We didn't make Cowes Week that year but ten days later, with the new parts installed, *Fujifilm* touched the water for the first time.

We had been anxiously waiting all morning for the tide to rise high enough to allow us to launch. *Fujifilm's* keel is an impressive ten feet deep so launching the boat so far up the river posed its own problems. We had to wait for a particularly high tide and then would have only a short window of opportunity before the tide changed in which to launch and head off down the river the eight miles to Dartmouth.

The question of whether the boat would actually float on her lines was finally answered. As the crane driver released the load from the hoisting straps our magnificent boat floated perfectly alongside the river bank. I jumped aboard for a swift photo opportunity on the bow while Rick and Ifor went below to start the diesel engine and check there were no leaks. I shook Martin's hand and thanked him for a job well done. This was the moment I had been waiting for, the moment when the build team officially handed over the result of their hard work.

I gave a thought to when *Team Philips* had been launched from the very same spot nearly ten years before. It was in stark contrast to today. Back then, forty thousand people had lined the banks of the river to watch the spectacle. Today, the twenty-five or so people who gathered for this launch somehow made it all the more personal.

The rest of the team climbed aboard, joined by my father and a

Launch day – looking
fabulous.

Posing on the bow just
after launch.

friend of mine Simon Ellyatt who has a lifetime of experience navigating the river. Simon had volunteered his services and although the River
Dart had become home for me too over the past ten years I felt pleased
to have him aboard for the journey downriver.

We were on the threshold of going sailing. Even Mum's little teddy
bear that has shared nearly all of my sailing adventures found his way
on board. Fuji bear, his new nickname, took pride of place perched
above the sat phone on the chart table. Wherever I go he goes, but
first we had the tricky task of navigating the River Dart so that the real
adventure could begin.

I felt relieved that we were finally in the water. Although there was
still a huge amount of work to do, I felt ready to embrace the future.
Sea trials started in earnest, with our first sail being a leisurely jaunt
from Dartmouth to Torbay. It was just a few miles, a chance to whet
the appetite and check that everything functioned as expected. It was
the middle of August and a whole year since the first planks of wood
had been laid onto the build shed floor.

Our first trip, down the
river Dart

I had given plenty of thought to the best way of working the boat up before the race start and had drawn up a plan that would give the best chance of being ready when race day came the following June. The first priority was to sail over to France before the end of the month and then make an appearance at the Southampton boat show for an official naming ceremony. I had booked a slot with the measurers in St Malo and arranged for the boat to be officially inspected for Class 40 rules. It's always a nail-biting time for skippers and their teams as their vessels are subjected to the full scrutiny of the measurers, but I wanted that process out of the way early in case of any problems. The measurement procedure takes an in-depth look at each boat to make sure that it conforms in every respect to the rules specified by the Class association. Everything from the overall length of the boat to the maximum depth of the keel and capacity of ballast is carefully measured. Safety is a major priority and the stability of each boat is also given serious consideration.

With the help of a crane, each yacht is pulled over to the ninety degree position with the masthead almost touching the water, a process to check the boat conforms to the technical rules relating to stability. The measurement team is responsible for ensuring every detail of each yacht is compliant. Any boats that don't pass the tests are refused an official certificate until their shortcomings are rectified. Without a

Stability tests in St Malo for Class 40 rules.

certificate you can't race.

The trip to France would be the first proper passage and served as part of the sea trials. I made sure we had a full crew for the early trips, so there was plenty of muscle to deal with any unforeseen circumstances. After all, at this stage we didn't even know if the boat was seaworthy, not that there had been any reason to think that she wouldn't be. But the thought had crossed my mind as my past experiences have taught me to continually expect the unexpected at sea. As far as I was concerned, at this stage *Fujifilm* was brand new and untested.

As the sea trials got underway the 'what if' thoughts were privately a real consideration for me. I was the guy at the business end of the project, I was the one who would have to sail this boat beyond the horizon into the desolate void of open ocean. *Fujifilm* needed to prove to me more than anyone that she was up to the rigours of such a demanding trip. I had faced the prospect of death at sea before and had no plans to face it again because of a lack of preparation. The experience of building the boat had been exciting but this was now the real world and I was looking for cast-iron proof that this boat was my friend and not my enemy. I never told anyone but if between then and the start of the race, I reached a point at which I didn't have confidence in the boat and had good reason to believe she wasn't up to the job, I was prepared to call it all off. I had already faced that unlikely prospect in my mind and was comfortable with the decision if I had to face it in reality. The North Atlantic is no joke.

The measurement process was a little stressful, not helped by my inability to speak adequate French, but was by and large a success, although we had passed the maximum draft test for our keel by the thinnest of margins. Apart from a couple of minor idiosyncrasies it was a pass and we returned to the UK pleased that that process was now behind us and the all-important certificate was in the post.

The naming ceremony was approaching. The whole team had been looking forward to the big day and I was particularly excited at the prospect of having the boat on display to the public in the heart of the Southampton boat show, even if it was just for a day. Fujifilm had wanted an official naming event and it was decided that the boat show was the ideal venue to mark the occasion. In the interests of making it a day to remember one of the big chiefs from Japan was coming to give the official seal of approval. It was important everything went smoothly on the day. As we tied up to the pontoon on the morning of the event there were already swarms of people milling about. I remember over-hearing various comments about how striking the boat appeared in her corporate livery. It seemed our lean green racing machine was already striking the right chords with the public.

The day was a bit of a whirlwind and passed very quickly. Some of the Fujifilm Graphics Systems team had pitched up early to lend a welcome hand with the final touches and together we were soon ready for the big moment. We had been blessed with dry but rather windy weather, but the strong breeze only helped to fuel the raptur-ous applause as the champagne cork finally popped off the bottle to release an impressive spray of France's finest. Just before the ceremony got underway I had been shaking the champagne bottle vigorously to ensure the moment passed with all the drama it deserved.

There is nothing worse than a tiny splash from the bottle when a celebratory moment is marked – better a fire hydrant than a water pistol in my book. The champagne engulfed the bow of *Fujifilm* and certainly had the desired effect, and several bystanders who were perhaps a

The naming ceremony at the Southampton Boatshow: Mr Saigusa, head of Fujifilm UK at the time, enjoys the moment.

little too close to the action enjoyed rather more than just the visual display, and were covered in the stuff. The crowd who had gathered to watch the event were full of enthusiastic applause and even Mr Saigusa, head of Fujifilm UK at the time, seemed genuinely excited as we both stood next to each other brandishing glasses of champagne while posing for the cameras. It was a great day and thanks to the support of the whole team it went without a hitch.

The journey back to the West Country brought with it our first test of rough weather. A fresh force seven near-gale was blowing from the west, exactly the direction we wanted to go. It would be a slow and bouncy trip home but would provide a good introduction to some challenging seas.

There was some urgency to leave Southampton. We needed to make an appearance at a corporate sailing event in Torbay hosted by our legal sponsors Michelmores. The Michelmores Cup is an annual one-day regatta hosted by the regional law firm and was part of our corporate sailing calendar.

As we punched our way down the Solent with heavily-reefed sails the lads were full of enthusiasm. Mike, Rick and Richard are all sailors and they had each played an essential role in the making of the boat so it was only fair that they should be part of the action. As we cleared the Needles channel at the western end of the Solent we could tell the weather was deteriorating. The motion started to get exciting as *Fujifilm* jumped over the crests of waves. It was our first proper test of rough weather and despite the uncomfortable motion on board, *Fujifilm* performed admirably. By the time we reached home waters my confidence in the boat was growing.

THE SINGLE-HANDED TRANSATLANTIC RACE

Many more people have climbed Mount Everest than have completed the Single-handed Transatlantic Race. The event provides more than just a competitive environment, it's an epic test of endurance, both physical and mental, a massive test of seamanship and navigational skill, and a challenge that at times will require astonishing determination to finish.

The Single-handed Transatlantic Race started the whole solo ocean racing revolution in 1960. The historic race was born out of a half-crown bet between two of the great pioneers of solo sailing, Cockleshell hero Blondie Hasler and Sir Frances Chichester. In those days solo ocean racing was a new phenomenon and the thought of crossing the Atlantic single-handed against the prevailing winds and currents was considered by many to be impossible. The inaugural event gained support from The Observer newspaper and as a result adopted the more commonly-known name OSTAR – Observer Single-handed Trans Atlantic Race.

For the first race, although interest in the event swelled to well over a hundred potential entrants, just five single-handed sailors set out from Plymouth for the long and lonely challenge of crossing the North Atlantic. Francis Chichester took victory, completing the course in little over forty days and cementing the foundations for a race that would become known as the grandfather of all the great solo ocean races.

Most recently, in direct response to the popularity of the event and a growing number of professional competitors with commercially-sponsored yachts, the race committee at the Royal Western Yacht Club of England took the decision to split the race into two separate events. There would be a professional race organised by a separate commercial entity to cater for professional competitors and a Corinthian event that remains unchanged from the original's ethos as a challenge for only the most ambitious of recreational yachtsmen.

This is without doubt one of the three toughest solo ocean races, three thousand miles across the North Atlantic from Plymouth to Marblehead near Boston Massachusetts and one of the greatest challenges I have ever faced. The professional race claimed my attention. This race offered the same route, the same harsh ocean conditions and the same challenge against the prevailing winds and currents. The only difference was the name, which was The Artemis Transat.

As time quietly ticked by, the countdown to the start was well and truly underway. In February 2008 the race organisers staged an impressive media launch in the heart of London, unveiling the race to the public. As a registered competitor, the event provided an excellent opportunity to engage the media and rub shoulders with some of the great names in our sport. The race launch was a classy affair with all the trimmings. The media turned out in force and while the venue was packed full of competitors and their sponsors, the atmosphere gained further electricity thanks to an impressive display of mood lighting, while an endless flow of canapés and drinks completed the ambiance. The icing on the cake was an engaging video which brought a Hollywood theme to the race. Its powerful visual effect was obviously designed to capture the attention of the media while highlighting just how challenging this race really is.

As I sat perched on my stool in front of a room packed with hundreds of people I listened intently as our host skilfully interviewed each competitor, probing us for our thoughts about the approaching adventure.

Part of the process for entering a race like the Artemis Transat is the requirement to complete a qualifying passage to prove that you and the boat are up to the challenge. For me that translated into a three hundred-mile passage. Nothing more than a formality for most competitors, the qualifier trip normally doubles up as a good opportunity to drum up some media exposure on your return as well as providing a good test for the race tracking beacons that pinpoint our exact positions at sea, essential for maintaining public interest during the race.

For my qualifier I wanted more than just a leisurely three hundred-mile cruise. This would be the last opportunity to put the boat through her paces before the real thing. For our trip we would leave Plymouth under true gale-force conditions. Normally good seamanship would prevent any mariner from leaving a safe port when such weather is raging but this time I would ignore my instincts and look at the bigger picture. If the wheels were going to come off the bus, I would rather they did so in the confines of the English Channel than in the middle of the Atlantic.

My departure for the qualifier was imminent. But before I put to sea a press launch at Sutton Harbour in Plymouth marked the official start of preparations for the Plymouth Summer Festival, a showcase for major national and international events running throughout the summer. The Artemis Transat and the Summer Festival were being promoted in parallel as partner events. As a local race competitor, I was invited along and was asked to bring the boat to create the necessary sparkle for the media. Being the type of guy who rarely declines opportunities to get in front of the cameras and promote my sponsors, I went along and took Mike and the boat with me. An excellent photo opportunity alongside the harbour wall showed around thirty people standing in the cockpit of *Fujifilm*, holding festival banners to mark the occasion. The event provided good exposure for our project while achieving the same goals for both the race and the festival.

During the morning I had spoken to several television reporters and one of them, on hearing about my imminent departure for the qualifier expressed an interest in coming along to document the voyage. It was an interesting proposition and one that would have certainly delivered some extra television coverage in the build-up to the race. The race control had previously agreed that each boat could take a member of the media on their qualifier for this very purpose. But when the young journalist presented the idea to her superiors they quickly declined the request on the grounds of health and safety. They wouldn't send a member of their staff but readily offered to provide one of their video cameras. I found that rather amusing.

The following day *Fujifilm* and I set sail from Plymouth Sound under a blustery wind with the threat of severe gale force nine imminent. The wind was in the south west, so the plan was to head east along the English Channel to somewhere near Brighton before turning around and coming home. The first night at sea, while feeling pretty cold, delivered easy sailing as we surfed along at great speed under the capable hands of the autopilot. I was never going to get much sleep during this trip because of our close proximity to land and shipping but as *Fujifilm* blasted along the coast I took time to relax and think about the journey so far in addition to the path ahead.

The qualifier presented the perfect opportunity to test out some new camera equipment that I would use during the race. A local company called Scanstrut had recently installed a new piece of equipment on board that could video all the action on deck at the flick of a switch. Essentially the device was a long pole that protruded from the back of the boat with a small camera and lens attached to the top. Simple, yet a great piece of equipment and it would be invaluable for capturing those action shots when the going got rough. I also had an excellent little pocket digital camera with video capability that *Fujifilm* had supplied. I would use this to capture quality digital images during the voyage as well as to record a video diary which with the help of my onboard laptop I would edit and then send home via the sat phone for distribution to the press.

Nowadays, a commercially sponsored sailor doesn't just have to worry about sailing the boat during a race. We also have to deal with the ongoing commitment to convey the story to the outside world. Sounds easy? Try doing it after a week at sea when your opposition are breathing down your neck, you're beyond exhaustion and the effects of sleep deprivation are well and truly kicking your arse. Just typing an email when the boat is launching off waves and slamming into the troughs with such force that it's all you can do just to hang on in the cabin requires a major effort. It's during those moments when you really could do without the intrusion of a reporter on the end of the sat phone, but it's exactly at those times that you have to remember that it is your sponsors who gave you the opportunity to experience this awesome side of life in the first place.

For the Artemis Transat my media commitments were shaping up to be pretty heavy. During the race, barely a day would pass when I didn't have interviews to do. The BBC were keen to follow my progress and wanted digital images and short video clips sent back almost daily. Modern technology is a wonderful thing, the onboard satellite phone and our ability to send and receive email while on the race track provide the perfect means to keep the world informed as events unfold. Nowadays, communication is everything.

There are always two sides to a yacht race: there is the actual race which you naturally want to win but equally important is the media race, which is the fight to get the spotlight fixed firmly on you more often than on your counterparts. If you crack that, you're laughing. We had worked hard during the winter months to keep the project in the public eye and now that the race was almost upon us I was determined to make sure the equipment on board worked properly so I could keep the news reports flowing once we set sail. The qualifier was probably the last opportunity to make sure the technology worked and as a result I spent most of the first night at the chart table sending emails to the BBC.

As we approached Portland Bill we had steady gale-force conditions and while not in race mode, I felt pleased with progress. By lunchtime the following day we were close to our turning point near Brighton. The seas had really picked up during the night and with a solid forty knots of wind breathing down our neck I knew that as soon as we turned around and started to head into the waves all hell would break loose. That was when we would start to see the true measure of the boat. With a healthy amount of sail set, *Fujifilm* was really smoking as we blasted down the face of short but steep waves. It was time to turn around but first I had to get organised. I needed to reef the mainsail and change the headsail for a small storm jib.

Trying to pull the mainsail down onto the deck with that amount of wind pressure proved nearly impossible in the conditions. For twenty minutes I struggled at the base of the mast giving it everything I had to pull the Kevlar-reinforced sail down to deck level. By now the torrential rain we had experienced earlier in the morning had turned into solid hailstones that pelted the decks with the kind of fury that made me wonder whether it had been such a clever idea setting off in such ugly weather after all. Eventually I managed to haul the remainder of the mainsail to the deck and after a hasty headsail change I set the storm jib and clambered back to the cockpit. I felt knackered and was soaked to the skin but we were ready to face the music and make the turn.

The trip back to Plymouth was not particularly comfortable. The rough seas gave us a real pasting and for a while we made slow progress under just the tiny handkerchief of a storm jib. The journey was

Left **Putting *Fujifilm* through her paces during sea trials.**

Below ***Fujifilm*** **at speed during a training session prior to the start of the Artemis Transat.**

Above **Surfing at over twenty knots.**

Right **Blasting downwind during the qualifier. Image taken by the Scanstrut stern camera.**

certainly less than enjoyable, but as Plymouth Breakwater came into view it confirmed more than just the end of the qualifier. We had achieved what I needed to know. *Fujifilm* handled the weather with ease and my confidence in the boat was now one hundred per cent.

As confirmation came though that my qualification passage had been accepted all that was left to do was make the final preparations to the boat and concentrate on keeping the story alive with the press. Race week arrived quickly and we soon moved the boat into Sutton Harbour in the heart of Plymouth city centre for the start of the official race festivities. Competitors were arriving and this was a chance for the general public to stroll through the race village and experience a rare close-up look at the stunning yachts that comprised our fleet. The atmosphere in the race village was fantastic. The harbour-side was regularly packed with thousands of people walking through the area and enjoying the entertainment. The sound of jazz and blues could be heard all day which all helped to create a real buzz as bands pitched up to share their music.

Sponsors came down throughout the week, keen to wish me luck but the night before the start I had an important dinner appointment with some of the Fujifilm management team who were bringing some VIPs down to see the boat and wanted to soak up the atmosphere. We had been flat-out all week with interviews and media engagements so a late night was the last thing I wanted. With dinner out of the way and just hours to go before the start I quietly bowed out of the evening celebrations to get a good night's rest. It was the last opportunity I would have to get several hours of uninterrupted sleep for the next three weeks.

The following morning, I arrived at the boat to find Mike standing on board having prepared everything for the off. It was the crack of dawn, the race village was deserted and almost silent, sponsor's flags lay limp in the rigging of competitors' yachts. The sun had only just appeared, but an appointment with the BBC demanded my presence. They wanted a final interview for breakfast television before the race got underway. That interview was going national and proved to be one of the most important of the project. Hundreds of miles away, Keith Dalton of Fujifilm Graphic Systems was standing in a hotel room getting ready for his day when our project burst into life across his television screen. I was standing right in front of the boat with the logos plainly visible, talking about the adventure that lay ahead. Apparently he saw the whole thing and was impressed that we had managed to get in front of network cameras.

Race day was not just about the obvious. As part of our commitments to our sponsors we had arranged for two powerboats to take our VIPs onto the water for a close-up view of the action as the race started. While the Fujifilm team and their clients enjoyed watching the action from the luxury of a spanking new motor cruiser our remaining partners and friends were treated to the excitement of a high speed RIB ride with my father as host.

It was time to slip the lines and head out for the start. Ifor, Mike and Dad initially jumped aboard to help with getting through the Sutton Harbour lock gates and into Plymouth Sound. I waved a triumphant goodbye to all the people who had come to wish me luck and gave Mum a big hug. As we motored out of the marina I could see thousands of people lining the Barbican. The spectators bunched together in a long line stretching all the way up onto the Hoe. It was an amazing sight, I remember thinking England had not seen this many people gather for the start of a yacht race like this in many years. Somewhere

Thousands of people stroll through the race village in Sutton Harbour, Plymouth.

Above **Well-wishers gather on the pontoon before the start of the Artemis Transat.**

Left **Dad and me before the start of the Artemis Transat.**

Mum and me share a last minute hug before I leave the dock.

amongst the crowds I knew Mum was waving.

As we passed Plymouth Hoe in a long parade with the other competitors Dad and the lads hoisted the mainsail. Soon after, the RIB came along side to collect Dad and Mike. We said our goodbyes and they left me and Ifor to sail out to the starting area. Ifor was keen to help with any last-minute sail changes before the start and as we waited patiently for the minutes to count down we discussed how the first few days at sea might pan out. With just twenty minutes to go the RIB pulled back alongside and Ifor jumped aboard to join the others.

The race start was a typical affair, a barrage of yachts zooming around the starting area looking for the best position to cross the line. We had very light winds, something I was quite pleased with. A soft introduction into a race like this is always a welcome sight for the competitors. We all know that the path ahead will deliver testing times, but there's nothing worse than setting out into the teeth of an Atlantic gale.

Boom! The deep-throated roar of the starting gun fired from the decks of *HMS Argyll*, an impressive Type 23 Class Frigate. I could feel my heart pounding, the Artemis Transat was underway and we were off! Despite the light winds, the fleet quickly gathered pace and set off for the first turning mark of the course, Eddystone lighthouse. Having waved goodbye to my family and friends it wasn't long before the last spectator boats gradually turned back to shore. *Fujifilm* and I were

finally on our own. Next stop America.

Everybody expected rough sailing but initially as the fleet clawed its way towards Land's End we were ploughing through thick fog and light winds. The first night had proved frustrating as we negotiated a fickle breeze close to Lizard Point Lighthouse. The fleet had been sailing within sight of each other since the start. *Fujifilm* was doing well but close to midnight we sailed into a patch of no wind. I could only watch as two competitors sailed past while I fought frantically on the fore-deck to get the spinnaker unravelled from the rigging. There seemed to be wind all around us, just not where we were. We drifted around in circles for a good fifteen minutes before finally managing to pick up

Sailing out of Plymouth at the start of the Artemis Transat. The yellow RIB in the foreground is packed with our sponsors.

the pace. It was early days and not the end of the world. The important thing to remember is that everyone has to deal with their fair share of problems and this was just the beginning. The treacherous Atlantic lay ahead. I knew it would be a challenge but I had no idea just how tough things would become.

The first couple of days delivered a constant stream of sail changes, necessary to keep the boat sailing at its full potential. Yacht racing is always an exhausting business, but never more so than when you're sailing solo. If anyone reading this wants to lose weight, I have an exercise programme that allows you to eat what you like yet still lose at least two stone in just three weeks – just sail a highly-strung racing yacht solo across an ocean. Keeping the boat going at full speed is a full-time job and solo racers spend their time constantly fighting the debilitating effects of sleep deprivation while watching the wind for any changes that will affect their performance in the race. Changing sails is one of the most demanding tasks at sea. Sails are big and heavy and when soaked with seawater their weight can almost double.

The second night out I was preparing to hoist the spinnaker when the sail ripped on its way up the mast. It turned into a real monty, my word for a bloody nightmare. I spent the following forty-five minutes perched on the foredeck with a can of spray glue and some sail repair tape making an ad-hoc repair. It was getting dark as well, which only added to the difficulty. The light of my head torch was all that guided me as I searched for any holes that I had missed. If the sail set with any damage to the cloth it could easily blow apart as the wind pressure increased. If that happened it would be a really bad day.

By the morning of day three we were well out of sight of land, scooting along under an uncharacteristic easterly wind. I could see a sail on the horizon behind me. It was definitely another competitor. The breeze was blowing hard and we both had a wall of sail set. The big masthead spinnaker was propelling *Fujifilm* along at thirteen to seventeen knots as we picked up the pace. I could see the boat behind was also pushing hard and for the next three hours we enjoyed our own private game of 'who dares wins'.

The breeze was steadily increasing and getting close to the maximum for our big sail. As I sat at the chart table talking to a reporter on the satellite phone I could feel the boat starting to get over pressed. The autopilot was beginning to struggle with the amount of canvas we had flying, so it was time to cut the conversation short and deal with it.

As I clambered into the cockpit I could see the other boat distant on the horizon, still carrying his big sail. The maximum wind speed alarms I had set to twenty-four knots of wind were now blasting constantly as a threatening reminder that the breeze was steadily climbing. There was no way I was going to take the sail down unless he did, but this was starting to become a risky business. I knew the other guy would be pushing hard to catch us and there would come a point where one of us would have to make the first move, but I was determined it wouldn't be me. *Fujifilm* was alive with speed and vibration, and in such conditions the autopilot could no longer be expected to steer the boat safely. It was now down to me to keep us on our feet and drive the bow down the waves. I could feel my adrenaline pumping as the big one hundred and eighty square metre spinnaker dragged us across the ocean. The pace was fast and furious. In these conditions, with that amount of sail set there is no room for error, especially when you are solo. If you mess up, you mess up big time and your world quickly ends up on its side.

I knew we were pushing our luck. I kept looking over my shoulder to check on the guy behind, waiting to see his spinnaker collapse as he either wiped-out or took it down. Neither of us did, and eventually the wind speed settled down to a more controllable twenty knots. Mid-afternoon, the latest weather reports arrived by email. It was important that we change our course to a heading slightly south of west to capitalise on the changing weather ahead. This meant gybing the boat which would not be an easy manoeuvre on my own with so much sail set. I considered for a moment the best way of carrying out the turn. The best option would have been to drop the spinnaker and gybe, then re-hoist the sail. That was the safest way of doing things but also the longest and slowest. The quickest way was to keep everything flying and just go for it like you were doing the manoeuvre on a dinghy. It was more risky, but way quicker if I could pull it off.

The guy behind must also have been thinking the same thoughts. As I went for the gybe I noticed his sail start to come down. He was thinking the safer route. Too late now, I thought, just go for it.

I waited for the right moment and sheeted in the mainsail. I had to be organised with all the ropes and sheets otherwise everything would mess up. The plan relied on timing. I was to make the turn the moment

Fujifilm took off down the face of a wave. In that instant, with the tiller between my legs and the spinnaker sheets in both hands, I would let go of the loaded sheet and start pulling on the other. In a split second as the back of the boat crossed through the eye of the wind the mainsail would fly across the cockpit inches above my head and settle on the new side. I had a couple of seconds to then get the spinnaker flying on our new heading. Then I must quickly lock off the sheet, engage the autopilot, winch on the new running backstay rope that holds the mast in place, release the opposite side backstay and then rapidly ease out the mainsheet before the boat wiped-out under the wind pressure. If I got any of it wrong, we would be in a world of trouble.

Fujifilm started to surf. Here was the moment. I took a deep breath and went for it. The following seconds were a frantic mixture of pulling lines and easing out sheets but somehow I managed to resist tripping over my own feet and pulled it off. As I eased out the mainsheet I cast an eye toward the boat in the distance to see the silent sight of my adversary's sail flogging in the wind. I spared him a thought while feeling pleased that it was not me having that nightmare. It was the last I saw of him.

Life soon started to settle into a routine and by the end of day three I felt well and truly dialled-in to the environment. The boat was going well and apart from not getting as much sleep as I would have liked, life was good and going to plan.

Nine days into the race the fleet was slowly losing the wind, and keeping the boat moving somehow was essential. The position rankings were so close that it was anyone's game. I hadn't seen another competitor since our ballsy duel on day three, but far out on the horizon I thought for a moment I could see a sail. The ocean was almost mirror-calm and had taken on an oily appearance in the absence of any significant wind. Despite being close to becalmed *Fujifilm* was ghosting along, making just over a knot through the water. We were well and truly in the middle of the North Atlantic by now, over a thousand miles from the nearest land. I was sure I could see a sail, but who it was could be anyone's guess. A further look at the radar screen on the chart table gave proof that I wasn't seeing things.

Indeed there was a boat out there. As we drifted on the ocean basking underneath a warm sun I could see we were closing in on them. I was anxious to know who it was and looked at the last position reports that had been sent from race control. It looked like it was probably my friend Miranda on *40 Degrees*. She was competing aboard an identical design to *Fujifilm*. Miranda is a first-class sailor, and we had been neck-and-neck as we sailed along the coast towards Land's End on the first day of the race.

Whoever it was, as we closed the gap I could see they seemed to be becalmed. In an effort not to become trapped like they seemed to be, I freed off our course and slowly sailed away into the distance.

Later that evening the long-awaited arrival of a stiff north-westerly wind picked up the pace for the whole fleet. Watching the race reports every few hours I could see that everyone was using the new wind to drop down onto a course similar to ours, although the separation between some of the boats was hundreds of miles from north to south. The race was becoming more and more tactical as time went by.

The following day was our tenth at sea. With little more than four hundred and forty miles to the ice gate, conditions were proving relentless. The ice gate was a mandatory rounding mark set on the race track to keep the fleet away from the bulk of icebergs floating on the Labrador Current sweeping across the Grand Banks of Newfoundland. In 2008 the Artemis Transat race control issued a set of coordinates to competitors prior the start of the race, intended to keep everyone away from the worst of the ice. Competitors were required to pass through these specified coordinates in order to comply with the race rules. The direct route from England to Boston is along the route mariners call a great circle. The trouble was that route would take the fleet directly through the bulk of the ice field and straight into hell. Big icebergs, the ones that are the size of a small building, show up on radar and are fairly easy to spot. It's the ones the size of a small car that float only just above the surface of the ocean that pose the biggest risk to a small yacht travelling at speed. They are impossible to spot and certainly don't show up on radar. They are the ones that will sink you. The ice gate was a precautionary measure and one that was by and large well-received by the sailors. Tactically, the ice gate became a major consideration for everyone and marked a significant turning point of the course.

I had just taken the Code Zero sail down and changed to our Genoa as the wind filled in. Ten days of seriously hot racing had left me exhausted and certainly feeling the biting effects of sleep deprivation. The sudden change of wind had caught me out. One minute *Fujifilm*

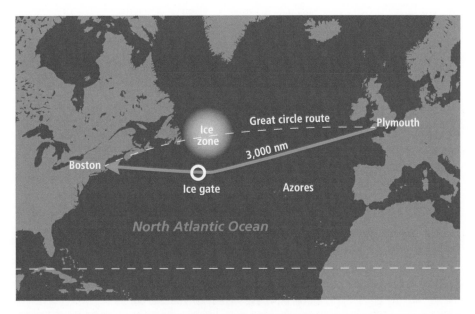

The Artemis Transat Race route showing ice gate.

was sailing along comfortably making about eight knots and the next, bang! The boat tacked through the eye of the wind and lay over on her side. I was in the cabin at the time and had to dodge the debris as food and equipment were thrown across the cabin. The following twenty-four hours brought much of the same tricky weather conditions.

The wind had been clocking, north west, west, west south west, and south as the various frontal systems passed overhead. It was hard sailing. I was soaked to the skin, not from spray but from sweat. The good news was that I had managed to keep the boat speed close to eight knots, about right for the conditions. The bad news was that I felt beyond knackered and if I wasn't before I was now definitely in the danger zone for exhaustion. As a solo sailor you have to quickly learn how to prioritise your time efficiently at sea. You learn more about your physical and mental capabilities on your own on the ocean than you would otherwise realise through normal life. It's a different world out here and right now I knew I needed to get my head down for at least a couple of hours to recuperate. With *Fujifilm* pointing in the right direction and making good speed I crashed out on top of the sails on the floor of the cabin.

Less than an hour later, I was woken by the uneasy motion of the boat. The moment my eyes opened I knew something was wrong. I was half-asleep but alert enough to realise that *Fujifilm* was bolt upright and hardly moving. Not now, I thought, initially assuming the mast had broken. It wasn't until I climbed into the cockpit and looked up that I realised the mast was fine but the headsail was hanging over the side. A quick look around the boat seemed to reveal no other damage so with *Fujifilm* dead in the water I ran onto the foredeck to try and retrieve the sail. It wasn't easy but eventually with the sail safely back on deck I could see the source of the problem.

The metal fitting that connects the headsail to the top of the fore-stay furler at the top of the mast had broken. The metal had torn completely apart. In an instant we had lost the ability to use our primary headsail. From the performance perspective, this was a serious problem. The other end, which was connected to the rope halyard, was stuck at the top of the mast. Normally, retrieving it would mean a climb up the mast, but in those seas, that wasn't an option. We would have to carry on under reduced sail until the sea state moderated enough for me to make the climb. It was a cruel blow. We were still in the race but without the use of that sail we would quickly drop off the pace. I think if I'd had the telephone number of the manufacturer on board I would have called them and gone ballistic, not that it would have achieved anything. We were on our own out here, just me and the boat, and only we could find a workable solution now.

The morning of our thirteenth day at sea delivered the most amaz-ing sunrise that illuminated the sky with a sumptuous red glow. Despite being beautiful it was a sign of weather to come. The thought of the old saying started to ring alarm bells in my mind: 'red sky at night, sailor's delight; red sky in morning, sailors take warning'. The latest weather reports confirmed my forebodings, the moderate conditions would soon be replaced by a big blow. The sole focus now was to prepare for the rough conditions ahead and do our best to get around the ice gate.

There was a short window in the weather that would allow me to have a crack at repairing the broken headsail fitting. After that, it could be days before another opportunity might present itself. Effect-ing the repair was not easy and as every hour passed I was conscious the competition would be gaining ground. It was a whole twenty-four hours before I managed to fix the damage. In the end, the makeshift

A spectacular sunrise on day 13 of the Artemis Transat.

repair was a relatively quick and easy fix; the biggest issue was retrieving the end of the halyard that was stuck at the top of the mast.

The solution was to release the rope halyard from the jammer block on the deck and pull plenty of slack through. After that all I could do was wait. The motion of the boat jumping over the waves was such that coupled with the weight of the furling fitting attached to the forestay and the effects of gravity it was enough to slowly pull the halyard down. I watched anxiously for hours as the fitting slowly slid down the forestay. Eventually it was just twenty feet or so above the deck and my patience had run out. With the aid of a fibreglass sail batten with a pair of pliers lashed to the end I managed to climb the mast and once high enough, I hooked the pliers around the halyard and pulled the fitting down to deck level. It was pretty dodgy hanging by just one hand about fifteen feet above the deck. If I had fallen I would have been stuffed.

With the halyard and fitting retrieved I was able to make the repair. I lashed some thin Vectran cord around the fitting to create a fixing point. Then by using another separate piece of cord I tied the head of the sail to the fitting. A quick check seemed to indicate a successful repair but I could see that I would not be able to apply the normal amount of tension to the halyard once the sail was set. At the time I was just pleased to be able to re-hoist the sail, though I did think we would be lucky if the repair lasted the remainder of the day, let alone all the way to the finish.

The repaired headsail furler.

Conditions were slowly deteriorating. I could only watch as the barometer started to drop like a stone. We were now sailing into the wind and waves, punching toward the jaws of a deep depression. As the sea state built, the motion on board became increasingly violent. *Fujifilm* was launching herself off the crests of waves and slamming down into the troughs with such force that I started to wonder how much punishment the boat could take before something important gave way. We were racing and I wasn't about to slow down for love nor money, although there would come a time when I would have to, just to keep the boat in one piece. I knew the fleet was experiencing the same conditions and Miranda on *40 Degrees* was certainly in my neighbourhood breathing down my neck. For now we would keep pushing.

Just walking around the cabin required serious effort. Later that evening with the sea continuing to build I went forward onto the foredeck to swap the reefed staysail for the tiny storm jib.

I had earlier changed my wet weather gear for the preferred security of my one-piece survival suit. Together with my trusty lifejacket and harness I clipped onto the safety lines, released the staysail halyard from the clutch at the front edge of the cockpit and while the sail started to flog violently in the wind I shuffled forwards on my hands and knees, working my way towards the bow.

We were approaching full gale-force conditions. The foredeck looked intimidating and was awash as big waves thumped into the side of the hull, sweeping wildly across the decks. I felt little reassurance in the knowledge that I was tethered to the boat. I knew that any one of those waves could easily wash me off the deck and into the sea. The shock loading of my hundred-kilo bodyweight on the lifelines could potentially break the tether. Definitely a risky business.

The storm jib was already attached to the bottom of the stay, something I had prepared before the going had gotten rough. I knew that when the time came to need it I would have plenty on my hands and wanted to be ahead of the game. That still left me with the not-so-easy task of lowering the reefed staysail, securing the sail to the deck and then changing over the halyard to the storm jib before I could fight my way back to the relative safety of the cockpit.

The bow felt like a tremendous bucking bronco as I secured my feet against the foot chocks on the foredeck. The motion was incredible. It's up there at the very front of the boat where the pitching move-ment is most accentuated. I held on as tightly as I could while the bow slammed down hard across every wave. A mixture of thoughts flashed through my mind. I hoped Martin and the lads hadn't cut any corners during the build; any imperfections in their craftsmanship would surely show up now.

I remember looking towards the back of the boat and being treated to an awesome sight. The ocean waves were starting to dwarf *Fujifilm* as they rolled past, and suddenly my forty-foot plastic world seemed very small. Nature is so beautiful, though and out here amongst all the turmoil I knew this was really living. I shouted into the wind at the top of my voice, "Yeah baby, yeah!" The release of emotion helped to focus my mind and stirred up my adrenaline, not that I wasn't already feeling that total buzz that makes people like me do this kind of crazy stuff in the first place. Very few people experience this kind of extreme, but for any adrenaline junkie I would suggest that this kind of experi-ence is right up there!

I pulled on the staysail for all I was worth. It was surprisingly easy to recover. With the sail on the deck I reached into my survival suit pocket for some sail ties that I had grabbed as I clambered on deck. Another wave thumped into my back and broke over the boat. Lashing the sail to the foredeck proved much more difficult than I had initially expected, but with so much water coming over the boat I could see that leav-ing the sail exposed to the elements was not the best option. I was worried the sail would be damaged so I decided to stash it down the foredeck hatch and get it safely below decks. I could see the weather was worsening and certainly didn't fancy having to come back up onto the foredeck if the sail broke free from the lashings during the night.

I knew the minute I opened the foredeck hatch solid water would pour into the boat. I needed to be quick and not mess about. With the sail unclipped from the stay and bagged up with the lashings I timed my moment and then opened the fore hatch and stuffed the Kevlar sail through as best I could. The bulky sail resisted going through the hatch so in the end I resorted to using my feet to force it though the tiny opening. Eventually the last of the sail dropped into the bilge and after quickly untying the sheets I slammed the hatch shut, untied the lashings on the storm jib and crawled back to the cockpit. A lot of water had poured down the hatchway and I knew I had to get below to sort it out, but first it was time to hoist the storm jib and get us back up to speed.

I climbed into the cabin and sprawled out on the sails to get my breath back. My whole body was shaking with adrenaline as I gasped for air. As I lay on the floor of the cabin I could hear the wind whistling through the rigging, a sure sign that we were now in gale-force conditions. The noise of water sloshing around in the bow was too much to ignore, I knew I had to go forward to deal with it and the staysail also needed re-packing into its bag. I had to keep the boat shipshape and couldn't just leave everything in such a mess. Exhausted as I was, I took a deep breath, pulled myself to my feet and climbed through the tiny watertight hatch to sort out the mess.

Half an hour later I was ready for a decent cup of tea. While I waited for the kettle to boil I stripped off my survival suit and wedged myself at the chart table to have a look at our position on the chart. It was time to make a quick call to Mum and Dad. I knew they would have the same weather information as I did, and they would know I was entering a particularly rough phase so I wanted to let them know I was OK.

The worst was yet to come. That night as we fought our way into hell the motion on board became increasingly ugly as the wind peaked at close to fifty knots. We were about one hundred and twenty miles from the ice gate, well and truly in the middle of nowhere, almost two hundred and eighty miles south-east of the Grand Banks of Newfoundland. Outside, the seas were huge, like office blocks looming over us. We were being knocked down by the force of the waves frequently and the noise inside the cabin was so intense I was convinced that structural damage was a possibility. Even in the confines of the cabin I remained fully togged-up in my survival suit, just in case. Despite desperately fighting the severe effects of sleep deprivation I felt I was still making coherent decisions. My senses had rarely felt so in tune with the surrounding environment.

The slamming motion was the worst. The flat-bottomed profile so typical of these modern flying machines provides an excellent hull shape for sailing with the wind behind you but in these conditions that same flat-bottomed profile makes for rough treatment as you slam into the waves. I remember thinking it was little wonder that a good proportion of the Class 40 fleet had decided not to compete in this race. Sometimes – like just then – it can prove to be just too demanding on both boat and skipper.

I had perched myself on the floor next to the engine box cover at the forward end of the cabin and was just cooking up some pasta when the first big knock-down occurred. I heard the wave approaching a second or two before it hit. The noise was unbelievable. We were knocked completely flat the instant it slammed into the hull, and the pasta bolognaise ended up on the cabin roof, becoming the first casualty. If we didn't want to be the next, I had to get on deck, pronto.

As I reached the cockpit *Fujifilm* popped back upright. It was pitch-black outside and difficult to immediately gain orientation but I could see the instruments clearly. I eased out a chunk of mainsheet to get the boat back on her feet and disengaged the autopilot so I could take charge and get us moving again. As my eyes adjusted to the darkness I could make out the impressive crests of waves towering above us. This was a wild place and certainly not an ideal spot for your grandmother.

I had taken the knock-down as a sign that my presence was required on deck so for a while I stayed at the helm and steered into the night. The change in sensation from the constant slamming motion in the cabin to the screaming pitch of the wind on deck was welcome, but listening to the continuous beating the boat was taking made it difficult to remain confident that she would hold together. I spent the remainder of the night on deck and catnapped in the cuddy at the forward end of the cockpit, just in case I needed to grab the helm again. A couple of times I heard the sat phone ping into life but by the time I climbed into the cabin it rang off.

We had the mast in the water twice that night. Both times were pretty wild but on each occasion *Fujifilm* came straight back up. When dawn finally broke, my eyelids felt like lead. As I looked around to check that everything was holding up, I noticed the fibreglass VHF radio antenna at the mast head. It had snapped off and was hanging from its wires, a sure sign that the mast tip had indeed seen the surface of the ocean during the night. Chuffing hell, I thought. Exhausted, I ventured into the cabin to make some hot noodles and take a glance at the charts to see where we were.

The ice gate was close. It was just a few miles before we could tack and free off our course. The gate had become a real psychological milestone for the race competitors. With such rough conditions, getting past it was all that occupied my mind, and no doubt everyone else was thinking the same. I knew as we got closer I would have to tack the boat and start heading north of west, and after that things would improve. We just had to keep going and bloody well pass through it. Tacking the boat would be hard work and potentially dangerous in those seas, so I decided to pour some hot food down my throat and recuperate. With daylight outside it was time to close my eyes for an hour. I flashed up the radar and set a perimeter guard zone of five miles around the boat before crashing out. If any vessel emitting a radar signature ventured into the five-mile zone, alarm bells would sound.

Later that day we finally rounded the eastern end of the ice gate. *Fujifilm* had taken a real pounding. I didn't know a boat could take that much punishment without breaking but the worst was now behind us. The tacking manoeuvre shortly before we passed through the gate was a bit brutal, with such huge seas running I found it difficult to make the boat tack through the eye of the wind, but eventually we got around and made the turn. We were now heading north-west and with the wind on our port side life instantly started to feel easier. That's not to say the going didn't remain tough, we still had close to forty knots of wind and huge seas, but our course and direction to the wind and waves allowed me to slip out of survival mode and start thinking about pushing the boat again.

I was on deck and holding on at the mast, trying to shake out the third deep reef in the mainsail. We needed to hoist some more canvas and start piling on the pace. I had just started the manoeuvre when I glanced out across the horizon. Bloody hell, it was another sail. One minute it was there and the next it disappeared into the troughs, but it was without doubt another yacht. In fact we were so close I could see they were carrying the same sail configuration as us. Blimey, this far out on the ocean and here we are, two competitors going for it. The sight was a stirring one. I could easily see them, so they must know I was here too.

The sight of another competitor spurred me into overdrive as I began hoisting the mainsail for all I was worth. Winching the mainsail from the third reef to the second normally involves less than five minutes of continuous work to complete. But this time, the third reefing line that secures the trailing edge or leech of the sail to the outboard end of the boom had jammed. The outer cover of the Dyneema rope had chafed at the end of the boom and become stuck as I released the line. It was every sailor's nightmare, with the boom hanging out over the side of the boat while we surfed along at nearly fifteen knots. I struggled to free the rope for a good ten minutes before deciding to just cut it. It was the easiest option and right now we had an intense duel to deal with.

While I was messing around in the cockpit I had been conscious that I could hear what I thought was a voice on the VHF radio. The antenna, although broken, was still hanging by its wire from the masthead and with the close proximity of the other yacht I assumed it must have been them hailing me. *Fujifilm* was back up to full speed, so I climbed into the cabin to see what all the fuss was about. I was intrigued to know who the other competitor was so I waited and listened to see if they would hail again.

The broken crackle of a human voice cut unmistakably through the noise in the cabin. Initially the transmission was almost unreadable, probably thanks to my dodgy antenna but then I heard the name. *Custo Pol, Custo Pol.* It was one of our fleet alright. The French skipper Halvard Mabire had seen me struggling with the mainsail and was calling to make sure everything was OK, a nice touch I thought. We had a welcome but short conversation, but the reception was poor and I could barely understand what he was saying. I could tell he had also experienced a rough couple of days, as he mentioned problems with the boat but nothing serious. We wished each other well and agreed

Pushing to the limit shortly after rounding the Ice Gate.

to have a beer in Marblehead after the finish.

The following hours were some of the most exciting of the trip. I spent a good deal of time on the helm that day, totally focused on gaining an advantage. The weather reports predicted that the rough conditions were on their way out and I was intent on pushing *Fujifilm* to the limit while we still had the big breeze. It was a high-power environment and visibility was very poor. White water was everywhere as we regularly surfed down the face of waves at over twenty knots. We were carrying a ridiculous amount of canvas and at times the boat was completely out of control, but I was haunted by the feeling that we had lost miles to the opposition when the headsail furler had broken. This was an opportunity to get some of those precious miles back and both *Fujifilm* and I were up for the cup.

Three hours later I ventured back into the cabin to grab some snacks and send a quick email home to let everyone know I had rounded the ice gate. The sat phone had registered several missed calls and just as I wondered who had been calling it burst into life. I answered with my standard greeting "Hello this is yacht *Fujifilm*". The voice on the end of the line was clear and composed. It was Slyvie Viant from Artemis race control. They had been trying to get through for over an hour. Another competitor, Yvan Noblet on board *Appart City* had suffered serious structural problems and was in trouble. Apparently Miranda on *40 Degrees* was the closest and had been asked to help in case the French skipper decided to abandon his boat. If he did abandon he would not be the first competitor to do so in this edition of the race. Just a couple of days earlier one of the larger sixty-foot mono-hulls had collided with a sea mammal while sailing at close to twenty knots. The impact was so severe that the damaged keel was threatening to become completely detached. The storm that we had just been through had been approaching, so the skipper requested assistance and the race leader diverted to pick him up.

Race control wanted me on standby in case they needed extra help. Wow, this race is a cruel one, I thought. I knew exactly how Yvan must have been feeling. Another big green wave thumped into the side of *Fujifilm*'s hull, sending a torrent of sea water into the cockpit. Chilling thoughts of when I'd had to make the heart-wrenching decision to abandon *One Dream One Mission* came to mind. I hoped he was alright. The sea temperature was close to zero out there and the air temperature was not much better. I plotted the last position of *Appart City* that race control had given me and agreed to wait for further instructions.

An hour later race control called back to say that the rescue had been called off, at least for the time being. Yvan's race was over but he thought the boat would probably hold together long enough to reach a safe port. He was heading under his own steam for the St Pierre and Miquelon Islands near Newfoundland. The news meant that Miranda and I could keep our focus on the racing and our ongoing duel.

Sixteen days in, and we were once again struggling in the grip of a high pressure ridge. The harsh Atlantic weather had given way to light, gentle conditions. We were entering the final stages of the race but even at this late stage most of the fleet were still close enough to each other to make forecasting who would finish in what place difficult. Miranda had opted to stay in the north of the high pressure ridge, while having sighted what I thought was her a couple of miles astern the evening before, I had decided to sail at a faster angle to the wind and dive toward the south. It was a gamble but everyone faced difficult tactical decisions as the final miles slowly unwound.

As we entered our eighteenth day of racing the fleet position reports from race control brought good news. My gamble had paid off and we had put fifty miles between us and *40 Degrees*. This brought me great relief, as we had been neck-and-neck for the past seventeen days and despite our best efforts, neither of us had been able to break away.

For me and *Fujifilm* the finish line was now in sight and the realisation that we were close to achieving our goal suddenly dawned as I sighted land for the first time in eighteen days. I felt both exhausted and excited, and decided to call Mum and Dad to let them know I could see the American coastline.

My girlfriend Rachel and the delivery crew had flown out from England the previous day and managed to blag their way onto a press boat that had motored out into the bay to greet me before I crossed the finish line. I called them to let everyone know I was closing in on the finish but they already knew. Apparently they had been following my progress on the race tracker all morning while enjoying cocktails on the balcony of the Corinthian Yacht Club in Marblehead.

As we made our last tack into the bay the sun was shining and with a beautiful blue sky I sat at the back of the boat to enjoy a final private moment before the press boat and cameras arrived. We had done it, we had successfully crossed the mighty North Atlantic. *Fujifilm* and I had taken a real pasting at times, but throughout, the boat had looked after me and pulled us through. I felt quietly proud and elated to have achieved what we had set out to do. We hadn't won the race, but somehow that didn't matter. We were here and in one piece.

Suddenly a fast-moving power boat appeared in the distance ahead. With flags flying and moving like it had a purpose, I just knew it was the press boat. As it drew closer, I could see the boat was full of people. Rachel was on the bow, intently taking photos that would undoubtedly be required for the inevitable press release as soon as I stepped ashore. Mike and Richard were waving, obviously pleased to see me and the boat in one piece. My safe arrival may have signified the climax of my adventure but it also confirmed that theirs was only just beginning. I knew both Mike and Richard were excited at the prospect of sailing *Fujifilm* back to the UK and I felt pleased that they were here to see the boat romping home in fine fashion.

Crossing the finish line was an amazing achievement, not just for me but for the whole team. It was the culmination of more than two years of hard work for the lads who had given their blood, sweat and tears to make the project a success. For me, hearing the sound of the finishing gun represented the realisation of a lifelong dream, a dream that I have held close to my heart since I was just a small boy gazing out of a classroom window and dreaming of adventure on the high seas.

Despite the problems with the broken headsail furler, after eight-

Above **Approaching the finish line at Marblehead.**

Right **No time to chill, the media want to hear all about it.**

een days, five hours, fifty-three minutes and just two seconds at sea, we were the top-ranked British boat and had done enough to secure sixth place overall, narrowly missing out on the podium. Today the Single-handed Transatlantic Race remains one of the toughest solo ocean races in existence. I'm proud to have taken my place amongst the few who have completed it.

We all have dreams and aspirations. Life is short, but achievement is within all of us, even though the journey of life doesn't always pan out the way we might plan or expect. I have come to realise that, but sometimes you just have to believe in yourself and go out and make things happen. That's how I live my life. Roll on the future...

Totnes, Devon, November 2010

We've done it! A proud smile as we motor into Marblehead harbour.

Alex gratefully acknowledges the support of the following people and organisations:

Fujifilm for making this book a reality, without your support it would not have happened.

Fujifilm Graphic Systems UK

Fujifilm FinePix Digital Cameras. Alex uses the Fujifilm Z33 waterproof digital camera when at sea

Duplo UK

David and Virginia Bennett

Mike Shand

Rachel Ellis

Ifor Pedley

David Ierston

John Wright

Shane Dickson

Richard Hatton

The master and crew of the *Hoescht Express*

The master and crew of the *EWL Central America*

Peter Earp, English Braids Yacht Ropes

Pete Neale, English Braids Yacht Ropes

Raymarine

Keith Dalton

Graham Leeson

Paul Hiscock & Anne Ransom, Hiscock Ransom Design

Michael Walker

Navionics digital cartography

Chris Pontet, Euronav

Graham Goff

Ian Dennis

John Brinkers

Scanstrut

Michelmores Solicitors

Malcolm Dickinson

BCB International

Musto Clothing

John Tilling

Phil Davies

Pro Rainer clothing

Richard Brown and Plymouth Sailing School

Whitby Yacht Club and its members

Dr Claire Bailey

Dave Scully

John Stacey Riley accountants

Vikki Penny

Karen Hamilton

Jonathon Harwood, County home search company

Harold Usherwood

Stratos communications

Adam Stone Rokk Media

Neil Devons, Proteus Media

Ben Allen A&G computers

Charles Allen

Pete Goss

Mark Orr

Gaye Sarma

Bank Sails USA

Alan Holmes

Alan Smith and family

John Beattie

John Chandler, Polaris yacht deliveries

Shaun Patterson

Pains Wessex

Rachel Amor

Phil Tucker

Baltic Wharf Boat yard, Totnes

Dave Sharp

Martin Boulter and the build team at Composite Creations

Merv Owen and Allen Clarke, Owen Clarke Design LLP

Metyx Composites

Mumfords Renault Plymouth

ACKNOWLEDGEMENTS

William Mumford

Andrew Lay, Brighton Marina Village

Dave (Red Ned) Hutchinson

Frank Rees

Rick Powell

Lisa Horton

Dimention polyant sailcloth

Robin Price Photography

The Littlejohn family

Mike Coates

Topper International

Lee Bruce, Tactical Weather

Paul (Larso) Larsen

Bob Siggsworth

Don Cowen

Plymouth Yachthaven

Tetrosyl paints

Andrew (Robbie) Robinson – Anything Stainless welding services Plymouth

Ocean Safety

Jane West

Explore technologies

Blakes paint

Richard Parslow

Rick Tomlinson Photography

Spex opticians

Jock Sheppard

Simon Ellyatt

Mark Turner

Two four productions

Sam Joseph – Silverstream Media

Brixham Harbour master

Clydesdale Bank

Charles Stanley

BBC Radio Devon

BBC Spotlight

The author acknowledges the rights of the following identified third parties whose copyright material is used, with their kind permission, in this publication:

Rick Tomlinson: pp.113, 114, 115, 162, 164, 165, 166, 167, 172, 174175, 182, 183, 194, 195

Paul Larsen: pp.185, 244, 245, 252, 256, 257, 258, 260 (bottom), 261, 262, 263, 264 (top)

John Wright: p. 293

Robin Price Photography: pp. 310, 314, 315, 394, 406, 407 (top)

Dr Claire Bailey: pp 327, 331, 334, 335, 336, 339, 340, 351, 352, 353

Tony Ellis: p. 409

Rachel Ellis: pp. 410 (top), 411, 412, 429, 430, 429

Jane West: pp. 410 (bottom), 411